*Making Meaning in*
*Indian Cinema*

# Making Meaning in
# *Indian Cinema*

Edited by
RAVI S. VASUDEVAN

OXFORD
UNIVERSITY PRESS

# OXFORD

UNIVERSITY PRESS

YMCA Library Building, Jai Singh Road, New Delhi 110001

Oxford University Press is a department of the University of Oxford. It furthers the
University's objective of excellence in research, scholarship, and education
by publishing worldwide in

Oxford New York

Auckland Cape Town Dar es Salaam Hong Kong Karachi Kuala Lumpur
Madrid Melbourne Mexico City Nairobi New Delhi Shanghai Taipei Toront

With offices in
Argentina Austria Brazil Chile Czech Republic France Greece Guatemala
Hungary Italy Japan Poland Portugal Singapore South Korea Switzerland
Thailand Turkey Ukraine Vietnam

Oxford is a registered trade mark of Oxford University Press
in the UK and in certain other countries

Published in India by Oxford University Press, New Delhi

First published 2000
Oxford India Paperbacks 2002
Sixth impression 2008

ISBN-13: **978-0-19-56867-5**
ISBN-10: **0-19-565867-1**

Typeset in Adobe Garamond by Wordsmiths, Delhi 110 034
Printed in India by Ram Printograph, Delhi 110 051
Published by Oxford University Press
YMCA Library Building, Jai Singh Road, New Delhi 110 001

# Preface

This volume was inspired by a seminar, 'Making Meaning in Indian Cinema', held at the Indian Institute for Advanced Study, Shimla, in October 1995. The IIAS has had a long and valuable tradition of supporting work in new fields of research, and I thank the Director, Professor Mrinal Miri, and his staff for their generous hospitality. Four of the articles published here are substantially revised versions of papers presented at this seminar: 'The Couple and Their Spaces: *Harano Sur* as Melodrama Now' by Moinak Biswas; 'From Subjectification to Schizophrenia: the "Angry Man" and the Psychotic Hero" of Bombay Cinema' by Ranjani Mazumdar; 'Formal into Real Subsumption? Signs of Ideological Re-form in Two Recent Films' by Madhava Prasad; and '*Kaadalan* and the Politics of Re-Signification: Fashion, Violence and the Body' by Vivek Dhareshwar and Tejaswini Niranjana.

Thanks to the editors at OUP who did their best to make the Introduction comprehensible and for their good-humoured pursuit of the manuscript across several continents.

# Acknowledgements

To the following editors and publishers for permission to republish articles from their journals:

*Economic and Political Weekly* for
  M.S.S. Pandian, '*Parasakthi*: Life and Times of a DMK Film', *Economic and Political Weekly* 26 (11–12), March 1991.
*Journal of Arts and Ideas (JAI)* for
  Vivek Dhareshwar and Tejaswini Niranjana, '*Kaadalan* and the Politics of Resignification: Fashion, Violence and the Body', *JAI* 29, 1996.
  M. Madhava Prasad, 'Signs of Ideological Re-form in Two Recent Films: Towards Real Subsumption?', *JAI* 29, 1996.
  S.V. Srinivas, 'Devotion and Defiance in Fan Activity', *JAI* 29, 1996.
  Ravi S. Vasudevan, 'Shifting Codes, Dissolving Identities: The Hindi Social Film of the 1950s as Popular Culture', *JAI* 23–24, 1993.
*Screen*, UK, for
  Lalitha Gopalan, 'Avenging Women in Indian Cinema', *Screen* 38(1), 1997.

# Contents

# Contributors

Moinak Biswas is Senior Lecturer, Department of Film Studies, Jadavpur University, Calcutta. He has edited two volumes of the Bengali writings of Hemango Biswas, *Ujan Gang Bayia* (1989) and *Ganer Bahirana* (1998). He has also written a monograph on Chaplin in Bengali in 1997.

Vivek Dhareshwar is the author of *History, Sovereignty, Politics* (forthcoming) and co-editor of *Interrogating Modernity: Culture and Colonialism in India* (1993). He has worked at the Centre for Studies in Social Sciences, Calcutta, and is currently Senior Fellow at the Centre for the Study of Culture and Society, Bangalore.

Lalitha Gopalan teaches Film Studies at Georgetown University Washington. She is currently completing a manuscript on genres of violence in contemporary Indian cinema.

Stephen P. Hughes teaches Anthropology at the School of Oriental and African Studies, University of London. He is working on film exhibition and audiences in Tamil south India upto 1950.

Sundar Kaali is completing his doctoral dissertation on the community theatres of Tamil Nadu. He researches and writes on various subjects in cultural studies, including film, theatre, festival and ritual.

Tejaswini Niranjana is the author of *Siting Translation: History, Poststructuralism and the Colonial Context* (1992) and the co-editor of *Interrogating Modernity: Culture and Colonialism in India* (1993). She has published extensively on popular south Indian cinema. She has taught at the University of Hyderabad and is currently Senior Fellow at the Centre for the Study of Culture and Society, Bangalore.

Ranjani Mazumdar is an independent filmmaker based in Delhi and a member of the Mediastorm film collective since 1986. She has recently completed her dissertation on Indian cinema titled 'Urban Allegories: The City in Bombay Cinema' from New York University.

M.S.S. Pandian is currently a Fellow of the Madras Institute of Development Studies. His publications include *The Image Trap: M.G. Ramachandran in Film and Politics* (Delhi: Sage, 1992) and papers in leading social science journals.

M. Madhava Prasad is Senior Fellow at the Centre for the Study of Culture and Society, Bangalore. He is the author of *Ideology of the Hindi Film: A Historical Construction* (Delhi: Oxford University Press, 1998) and is currently completing a study of the politics of stardom in south India.

Ashish Rajadhyaksha is the editor, with Paul Willemen, of the *Encylopaedia of Indian Cinema* (London, Delhi: British Film Institute, 1994, Oxford University Press, 1995). He is on the editorial board of the *Journal of Arts and Ideas*, New Delhi, and a Senior Fellow at the Centre for the Study of Culture and Society, Bangalore.

S.V. Srinivas is Post-Doctoral Fellow, Centre for the Study of Culture and Society, Bangalore. He completed his Ph.D., 'Fans and Stars: Production, Reception and Circulation of the Moving Image' from the University of Hyderabad in 1997. He has written on cinema in the *Journal of Arts and Ideas* and various journals.

Ravi Vasudevan, Fellow, Centre for the Study of Developing Societies, Delhi, studied history at Jawaharlal Nehru University in Delhi, and film studies at the University of East Anglia, Norwich. He has taught film studies at universities in India and the USA, and is visiting faculty at the Department of Film Studies, Jadavpur University. Vasudevan in on the advisory boards of *Screen*, the Public Service Broadcasting Trust and is Co-Director, Sarai, the new media initiative.

# Introduction

RAVI S. VASUDEVAN

## The Politics of the Popular

THE DISTINCTIVE FEATURE of the emerging academic and professional institutionalization of film study in India is the prominence now given to the popular-commercial cinema, so long denied legitimacy as an object worthy of study.[1] When the Indian Institute of Advanced Study, Shimla, organized a seminar on Indian film in 1995, the majority of presentations were concerned with popular commercial films, although the brief had been much broader. However, this generalization has to be broken down to assess the different drives underlying current research. In the clearest of these, popular film is treated as an entry point for understanding the legitimization of social and political power through narrative forms commanding the widest of social constituencies. Such approaches can range from an instrumentalist treatment of the popular cinema to more generous assessments which reveal the contradictory character of the views and experiences it channels. What is notable, too, is the overwhelming focus on contemporary cinema, especially on the period after 1970. This could owe something to the importance which the key left-wing intellectual periodical, the *Economic and Political Weekly*, began to give to film as a vivid, highly public and politically immediate document. An exemplary instance is the debate on *Roja* (Mani Ratnam, 1994) inaugurated by Tejaswini Niranjana's crisply polemical 'Whose Nation? Tourists and Terrorists in *Roja*'.[2] A series of contributions followed, animated by arguments concerning the politics of Tamil Nadu and Kashmir, and how the film represented relations between class, community and nationhood. This debate generated methodological arguments as well, about ways of analysing film narrative, understanding the politics of different traditions of film realism, and developing approaches to reception. But there is little doubt that the debate derived its energy from the approach to film as a contemporary political document.

If there is a unifying theme to this volume, it derives from the current drive to understand the political implications of Indian popular cinema. But how exactly does one approach the politics of a cultural product such as film with some specificity? Film study has begun to feel the need to define a coherent domain in terms of archival resources: the films themselves; documents on cinema production, distribution and exhibition; information about the cinema's personnel at various levels; the geography of cinema in society, both its urban geography as well as the geography of itinerant cinema. The research agenda should include a historical knowledge of technologies and techniques, and a history of perceptions about the cinema. We would also have to stay alert to the cultural histories of advertising, radio, recording and television industries as they intersect with the history of cinema.[4] This more formal, archivally grounded and theoretically specific approach to film study is slowly taking place both officially, in the National Film Archives of India, in regional initiatives such as the 1997 Chennai workshop on Tamil cinema, and through the large number of individual collections of film-related material. The quest is for a more specific political framework, in which an apparently unself-conscious and routinized leisure practice may be investigated for the politics of how films are produced, of what is shown to whom, and how desires centred on stars, life-styles, commodities, and social identities influence the politics of everyday life and imagination.[5]

Some of this initiative has left its mark on this collection, but apart from Pandian's and Hughes' use of government archival material and contemporary documentation, and Srinivas's collection of oral testimony from Chiranjeevi fans, the focus is on the analysis of narrative form. The broader issues of social and political ideology are refracted through the characteristic concerns with genre and stylistic analysis, dwelling on *mise en scène*[6] and *découpage*[7] in the wider perspective on the place of film within changing cultural and political arrangements.

An important context for such work was provided by the cultural and gender studies workshops organized by the Centre for the Study of Social Sciences, Calcutta, the Madras Institute of Development Studies, Chennai, and the Central Institute for English and Foreign Languages, Hyderabad, between 1995 and 1998. Here the theoretical objects were re-framed through the cultural categories of self, subjectivity and the imaginary. Literary material was inducted to understand the formation of ideas about public life, community, nationhood, and citizenship. This proved an influential framework for the study of film as well. The present volume emerged to understand this particular meeting of disciplines and research agenda. At this juncture, the narrative analysis highlights the politics of representation, of nation, community, gender, caste and class. In particular, a group of articles in the latter part of the book juxtaposes concepts of film representation with ideas about political representation. With the deepening of the archival and research agenda outlined earlier, the location of the political in film will become more elaborate, signposting a variety of directions.

The subject matter of the volume is, by and large, the popular cinema, but defining the popular is hardly a straightforward matter. One issue is the analysis of how the difference between elite and popular forms was conceived at any moment in time. The related question is of cultural recognition and assertion. How can our understanding of form avoid complicity with a hierarchical outlook on aesthetic sensibility and cultural consumption and focus instead on how audiences recognize and identify with particular codes of entertainment?

## EXISTING PARADIGMS

A dominant narrative has governed this understanding of the relationship between elite and popular forms in the history of Indian cinema. The tale runs something like this. Following a brief inception in which the films were exhibited as a scientific curiosity, film-makers introduced the genre of the mythological film to cater to popular taste. Subsequently, in alliance with literary culture, a middle-class social cinema of reform evolved in the sound period, one at variance with other genres such as the stunt, mythological and costume films which catered to the plebeian film-goer. These currents continued, with greater or lesser influence after Independence and into the 1950s, the heyday of a nationalist ideology with socialist aspirations. From this period, too, a more specifically art enterprise, one attuned to cinematic language, emerged, supported towards the close of the 1960s with systematic state investment in art cinema. The 'parallel' cinema emerged as the object of middle-class spectatorship, especially in the wake of the 'massification' of the commercial form into an encompassing and alienating package of spectacle, action and titillation.

This stock account is echoed in analyses with very different agendas. A very interesting contrast is that between the writings of Chidananda Das Gupta and Ashis Nandy, who could be considered the forerunners of current discussions on the politics of popular cinema. The former, one of the founders of the Calcutta Film Society in 1948 along with Satyajit Ray, has written extensively on cinema and made films as well. With a few exceptions,[8] Das Gupta's writings were devoted to promoting a cinema of rational perception and reformist sensibility. In the recent past, this commitment has assumed a polemical edge arising from the debates on secularism and national identity which have governed Indian political and academic life. The context is that of a Hindu majoritarian nationalism mobilizing affiliation to apparently archaic religious and mythical symbolism. Das Gupta argues that the popular cinema has provided fruitful ground for this ideology from its very origins in film-makers such as Phalke and his development of the mythological genre.[9] To state his thesis baldly, he attributes an irrational, pre-modern outlook to the spectator of contemporary popular cinema, and urges support to the art cinema in defence of rationalist, enlightened attitudes.[10]

In his book on popular cinema, *The Painted Face*[11] Das Gupta views the spectator of popular cinema as incapacitated by pre-modern cognitive features, unable to distinguish between screen image and reality. Believing what he sees, the mass spectator is eminently susceptible to a totalitarian politics founded on the image of the leader. In his understanding, this weakness is dramatically underscored by the way film is put to political use in certain regional cultures as in Tamil Nadu, Andhra Pradesh and, less successfully, Karnataka. Here the contemporary popular cinema seems to signpost an impending and paroxysmic political collapse, as the political system careens away from its rationalist origins in the epoch of Nehru towards a demagogic form. The book is dedicated to Ashis Nandy, and, on the face of it, one could not ask for better, if unintended, irony. For Nandy has been one of the most passionate critics of rationality and enlightenment.[12] For him, such cognitive currents have unleashed state-sponsored projects of large-scale social engineering in the name of development which, far from exercising a liberatory effect on society, have uprooted communities and imposed the deadening standardization of modernity over a rich variety of traditional beliefs. The paradox emerges fully when Nandy, analysing the cultural conflict between the rationalist, modernizing state and traditional, local communities, suggests that the commercial cinema retains the traces, however distorted, of affiliation to forms of community, cultural languages and moral concerns endangered by the homogenizing imperatives of modernization.[13] This cinema provides a fictive arena in which the depredations wrought by modernity can be worked out and imaginary compensations rendered to the victim.

There is a fascinating, distortive mirroring involved here, where Das Gupta's bad object becomes the repository of a residual communitarian virtue for Nandy. A shared characterization of the spectator generates two entirely different political positions, indicating that different values and theoretical inclinations do not necessarily lead to differences in modes of description. At the root of this paradox is the tendency of both writers to describe the mass entertainment film as grounding its characters in certain stable ways of organizing subjectivity. The self is not based on individual self-perception but is dependent on others and other formations for its psychological and moral coherence. Central to a character's subjectivity is the social form of the family and the idioms of filial duty and obedience that arise from it.[14] In turn, the decisions taken by characters derive from a larger moral frame reposed in figures outside them, especially in certain iconic figures such as the mother.

The absence of the modern individual in popular cinema is, therefore, central to the overlap between the arguments of Das Gupta and Nandy.[15] The most significant correlation here is the perceived lack of a critical outlook in the subjectivity retailed by the mass film. The non-individuated subjectivity, stigmatized by

Das Gupta as the locus of a personality that is submissive to authority, is converted in Nandy's diagnosis into a defence of 'traditional' social mores against an atomizing modernity. For the latter, the political dynamic of popular film lies in its symbolic enactment of 'traditional' society's self-exclusion from the domain of an instrumentalist rationality.

## AN AGENDA

In a fresh formulation of an agenda for film studies, the categories of the traditional and the modern need to be placed more contextually against the historical and institutional conditions which produce these oppositions. The question of who fashions these categories is central here, and may suggest a variety of usages at any point in time. The job of historical research would be to locate the key moments at which influential usages were formulated. The state as it evolves policies of censorship, taxation and institutional formation, is an influential player in the processes which define the status of cinema as a cultural institution. The nature of the discussions changed in the transition from the colonial to the national governments, the latter demonstrating a more purposeful sense of the ideological tasks to which cultural institutions should be oriented in the vision of an independent India. Here government representatives, intellectuals and an interested public discussed how the cinema could be shaped to nurture desires for a 'traditional' and 'authentic' India while fulfilling the imperatives of a modern national identity. Alongside this were discussions about ways to regulate and stabilize industrial conditions to achieve desirable cultural goals, in which questions of censorship, financial support and exactions were highlighted. The major cinematograph committees, film enquiry committee reports,[16] and home department proceedings constitute major sources for such an investigation.[17] These are crucial to an understanding of how the state and various sectors of public discussion fashioned a cultural image for the cinema, and are yet to be adequately tapped.

The ongoing engagement of various strands of the literary, artistic and journalist intelligentsia in the cinema constitutes a rather complicated series of positions, a substantial part of which is yet to be identified and excavated. In my article I indicate one fairly coherent outlook, the film society/art cinema intelligentsia of the post-independence period, which demanded an alternative cinema committed to a realist observation and style which they believed would ensure an authentic rendering of Indian culture. This overtly elitist strand of argument, of which Das Gupta's *The Painted Face* is the latest product, has been an extremely influential one in its impact on public discourses and state policies. But there are other discourses to be attended to. There was a broad engagement in the popular cinema by the left-wing intelligentsia and those more loosely associated with the Progressive Writers Association and the Indian People's Theatre Association: Bijon Bhattacharya, Ritwik Ghatak, K.A. Abbas, Rajinder Singh Bedi, Saadat Hasan Manto, Ismat Chughtai, Bimal Roy, Zia Sarhady, Shaheed Latif, Shombhu Mitra, Chetan Anand, Krishan Chander amongst the better-known directors and scenarists; Balraj Sahni, Dev Anand, Prithviraj Kapoor amongst the actors; Kaifi Azmi, Anil Biswas, Salil Chowdhury, Bhupen Hazarika, and Sahir Ludhianvi amongst lyricists, dialogue writers and music composers. Another current was the specifically regional, alternative nationalism inspired by the engagement of the radical Dravidian intelligentsia in the popular cinema of Tamil Nadu from the 1940s. Therefore, the criterion of the intelligentsia's involvement was not the determining factor in the opposition between art and popular cinema. The complex nature of this intellectual engagement with the popular needs to be analysed.[18]

In developing a nuanced sense of the attitudes of those working in the popular cinema, we must nevertheless acknowledge that they accepted and worked creatively within the framework of attractions—musical, performative, narrative—that compose the dominant Indian cinematic experience. In this milieu, a straight-forward linearization of the narrative form, into a pattern of cause and effect on the Hollywood model, did not emerge as a clear-cut agenda. Here one steps down from the domain of discourses about the popular cinema to discourses within it, where its conventions are inhabited and employed with a certain confidence and ease. It is here that the question of cultural recognition surfaces. Insofar as there is a consensus between producers of a fairly broad-ranging intellectual/perceptual and ideological hue, and a continuing demand for a certain type of cinema, we may assume that there is a circuit of communication, of narrative and performative intelligibility, in the relationship between films and their audiences.

This is the domain of recognition which must constitute a second stream of investigation. It implies a focus on local cinematic cultures rather than a comprehensive and differentiated sense of what the cinema means in a society. One resorts to this term—the local—for strategic reasons, to get away from the ideologically loaded concepts of the national and the indigenous.[19] The investigation of such local forms has been important in film study at large, in acknowledgement of the cinematic experience generated outside the international coordinates of narrative film language associated with Hollywood and with the various national art cinemas that flourished after the Second World War.[20] The cultural transactions involved in the mobilization of local forms are central: performance practices, musical and linguistic idioms, the formulation of personality types who condense social consensuses about the representative image.[21] Of course, such local cultures result from fairly recent historical construction, and, as with any modern phenomenon, date from the nineteenth century. Further, the positioning of products to cater to particular constituencies, that is, the logic of the market, often reveals a layered structure to the popular.[22] The local popular product may also be subordinate to the foreign import in terms of total audience attendance. This has been the case with the relationship between European cinema and Hollywood cinema.[23] Nevertheless, the popular local film clearly has a significant presence, and may prove durable in certain sectors and periods. In Latin America, for instance, there has been the significant Brazilian musical film genre of the *chanchada* in the 1940s[24] and in Mexico the *cabaratera* of the 1950s,[25] both under-analysed but influential genres. In the Indian case, of course, the local cinematic culture has dominated its own market.

In an extreme sense, such a local culture should not be understandable outside the community or society within which it is produced and consumed; it should be 'unexportable'. In practice the local inevitably attends to and assimilates the foreign norms of narration it appears indifferent to. Nevertheless, distinctive features remain. Even when such products acquire a largeness of scale and reach, both national and international, they still retain a strongly bounded identity address. In the Indian case, this is notable in the way the popular cinema has been important to Indian diasporas. Where this cinema's reach has extended beyond the moorings of the 'original community' and its international extensions, interesting issues arise about the nature of its attractions. It is possible that the success of the Indian cinema in North Africa, the countries of the Middle East, Eastern Europe, the former Soviet Union and China points to a suggestive international constituency for a narrative form addressing the problems associated with modern social and political transformation.[26]

The disaggregated form characterizing the 'local' in Indian popular cinema has been variously evaluated, both in a notionally historicized way, as well as a fixed and eternal attribute. In the first group, Madhava Prasad has proposed that the form emerges from the dispersal of the mode of production into a heterogeneous field. Autonomous units of production generate different components, such as dialogue, dance and music whose product is then combined. Such a 'heterogeneous mode of manufacture' may be attributed, Prasad suggests, to the way merchant capital financing the distribution sector leaves these different units unintegrated, but also to the ideological imperatives of dominant social and economic forces.[27] We will return at a later point to the complexity of this primarily ideological analysis. The more cultural explanation characterizes the popular film as repository of a traditional aesthetic that composed different *rasas* or moods, in line with the ancient canons of Hindu aesthetics.[28] In a folkloristic rendering, the popular film is rooted in the persistent orality of Indian culture, in which music has an expressive equivalence to speech.[29] In contrast to a literary disposition whose reading practices interiorize the reader/viewer's relationship to the text,[30] such orality is said to sustain an externalized, declamatory and musical form in the Indian popular cinema.

Both the ideological-economic and folkloristic explanation might suggest a transitional situation which could change, whereas the notion of a 'traditional' aesthetic suggests something constant and invariant. At first glance, the cinema indeed seems to reproduce the traditional, its entertainments being organized along different registers, edificatory and pleasurable, on the lines of *rasa* theory. This is often accompanied by an indifference to coherent character development, as if the objective of the entertainment is the display of a (structured) variety of attributes rather than the outlining of a plausible personality. However, while popular film does appear to have condensed an entertainment which incorporates elements reminiscent of earlier folk and urban theatrical forms, this does not mean that the mode of combination and expression of the different elements has remained static.

Of significance here is the nature of opinion for change. In arguments for emulation of the Hollywood model, the economic rationale has been that it would enable a more cost-effective functioning at the industrial level[31] and that adoption of the Hollywood narrative form would bring greater success in the export market.[32] But there has also been an implicit cultural and political agenda, that of refashioning the spectator on rationalist terms.[33] Within India, the practice of doing away with the performance sequence has resulted in rare and often ungainly instances which have failed to streamline the product. The more important consequence of drives for change has been to integrate song and dance more systematically into an overarching narrative and affective shape. Such a disciplining of the dominant form, or, to put it less repressively, intratextual shaping and tonal coordination, as for example, in the work of the great Guru Dutt, has always been undermined by the comic function. This is a unit which has been under-analysed, one whose anarchic dimensions gesture to dissonances in the system of meaning in a film. The disaggregated nature of the popular form, the various 'niches' and forms of address which compose it, have been used for pedagogical purposes by reformists, especially in the 1930s, leftists, in the 1940s and 1950s, and for various types of patriotic address throughout the history of the cinema. The articulation of such views from various positions, heroic, moral, and comic, do not necessarily reinforce each other, resulting in an often suggestive tapestry of images and types.

## TRADITION AND MODERNITY IN THE CINEMA

The locally recognizable cultural form has been formulated as a political issue by Partha Chatterjee in evaluating the cultural response of Indians to the colonial experience.[34] He poses the question of how a self-affirmative politics can be cognitively organized in circumstances in which the state is an alien form, alongside a series of other 'outside' institutions and practices of modernity such as science, impersonal bureaucratic codes, and even aesthetic choices such as realism. The suggestion here is that the power-laden circumstances in which modernity was introduced caused culturally defensive reactions against it; but that the 'inner' or 'traditional' stance which developed in response inevitably employed modern perceptual, technological and organizational developments to institute itself.

Ashish Rajadhyaksha anticipated this argument in one of the key writings in Indian film studies, 'The Phalke Era', where he used the concept of neo-traditionalism to explore the way in which traditions of representation and performance had been refracted through the new technologies in theatre, painting and cinema. In the manner of Chatterjee's interiorizing cultural imaginary, he argued that a traditional aesthetic was re-enshrined within the armature of the new medium through an assembly of cinematic techniques of narration. Frontal staging, direct address to the camera, decorative and presentational *mise en scène*, highlighted a certain organization of space over time and image over movement in a strategy of foregrounding familiar 'traditional' images to re-assure and stabilize audience perspective. To use Thomas Elsaesser's point about early Euro-American cinema, this was a cinema which imagined its audience to be present, and was therefore, alert to its cultural expectations.[35] This form of cinema often assumed that its audience already knew the story being told, or would have interlocutors to explain gaps in the narrative.[36] Elsewhere, Rajadhyaksha has extended his argument about the way in which early cinematic narration embedded itself in culturally familiar narrative and performative circumstances. He suggests that a transaction was undertaken between audience and apparatus to bring about a look that was both interior and public; that is, interior to a public whose terms of imagination are other than those of the unadorned rationality, reasonability and realism of modernity.[37] However, we should pause at this point to note the complexity of early cinematic forms as vehicles of modern experience. Steve Hughes, for example, has shown that the action serial, devoted to stunts, fights and chases, was a crucial attraction for early southern film audiences,[38] and his findings would require us to account for a new, visceral dynamic afforded to the spectator of the cinema. Was 'neo-traditionalism' redeployed in such forms of filmic address, or were narrative forms and modes of audience address considerably more varied?[39]

Traditional form, far from being fixed or fixing of cinematic convention, has been selective and open to revision. In his essay here, Sundar Kaali indicates that traditional reference points in popular Tamil cinema were encoded in the nativity genre, which narrated the symbolic triumph of rustic village hero and the village community over a modernity/city represented as woman. Kaali historicizes the genre by suggesting that industrial changes in the 1970s led to changes in the modes of shooting and staging and in the star system, resulting in a re-coding of generic elements and a more ambiguous status for the 'traditional' village community. Further research will doubtless yield more precise observations and qualifications around the original codification. Representations of virtue have not inevitably centred on images of the bucolic; for instance, the rationalist Dravida Munnetra Kazhagam's interventions in the popular cinema do not seem to disavow modernity to the same degree. As M.S.S. Pandian shows in his analysis of *Parasakthi* (Krishnan-Panju, 1951), reproduced here, the Tamil people are pictured as fallen into a state of immiseration and exile, an experience centred on the figure of a woman, Kalyani. Conventional as this vehicle of virtue may be, the village or countryside is not the primary unit in the semantics of a radicalized Tamil culture. It is the small town with historical ramifications, such as Madurai and Tiruchi, which provides the major itinerary for this reclaiming of Tamil identity, one perhaps implicitly pitted against the large city as an ungovernably alienating space, as in the representation of Madras.

Pandian shows that traditions are quoted but these are carefully selected to effect a junction with more contemporary references to the Tamil politics and culture of the period. Tradition is strategically invoked, it does not simply exist for invocation, a point reiterated in Kaali's analysis of *Annakilli* (Devaraj–Mohan, 1996). Here the heroine is associated with images of powerful mythical women such as Kannagi in her destruction of a corrupt modernity. But as Kaali argues, modernity in the genre of neo-nativity has two faces. In this film a desirable tradition is relayed, in a self-reflexive way, through the cultural technology of cinema. Annakilli, the heroine, is an enthusiastic film-goer, and she is watching the film *Kannagi* (T.R. Raghunath, 1942) when she is pitted against the threatening figure of the cinema-owner. Perhaps this thematizes an opposition of interests and desires in the split between cinematic institution and spectator. As we shall see, this is an issue elaborated in Srinivas's analysis of the relationship between fans and the industry.

In identifying how imperatives of cultural recognizability

influence narrative procedures, certain studies have examined the way 'traditional' codes mesh with 'modern' codes. Codes such as the Hollywood eyeline match and point of view editing, used to highlight individualized perception,[40] may acquire a different function in a different system of narration. But there is no doubt, too, that the induction of such codes complicates the way selfhood is constructed. In this connection, the argument of my article could be rephrased in the following way to understand the reconstruction of self under conditions of colonial modernity: the forms of filmic representation are mixed, gesturing to different types of subjectivity, and the look of the spectator operates at the interstices of these forms, initiating a dialogue between various forms of selfhood.[41]

This article focuses on the post-Independence Bombay film, and has been placed along with Moinak Biswas' analysis of an 'Uttam-Suchitra starrer', a current in Bengali melodramatic narratives. This has been done to suggest differences in the way modern, Hollywood filmic codes were employed at the time, and thereby a sense of the variety of ways in which film contextualized ideologies of modernity. *Harano Sur/Forgotten Melody* (Ajoy Kar, 1957) stands in contrast to the broad strokes and emotive flourishes of the Bombay film melodrama, with its drive to constantly externalize meaning in a bipolar, non-psychological delineation of character. In its melodramatic tale of virtue disempowered, victimized and finally ascendant,[42] the Bengali film exhibits a more 'modern' occult, a dark 'underside' of perception composed of individual sensibility and interiority. What is remarkable here is an uncanny sense of recognition. The recognition is not only of the way *Harano Sur* evokes the Hollywood mode of narration but also of Biswas' successful deployment of the critical apparatus used to understand Hollywood melodrama.

Euro-American film studies used psychoanalytical methods to identify the conversion of repressed meanings into the objects and textures which composed the filmic scene, and Biswas employs these with similar results. This suggests a highly unusual conjuncture in 1950s Bengal. The fragile sense of self inscribed in the film is achieved in a fantasy space outside society, a fantasy underlined by our ability to apprehend it through a method not normally productive for understanding Indian popular film. The phantom 'longing for form' of this imaginative world is replayed in the more recent exhibition of this cycle of films on television. The contemporary looks to the evanescent moment of the 1950s which, in turn, looks to another, unspecifiable moment. There is a desire here to return to a not yet and never to be realized sense of the self. In effect, the film seeks to neutralize the differences wrought by time, and we may perceive again that spatializing, iconicizing and fixing of the narrative moment rehearsed in the form of the early cinema. Ironically, where that earlier moment was a symbolic reinstatement of a traditionalizing compact with the audience, this instance is a fantasy of the modern couple constituted away from the arid and threatening features of modern public authority and psychological vulnerability that govern the world of the film.

Though very different from each other, the cinemas in these two articles suggest a particular set of desires that developed in the 1950s: the mobilization of an image, a space, and a filmic technique of the couple that made it the idealized emotional unit for a new society. But these films are distinct from each other in the way they frame the relationships of authority and subjecthood within which new forms of romance flourish. Here the recurrent importance of the courtroom as the space in which mysteries of identity are sorted out, quite common within the narrative format of melodrama and the popular cinema generally, is notably absent in the Bengali film. Authority, in its exclusions and its marginalizing effects, ultimately lies in the person of the hero himself rather than institutions outside him. And resolution is achieved by the triggering of his memory to recover a repressed identity. Does this alert us to a different cinematic imagining of identity in which the state is not a dominant reference?

## CINEMA AND CITIZENSHIP: BRINGING THE STATE BACK IN . . .

The state as a prominent factor in the shaping of cultural forms is observable in several articles in this volume. It is also recurrently invoked as a political concept produced by film narrative in the form of the emblematic character, the narrative agent, and, perhaps most complicatedly, the imaginary authority involved in the organization of narrative. It is as if the overarching political form governing our lives has intruded into the autonomous domains of

cultural production, inviting us to imaginatively participate in the
(re)fashioning of authority into an object of desire. In this role, it
invites us to surrender our subjectivities to it, and does not operate
as a brute vehicle of power. Thus in films such as *Roja*, there is an
argument for a bridging of the emotional distance between state
and nation.

The state as an institution governing the cinema is on display in
Pandian's and Steve Hughes' archivally grounded articles. Hughes
gives us a vivid sense of how the civic administration of the colonial
government in Madras believed the cinema posed a threat to public
order. At this point, the language of administration did not single
out the cinema as a distinct object of regulation. Thus, the earliest
administrative orders on the cinema were municipal safety regulations, concerning fire and crowding, although the concern was
clearly with the moral ramifications of the new cultural form. Here,
the state emerges as arbitrator of leisure practices and the imaginary
life, operating through a medley of administrative mechanisms to
control what people can see and hear. However, the imprecision
of the categories used in official discourse to deal with the cinema
indicates its somewhat phantasmagorical character. Administrators
anticipated that the cinema would endanger race authority by the
terms on which it represented white civilization, and that it would
disrupt public morality and harmony more generally, these fears
often running ahead of any actual display of unrest or protest.

This phantom quality to administrative perceptions of the
cinema is echoed in public complaints about the social effects of
film-going. Such organized forms of public opinion suggest a
motivated form of reception quite distinct from that of film-going
oriented to pleasure. Its cinephobia sprang from fears that the
accelerated circulation of images and ideas through the technologies
of the modern public sphere might result in animosity between
groups and cause civil strife. Would-be representatives of social and
religious groups stepped in to claim that filmic representations
affected the dignity of their constituency. Cinema seemed to elicit
greater anxiety than other forms of public discourse because its
audio-visual dimension threatened to reach the illiterate masses.

Pandian's article also looks at the relationship between public
opinion and the state, but in the case he examines, such cinephobic
lobbies were not paranoid at all in their reaction to the DMK-

inspired *Parasakthi*. The film hardly makes a secret of its intention to challenge both contemporary (Congress) government and (brahmanical) religious authority. In this sense, *Parasakthi* did not conform to the entertainment cinema's norm of avoiding the alienation of any particular group in its modes of address, and was seen to threaten social stability and political authority.[43] Within the fiction, the state is denied legitimacy, and outside, the cinema affords a space ranged against the state, a space for Tamilness.

Lalitha Gopalan takes up the issue of censorship to investigate the effect of state intervention on cinematic form. Her article on the cycle of avenging women films in Bombay and Telugu cinema examines the terms on which violence on the body of the citizen can be enacted in cinema, a theme also taken up by Dhareshwar and Niranjana. Gopalan argues that the intervention of the state to censor representations of sex, shapes the ambiguous depiction of rape. As 'normal' sex cannot be represented, the tendency of collapsing rape with consenting sex within the rhetorical field of the narrative (invariably voiced by corrupt lawyers) is only retrospectively denied, when the rapist is violently punished by his victim. Gopalan demonstrates a second equivalence in the formal paralleling of rape and revenge, and their common unrepresentability. In both instances devices such as cut-aways, displaced images and negative film screen off direct representations.

Gopalan's observations are important in identifying the role of a prohibitive authority in the elisions and instabilities of representation in the popular form. This structure of prohibitions puts a question mark over the terms on which the narration pronounces judgement on what we are allowed to see. The ambiguity sustains the sado-masochistic possibilities open to the spectator of this genre. While acknowledging that these films of female revenge offer vicarious pleasures to the male spectator, Gopalan complicates this account by arguing that masochistic and sadistic elements are distributed *between* the events of rape and revenge. She thereby broaches the possibility of a woman's point of view, one which may even invite cross-gender identification.

Gopalan has a suggestive argument about how the industry parallels the authority of the state in its positioning of female subjectivity. It is therefore only at the extreme limit, where the moral coordinates of authority seem to have largely broken down, that the powerful female emerges and, in turn, a leading position opens up for the female star.[44] This is quite at variance with the dominant maternal archetype of vengeance. As dramatized in *Mother India* (Mehboob Khan, 1957), the maternal figure, Radha, is vested with a narrative authority based on constancy to a husband who has deserted her. Her chastity gives her the symbolic authority to represent and refigure the village community into a national community benefiting from the struggles and sacrifices of her family. The film's framing narrative underlines that the village is now undergoing transformation under the aegis of a developmental state which derives its legitimacy from Radha in the figure of her son turned Congressman. In contrast, the avenging woman genre, centred on a daughter who is family leader in the absence of male authority figures, outlines a clear disjuncture between state and community. While the daughter achieves some form of community sanction (most notably in the community of victimized women) she is ultimately not involved in a project of strengthening the state, although she must inevitably submit to its order.[45]

What is the nature of the authority reinforced in this final 'interpellation'? Is the heroine subject to a formal exercise of power, as in censorship, or is it an expression of the unoffical domain of patriarchal authority that rules society and which may over-rule or co-opt transcendent forms of power as well? The ambiguities around this question of how authority is figured in filmic story-telling has been most elaborately addressed in Madhava Prasad's notion of the feudal family romance. Prasad argues that relations of authority in the narrative world of popular cinema are distributed among a number of points with the transcendent state occupying only one such position. These locii have to generate an alliance to preserve their authority. In this analysis, an alliance between the state and traditional patriarchy constrains the formation of a nuclear family and the representation of privacy and intimate relations. Here Prasad identifies traditional visual forms of authority in the culture of *darsan* as central to the reproduction of traditional patriarchies.[46] However, the term 'feudal' refers only to the dominant feature in the ideological organization of narrative. Other contesting elements exist but remain subordinate. For Prasad this symbolic form mirrors the coalition between old landed authority, capitalist elements and bureaucratic elites composing the political and social order. However, the work on the 1950s in this volume suggest that this formulation would not hold for the popular cinema of that period. Here representations of authority and techniques of subjectivity do not conform to the notion of a feudal form dominating all other ideological possibilities. Prasad's concept seems more apposite both for the cinema of the 1940s and again for the 1960s and after, which alerts us against the notion of any steady 'development' of narrative mode. Instead one could explore the possibility of a separation of forms which culminated in the mass, middle and parallel cinemas of the 1970s.[47] Secondly, the very notion of privacy as an issue in representation might be considered through the array of techniques used to implicate the spectator in the intimacy of the couple. Even if films exhibit prohibitions around the explicit representation of sexuality, they also display complex strategies to engage the spectator in the aura of the couple. Here one thinks of the way editing and camera movement, in shot-reverse-shot, close-up and reframing, can alter the terms of a space otherwise governed by an authoritarian patriarchy. And sound can also be used to conjure up an intimate communication, as Biswas shows for the song in| *Harano Sur.*

These qualifications noted, Prasad's is a powerful argument about the forceful assertion of the state within the cinematic imaginary of the 1990s, and the way it is re-conceptualized in filmic story-telling to constitute new discourses of citizenship. Prasad argues that in *Roja* and *Damini* (Raj Kumar Santoshi, 1993), there is a significant development of an enunciating or narrating instance which stands above narrative and organizes the segmentation of the story in ideologically purposeful ways. This lifts the romance of the couple out of the dominant arrangements of marital alliances and nucleating drives, to resituate it in a large-scale theatre of identity centred on the state. In *Roja* the drama centres on the justness of an ideal territoriality incorporating Kashmir, while in *Damini* the law becomes the arena to ward off the brute excess of familial authority. The achievement of the goals set by these new political and legal entities becomes absolutely necessary to the fulfilment of romance, which in turn becomes central to the reproduction of the state's legitimacy.

Prasad employs a theoretical construct from Marxist economic theory, the formal subsumption of labour to capital, explaining why the appearance form of independent petty commodity production continues to exist even in conditions where the labour process is subordinate to capitalist control. Under classical conditions of capitalist development such appearances dissolve to produce the 'proper' form of wage-labour. The labourer is now separated from the means of production, and labour itself becomes a commodity, really subsumed to capital. Transposed to the question of the narrative form of Indian popular cinema, the characteristic dispersal of the story into a series of autonomous segments, with their own conditions, expertise and economy of production, as in the song, dance, stunt and dialogue elements of the popular film, has the aspect of a pre- or early capitalist putting out system.[48] However, changes in form are not attributed to economic reasons alone. Prasad stresses the commanding role played by political and ideological elements in the transformation.[49] In his formulation, 'real subsumption' requires the altering of authority structures and subjecthood through a reordering of forms, so that one form, the feudal family romance, is subordinated to a form in which the modern state and modern romance are the dominant elements.[50] In this movement towards the transcendent state, modes of performance and representation associated with the middle cinema, oriented to the ordinary and plausible, are taken over and integrated into the larger entertainment form.[51]

In this intricate, fascinating argument the narrative process charts a series of mutually reinforcing exchanges between the state and the couple which ultimately subordinates older forms of authority and subjecthood. But what exactly is the nature of the new narrative process and subjectivity heralded in these films? Here Prasad's observations on form can be used to think afresh about the way the spectator's attention is attuned to new political formulations about citizenship through changes in the narrative process. The Hollywood strategy of continuity editing is the commonly valued way of achieving this narrative economy, in which the spectator's attention is moved coherently from point to point within a narrative design centred on the drives of individual character formation. However, from Prasad's article, as well as from other contributions, it becomes evident that the transaction between state and citizen can be expressed to the audience with a directness that disrupts the smooth channeling of emotional effects in character-driven narration. Thus Arvind Swamy, the hero of *Roja*, can shift from the mood of romantic dalliance into the hortatory mode of the passionate citizen. The rhetorical dimensions of popular film therefore continue to be important, employing elements of spatiality and frontality to highlight characters as vehicles of direct address.[52] This puts a question mark against the notion that existing models of cinematic modernity are an inevitable or, indeed, even possible destiny for Indian popular cinema. Prasad's is not a teleological argument, and he strongly argues against the likelihood of the Hollywood system being reproduced. Nevertheless, the category of real subsumption may evoke a teleology of systemic integration which seems rather remote in the context of the technologically and institutionally dispersed audio-visual regimes that characterized both earlier and contemporary contexts of Indian cinema, if in rather different ways.[53] One may also wonder whether other elements significant of earlier modes in the production of narrative meaning and pleasure are fully subordinated, or whether they are refashioned to fulfil certain new requirements.

Even for the Hollywood case, it has been argued that a much more anarchic, popular and modernist set of practices was at play than has been allowed for in the well-established paradigm of narrative integrity. Here, the attributes of classicism, balance, symmetry, aesthetic composition, suggestive as they are of a nineteenth-century fascination with the lineages of the ancient world, seem inadequate to the characterization of a twentieth century cultural project. The argument is that such projects would be based on interruption, discontinuity, and jaggedness rather than classical harmony. Revisionism can sometimes develop to the other extreme in discounting substantial accounts of the Hollywood system. But the Hollywood mode was itself preceded by a much less disciplined employment of the camera and of editing techniques.[54] The continuity system, and the various forms of industrial regulation and self-censorship involved in the systematizing of the Hollywood industry, also took time to come into being.[55] Even when the system was instituted, it was never monolithic in its characteristics, generating different processes of production within the studios, especially in what were referred to as B films and in marginal genres.[56] Finally, while the classical conception of the Hollywood film has a modular status in the cinematic imagination, and functions as a horizon for commercial cinemas at large, the nature of the model may itself be undergoing change in the post-classical period.[57]

By this logic, just as we need to think about the peculiarities in the adaptation of popular third world forms to new social and political circumstances, perhaps Hollywood should also be reinvestigated for the different constructions of subjectivity it solicited. The work on Indian cinema represented here may, therefore, address certain larger issues in cinema studies.

In contrast to the drives to 'modernize' the cinema, Niranjana and Dhareshwar's article appears to move a step beyond, drawing our attention to the politics of the non-realist, non-linear dimension of cinematic narrative. As in Niranjana's earlier articles on the films of Mani Ratnam, we are given an important agenda for film and cultural history, that of placing the image in histories of consumerism.[58] In *Kaadalan* (Loverboy) (Shankar, 1995), the authors argue, the mode of narrative construction, emphasizing the episodic, discontinuous and fragmentary, focuses attention on the screen as a surface rather than one inducting our view into narrative/character depth; and this forms one among the array of commodity surfaces that surround us in the liberalized Indian economy of the 1990s. The fluidity of this aesthetic is contrasted favourably with Mani Ratnam's attempts to shape a humanist realism, which they characterize as part of the hegemonic cultural strategy of a modernizing, high-caste, Hindu elite. In *Kaadalan*, Niranjana and Dhareshwar argue that the freeing of sign from referent allows for a greater play around the body of the character. In the process, many of the hallowed conventions of the commercial cinema, such as the valorization of the countryside, the benevolent role of the state, and the implicitly upper-caste figuring of the hero, are subjected to a different narrative economy. The emphasis is now on pastiche, irony, and open contest of older forms, as in the way the hero effortlessly learns and upstages the high-caste coded classical mode of dance.

This energetic engagement with the deployment of new technologies of filmic representation provides a suggestive entry-point for thinking about recent transformations of the cinematic medium. This is especially so with the impact of post-satellite media-space on the audio-visual domain. Here again, advances in conceptual approaches also generate certain queries. How exactly is this new form distinguished from the old popular cinema, which also had a tendency to pastiche, and complicated coherent identification by dispersing narrative into different sites for the expression of character? Secondly, how univocally modernizing, as opposed to modernist, is the Mani Ratnam oeuvre, which also routes its formulation of character through investments in narrative and performance? Indeed, his work seems to retain strong connections with the transcendental nature of popular performance, rather than simply using performance for identification.[59] Clearly, many of the distinctions that the authors make sound right, but we are still to shape the critical tools to adequately characterize changes in film form. And one might query the rapid re-anchoring of the new technical fluidity of the cinematic signifier in the politics and sociology of contemporary India. Rather than see this too immediately as an issue of dalit versus high-caste culture, a less precise category, such as youth culture, with its connotations of generational rebellion, narcissism and investment in style, might speak to the issues they raise. This category has its own inversionary and democratic implications, even if not those of a precisely identifiable social group.[60]

Ranjani Mazumdar also seeks to plot substantial transformations in the nature of popular narrative through an analysis of changing paradigms of stardom between the 1970s and 1990s. Her focus is on two actors who could be considered emblematic of the period in which they were ascendant, Amitabh Bachchan and Shahrukh Khan. She argues for a substantial contrast between the two stars and the way body, character, and notions of interiority are shaped in their films, and how the city and nation are represented. The particular star vehicles, *Deewar/The Wall* (Yash Chopra, 1975) and the Shahrukh Khan films *Darr/Fear* (Yash Chopra, 1994) and *Baazigar* (Abbas–Mustaan, 1994) are read as dystopian texts about nationhood. *Deewar* is seen to represent the unleashing of a frustrated energy against the inequities of a 'national development' which films of the immediate post-Independence period had invested so much in.[61] She suggests that, through the Bachchan persona, there is a coherent channeling of the energy generated by the physical and psychical scarring inflicted by the loss of his trade-unionist father. However, even if the character is sketched in as working class, there is a cross-class audience address in the framing of the star's charismatic personality. His carriage and demeanour are of a social mix, in turn plebeian and middle class. All of this is sharply contrasted with the Shahrukh Khan persona, where the psychology is conflicted and the persona schizophrenic. Mazumdar argues that these figurations are carried into the body of the narration, in the way point of view and sound are mobilized. She suggests that these narrative devices invite the audience to assume the imperilled subjectivity of the protagonist. There is a dissipation of motivation, and the city, seen as the repository of a community of the poor and working people in the Bachchan films, is rendered abstract and anomic.

This suggestive analysis may rely a little too much on the belief that there was an original coherence to the imagining of nationhood. It has been argued that there were much darker currents to the filmic fiction in the 1950s, a sense of sacrifice and victimhood built into the very dynamic of development.[62] To push the argument further, one would have to think through some of the micro-social and micro-narrational coordinates of character motivation. For example, while the mother remains significant in the justification of the hero's actions, a scrutiny of changing motivational features is needed. There are changes in narrative strategies, as for example, in the unusual way in which *Baazigar* manipulates the knowledge given the spectator, introducing elements of mystery and enigma in its address to the spectator. Finally, to picture allegories of the nation through a single narrative, body or voice, may simplify the series of images which constitute the cinematic imaginary at any one point in time. Bachchan and Shahrukh Khan have themselves enacted a series of different roles, not to speak of their contemporaries.

## INDIAN FILM, FILM THEORY AND DEMOCRACY

In this account of the political domain of the popular cinema, the ideological dimension of film form has been privileged by most writers, whether to explain the reproduction of political authority or its subversion. We seem to have mislaid the question of how a compact is formed between popular films and their audiences through mechanisms of cultural recognition. At one level, however, even the problems of form, whether the convolutions of segmentation and 're-housing' of forms observed by Prasad, or the obfuscations resulting from the prohibitions identified by Gopalan, are not abstractly universal. A formal solution, when it becomes a stable way in managing conflicts, provides an archaeological image, various past forms inhabiting the present in a layering of time. Cultural recognition may be evoked in the process of registering the embedded histories to which we are heir.

Central here is the issue of recognizing authority. If Prasad is right, then traditional form is centrally a form of authority. But instead of assuming that the compact between traditional and modern forms of authority operates unilaterally to subordinate its subjects, we could also examine its moments of self-persuasion. The ruling forces have to convince themselves as much as their subjects of their capacity to adapt to new conditions. Here tradition is cultural necessity as well as ideological instrument. But we also need to think of the subject negotiating new conditions while appearing to accept the reproduction of older relations of authority and subjectivity. As we have seen, tradition is not fixed but varied in the array of resources it offers. When cultural subjects choose or invent traditions, those choices may involve an adaptation to modernity, to make it 'our modernity',[63] rather than a rejection or neutralization of it. In this sense the neo-traditional encompasses more than the original encounter with colonial modernity outlined by Rajadhyaksha; it may also suggest a molecular adaptation to the modern. Such a shift in perspective requires historical analysis and specification, and is quite different from the hypostasis that fixed notions of tradition convey. This historicized version of the traditional would specify ideological operations and their contradictions, and also the various locii of tradition within a form. Looking further afield from the overarching system of ideological coherence, we may simultaneously explore local moments and disaggregated elements for the different stances and resources mobilized in the accession of Indian fictional processes and spectator situations to the realm of modernity. These need not be dominant elements, but that does not make them negligible.

Rajadhyaksha's essay touches on some of these issues in rethinking the question of the look as formulated in Euro-American film theory, and especially in the classic 1975 article by Laura Mulvey, 'Visual Pleasure and Narrative Cinema'.[64] Mulvey argued that there are three looks in the cinema, that of the camera, that of the viewer, and that of characters in the fiction. The Hollywood system has been considered especially important to the codification of this third look within the fiction, the intra-diegetic look. From the late 1910s, the Hollywood film industry fashioned a system of continuity editing that directed the spectator to look at the flow of character perceptions and actions within the fiction; she was to disavow her look in favour of that of the fictional agent or character.

In an insightful analysis of this formulation, Rajadhyaksha argues persuasively that there is never an unmediated spectator or camera 'look' in the cinema. When a film is shot, the 'look' of the camera presumes the look of the spectator in front of the screen. This assumption of a frontal baseline address to the spectator is built into the way shooting, composition and, subsequently, editing takes place. In these successive stages, the frontal baseline address is invoked *and* shifted; and the 'actual' spectator is mobilized into an inscribed spectator.

This dual quality to the camera's narrating functions, both acknowledging and effecting the disavowal of the viewer's look, constitutes the crucial political terrain of cinema for Rajadhyaksha. The moment of acknowledgement of the spectator in front of the screen within the procedures of narration, constitutes a form of consumer/viewer democracy. The camera/narrating instance does not initially insist on certain attributes, about how the spectator should view and make sense of the fictional world. Instead it assumes an enumerative relationship to the audience, in a sense accepting its rights to a view arising from the purchase of a ticket. Such 'democracy', has its own process of differentiation, through the hierarchy of tickets, seating arrangements, and the social geography of theatre location.[65] But the medium, its characteristic technical forms of presentation and of public exhibition, heralds a qualitatively new domain within the field of social and political life. Karthigesu Sivathamby, for example, has argued that the cinema offered an alternative to earlier forms of performance that limited access on the basis of social and ritual hierarchy.[66]

In contrast to Mulvey, Rajadhyaksha's argument suggests that the spectator's look is not separate from, but overlaps and develops in close relationship to that of the camera. By focusing attention on the camera's look as already partially constructing the viewpoint of the spectator, Rajadhyaksha points again to the question of the relation between authority and subjectivity in film. Regarding the third look, Rajadhyaksha argues that its systematic coding on the Hollywood model is probably unrepresentative of world cinema trends. Instead of an 'excessively obvious' mode of film narration,[67] as if the story tells itself, Rajadhayaksha suggests that it is more common for the process of story-telling to draw attention to itself and the authority underlying it. The organization of the frame works not to obscure the interval between shots, but to highlight it, to emphasize the camera or narrating instance and, in turn, the viewer as the object of its address.[68]

The foregrounding of the look of camera and spectator over that of character suggests that the third look is always a negotiation between the narrator or narrating instance and the spectator. It is not just a system of shots coded to construct a seamless scene or sequence. Contributions such as my own and Biswas's indicate that such a disestablishment of the third look is somewhat excessive, but one can put these reservations aside for the moment and attend to the political resonances of this formulation.

These lie in the following set of transpositions of narrative and aesthetic categories onto political concepts: of realism onto civil society, of story onto communal narrative contract, and of viewership onto citizenship. As we have observed, one strand of film criticism faults the Indian popular cinema for its failure to be properly realist, and character-centred, that is, for its failure to achieve a 'modern' procedure of narration which develops the intellectual and perceptual attributes of the individuated citizen in the spectator. But just as recent Indian political theory has critiqued the assumption that the inevitable and most equitable form of political representation rests on the freely associating individual citizen of civil society,[69] Rajadhyaksha suggests that the unachieved third look is in fact not a lack but an indicator of the transactional relationship between authority and subjectivity, between the first and the second looks. This is not an advocacy for the cultural peculiarity of Indian cinema, but for a reworking of existing theories of film spectatorship.

However, Rajadhyaksha also emphasizes the significance of cultural recognition in this relay between the first and the second looks, a relay emblematized by Phalke's famous expression of a desire to show Indian images of gods and natural surroundings on the screen. The project of instituting culturally recognizable images then becomes a significant field within which the second look is constituted. In rendering a primacy to this relation between the first two looks over the third, there is a disestablishment or subordination of the intra-diegetic look as a hegemonic universal form.

The second point to note is the politics of this relay of looks, not as a textual or logical system which unilaterally produces the spectator, but as a framework for social initative and micro-political group action. If Sivathamby points to the democratic implications of the cinema over earlier, hierarchized, cultural forms, then recent discussions of fan clubs show that the audience for the cinema as a social institution has a dynamic relationship to the cinema event. I will suggest that this is akin to a fleshing out, a social elaboration of the look of the spectator.

Here Srinivas's work on the fan club presents us with an important agenda. He not only illuminates processes of industrial publicity, where the industry has a direct institutional relationship to the fan and fanzine as vehicles of public enthusiasm for the star; he also shows that this is not a perfectly controlled and instrumentalized activity. Ironically, the framework of fan response need not accord with the democracy of choice and interpretation favoured by audience ethnographies. Instead of fans subjecting the star to interpretation, there is a significant drive to control, indeed to fix the image of the star, as an assertion of a collective self. The spectator's look here functions as an extensive field of force, generating a territoriality around distinct fan organizations. And the cinema hall becomes an arena for ritualized contests and assertions of identity in the relation between fan and industry. Here the city is redefined by the cinema. Under the micro-regime of the fan, it is no longer an unproblematic space for the consumption of images relayed by the industry. A plebeian culture of the image now refracts the urban space as one of embattled enclaves. The cinema as an arguably low cultural form is further 'lowered', a subalternity further subalternized. In all this, one hesitates to use the connotations of subalternity positively because, while exhibiting autonomy, the spaces it carves out for popular culture are politically ambivalent. On the other hand, Srinivas argues that certain fan clubs also demonstrate a sustained cultural engagement, in terms of evaluating forms of production and meanings, and this is a dimension of the spectator's activity focused on by J. Michael Kennedy.[70] His work, which we were unfortunately unable to excerpt for this volume, looks at questions of fandom through the phenomenon of the fanzine. Not only does the question of multiple interpretations of film narrative and of the significance of the star emerge from his work, so too does the complicated process of popular legitimation. Kennedy looks at the whole question of how the fascinating but also potentially alienating distance beween star and fan are worked over through star narratives, of ordinariness (he was like anyone else . . .), of philanthropy, worldly transcendence, and narratives which seek to neutralize the yawning social and economic chasm which separates star from fan.

This volume is an exploratory one, highlighting themes and questions which we hope will stimulate further research on Indian popular cinema. The limited spread of this kind of work has imposed certain boundaries on what is addressed. One lacuna is the absence of discussion on the musical features of Indian popular cinema, so central to its character. The regional basis of popular cinema which must emerge as one of the major concerns of film studies in India also remains undeveloped here. This dimension is crucial to a democratic cultural practice concerned to investigate and historicize the boundaries of such avowedly fixed entities as nation and region. We have to explain how these categories are culturally produced and how they may constrain our understanding of the complexities of exchange and constituency that compose cultural products.

As I have suggested at the outset, the contours of theory are likely to shift, as the question of what the political means in cultural practice emerges with greater complexity through interdisciplinary exchange. The evolution of cinematic and audio-visual institutions, which will include the new interactive technologies, will force new agenda and methods on our attention. So too will the different senses of time that come together in any intellectual project—the longer duration of archival collection and the shorter, contextual span governed by academic and intellectual institutions. For the present, we can only hope to convey some of the excitement and

engagement we have experienced in writing on this most dynamic
of cultural institutions.

## NOTES

1. Except when tied very powerfully to the domain of politics, as in Tamil
Nadu, e.g., S. Theodore Baskaran, *The Message Bearers: Nationalist Politics and
the Entertainment Media in South India*, Madras: Cre-A, 1981; *The Eye of the
Serpent: An Introduction to Tamil Cinema*, Madras: East-West Books, 1996;
Venkatesh Chakravarty, 'The Alternative Film and Tamil Cinema', in the
Seminar on 'Making Meaning in Indian Cinema', Indian Institute of Advanced
Study, Shimla, October 1995; Robert L. Hardgrave Jr, 'The Celluloid God:
MGR and the Tamil Film', *South Asian Review* 4, 1971; *When Stars Displace
the Gods: The Folk Culture of Cinema in Tamil Nadu*, Austin: University of
Texas Press, 1975; with Anthony Neidhardt, 'Film and Political Consciousness
in Tamil Nadu', *Economic and Political Weekly* (hereafter *EPW*), 1 January
1975; M.S.S. Pandian, '*Parasakthi*: Life and Times of a DMK Film', *EPW* 26(11–
2), March 1991, reprinted in this volume; *The Image Trap: M.G. Ramachandran
in Film and Politics*, New Delhi: Sage, 1992; 'The Tamil Elites and the Cinema',
in the Seminar on 'Making Meaning in Indian Cinema', October 1995, and
published in *EPW* 31(15), 13 April 1996: 950–95; Karthigesu Sivathamby, *The
Tamil Film as a Medium of Political Communication*, Madras: New Century
Book House, 1981.

2. *EPW* 24(3), 15 January 1994.

3. Other contributions included Venkatesh Chakravarty and M.S.S. Pandian,
'More on *Roja*', *EPW*, 12 March 1994; S.V. Srinivas, '*Roja* in Law and Order
State', *EPW*, 14 May 1994; Tejaswini Niranjana, '*Roja* Revisited', *EPW*, 21 May
1994; Rustam Bharucha, 'On the Border of Fascism: Manufacture of Consent
in *Roja*', *EPW*, 4 June 1994; Arun Kumar Patnaik, 'Idealistic Equations', *EPW*,
6 August 1994; Ravi Vasudevan, 'Other Voices: *Roja* against the Grain', *Seminar*
423, November 1994.

4. Ashok D. Ranade (ed.), *Sangeet Natak*, special issue on film music, no.100,
New Delhi: Sangeet Natak Akademi, April–June 1991; Peter Mandel, *Cassette
Culture: Popular Music and Technology in North India*, Chicago: University of
Chicago Press, 1993.

5. The compilation of the *Encyclopaedia of Indian Cinema*, London: British
Film Institute, 1994, was a landmark in the construction of an archive for film
study. Its editor, Ashish Rajadhyaksha wrote a pioneering article on Phalke
which drew on the wider history of the transformation of representational
practices in painting, theatre, and popular prints. 'The Phalke Era: Conflict of
Traditional Form and Modern Technology', *Journal of Arts and Ideas*, 14–15,
July–December 1987; reprinted in V. Dhareshwar, T. Niranjana and P. Sudhir
(eds), *Interrogating Modernity: Culture and Colonialism in India*, Calcutta:
Seagull Books, 1993. Madhava Prasad has used committee reports and trade
magazines to understand the debates on Indian film which took place in the

1970s in his *Ideology of the Hindi Film*, New Delhi: Oxford University Press, 1998. Cf. also Ravi Vasudevan, 'The Cultural Space of a Film Narrative: *Kismet* (Bombay Talkies, 1943)', *Indian Economic and Social History Review*, April–June 1991; and '"You Cannot Live in Society—and Ignore it": Nationhood and Female Modernity in *Andaz* (Mehboob Khan, 1949)', *Contributions to Indian Sociology* 29(1 & 2), 1995, for the use of various forms of archival material to understand film reception.

6. This refers to how objects and figures are enframed and spaces embellished through lighting and lensing.

7. The mode of arrangement of shots in a sequence.

8. One interesting detour is his 'In Defence of the Box Office' (1958), discussed in my article in this volume.

9. The edge to this polemic surfaced strongly in Das Gupta's article in Aruna Vasudev, *Frames of Mind*, Delhi: UBS Publishers, 1996.

10. Interestingly, this viewpoint is echoed in Satyajit Ray's cinematic interpretation of *Ghare Baire/The Home and the World* (1983), in which Tagore's multi-voiced novel is narrowed into the perspective of the enlightened, reformist protagonist, Nikhil alone. The particular energy conjured up in the other characters, a passionate relationship to a more varied cultural conception of self, is regarded as mired in reactionary cant.

11. Delhi: Roli Books, 1992.

12. For example, *The Intimate Enemy* (1983); *Tyrannies, Traditions and Utopias* (1987); (edited) *Science, Hegemony and Violence* (1988).

13. 'The Intelligent Film Critic's Guide to the Indian Cinema', in Ashis Nandy, *The Savage Freud*, New Delhi: Oxford University Press, 1995.

14. In contrast, Madhava Prasad would see the family as a political entity. See *The Ideology of Hindi Cinema*; and his article published in this volume.

15. This argument is echoed in other discussions of selfhood, as in the psychoanalyst Sudhir Kakar's *The Inner World: Childhood and Society in India*, New Delhi: Oxford University Press, 1978.

16. *Report of the Indian Cinematograph Committee 1927–28*, Calcutta: Government of India Central Publications Branch, 1928; *Report of the Film Enquiry Committee*, New Delhi: Government of India Press, 1951; *Report of the Film Enquiry Committee on Film Censorship*, New Delhi: Government of India, 1969; *Report of the Working Group on National Film Policy*, New Delhi: Government of India, Ministry of Information and Broadcasting, 1980. Existing accounts include E. Barnouw and S. Krishnaswamy, *Indian Film*, London and New York: Oxford University Press, 1963, 1980; Sumita S. Chakravarty, *National Identity in Indian Popular Cinema, 1947–1987*, New Delhi: Oxford University Press, 1996, ch. 2; Manjunath Pendakur, 'India' in John A. Lent, *The Asian Film Industry*, Bromley: Christopher Helm, 1990, pp. 229–52.

17. These are available in all major state archives.

18. The compilation of writings for this subject has started slowly, with the recent workshop on Tamil film held by the Madras Institute of Development Studies showing the way in an archival project for collecting Tamil language materials on the subject of the cinema.

19. For an interesting discussion on 'The Production of Locality', cf. Arjun

Appadurai, *Modernity at Large*, New Delhi: Oxford University Press, 1997, pp. 178–99.

20. David Bordwell, *Narration in the Fiction Film*, London: Methuen, 1985, for an elaboration of art cinema exhibition after the Second World War; and Steve Neale, 'Art Cinema as Institution', *Screen* 22(1), 1981: 11–39.

21. For example, Ginnette Vincendeau, 'The Exception and the Rule', *Sight and Sound* 2(8), 1994, which demonstrates that Renoir's *Rules of the Game* (1939), invariably highlighted in the canon of world cinema by critics, should be understood within a set of local parameters of narrative form, performance tradition (boulevard plays) and cinematographic style (long takes and shooting in depth) that were shared by a number of French films of the time. Other stimulating writing on the importance of local industrial and cultural contexts includes: Ana M. Lopez, 'Tears and Desire: Women and Melodrama in the "Old" Mexican Cinema', in John King, Ana M. Lopez and Manuel Alvarodo (eds), *Mediating Two Worlds: Cinematic Encounters in the Americas*, London: BFI Publishing, 1993; Thomas Elsaesser, *A Second Life: German Cinema's First Decade*, Amsterdam: Amsterdam University Press, 1996; James Hay, *Popular Film Culture in Fascist Italy: the Passing of the Rex*, Bloomington and Indianapolis: Indiana University Press, 1987; Sue Harper, *Picturing the Past: The Rise and Fall of the British Costume Film*, London: British Film Institute, 1994, for an understanding of how the historical film reflected popular perceptions about British history; Susan Hayward, *French National Cinema*, London: Routledge, 1993, who notes the importance of systems of gesture and morphology in condensing social and political consensuses through the vehicle of the star. More generally, there is the elegant introduction on the problems and possibilities of the notion of popular cinema in Ginette Vincendeau and Richard Dyer, *Popular European Cinema*, London: Routledge, 1992. Such writing is yet to evolve substantially for the 'Third World cinema', as much recent writing has been centred on avant-garde 'third cinema' studies.

22. Christopher Wagstaff, 'A Forkfull of Westerns', in Vincendeau and Dyer, *Popular European Cinema*, is excellent in showing the layered nature of the popularity of Italian Westerns. He distinguishes between the big budget Italian Western run in prestigious outlets and its poorer relation, the small budget genre version exhibited perhaps often more extensively in low-priced small town and 'interior' theatres. The former may be more lucrative and elicit national attention, but the latter may actually reach a larger number of people.

23. For example, Andrew Higson, *Waving the Flag: Constructing a National Cinema in Britain*, Oxford: Clarendon Press, 1995; Hayward, *French National Cinema*, ch. 1; Stephen Crofts, 'Reconceptualizing National Cinema/s', *Quarterly Review of Film and Video*, 14(3), 1993.

24. Robert Stam and Randall Johnson, 'The Shape of Brazilian Film History', introduction to Stam and Johnson (eds), *Brazilian Cinema*, Rutherford, NJ: Fairleigh Dickinson University Press, 1982.

25. Ana M. Lopez, 'Women and Tears'.

26. For example, my 'Addressing the Spectator of a "Third-World" National Spectator: The Bombay Social Film of the 1940s and 1950s', *Screen*, 36(4), 1995.

27. 'The Economics of Ideology: Popular Film Form and Mode of Production', in *Ideology of the Hindi Film*, ch. 2, pp. 30–52.

28. Lothar Lutze, 'From Bharata to Bombay: Change and Continuity in Hindi Film Aesthetics', in Beatrix Pfleiderer and Lothar Lutze, *The Hindi Film: Agent and Re-agent of Cultural Change*, New Delhi: Manohar, 1985. This argument is also present in Gaston Roberge, *Chitra Bani: A Book on Film Appreciation*, Calcutta: Chitrabani Publications, 1974.

29. William O. Beeman, 'The Use of Music in Popular Film: East and West', in Pradeep Krishen (ed.), *Indian Popular Cinema: Myth, Meaning and Metaphor, India International Centre Quarterly* special issue, 8(1), March 1980; Ashok D. Ranade, 'Chitra, Pata and Sangeet in India: an Aesthetic Appraisal', in idem (ed.), *Sangeet Natak*, no. 100.

30. However, this too, needs to be qualified, and the forms of reading themselves historicized, as Chartier informs us. Roger Chartier, *Cultural History: Between Representations and Practices*, Oxford: Polity Press, 1989.

31. From its inception, *Filmfare*, the Bombay-based film magazine brought out by Bennett Coleman and the Times group of publications, has regularly editorialized and included articles arguing for such changes. Along with this role of advisor, the magazine instituted a system of awards, and engaged in hunting for new talent with a view to creating incentives for change and dynamizing the industry.

32. Partharasarathy, 'India in the Film Map of the World', *Indian Talkie 1931–56*, Bombay: Film Federation of India, 1956; Manjunath Pendakur and Radha Subrahmanyam, 'Indian Cinema beyond National Borders', in John Sinclair (ed.), *New Patterns in Global Television: Peripheral Vision*, London and NY: Oxford University Press, 1996.

33. In this context, one area worth investigating is exhibition practices abroad. Rosie Thomas pointed out that before Channel 4 ensured a greater integrity to the programming of minority television in Britain, it was common to cut out musical sequences from popular Indian films. Rosie Thomas, 'Indian Cinema: Pleasures and Popularity', *Screen* 26(3-4), 1985.

34. *The Nation and its Fragments: Studies in Colonial and Post-colonial Histories*, New Delhi: Oxford University Press, 1994.

35. 'Early German Cinema: A Second Life?', in Elsaesser, *A Second Life*.

36. For these aspects of early cinema, cf. Thomas Elsaesser, *Early Cinema: Space, Frame, Narrative*, London: British Film Institute, 1990 and Miriam Hansen, *Babel and Babylon: Spectatorship in Early American Cinema*, Cambridge, MA: Harvard University Press, 1991.

37. 'A Viewer's View', in Suresh Chabria, *Light of Asia: Indian Silent Cinema 1912–1934*, National Film Archives of India, 1994.

38. Stephen P. Hughes, 'The Pre-Phalke Era in South India: Reflection on the Formation of Film Audiences in Madras', *South Indian Studies 2*, July–December 1996.

39. While the early Indian cinema collection up to 1931 is very limited, it has still not been adequately analysed, and we are likely to develop a much more complicated account of narrative methods than is presently available. I have suggested elsewhere that film-style and forms of address in Phalke's cinema

was composed of mixed forms rather than a dominant form. 'Reflections on the Cinematic Public, 1913–43', in Seminar on 'Making Meaning in Indian Cinema', Indian Institute for Advanced Study, Shimla, October 1995.

40. For the most systematic account of this mode of production, see David Bordwell, Kristin Thompson and Janet Staiger, *The Classical Hollywood Cinema: Film Style and Mode of Production to 1960*, Routledge, 1985, 1988.

41. See also my 'Addressing the Spectator'.

42. There is a body of work which understands melodrama as dramaturgy and meaning system to address the experience of the transition to modern social and political forms. In this reading melodrama strives to recover sacred meaning but, failing to do so, comes to locate significance in the personality. The ambiguities of the system are encoded in its drive to figure the 'truth' of relationships through the surfacing of a hitherto concealed moral occult. See especially, Peter Brooks, *The Melodramatic Imagination: Balzac, Henry James, Melodrama and the Mode of Excess*, New York: Columbia University Press, 1985. In international film studies, a register of disempowered perception is observable in the dramas of suffering and alternative subjectivity conjured up by the Hollywood 'women's film'. See Christine Gledhill (ed.), *Home is Where the Heart is: Studies in Melodrama and the 'Woman's Film'*, London: British Film Institute, 1987.

43. Censorship is also an issue here. As Pandian shows, the centrally administered structure of government censorship proved an obstacle to the Madras government's efforts to censor the film, though this was a problem of administrative structure rather than political difference.

44. The avenging woman may then represent something of the 'in-between' agency which Prasad refers to, a position whose power arises from not being fixed within the hierarchies of symbolic order. 'The gulf between two patriarchal zones is bridged . . . by the figure of woman. It is through her agency that it becomes possible to allegorize historic transformations . . .' 'Signs of ideological re-form', below. However, in Prasad's formulation the transformation is completed, whereas circumstances are much more ambivalent in the final submission of the avenging women cycle. This is akin to a gothic excess where feminine subjectivity, instead of being suppressed and subject to suffering as in melodrama, returns with a demonic vengeance, thereby keeping male fears of its power alive at the moment of narrative resolution. For an interesting discussion of gothic representations and female subjectivity, see Laleen Jayamanne, 'Post-colonial Gothic: The Narcissistic Wound of Jane Campion's *The Piano*', in Seminar, 'Under Capricorn: A Conference on Art, Politics and Culture', Wellington, New Zealand, March 1994.

45. Where would one locate *Bandit Queen* (Shekhar Kapur, 1995), within this framework which places the avenging woman film in the interstices of state-forms and at the margins of industrial enterprise? Funding from Channel 4 of British television meant *Bandit Queen* was produced under a different state-form and oriented to a different constituency. This permitted a depiction of nudity, sex and rape with an unprecedented directness and rawness, quite the reverse of the displaced cinematic idiom of Gopalan's description. The film is definitely merchandized for foreign audiences and awards, and is therefore

part of an orientalist tradition. But arguably, it is also an intervention in the culture of diaspora and in the local culture of the original national entity. This location has accentuated some of the problems already apparent in the way parallel cinema in India represented socially oppressed groups. As with the latter, atrocities are located with the dominant groups and low castes are championed as the victims in the politically correct fashion. Yet backward rural society seems to emerge in a very discomfiting way as a space inhabited only by the bestial or the submissive. The avenging woman and her lover have to be separated out from this brutal environment, using the conventions of romance and rebellion to provide a surrogate position for the modern spectator. This becomes an invitation to underwrite a cultural separation of the modern from the backward and barbaric in the constitution of Indian society.

46. See also my 'Addressing the Spectator' and 'Dislocations: The Cinematic Imagining of a New Society in 1950s India', *Oxford Literary Review* 16, 1994 for further discussions on how the culture of *darsan* is employed in popular film.

47. Nandy was the first to address this divide in his 'The Intelligent Film Critic's Guide to the Indian Cinema'. He was particularly concerned about understanding the character of middle-class culture. In his account, this is a complex formation with sections of it sharing in mass cinematic culture. The latter is then not just a plebeian mode of consumption, and its 'traditional' character caters to a much wider segment of society. As in other aspects of Nandy's work, class is not a central category, and the culture of the supposedly marginal has an encompassing quality to it. Indeed, on closer view, it may be the culture of the silent majority. Interestingly, Prasad's Marxist approach may in some ways overlap with Nandy's: for he too sees popular film as vehicle of tradition: 'traditionally regulated social relationships'. But in Prasad's account, the traditional does not palliate a victimized public, it is marked by relations of power and subordination. For him, the popular film also exceeds the traditional, providing a framework of desire, for new senses of self, romance, and familial relations, and hence for that modernity which is anathema to Nandy. It is with the 1970s 'mass film' that a more specifically class-related definition of consumption emerges for Prasad, with the suggestions that the Bachchan film is in fact catering to class-based senses of subalternity. See his seminal account of the diversification of the cinematic institution in the 1970s in *Ideology of the Hindi Film*, part II, pp. 117–216.

48. *Ideology of the Hindi Film*, pp. 29–51.

49. 'There is a political problem here which outweighs all the efforts focused on finding economic or purely cultural solutions to the industry's problems. Only if and when that transcendental point of emanation of meaning ceases to regulate the discourse of cultural texts will the occasion arise for searching for other ways of organizing the text'. Ibid., p. 50.

50. '. . .the Indian social formation is best characterized as structured by "formal subsumption" . . . a certain structured coexistence of the modern state and its instruments of passive revolution with pre-capitalist ideologies and social relations . . . The ideology of formal subsumption, which insisted on the difference between the modern and the traditional, and the need to protect

that difference, resulted in the protection given to the feudal family romance as the appropriate form of entertainment for the masses. This difference and the apparatuses that are meant to preserve it are no longer sustainable . . .' 'Signs of Ideological Re-form', below.

51. This argument was also made by Niranjana in her 'Tourists and Terrorists in *Roja*'.

52. For example, see my 'Voice, Space, Form: *Roja* (Mani Ratnam, 1994), Indian Film and National Identity' in Stuart Murray (ed.), *Not on Any Map: Essays on Post-colonialism*, Exeter: University of Exeter Press, 1997.

53. I am referring to the new contexts of television music programmes and music videos in changing the nature of the cinematic institution.

54. Elsaesser, *Early Cinema*; Hansen, *Babel and Babylon*; Tom Gunning, 'The Cinema of Attractions', *Wide Angle* 8(3-4), 1986.

55. Bordwell et al., *The Classical Hollywood Cinema*, p. 254.

56. For example, Paul Kerr, 'Out of What Past? Notes on the B Film Noir' in *Screen Education* 32-3: 45–65, Autumn 1979–80.

57. Miriam Hansen, 'Early Cinema, Late Cinema: Permutations of the Public Sphere', *Screen* 34(3): 197–210, Autumn 1993.

58. Tejaswini Niranjana, 'Cinema, Femininity and the Economy of Consumption', *EPW* 26(43), 26 October 1991.

59. By transcendence I imply here a move, via performance, which impresses the common mechanisms of identification—empathy and pathos—with a drive to exceed the bounds of the social and the real, in a burst of choreographed energy. This transcendent dimension relates to the utopian qualities of entertainment, as conceived by Richard Dyer in his seminal article, 'Entertainment and Utopia', Bill Nichols, *Movies and Methods*, vol. II, Berkeley: University of California Press, 1985. I have suggested how such modes of performative excess allow for the circumvention of communal differences in an analysis of *Bombay* (Mani Ratnam, 1995) in '*Bombay* and its Public', *Journal of Arts and Ideas*, 29, 1996, to be re-published in Rachel Dwyer and Chris Pinney (eds), *Pleasure and the Nation*, London: Curzon Press.

60. As the reader will observe, the article locates its interpretation in the conflicts that erupted in India after the government-instituted Mandal Commission advocated reservations in government service for 'backward classes'. This caused extensive unrest amongst a middle-class, upper-caste public, particularly in north India. While some of this unrest related to the anxieties of socially and economically marginalized sections of the upper castes, media reportage and analysis was dominated by an elite professional public. This discourse denounced reservation as inimical to the cultures of merit and excellence required for national economic and social transformation, and represented a callous indifference to the histories of economic and educational backwardness and social ignominy that lower-caste groups have had to contend with.

61. This analysis is quite in contrast to an earlier attempt to think about the politics of 1970s Bachchan films. Siddhartha Basu, Pradip Krishen and Sanjay Kak argued that the 'angry young man' films should be situated against the perceived decline of state institutions, which resulted in the emergence of a series of extra-constitutional figures and movements, from the Naxalites through

Nav Nirman to the Youth Congress. As such there is considerable ambivalence about what the anti-hero represented. 'Cinema and Society: A Search for Meaning in a New Genre', in Pradip Krishen (ed.), *Indian Popular Cinema*. In his interpretation, Prasad seems to come closer to Majumdar, in arguing for a tragic rendering of the Bachchan character, rather than conjure with the possibilities of a potentially fascist personality. *Ideology of the Hindi Film*, pp. 144–51.

62. For example, Rosie Thomas, 'Sanctity and Scandal: The Mythologisation of Mother India', *Quarterly Review of Film and Video* 11(3), 1989; Ravi Vasudevan, 'Dislocations'.

63. Partha Chatterjee, 'Talking About our Modernity in Two Languages', *Studies in Humanities and Social Sciences*, 2: 153–69, Shimla, 1996; reprinted in Idem, *A Possible India: Essays in Political Criticism*, New Delhi: Oxford University Press, 1997, pp. 263–85.

64. *Screen* 16(3), Autumn 1975.

65. The first attempt to examine these issues for Indian cinema is Steve Hughes' dissertation on early south Indian cinema. See Stephen P. Hughes, 'Is There Anyone Out There?', Ph.D dissertation, University of Chicago, 1996.

66. Karthigesu Sivathamby, *The Tamil Film as a Medium of Political Communication*, Madras: Century Publishing House, 1981.

67. Bordwell outlines the objective of *The Classical Hollywood Cinema* as explaining, 'in a systematic way how [some familiar film-making practices] work together to create a distinct film style which, like Poe's purloined letter, "escapes observation by dint of being excessively obvious" ' (p. 11). See also Raymond Bellour, 'The Obvious and the Code', *Screen* 15(4), Winter 1974–5: 7–17.

68. I think this is Rajadhyaksha's objective, although he does not put it this way; for, subsequently, he argues that local forms of cinematic practice will gradually develop languages through which the frame will no longer exercise a disjunctive function.

69. Sudipta Kaviraj, 'Dilemmas of Democratic Development in India', in Adrian Leftwich (ed.), *Democracy and Development: Theory and Practice*, Oxford: Polity Press, 1996; 'Democracy and Development in India', in Amiya Bagchi (ed.), *Democracy and Development*, London: St Martin's Press, 1995; Partha Chatterjee, 'Communities and the Nation', in idem, *The Nation and its Fragments*; 'Beyond the Nation—or Within?', *EPW*, 4–11, January 1997; Veena Das, 'Communities as Political Actors', in idem, *Critical Events*, New Delhi: Oxford University Press, 1996.

70. J. Michael Kennedy, 'Reading the Popular Text: a Study of Cultural Contestation', M.Phil dissertation, Centre for the Study of Social Systems, Jawaharlal Nehru University, New Delhi, 1992.

# I

# The Sociology and Politics of the Cinematic Institution

# 1

# Policing Silent Film Exhibition in Colonial South India

## STEPHEN P. HUGHES

FOR CRITICS IN both colonial and independent India, film censorship has deservedly been an important and persistent problem throughout this century which continues to be the subject of lively debate. However, the topic of censorship has dominated historical accounts of the government's relationship to the cinema in India to the point that the spatial definitions and aspects of official power at the places of film exhibition have been for the most part ignored. Even the most complete historical accounts of both the colonial and independent Indian government's efforts to control the cinema barely mentions anything about their interventions at the public spaces and institutions of film exhibition or the system of licensing cinema theatres.[1] Likewise, in S.T. Baskaran's otherwise worthy account of government policies on silent cinema in south India, official intervention is portrayed as being a matter of censorship.[2]

In part, this tendency can be explained as part of the general historiographic privileging of film production, texts, content and star personalities to the exclusion of the places, contexts and institutions within which film-goers have had access and engaged with the cinema in India. Certainly, in the now dominant formulations of Indian film history, there has been little effort to consider the conditions of circulation and exhibition which preceded and exceeded the films themselves.[3] For my purposes, the historical emergence of film exhibition in south India is important insofar as

I would like to thank Sarah Hodges, Raphael Cohen and Awadhendra Sharan for helpful criticism and comments on earlier drafts of this essay.

it provided the sites for regular access to film shows and created the primary conditions where audiences engaged with the projected images and live entertainment of the cinema. Especially in the early years before Indian cinema became enmeshed in a larger network of mass media ( that is, before there was any significant film journalism, a parallel music industry, radio or TV to extend and support it), exhibition was the primary mediation where widely circulated films met their local audiences.

In this essay, I seek to restore a sense of exhibition place to discussions about the relationship between the colonial state and the cinema in India, to recast the history of colonial efforts to control the cinema from their inception in terms of an ongoing engagement with cinema exhibitions. Only in recognizing the historical articulation of colonial power and the cinema at the sites of exhibition, can we begin to appreciate the material conditions and concrete situations which brought film texts together with Indian film audiences. The argument here is part of a larger project to critically rethink the history of the cinema in India to include not only films, but the emergent social institutions of exhibition, the growth of audiences and the conventions of film-going based on local perspectives from south India.[4]

During the first decade of this century there was very little in way of cinema entertainment available in south India. Up to about 1910 touring cinemas only occasionally visited Madras city, a few of the major cities and hill stations of the south where they catered to relatively small audiences of largely European and elite Indians. By the early 1910s, film exhibitors were beginning to open permanent cinemas, first, in Madras city, and then in the other major cities of the south by the end of the decade. Even though they were still quite limited in number, these permanent exhibition outlets represented a new public institution of commercial entertainment with regular and daily film shows capable of attracting steady crowds. The cinema in south India was catching up with the phenomenal growth of cinema entertainment worldwide. Most of the films which were being distributed the world over found their way to south India where virtually all films screened during this period were of foreign make.

During this period between 1910 and 1920, when it became obvious that the cinema in south India was going to be something more than a passing curiosity, the colonial government perceived this new form of entertainment as a vague, but potential threat. As the cinema business established itself permanently in Madras during the 1910s, the Government of India grew increasingly concerned about their ability to manage and mediate the spread of silent cinema exhibitions. Colonial officials were both uncertain about the effects of cinema viewing on their subject population and juridically unprepared to regulate the growing film trade. The cinema posed problems for the colonial administration of what exactly this presumed danger posed by the cinema was, and what they could possibly do about it. These questions were initially left to local authorities, police, district magistrates and a zealous Electrical Inspector in Madras Presidency who variously worried about the fire hazards and physical safety of film audiences inside theatres, the geographic location of cinema halls and gathering of film crowds within certain neighbourhoods, the alleged harmful (ideological) effects of cinema content on public morality and the possible propagation of discontent with colonial rule. Officials variously mobilized this cluster of confused, presumed, vague yet seemingly urgent anxieties about the cinema in regulating the places of exhibition where audiences had access to cinematic entertainment.

In this essay I consider how various local government officials responded to the spread of cinema exhibition in Madras Presidency—from the first official action on the cinema implemented by local authorities in Madras city during 1913, to the extension of exhibition regulations to cover most of the Presidency in 1915 and then finally, the establishment of all-India legislation in 1920. The focus here is on how the early discourses and practices of government regulation related to the emerging patterns of commercial film exhibition in south India. I discuss a series of episodes—a failed dance performance, the construction of a cinema hall, the personal efforts of the Madras government's Electrical Inspector and the enforcement of cinema regulations dividing permanent and touring cinemas—to suggest how local government's anxieties and actions addressed the growth of the cinema at the places of exhibition. I, thus, follow the colonial government's changing engagement with the cinema in south India during the 1910s and 1920s as it produced standards, regularized surveillance and institutionalized a hierarchy of exhibition practices.

## MAUD ALLEN AND THE LICENSING OF CINEMA SPACE BEFORE 1918

The first government moves to control the cinema in south India were based on the reputation of a woman dancer who never performed in Madras. Nonetheless, the dancer's non-incident established government precedent in Madras city which defined official power over the space of cinema exhibitions and what could be performed in that public place which served as the basis for creating regulations for the rest of the Presidency at a later date. This early example drawn from the colonial archive in Madras, reveals how the threat of a live performance at a cinema hall provoked local officials into taking their first actions to control exhibition.

In November 1913, the Government of India requested the Presidency governments to take action to prevent the performances at cinema halls in response to the announced India tour of Maud Allen, a British ballet and exotic dancer known for her virtual nudity and sexually suggestive style. At first the Secretary of State for the Government of India tried to dissuade Allen from undertaking the tour. Upon Allen's refusal to cancel, he issued a circular to the provincial governments warning of her arrival and suggesting that appropriate local action be taken to prevent her performances. The directive explained that, '. . . the objections to performances in this country by a white woman of her dramatic reputation, with dances of the type that have been associated with her name, are obvious.'[5] The government was concerned that this 'indecent performance' would reflect poorly on the moral character of British people as a whole and, in so doing, damage the authority of colonial British rule in India.[6] Conceived as a threat to British prestige, colonial officials acted out their duty to protect and, in this case, police the virtue of white women as represented on stage against what they perceived as the lustful desire and gaze of Indian men in the audiences.[7] These concerns were not limited to government officials, but also greatly vexed members of the European community more widely. In Madras city, three months before the proposed tour, the local branch of the European Defence Association convened a special meeting in order to consider the question of Maud Allen's visit to India.[8]

As part of an ambitious tour throughout the 'East' Maud Allen was to perform in Madras city at the Lyric Theatre, which was located on the first floor of the Misquith and Company music store building at the intersection of Walaja and Mount Roads. In early 1913 Misquith leased the Lyric out to the Empire Cinema Company and thus established the first of the eventually numerous permanent cinema halls to open along the European shopping district on Mount Road. The Empire was owned and managed by D.E.D. Cohen, who after running the cinema hall successfully for over eight months, purchased the Lyric from Misquith and immediately closed it down in order to make extensive alterations. At that time Cohen was also closely involved with Maud Allen's tour, working as a promoter who 'booked and directed' Allen's performances in 'South India, Ceylon, Burma and the East'.[9] The plan was that Maud Allen and the Cherniavsky Brothers music trio, advertised as 'The Most Powerful Attraction in the History of India', were to inaugurate the new ownership and management of the Lyric Theatre as well as open the Christmas performance season.[10] The Presidency government was alerted to this impending performance about one month in advance, and charged with the duty of protecting the central government's conception of public morality. In turn the Madras government further delegated the administrative problem of how to prevent the event from happening to the municipal officials of Madras, as Allen's performance at the Lyric was considered to be a matter of local jurisdiction.

When considering what to do about Allen's performance, Madras city officials first turned to already established regulations governing 'places of public resort' and dramatic performances. The Public Performances Act of 1876 provided a model for the Madras government to deal with the threat of morally and politically undesirable live entertainment. The 1876 Act was aimed at prohibiting what the government considered to be seditious drama performances, that is, those likely to excite feelings of discontent and rebellion against British colonial rule. The law required managers or promoters of a 'place of public resort or amusement' to notify the local police authority about any planned drama performance. Though the Madras government was legally empowered to ban any performance it saw fit, this was not enforced locally to stop dramas until the 1919 agitation against the Rowlatt Act.[11] However, in the case of Maud Allen, Madras city officials were doubtful about stretching the existing rules about drama performances and places of public resort to cover a dance performance in a cinema hall and did not believe that they had the legal authority to prevent a non-dramatic performance at a cinema hall or otherwise.

Faced with Allen's impending arrival, the city officials prepared a different legal basis to prohibit her performance by introducing new measures to assert control over the content of all performances at places of film exhibition. The city government added a provision to the Public Resort Act of 1888 to include cinema shows: 'No cinematograph exhibition shall be held without special sanction of the Commissioner of Police. . . . The licensee shall furnish the Commissioner of Police with full information of any performance at least seven days beforehand.'[12] Even though the explicit purpose was to stop a particular performance at a specific cinema hall, police authorities in Madras city suddenly gained new powers over all performances held in the public spaces of cinema exhibition.

With this move the Madras officials created police jurisdiction for approving the material to be performed at film shows, whether live or celluloid, which was similar to what had been established for public dramas and songs. The Commissioner had the power to prohibit any performance in the city, which in his judgement did not conform to the requirements of decency or was likely to lead to disorder.[13] This meant that the Commissioner of Police was institutionalized as the local authority over film shows with *de facto* power of censorship at the sites of exhibition, a position which was later formalized in the creation of regional film censor boards by 1920 and was even retained after Independence. In the end Maud Allen never performed in Madras due to a well-publicized injury and city officials never had to exercise their newly created powers to ban the show. Since there is no indication that Cohen had planned to screen any films in conjunction with Maud Allen's dance performance in Madras, just the threat of a live performance at a cinema hall was enough to prompt the government to initiate its first steps in a long history of regulating the spaces of cinema.

## GREENWOOD RULES: THE ELECTRICAL SURVEILLANCE OF THE CINEMA

The failed Maud Allen event encouraged government officials in south India, at least sporadically, to consider ways of expanding their power to regulate and control cinema shows. However, it would be a mistake to assume that there was a centrally organized and collective government plan of action in relation to the cinema. Before specific regulations were drafted for the cinema in all of colonial India, local authorities in Madras acted on their own, sometimes idiosyncratic, initiatives to control the public spaces of entertainment. The Electrical Inspector for the Public Works Department of Madras Presidency, E.J.B. Greenwood, took it upon himself to examine every cinema hall in the Presidency and in so doing, sought to create the administrative means to make the Presidency safe from a variety of dangers—ranging from fire hazards and physical safety to immorality and presumed ideological effects—posed by the cinema.

In 1915, Greenwood personally appealed to the Madras government to extend the rules of the Indian Electricity Act of 1910 and the Places of Public Resort Act, 1888, to make it necessary for all film exhibitors to obtain a certification of electrical safety in order to run cinema shows. Greenwood's proposal was most likely based upon the example of the British Cinematograph Act of 1909 which sought to regulate the public safety threat of the new entertainment. This Act empowered local authorities in Britain to issue licences for buildings where 'pictures or other optical effects' were exhibited on the basis of whether they conformed to certain safety criteria. The explicit concern motivating this Act was that the inflammable nitrate film stock used at cinema halls presented a special risk of fire and was, thus, a public safety hazard.[14] With no mention of any ideological or moral problems with the content of film shows, this first legislative effort in Britain defined the public problem of the cinema strictly in spatial terms and located it in specific buildings of public entertainment.

Using the precedent established in the Maud Allen affair, Greenwood suggested that 'a special set of rules based on those already worked for Madras city be extended for the rest of the Presidency.' The Madras government implemented his plan three years before the Government of India took any action to regulate the cinema.[15] This move constituted the first attempt by the provincial government to exert control over cinema shows, both touring and permanent, through necessary compliance with electrical codes, inspections and licensing. Almost five years before the first official board of film censorship in Madras, the government assigned the

Electrical Inspector to keep track of exhibition activities throughout the Presidency. Under this plan, Greenwood inspected a cinema theatre for the rather costly fee of Rs 64 and issued a certificate which was presented to the Chairman of Municipal Councils and Subdivisional Magistrates who issued licences for cinema shows within their areas. The owner or manager of each touring cinema was also responsible for informing the District Magistrate at least seven days in advance of every time a relocation was proposed. In this way Greenwood became the mediating broker between film exhibitors and the District Magistrates whose intervention made commercial film shows possible.

Greenwood assumed direct responsibility and evinced a personal interest in inspecting all cinemas, both permanent and touring, operating in the Presidency. In this capacity, he acquired a great deal of first-hand experience relating to the conditions of cinema exhibition. In the 1910s the number of cinema outlets in the Presidency were few enough for Greenwood to look after the matter personally (though in later years he had to delegate his responsibilities). In fact, Greenwood attended to all matters of public safety, broadly conceived, at all film exhibitions in the Presidency, including exits, air quality, ventilation, electric installation, fire appliances, the strength of balconies and staircases, storage of films, eye-strain, and certifying that the age of the operator was over twenty-one.

Despite Greenwood's concerns, the physical safety threat posed by cinema theatres became less of an issue for the government throughout the 1920s. As it turned out, there were very few accidents at cinema theatres in south India.[16] They were much safer than officials had feared. In 1928 Greenwood claimed that since there had been no cinema-related fatalities during his entire fifteen years of inspecting exhibition sites, '. . . the present standard of safety cannot be insufficient.'[17] This assertion can, in part, be read as Greenwood congratulating himself, but also marks an important shift in the perceived danger of the cinema, especially coming from a man who had more than anyone else in the south, been obsessed with the physical safety at cinema theatres.[18] By the late 1920s, the government was generally satisfied that the system of licensing cinema theatres worked well enough to protect the public safety of film-goers.

From the mid-1910s through the mid-1930s, Greenwood acted

in a capacity which went well beyond being just an electrical inspector concerned with physical safety. Greenwood did not stop with an inspection of the material conditions of exhibition, but also concerned himself with moral and political issues raised by the exhibition of objectionable films in ways that prefigured and paralleled later censorship policies. However, in pursuing his duties, Greenwood did not clearly make the distinction between physical safety conditions and the harmful moral and political effects of film content, which was institutionalized along with censorship. Greenwood used his expertise and involvement with film exhibitions to advise the government on all dangers—physical, mental and political—posed to film audiences. In 1921, Greenwood went so far as to write a letter to the Madras government which proposed his own censorship criteria for determining which films were unsuitable for exhibition, even though official censor boards had already been formed. With a clear acknowledgment of the current political climate, he suggested that films '. . . dealing with inflammatory matters as Gandhi doctrines, religious feelings of the Mohamedans, and universally condemned scenes of inchastity or immorality' were particularly dangerous in the current situation.[19] Greenwood always used his position as electrical inspector beyond building safety to help the government police the moral and political aspects of film exhibition.

Greenwood's overall concerns about the cinema were indicative of the colonial government's difficulties in sorting out the issue of what the cinema was potentially capable of doing to its audiences. While the officials clearly recognized that cinema could be both physically and morally harmful to the public, they initially dealt with the moral and political threat through the regulation of the theatre spaces. Before the Government of India stepped in to regularize and institute central controls in 1918 and before it came into effect in 1920, the regulation of the sites of exhibition in Madras Presidency was largely left to the personal initiative of one man. In the absence of clear, officially mandated guidelines, Greenwood took pride in applying his own strict standards for protecting the physical and moral safety of the film-going public through surveillance at the sites of exhibition as a self-appointed representative of the colonial state in Madras Presidency on all matters relating to the cinema.

## CONTESTING THE PLACE OF THE CINEMA IN MADRAS

Greenwood was undoubtedly an important figure in defining the Madras government's emerging engagement with the cinema, but he was not the only official concerned about the increasing dimensions of the cinema trade in south India. Indeed there was a wider debate among local officials about their authority and power to control cinema exhibition in relation to their attempts to prevent the construction of an Indian cinema hall in the Georgetown area of Madras city during 1916. Once again, the physical space of the cinema became a primary site at which the Madras government both tested its powers and confronted its limitations in the control of the cinema.

The cinema hall in question was the Crown Theatre, the second of R. Venkiah's three Madras city theatres. The site for the hall had previously been a hand-cart stand, located on Mint Street next to an alley used as the entrance to the Government Press and across from the Government Stores Depot. This plot of land and its surrounding Georgetown neighbourhood opened possibilities for Venkiah to cater to new Indian film audiences in Madras city. Venkiah drew up the plans for constructing the hall in October 1915, obtained a building licence by the beginning of November and began construction in December.[20] The plan was more functional and less ornate compared with the most recent picture palaces in the Mount Road neighbourhood, which catered to more affluent and European audiences. The hall was to measure 140 feet by 50 feet and was to accommodate up to 1,200 on the flat floor without a balcony. However, before the project could be completed, Venkiah ran into resistance from the British authorities in Madras.

Some highly placed British officials in the Government of Madras Presidency and in the Municipal Corporation worked together to stop the construction. Responding belatedly, five months after construction commenced, the Commissioner of Police warned Venkiah in early May 1916 to discontinue the building work. The exact motives behind this move are not clear but the official charge was that the new cinema was located too close (sixty yards) to the Government Medical Stores Depot which, in 1916, was producing medical dressings for the war effort. The stated fear was that a cinema hall represented a serious fire hazard due to the arc light used in projection, thus threatening the medical dressings 'which would be irreplaceable at the time of war and are very urgent for the Expeditionary Force in Mesopotamia.'[21]

This official excuse for halting the construction of the Crown Theatre proved to be rather thin. When the Madras government asked the British military authorities to intervene under the Defence of India Rules, they declined because they were not concerned enough with the safety risk posed by a cinema hall to their bandages. The Madras government next sent the Electrical Inspector, E.J.B. Greenwood, to check the construction. However, Greenwood also failed to find any fault, certifying the theatre to be up to electrical standard and presenting only a small risk of fire spreading from the building. The hall had been built using the latest fire-proofing methods: a zinc-and-iron trestle roof covered with corrugated iron, brick walls and a concrete floor. The only wood in the building was used for the doors and windows.[22] The government's position was further complicated by the fact that Venkiah had originally been granted a building permit without objections. However, the Madras officials, still not satisfied, continued their ban and searched for other legal means to enforce it, even after their original complaints had been dismissed.

Venkiah, for his part, contested the ban on his building the Crown and hired a lawyer to represent his case and help pressure the government on his behalf. He wanted to know why the government had waited through five months of construction before raising its objections, if the danger posed by a cinema was so great. Further, Venkiah was anxious not to lose the substantial investment for the construction of the theatre which he claimed was close to one lakh (100,000) rupees. He estimated that for every day that the theatre was delayed he would lose something close to Rs 400 in profits from ticket sales. Perhaps it was precisely this projected success which most concerned the Madras government.

Rather than the expressed anxiety about possible fire hazard being a threat to the war effort, one can speculate that there were other concerns at work as well. The idea of crowds of Indian working-class men gathering for film shows in close proximity to important government institutions would have made Madras officials uneasy. The daily collecting of crowds in the street outside the Crown Theatre at regular intervals before a film show and then, after being emotionally galvanized through the collective experience of film-watching, exiting together on to the streets again, would have made the police authorities particularly concerned. The colonial government of India had long recognized crowds, especially those of religious processions and at dramatic performances, as a potentially uncontrollable threat to the political and social order. The very notion of collective gatherings, even at places of public entertainment, carried assumed connotations of riotous mobs and revolutionary masses which could be mobilized against colonial authority. This was especially the case for the Crown, since it was the first cinema hall in Madras which explicitly was designed to cater to a clientele of the Indian lower classes who lived and worked in north Georgetown. The relatively European and higher-class Indian audiences of the Mount Road cinema establishments did not seem to provoke the same anxieties for Madras officials and none of these previously constructed cinema halls in this European area of Mount Road had been contested. Rather, it was the class specificity of the anticipated Indian audiences of the Crown Theatre which distinguished this cinema hall as a particular problem for those most invested in maintaining the colonial order of urban Madras.

Yet, beyond the official excuse about the fire hazard to the bandages which in any case proved to be hollow, the government was either unable or unwilling to state why the presence of the Crown Theatre was so objectionable. Still searching for a legal basis to enforce the ban on the cinema, it even considered appropriating the site under the Land Acquisition Act. However, on further legal advice, the government finally capitulated three months after halting the construction and decided not to take further action to prevent the completion of the theatre. This temporary government interference in the construction of the Crown was just the first of many more official interventions in both colonial and independent India to prevent the construction of cinema halls in what officials considered to be inappropriate locations. Most of these continuing efforts to control the spread and access of cinema entertainment involved anxieties about the congregation of certain Indian classes and communities at the sites of film exhibition.

## THE RATIONALIZATION OF CONTROL: PUBLIC SAFETY AND MORALITY AT THE FILM SHOW

For almost a decade, the Government of India had left the regulation of the cinema to local authorities, who patched together whatever administrative means they had at their disposal. The result was that the existing laws relating to the cinema were 'scattered over various Provincial Police Acts and Municipal Acts.'[23] They were concerned that not only was there a great deal of variability, but also confusion and ineffectiveness in what local governments were doing about the growing dimensions of film exhibition. One official at the time observed, '. . . the existing law on the subject was for the most part framed long before the cinematograph was dreamt of and is altogether inadequate to deal with film which may be objectionable.'[24] The Government of India had come to recognize that the cinema represented a new kind of administrative problem which necessitated a set of regulations designed specifically to cope with it.

By 1917 the Government of India believed that more than anything else, the power of the cinema lay in its ability to propagate ideas, to shape the consciousness of its audiences. Prompted by Britain during the First World War, the Government of India experimented with the possibility of using films as propaganda for encouraging cooperation with the war effort. In the short term, very little came out of this initiative except a flurry of government circular memoranda alerting local officials to both the dangers of enemy film propaganda and the new possibilities of screening films which helped educate and explain the purposes of the war to Indians.[25] If nothing else was accomplished from these propaganda efforts, it indicated an official recognition of the potentially vast powers of the medium to reach and mould public opinion which were significant enough to warrant government action in the matter.

In 1918 the Government of India made its first significant legislative intervention covering the cinema, when it drafted the Indian Cinematograph Act of 1918 based on two main objectives for the control of the cinema: to ensure the safety of film audiences and to prevent the exhibition of objectionable films. With this Act, the government clearly articulated a distinction between physical and moral safety in so far as these objectives were to be realized through the separate administrative strategies of licensing theatres and film censorship. Similar to what was already in place in Madras Presidency, no cinema exhibitor could operate in any public place without first obtaining a licence granted by the District Magistrate or by the Commissioner of Police in the Presidency towns.[26] The earlier licensing system of 1915 was carried over into the new legislation, but with the addition of regionally centralized film censorship, the moral qualifications of films were to be decided in advance as a matter of colonial policy.

While earlier government efforts focused solely upon the sites of exhibition and struggled to keep up with their proliferation, censorship attempted to deal with the problem of the cinema in a very different manner. Compared with earlier controls over cinema which had been implemented spatially across the entire Presidency at specific theatre locations, censorship seemed to offer a centralized means of controlling the supply of films before they went out for exhibition. Censorship held the promise of offering a unified solution for all of colonial India to what had previously been delimited as a regional and local problem at exhibition spaces. Further, the government hoped that censorship would standardize the regulation of film content from above and impose a standard moral and political code for the cinema. Thus conceived, the work of censorship seemed far removed from the exhibition spaces where the public had access to films. The institution of censorship abstracted films from their conditions of circulation and exhibition and confined their evaluation to the isolated comfort of a darkened room in a government bungalow where police and officials met with a few elite and representative leading citizens.

The Indian Cinematograph Act of 1918 empowered the provincial governments to form Boards of Censors in order to examine and grant or deny certification for films as suitable for public exhibition. No film was to be exhibited unless it had received a certificate of approval from one of the regional Board of Censors at Bombay, Calcutta, Madras, Rangoon and then later, in the Punjab. To ensure representation of all public interests on the Board it was required that no more than half its members could be in government service. In practice the final authority was exercised by the Commissioner of Police in the Presidency towns who served as President of the Censor Boards. Most of the early work of film censorship took place in the cities where imported films entered the country, which meant that the Censor Board in Bombay and to a lesser extent in Calcutta, handled the vast majority of films in the 1920s.

Though it was set up to operate independently and with a completely different moral and political agenda, even the censorship of films could not be entirely separated from the contexts of their exhibition. Censorship could not be effective if there was no way to make sure that the exhibitor screened approved films. Cinema hall managers were required to send a copy of their entertainment programme in advance to be scrutinized by an Inspector of Police who was then responsible for determining whether each film had proper censorship certificate numbers. Every film which passed through a Board of Censors came with an accompanying certificate (which was later spliced to the beginning of the films) with a registration number. The certificates were cross-checked with the lists of censored films regularly published in government gazetteers. Greenwood put it simply, 'If you cannot show the number, the film is obviously unproved.'[27] In order to prove censorship, the certificate had to be shown to someone, usually the police, who represented the authority of the state in the matter of regulating film exhibitions at the site of the cinema hall.

The government was well aware of the fact that the censorship process could easily be eluded by exhibitors who used smuggled film prints. The establishment of censorship immediately created a black market for films which might not have been passed by the regional Boards. The extent of this illicit trade of smuggled films was relatively small and mostly limited to erotic entertainment at private screenings, but seemed both significant and vague enough to worry government officials in the early 1920s.[28] Uncertified films could easily be screened since the local authorities were not always present at every public exhibition.

In 1921 a committee of publicity advisors warned the Madras government of a small but highly profitable market for indecent films in south India: 'At present these films are smuggled in clandestinely from France and South America and are believed to fetch a very high price.'[29] Greenwood echoed this concern, but added that more than any other mode of exhibition, touring cinemas were the ones likely to screen uncensored, smuggled and undesirable films.[30] As government officials episodically constituted the cinema as an object of regulation, they constantly confronted the limits of their own power to control its alleged effects. While censorship appeared to offer a centralized mode of power over the ideological content of films before their distribution, the circulation of these films to diverse audiences at the widely dispersed sites of film exhibition always exceeded the bounds of direct government control.

Greenwood, as on anything related to the cinema in south India, had very strong opinions about the enforcement of censorship at the point of exhibition: 'I say there is no definite machinery for seeing whether films exhibited are approved or unproved. . . . The police may amble in or not. It is nobody's duty in the mofussil at the opening night of a film to see to this [check the certificate].'[31] Film shows in remote areas presented obvious limitations in the government's surveillance of licensed theatres, but those in the urban centres of south India were more vigilantly followed by local authorities. In Madras city, the Commissioner of Police employed three inspectors, 'a Muhammadan, a Brahmin and a non-Brahmin' who were regularly sent to film theatres, to examine whether a film being screened related to their community's interests or religious feelings.[32] It is highly unlikely that exhibitors screened uncensored films at Madras city cinema halls which maintained prominent public profiles with newspaper advertising, posters and handbills.

Moreover, the police seem to have frequently attended Madras silent film shows on their own and for their own ends. Police officials throughout the south used their positions of authority to go beyond their official duties in regard to enforcing censorship at their local cinema halls. The police presence at cinema theatres seems to have been more often related to their interest in taking in the show for their own entertainment rather than as representatives of the colonial state. Exhibitors found it difficult to refuse the police any number of free passes, which were used more for their own enjoyment. Greenwood speculated about police attendance at cinemas: 'I think they go there more for amusement than in an official sense. It is not their definite object to see whether a film has been passed or not passed; whether it is approved film or not. They may get there late or early, just as they please.'[33] Local police may have been the foot-soldiers of the government's cinema policy, but they attended their duties with widely variable interests, which undoubtedly included their own amusement.

For the most part, the police remained unwanted, unpaying guests who personally represented the official power at local cinema halls, even though they may have also enjoyed the show. Despite shifting the process of making censorship decisions to an all-India level, police officials were still necessary at local cinema theatres to enforce the licensing system, ensure compliance with cinema building safety regulations and check the certification of censorship on the films screened.

## TOURING CINEMAS AND THE LIMITS OF OFFICIAL SURVEILLANCE

Even though the Madras government acquired broadened powers to censor and license film exhibitions, it continually confronted the limits of its abilities to monitor and control the events of film exhibition. More than any other mode of exhibition, touring cinemas presented special problems for government licensing and surveillance.

From the 1910s, permanent and touring cinemas developed in tandem as the two main aspects of the same commercial exhibition business in south India. Both kinds of cinema outlets were separated and related through a division of exhibition practices worked out in terms of different locations, levels of capital investment, film programmes, and audiences. Though touring exhibitions were the rule before 1910, the trend toward large, capital-intensive, permanent cinema halls in the 1910s, displaced touring cinema companies from the best urban locations and appropriated the more affluent classes which touring cinemas had been able to attract during their early years in Madras. This left the touring cinemas on the margins of the growing film trade in south India where they provided entertainment in rural areas and on the outskirts of larger towns to audiences relatively removed, if not completely cut off, from the cosmopolitan life in Madras city. During the silent period touring cinemas in south India struggled as low budget, small-scale operations which moved periodically, often by means of bullock-carts, with their own projector, tents, benches and chairs. They tended to screen films which were the least expensive and of the worst picture quality, for admission prices which were about half that offered at permanent theatres.[34] In short, almost everything about touring cinemas put them in a class below permanent cinema establishments.

The government was especially concerned about its ability to control these touring cinemas, because, as it reasoned, any temporary or mobile cinemas were, by their transitory nature, inherently difficult to control. Touring exhibitions exacerbated existent anxieties about the porous limits of government regulation and hence were considered uniquely dangerous.[35] From the mid-1910s, the Madras government was well aware and increasingly concerned about the fact that touring cinemas were 'not uncommon' in the districts of Madras Presidency.[36] When in 1915 the government extended the rules regulating cinematograph shows, which had been worked out for the city of Madras to the rest of the Presidency, they included both permanent and touring cinemas under their new licensing requirements.[37] Permanent theatres were issued licences for a particular building only, while touring ones had to obtain a licence for every district within which they operated.

The licensing system for touring cinemas had the unintended effect of limiting their movements within a small number of districts in Madras Presidency. Since the licences originally issued to touring cinema companies by District Magistrates were good for a period of one year within each district, it was much easier, less expensive and more convenient for exhibitors to confine their movements to districts for which they already had acquired a yearly licence. By 1917 the results of this policy were already obvious to government officials, who discerned patterns in the geographic distribution of touring cinemas. They found an uneven distribution, with the majority of touring cinema companies confining their movements to only a few districts while avoiding others altogether.[38]

After the implementation of the system of touring cinema licensing in 1915, the government was able to quantify and monitor the movements of these cinemas for the first time, with information provided by the local licensing authorities and the Electrical Inspector for the Presidency. As a result of these initial licensing efforts, the Electrical Inspector was able to estimate in 1917 that there were seventeen touring cinema companies operating throughout the Presidency.[39] The Madras government, especially through the efforts of Greenwood, became much more knowledgeable about the local conditions of exhibition at touring cinemas than had previously been the case.

Yet, despite these new measures, better surveillance and more knowledge of touring cinemas, government officials were still sceptical about their ability to control their entertainment content as well as follow their movements. The more the Madras government involved itself with regulating touring cinemas the more it realized the problems, limitations and uncertainties of this endeavour. Greenwood reported to the Government of Madras that because travelling cinema shows in the rural areas usually moved on after a few days to a maximum stay of two months, it was possible for them to move quickly through the Presidency while escaping the notice of the government. In 1917 Greenwood admitted that he 'could not make long sudden tours to catch one or two travelling shows, so that in general these cinema shows are subject to little technical control.'[40] Even if Greenwood could have kept up with these movements, touring cinemas tended to change their film programmes daily, making it virtually impossible to monitor the content of these exhibitions with anything less than constant surveillance.

In addition to these difficulties, the government also recognized there were a number of holes in its legal authority to control touring cinemas. First of all, the electrical codes first used to regulate the public safety of cinema shows did not apply to exhibitors who still used limelight. When the rules had been drawn up for Madras city, electricity had already supplanted limelight as the norm for cinema illumination and no rules had been written to regulate its use. This was especially a problem for controlling touring shows, since in 1915 Greenwood estimated that touring cinemas outside of Madras city usually used limelight.[41] If an exhibitor used limelight for illuminating projectors, then certification of electrical safety was not necessary and, thus, such shows escaped Greenwood's personal attention. Also, there were a few places in the Presidency where the Place of Public Resort Act 1888 did not apply and officials had no legal authority to license or regulate cinema shows. In some areas such as Tirunelveli, Tuticorin and Nilakottai, touring cinemas seem to have gone unlicensed before the Cinematograph Act of 1918 was implemented.[42]

Some of the problems outlined above were addressed with the implementation of the Cinematograph Act of 1918 which applied uniformly to all cinema shows throughout British India, no matter what illumination was used. Despite these ongoing efforts to further rationalize and extend their power during the first decades of this century, government officials in India only had a tenuous and provisional control over cinema exhibition. Less than one decade after the Cinematograph Act was supposed to have solved the

problems of cinema policy in colonial India, the uncertainty, feared
ineffectiveness and political sensitivity of these government
regulations directly led to the enormous inquiries of the Indian
Cinematograph Committee of 1927–8.

## OFFICIAL DIVISION OF EXHIBITION PRACTICES

While the relations of power between colonial authorities and silent
cinema worked to simultaneously restrict and prohibit, they also
helped produce and shape film exhibition in south India. As colonial
officials struggled to establish and define the state's power over the
sites of film exhibition, they helped to institutionalize an official
two-tier distinction of exhibition practices. Apart from the issues
of film censorship, the Cinematograph Act of 1918 also established
regulations to protect the physical safety of audiences as a matter
of licensing cinema theatres. However, in so doing, they instituted
an official division between the two modes of exhibition, which
framed a separate set of rules for the operation of permanent and
touring cinema outlets.

The governmental measures for regulating the cinema theatres
defined a set of differences between permanent and touring cinemas,
which privileged certain exhibition practices while discouraging
others. The Cinematograph Act of 1918 elaborated detailed safety
regulations for cinema shows in permanent buildings, which mandated certain standards for fire-proof construction materials, sanitary
conditions, ventilation and exits. The Act stipulated that permanent
theatres be constructed out of more expensive fire-resistant
materials, such as iron, brick and cement. However, touring
cinemas, which operated out of temporary structures (first tents
and later thatched halls) were not held accountable for the same
building safety requirements.

Greenwood himself justified the differential treatment of permanent and touring cinemas:

A travelling cinema using a tent does not require the careful examination
and approval that a cinema working in a building requires. The tent is
always the same, it must be pitched in an open space and there are
never any difficulties as to exits or proximity of fire spreading to
neighbouring houses.[43]

Greenwood made this assertion based on the assumption that

touring exhibitors usually used tents or temporary thatched sheds located in open areas on the outskirts of towns with no residential quarters nearby. Touring cinemas with their tents or other temporary structures were an easier, less expensive means of extending or entering the exhibition business. In legislating the disparity of standards between touring and permanent, the government helped to officially institute touring cinemas as both less prestigious and more profitable.

The government used the length of stay at one venue to define the exhibition category of touring cinemas. The Act dictated a somewhat arbitrary frequency of movement which defined the distinction between the two kinds of exhibition. In order to qualify under the rules for touring cinemas, exhibitors were required to move from a location after three months. Local authorities issued licences to touring cinemas only for a maximum of three months in one location. By defining and enforcing exhibition as either permanent or touring, these regulations placed the government in the middle of increasing competitive tensions and struggles between these modes of exhibition and figured centrally in both sides' claims and counter-claims about the government's supposed preferential treatment of the other.[44]

Officials followed touring cinema operators in order to make certain that a film show using a temporary structure was not covertly turned into a permanent establishment, disguised as a touring outlet, to avoid the more strict building codes. In offering touring cinemas concessions on safety requirements, the government did not want to give an unfair competitive advantage to touring exhibitors over other exhibitors who had invested large amounts of capital in permanent facilities. The three-month rule put government regulation in the middle of an emerging competition within the exhibition trade for the best locations with the highest collections.

The Cinematograph Act also created some new and unintended administrative problems in trying to enforce the distinction between touring cinemas and permanent theatres. Exhibition situations did not always conform to the government's definitions. Just as they had done in Madras city ten years earlier, many touring cinema companies used existing theatres for their film shows.[45] However, once touring cinema companies did so, they became subject to government regulations similar to those in effect for permanent cinema theatre buildings. Insofar as touring cinemas were performed at permanent buildings, they fitted the official category of a 'place of public resort', and required an examination to certify their suitability for hosting a film show.

In addition to this older requirement, the touring cinemas also came under the Cinematograph Act of 1918 and required another certification by Greenwood. The result was that exhibitors sometimes needed to obtain two separate licences and pay two licensing fees for one engagement.[46] These cases presented problems in issuing licences in a timely manner, which sometimes caused long delays before approval.[47] Though the government attempted to expedite these licences with the direct intervention of Greenwood, delays in obtaining official approval may well have discouraged touring companies from using such venues since the use of tents or thatched sheds presented fewer administrative delays and complications. This probably contributed to the fact that the practice of using existing halls on a touring basis tended to decline throughout the 1920s.[48]

The problems concerning the regulation of touring cinemas raised by Greenwood were registered in the collected evidence of the Indian Cinematograph Committee in 1928, but were not directly answered. By that time the government was more concerned with centralized film censorship, and touring cinemas seemed to be only a small and local factor in the comprehensive totality of the cinema in India as it was constituted by the Committee's investigation. When compared with permanent cinemas, touring cinemas represented a much smaller proportion of cinema outlets in British India. Government sources figured that in 1927 there were about 350 (75 per cent) permanent theatres as opposed to only 116 (25 per cent) touring cinemas.[49] In the Madras Presidency there were 16 touring cinema companies in 1917 and by 1928 that number had only gone up to 26.[50]

The Indian Cinematograph Committee found that, 'The people in general of the mofussil places, both small town and villages, have absolutely no access to these [cinemas in the cities and important towns] in spite of a few moving cinema companies.'[51] In their estimation, the cinema in India was still mostly exhibited at permanent theatres in urban areas and the impact of the medium 'has yet scarcely touched the fringe of the rural population.'[52] The problems posed by touring cinema exhibition at the all-India level may not have seemed significant, but the government's regulations pertaining to them helped to create a preferential system of licensing, upon which touring cinema operators in the south eventually capitalized. This officially brokered division has significantly structured the development of the exhibition trade in south India to the benefit of touring exhibitors. Especially from the 1930s, the rapid expansion of talkie films in south Indian languages, low operating costs, better electrical facilities and government regulatory concessions, all helped touring cinemas emerge as an increasingly important part of the exhibition business in south India.[53] Despite their temporary status and generally smaller seating capacities, by the 1950s touring cinemas reached larger audiences in more places than any other mode of exhibition in south India.

As an alternative to a narrow historiographic focus on the censorship of film texts, the point of this essay has been to suggest various local ways in which colonial officials constituted their efforts to control the cinema at the point of exhibition. Following various episodes during the 1910s and 1920s, drawn mostly from the colonial archives, my narrative examined the ongoing government strategies to cope with the growth of the cinema in south India, which were worked out at exhibition sites. Initially, even the colonial government's concerns about morally offensive or politically dangerous cinema representations were also addressed entirely as a matter of intervention, control and regulation at the public exhibition spaces. This articulation of official power at exhibition sites was eventually modified with the introduction of a coordinated all-India system of regional censor boards in 1920, which was nonetheless still predicated upon surveillance at local cinema halls. Moreover, the changing government rules relating to exhibition and film censorship not only imposed limitations and standards on the cinema but also helped to produce and shape the basic conditions of the cinema's availability in south India. From this point on, censorship eclipsed the regulation of exhibition space as the more important, contested and discussed mode of regulation, even though cinema licensing and exhibition spaces have remained, less controversially, a constant concern of government regulation.

NOTES

1. See Aruna Vasudev, *Liberty and License in the Indian Cinema*, New Delhi: Vikas Publishing House, 1978. For a more journalistic account see Kobita Sarkar, *You Can't Please Everyone! Film Censorship: The Inside Story*, Bombay: IBH Publishing House, 1982.

2. See S.T. Baskaran, *The Message Bearers: The Nationalist Politics and the Entertainment Media in South India, 1880–1945*, Madras: Cre-A, 1981, pp. 127–50.

3. Someswar Bhowmik's recent book has, at least, also recognized this point. He celebrates 'small itinerant showmen' as the 'unsung heroes' who created the film trade in India from nothing and provided a solid basis for the later development of the Indian film industry. *Indian Cinema, Colonial Contours* Calcutta: Papyrus, 1995, pp. 15–17.

4. See Stephen P. Hughes, 'Is There Anyone Out There? Exhibition and the Formation of Silent Film Audiences in South India', Ph.D. dissertation, University of Chicago, 1996.

5. Tamil Nadu Archives, Judicial, G.O. no. 2335, 18 November 1913; also see Baskaran, *Message Bearers*, pp. 128–9.

6. For a related discussion of these issues, see Poonam Arora, 'Imperiling the Prestige of the White Woman: Colonial Anxiety and Film Censorship in British India', *Visual Anthropology Review* 11(2), Fall 1995.

7. Since the revolt in 1857, the sexual threat to white women in India figured as a major trope in the colonial discourse justifying the continuation of the British civilizing mission. See Jenny Sharpe, *Allegories of Empire: The Figure of Woman in the Colonial Text*, Minneapolis: University of Minnesota Press, 1993. Also see Kenneth Ballhatchet, *Race, Sex and Class under the Raj: Imperial Attitudes and Policies and Their Critics, 1793–1905*, New York: St Martin's Press, 1980.

8. *Madras Times*, 22 September 1913.

9. Ibid., 1 December 1913.

10. Ibid., 3 December 1913.

11. See Baskaran, *Message Bearers*, pp. 21–42.

12. Tamil Nadu Archives, Judicial, G.O. no. 2335, 18 November 1913.

13. Ibid.

14. See Annette Kuhn, *Cinema, Censorship and Sexuality, 1909–1925*, London: Routledge, 1988, pp. 114–25; also, Rachael Low, *The History of the British Film, 1906–1914*, London: George Allen & Unwin, 1949, pp. 58–61.

15. Tamil Nadu Archives, Judicial, G.O. no. 1348, 16 June 1915.

16. The only mishap at a Madras cinema hall during the 1920s was reported at the Empire Theatre on Walajah Road near Mount Road at the site of the present-day Paragon Theatre. On the night of 5 June 1921, there was a slight fire in a dustbin, which was put out before anything serious could happen. From an unsigned letter to the editor, *The Hindu* (Madras), 21 June 1921.

17. *Evidence of the Indian Cinematograph Committee, 1927–1928* (hereafter *ICC Evidence*), New Delhi: Government of India Press, 1928, vol. 3, p. 42.

18. Even as early as 1921, Greenwood took personal credit for the fact that

there had been no cinema fire or accident during his tenure administering the public safety precautions at cinemas. See Tamil Nadu Archives, Law (Gen.), G.O. no. 1545, 29 September 1921.

19. Letter no. 29 (Confidential) in Tamil Nadu Archives, Law (Gen.), G.O. no. 804, 24 March 1922.

20. Tamil Nadu Archives, Judicial, G.O. no. 1297, 18 May 1916.

21. Ibid.

22. Ibid., G.O. nos. 1616–17, 23 June 1916.

23. *Report of the Indian Cinematograph Committee, 1927-1928* (hereafter *ICC Report*), New Delhi: Government of India Press, 1928, p. 105.

24. Legislative Council Debate, 5 September 1917. As cited in Vasudev, *Liberty and Licence*, p. 11.

25. See Philip Woods, 'Film Propaganda in India, 1914-23', *Historical Journal of Film, Radio and Television* 15(4), 1995: pp 543–53.

26. *ICC Report*, p. 105.

27. *ICC Evidence*, vol. 3, p. 46.

28. By 1928 the Indian Cinematograph Committee dismissed this problem as unfounded at public exhibitions and efficiently prevented by existing censorship channels. See *ICC Report*, p. 134.

29. From a confidential letter from the Advisory Publicity Committee located in Tamil Nadu Archives, Law (Gen.), G.O. no. 1237, 12 May 1922.

30. Ibid., G.O. no. 804, 24 March 1922.

31. Ibid.

32. Oral evidence from the Madras Board of Film Censors, in *ICC Evidence*, vol. 3, p. 75.

33. Ibid., 48.

34. Starting as low as one anna for a space on the floor or ground at the front closest to the screen and going as high as one rupee for a chair at the back, the norm for tickets at touring cinemas was two to four annas for a bench seat. E.J.B. Greenwood as cited in ibid.

35. E.J.B. Greenwood as cited in Tamil Nadu Archives, Law (Gen.), G.O. no. 2063, 23 August 1922.

36. E.J.B. Greenwood as cited in Tamil Nadu Archives, Judicial, G.O. no. 1348, 16 June 1915.

37. Ibid.

38. Tamil Nadu Archives, Judicial, G.O. no. 132, 18 January 1917. Another reason for the localized movements of touring cinemas was that in the 1910s and 1920s these companies mostly concentrated on the districts without any permanent cinema theatres, such as Tirunelveli, Ramnad, North Arcot, and Tanjore. See Tamil Nadu Archives, Law (Gen.), G.O. no. 1545, 29 September 1921.

39. Tamil Nadu Archives, Judicial G.O. no. 132, 18 January 1917.

40. Ibid.

41. Ibid., G.O. no. 1348, 16 June 1915.

42. Ibid., G.O. no. 132, 18 January 1917.

43. Tamil Nadu Archives, Law (Gen.), G.O. no. 466, 27 May 1921.

44. See, 'Permanent Theatre vs. Touring Cinemas', *Talk-A-Tone*, April 1949.

45. For example, until the Kamatchi Amba Cinema started in 1921, Tanjore district had no permanent theatres, but listed three buildings which were used for film exhibitions—Alahambra Theatre (seating 500) in Tanjore, the Havelock Theatre Hall (seating 800) in Nagapattinam and the South Indian Railway Institute (seating 300) also in Nagapattinam. Tamil Nadu Archives, Law (Gen.), G.O. no. 1545, 29 September 1921.

46. E.J.B. Greenwood as cited in the *ICC Evidence*, vol. 3, p. 39.

47. Tamil Nadu Archives, Law (Gen.), G.O. no. 466, 27 May 1921.

48. See A. Venkatarama Iyer, B.A., B.L., as cited in the *ICC Evidence*, vol. 4, pp. 241–3.

49. *ICC Report*, pp. 180–2.

50. Tamil Nadu Archives, Judicial G.O. no. 132, 18 January 1917.

51. N.R. Balakrishna Mudaliar, Acting Superintendent, School of Arts and Crafts, Madras, as cited in the *ICC Evidence*, vol. 3, p. 230.

52. *ICC Report*, p. 21.

53. By the early 1940s touring talkies, as they were commonly known, were the fastest growing sector of the exhibition business and by the late 1940s they had reached a position far more important and numerous than in any other part of India. See B.D. Bharucha (President, Cinematograph Exhibitors Association of India), 'Exhibition Trade in India' in *Handbook of the Indian Film Industry*, Bombay: The Motion Picture Society of India, 1949, p. 379. In 1948, touring cinemas outnumbered permanent outlets in the southern exhibition circuit (Madras, Mysore, Travancore-Cochin and Hyderabad) 743 (54 per cent) to 630 (46 per cent). See *Report of the Film Enquiry Committee, 1951*, New Delhi: Government of India Press, 1952, p. 336. Ten years later in Madras state alone, touring cinemas outnumbered permanent cinemas 706 (67 per cent) to 355 (33 per cent). See *Madras Film Diary, 1958*, Madras: Vi. Rama Rao Publisher, 1958.

# 2

# Parasakthi:
# Life and Times of a
# DMK Film

M.S.S. PANDIAN

I

> I witnessed there [at Ashok Theatre, Madras] such scenes which I have
> never witnessed so far in my life. My age is 25. Like animals, people
> have been expending great efforts trying to enter the narrow stair. All
> this under jostling by the police. Bhagirdha wouldn't have suffered so
> much to bring Ganges to the earth.[1]

THIS LITTLE DESCRIPTION about the scenes in a Madras
cinema hall on 17 October 1952, Deepavali day, gives one an
idea about the popular enthusiasm generated by a Dravida Munnetra
Kazhagam (DMK)[2]-inspired Tamil film *Parasakthi*. The film was
marked by such popular appeal not merely on the day of its release
or for a few more days. It ran for over a hundred days at
several places in Tamil Nadu, including in Madurai Thangam,
which was credited with being the largest cinema hall in Asia at
that time. Its dialogues became so popular that roadside entertainers
used to recite long passages from the film in the crowded Moore
Market area of Madras city and collect money from the bystanders
(Thirunavukarasu 1990: 55). Memorizing the dialogues of the film
became a must for aspirant political orators.

*Parasakthi* was scripted by M. Karunanidhi, a front-ranking
leader of the DMK and a future chief minister of Tamil Nadu, and
the hero's role in the film was enacted by Sivaji Ganesan, a DMK
activist in those days. Significantly, the film enunciated DMK's
politics—anti-Congressism, anti-Brahminism, attack on the religious
order and north Indian imperialism, Tamil nationalism, etc. The

film, as we shall see soon, was received by the audience as a quintessential DMK film. And it encountered bitter opposition from the opponents of the DMK.

Given the fact that the Dravidian Movement had effectively employed films as a medium of political communication (Hardgrave and Neidhart 1975; Hardgrave 1979; Sivathamby 1981; Pandian 1989), the present essay, on the one hand, analyses *Parasakthi*'s politics. On the other, it recounts the course of events that marked the career of *Parasakthi* as a hitherto unexplored element of Tamil political history. Moreover, it places this film in the history of the Dravidian Movement and analyses the ideological trends it represented.

## II

*Parasakthi*, which was based on a popular play by Pavalar Balasundaram of the Dravidar Kazhagam (DK) and directed by Krishnan-Panju, opens with an evocative poem of Bharathidasan, a poet of great eminence closely associated with the Dravidian Movement. The poem, in keeping with the early DMK's demand for a sovereign Dravidanadu, celebrates the greatness of the Dravidian nation and adulates its indestructible hills with teak trees, oceans with beautiful pearls, breezy paddy fields, fragrant jasmine shrub forests, rivers and springs, valorous men, beautiful and chaste women, etc. As if to disrupt this glorious picture of Dravidanadu and to bring the audience to the immediate realities of despair, the poem is followed by a long monologue which laments and grieves over the deplorable state of the present-day Dravidanadu:

The children of this beautiful country, without crawling in the lap of this motherland, are migrating to other countries. When thinking of this, what the *Arignarar* said comes to mind. Why is the sea water salty?. . . [He] said, [it is so] because of the tears shed by the Tamils who have gone to foreign lands without having the means to live in their own country . . .

*Arignarar*, which means 'a learned one' in Tamil, is a honorific title of C.N. Annadurai, the founder of the DMK. Thus, at the beginning itself, *Parasakthi* dramatically informs the audience about its politics.

The film narrative, then, revolves around the ups and downs

faced by a middle-class Tamil family. Manickampillai (Duraiswamy) lives in Madurai with his only daughter Kalyani (Sri Ranjani). His three sons—Gunasekaran (Sivaji Ganesan), Chandrasekaran (S.V. Sagasranamam) and Gnanasekaran (S.S. Rajendran)—have migrated to Rangoon. Chandrasekaran becomes a barrister-at-law and leads an affluent life with his wife Saraswathi (Susheela) and also his two brothers. Meanwhile, Manickampillai arranges Kalyani's marriage with Thangappan (Venkataraman), a writer with DMK-kind inclinations, and raises the necessary money by pledging his moderate house. The three brothers and Saraswathi plan to visit Madurai to attend Kalyani's marriage, but because of the war (the story of *Parasakthi* is set in World War II-ravaged 1942), the shipping company offers them only one ticket and Gunasekaran sails off to Tamil Nadu. The ship fails to reach Madras in time. Kalyani's marriage takes place without any of her brothers attending it, but with the mandatory Brahmin priests and Sanskritic chantings.

In course of time, Kalyani becomes pregnant; and she, along with her husband Thangappan, decides to christen their child Pannirselvam, if a boy, and Nagammai, if a girl. One may bear in mind that A.T. Pannirselvam was a prominent and respected leader of the Justice Party, and Nagammai was a leading activist of the Self-Respect Movement and the wife of Periyar E.V. Ramasami. Both the Justice Party and the Self-Respect Movement were the earlier phases of the Dravidian Movement. But unfortunately, the very day Kalyani gives birth to a son, Thangappan dies in an accident. Manickampillai too dies of shock. Their house is auctioned off. Impoverished, widowed and orphaned, Kalyani is advised by a well-meaning neighbour, Parvathi (A.S. Jeya) to start an *idli* shop to eke out a living and be able to feed the child, and she does so. Pointing to the sorry state of Tamil Nadu, Parvathi also makes a laconic, but politically weighty, statement: 'Running *idli* shops is the prime job for all those who lost their *tali* in Tamil Nadu.'

After several months' delay on the high seas, Gunasekaran at last reaches Madras. As soon as he lands in Tamil Nadu, beggars swarm around him, seeking alms. Reacting to this pitiable state of Madras city, he cynically remarks, 'Oh! Yes! The very first voice in Tamil Nadu sounds very good. . . .' Seeing him exchanging large chunks of money in a bank, a vamp-like character, Jolly (Kanamma), pursues Gunasekaran. She dissuades him from going for a film and tells him, 'If there is an association to finish off films, I will be its president. Only Bharata Natyam is fit for our country . . . There is a good dance performance in a place known to me. Let us go.' While films were closely identified with the DMK and its unsophisticated subaltern followers, Bharata Natyam was identified with the Brahmins and treated as a high-brow art form. The DMK of those days, on the other hand, exhibited a strong liking for anti-Brahminism. At a *dasi*'s house, where Jolly and a reluctant Gunasekaran have gone to watch the dance, Gunasekaran is given an intoxicating brew, robbed of all his money and thrown out on a pavement. Reduced to beggary, Gunasekaran laments the current state of the once glorious Tamil nation. In a long monologue, he wonders—for how long has Tamil Nadu been exploiting its own men; how come it, a land which once prospered by celebrating its valorous women, is blind to the prostitutes walking its streets; why are there men who have sunk into dishonour amidst soaring buildings that reach out to the distant skies, and so on. He encounters a heartless and unhelpful world: a policeman who chases him away for sleeping on a pavement, a woman fruit vendor who curses him for stealing some bananas to appease his hunger, a Madras Corporation water tap which is dry. . . . When he tries to pawn his only possession, a pair of expensive tweed pants, the north Indian moneylender, in his amusingly Hindi-ized Tamil, offers a paltry eight annas. Then, seeing a mad man being tolerated for his pranks by everyone, including a policeman, Gunasekaran begins acting as one and makes a living by playing tricks on people.

Gunasekaran finally reaches Madurai and learns from Parvathi that his father is dead and his widowed sister, who lives in poverty, is running an *idli* shop to survive. He continues to pretend to be mad and does not reveal his true identity, but hovers around Kalyani. In his self-assumed role as a mad man (a socially marginal figure with a certain amount of freedom), Gunasekaran holds forth in a long soliloquy, making fun of people praying to Lord Varuna to bring rain and going to temples seeking solutions to poverty. He irreverently points to a piece of stone and ridicules those devotees who treat it as God. (Interestingly, *Parasakthi* was released at a time when the Madras Presidency suffered a major drought and the then chief minister C. Rajagopalachari asked the people to pray to 'Varuna Bhagavan' for rain). Meanwhile, Kalyani gets into

more and more trouble. Venu (T.K. Ramachandran), a local vagabond, helps Kalyani when she is harassed by a north Indian
moneylender who persistently asks her to repay an earlier loan.
She thinks of Venu as an elder brother, but he has other plans.
Taking advantage of Kalyani's helplessness, he attempts to rape
her, but Gunasekaran appears on the scene in time to save her. In
desperation, Kalyani leaves Madurai and finally reaches Tiruchi.
At Tiruchi, she gets a job as a maidservant in the house of
Narayana Pillai (V.K. Ramasamy), a miserly blackmarketeer who
presents himself to the world as an extremely religious person. He
is also the president of the local 'Sanmarga Sangam'. Narayana Pillai
sends away his wife Kantha (Muthulakshmi) to a film *Krishna
Leelai* (!) and attempts to seduce Kalyani. He tells her, 'In the bedroom of big people, there is no difference between the owner and
the worker.' With the timely return of Kantha, who accuses her
husband of indulging in 'Narayana Leelai' and threatens to rape a
man herself (as if in retaliation), Kalyani is saved. She leaves her
job and wanders about, suffering hunger and an inhospitable world.
    Gunasekaran, searching for his sister, reaches Tiruchi and meets
Vimala (Pandaribai), a woman with DMK-kind progressive views,
whose brother is a political activist. Gunasekaran narrates his dis-
consolate tale to Vimala and she points out to him that he is selfish
to be worried only about his sister Kalyani, while the world is
populated with innumerable Kalyanis with similar tales of incon-
solable sorrow behind them. She absolves and even congratulates
Jolly, who has cheated Gunasekaran of all his belongings, for
opening his eyes to the world of suffering: 'She [Jolly] is the one
who opened your eyes. If you were not reduced to poverty, you
wouldn't have [ever] thought of the world of the poor. You
wouldn't have even known that such a world exists. . . .' She tells
Gunasekaran that she has learned this from her 'Anna'. ('Anna',
which means 'elder brother' in Tamil, is at once shorthand for
C.N. Annadurai). Gunasekaran, without informing Vimala, leaves
her house in search of Kalyani. And Vimala thinks to herself, 'You
have left (me) thinking that I am an idealist. Why should an idealist
be like Manimekalai detesting love? She can be like Kannagi too.'
Kannagi, a female character created by Illanko Adigal in his Tamil
classical text *Silapathikaram*, is a quintessential symbol of chastity
in the Tamil political and cultural milieu.
    Chandrasekaran and Gnanasekaran, the two other brothers of

Kalyani, also leave Burma due to the war. Chandrasekaran, with his wife Saraswathi, reaches Tiruchi in safety, and becomes a judge under a newly assumed name, S.C. Sekar. But Gnanasekaran, while trekking back to India from Burma, loses a leg in a Japanese bombing. The north Indian officer in charge of the refugee camp denies him and other Tamilians entry into the camp, while he welcomes healthy north Indians. Gnanasekaran, along with other Tamil refugees, is forced to eke out a living by begging. Finally, they decide to call for a conference of beggars and spur the government into action with their resolutions and demands.

Kalyani, begging for food, reaches Chandrasekaran's house but he does not recognize her and throws her out of his palatial house, where the social elite have gathered to feast. Desolate and hungry, Kalyani goes to the temple of goddess Parasakthi and seeks her help. The *poojari* (temple priest) tricks her into the sanctum of the temple and tries to rape her. The *poojari*'s assistant, Kuppan (M.N. Krishnan) rings the temple bell and in the ensuing confusion, Kalyani escapes. Unable to feed her starving child, she throws him into a river, tries to commit suicide, and is arrested. She is brought for trial before her own brother Chandrasekaran, who still does not recognize her. Kalyani defends her act of throwing the child into the river by invoking the popular folk story of Nallathangal, who, because of poverty, threw her seven children into a well, and that of Siru Thondar, who cooked his own son to please Lord Siva. She cynically mentions that her son was no 'Thirugnansambandar' that goddess Parvathi would feed him milk. When Kalyani tells her story, the judge realizes that she is his own sister and swoons in the courtroom.

A political speech by Vimala's brother, who has lectured on how mothers were selling their children like bunches of spinach ('big ones for Rs 5 and small ones for Rs 3'), refers to Kalyani's story as an example of the state of affairs in Tamil Nadu. Listening to the speech, Gunasekaran learns about Kalyani's whereabouts. He also learns from Kuppan about the *poojari*'s attempt to rape her. An enraged Gunasekaran enters the temple and from behind the imposing idol of goddess Parasakthi addresses the *poojari* who mistakes the voice of Gunasekaran to be that of Parasakthi herself. Gunasekaran corrects him, saying, 'Fool, when did Parasakthi speak? That will not speak; [that is a piece of] stone. [If that can speak], wouldn't it have . . . stopped you, when you tried to rob my sister's chastity?' The word 'stone' was removed from the soundtrack of the film, but Sivaji Ganesan's lip movements explicate the word so clearly on the screen that the audience can understand. In fact, the silencing of 'stone' is an intrinsic part of the legends that surround the film. The *poojari* shouts of sacrilege to the devotees assembled in the temple. Gunasekaran then snatches the knife from the *poojari*'s hand and plunges it into his head.

Gunasekaran is brought to the court for trial. He narrates his story in long monologues:

One country to be born. Another to survive. I am no exception to this fate of Tamil Nadu. . . . There is no means for a Tamilian, who has returned [to Tamil Nadu] from foreign lands, to live. A woman born in Tamil Nadu does not have the protection to live. . . . Glamour chased my sister. [She] got scared and ran. Money chased my sister. [She] ran again. Devotion threatened my sister. [She] ran and ran, and ran to the very edges of life. That should have been stopped. . . . Have those who talk of laws today, done . . . that? Have they allowed my Kalyani to live?

He goes on,

I created trouble in the temple; not because there should not be temple, but because temple should not become the den of dangerous men. [I] attacked the *poojari*. Not because he is a devotee, but because devotion has become a day-time disguise.

As the trial proceeds, Vimala enters the courtroom with Kalyani's child who was believed dead, but was actually saved by Vimala who was boating in the river. Kalyani and Gunasekaran are acquitted of the charges against them and they reunite with Chandrasekaran's family. The other brother, Gnanasekaran, in the course of collecting donations for the beggars' conference, also unexpectedly reaches Chandrasekaran's house. The film ends with Gunasekaran and Vimala planning to get married without any rituals, including the *tali*, and the inauguration of a welfare home for the orphans. Note here that conducting a Self-Respect Marriage without the mediation of Brahmin priests, religious chanting and other rituals was a well-propagated programme of the Dravidian Movement, especially during its Self-Respect Movement phase.

What does one find from this brief synopsis of *Parasakthi*? First and foremost, the film deploys Kalyani's so-called inauspicious and unprotected state as a widow and the consequent threat to her chastity as a sign of the current state of the Dravidian nation. Revealingly, the very name 'Kalyani' is chosen by the script-writer to emphasize the contradiction between her auspicious name and her pitiable life. Gunasekaran, in the course of his arguments in the court, despairs, '[My] sister's name is Kalyani. An auspicious name indeed. But there is no 'mangalyam' around her neck.' The film also presents powerful images to underscore Kalyani's unfortunate status. For instance, after she leaves Madurai to escape the sexual advances of the vagabond Venu, she is shown with her child, dwarfed against a huge barren tree with a cactus plant in the background. The camera lingers on. The barren tree, the tabooed cactus and the haunting loneliness all around, accentuate and effectively communicate her deplorable status to the audience. In fact, reference to Kalyani's chastity and the ever present threat to it, is repeated in the film, especially during the sequences of Kalyani's and Gunasekaran's court trials. Also, Vimala, who becomes Gunasekaran's bride, compares herself to Kannagi, a popular signifier of chastity in Tamil culture. If threats to Kalyani's chastity act as a trope for the current state of the Dravidian nation, Gunasekaran's constant vigil to help Kalyani from this threat stands undoubtedly for the DMK's promise of a glorious 'Dravidanadu'. Sivaji Ganesan, who enacted the role of Gunasekaran in *Parasakthi*, was in 1952 still a DMK activist in real life!

Secondly, the film, in portraying the tragic course of events that marks Kalyani's life, exposes the fraud in the name of religion and even the futility of religion itself in a certain sense. Equally important, the film succeeds in importing into the narrative a powerful critique of the Congress rule in the Madras Presidency. *Parasakthi* was indeed an explicit DMK film.

## III

While what we have seen so far is the story of *Parasakthi*, it will be instructive to know what elements of the film appealed to the audience and made it such a great box-office success. Fortunately, we have a sixteen-page letter written in Tamil by a twenty-five-year old youth under the pseudonym 'Tamilan', which gives a blow-by-blow account of the audience response to the film during one of its screenings on the very first day of its release. The venue was the Ashok Theatre in Madras city. Tamilan, a reluctant witness to *Parasakthi*, was so disgusted with the film that he made a vow not to watch any more films, and sought divine grace to fulfil this vow.[3]

First of all, Tamilan's letter makes it abundantly clear that M. Karunanidhi's image in the extra-cinematic sphere as a person who wields his powerful pen as a means to political ends had already given rise to certain expectations in the audience even before they watched the film. They went to *Parasakthi* to listen to Karunanidhi's dialogues—other elements of the film taking a back-seat in their minds: as if it was a film to be heard, rather than watched. Moreover, they expectantly looked forward to the political message of the film, well aware that the Karunanidhi's earlier works had run into trouble with the Congress government. Tamilan wrote,

When the credit 'Screen Play and Dialogue: M. Karunanidhi' was flashed on the screen, there were claps which shook the theatre. When I enquired from the man sitting next to me, [he] said that he [Karunanidhi] is the best dialogue writer in the film world. . . .

I have also learnt from him a few things about the film. . . . I learned that . . . this is the best among the unique creations of that fool Karunanidhi and that earlier it was staged as a play [with the name] 'Thookumedai' ['Gallows'] and was unjustly banned by the government.

Tamilan goes on to log meticulously those sequences which drew the wildest cheers from the audience. We may have to remember here that when Tamilan recalled these sequences in his letter, he was inaccurate in specific details, but broadly right in identifying them.

As Tamilan's elaborate letter shows, dialogues and film sequences which directed trenchant criticism against the Congress government, earned the appreciation of the audience. Let us see some excerpts from his letter:

(1) 'The youth who lost the money abuses his motherland of Tamil Nadu. It is as if all Tamilians are thieves. There are claps for this. They [the audience] do not have the sense to understand that this statement implicates them too.' (2) 'They portray the [Madras] Corporation to be a sleepy place, the mayor as useless and the [district] collector as a fool, because there is no water in a [drinking water] tap. For this, there were claps all around.' (3) 'In another place, they show that due to famine in Madras Presidency, mothers are not able to feed (*sic*) their

children and they sell them by their weight. For this there were claps all around.' (4) 'That woman [Kalyani] . . . says, "If I had become a prostitute, ministers and police officers would be sitting on my lap. But I didn't like it." There were claps which shook the theatre.'

(5) More importantly, Tamilan pointed out, when Anna[durai]'s politics is obliquely referred to on the screen, 'there were claps as if the cinema hall would fall apart.'

The other set of sequences and dialogues from *Parasakthi* which immensely enthused the audience were related to its critique of religion: 'When an orphaned and wailing woman comes to the temple with her child, the elderly *poojari* decides to indulge in prostitution in the sanctum of the goddess herself. For this, there were claps all around.' Tamilan was very upset about this:

When that woman wails, a boy [Kuppan] . . . who is initially portrayed as a [sleepy] Kumbhakarna, suddenly wakes up, rings the bell and saves her. No one claps for this. But when the woman's elder brother later on comes and shouts, 'This goddess is a mere stone. A useless stone. If there is a god, why did it not kill that elderly *poojari*? So there is no god. That is an irrational idea. All temples are whore joints,' there are claps. It didn't occur to anybody that that boy saving [Kalyani] by ringing the bell is an act of divine [intervention].'

Thus, the film did succeed in its pro-DMK campaign. Its anti-Congress slant as well as its anti-religious postures went down well with the enthusiastic audience.

## IV

*Parasakthi* evoked instant opposition and there was a demand for its ban. The Congress government in Madras headed by C. Rajagopala-chari (hereafter Rajaji), was flooded with representations against the film and the Brahmin-controlled press published vituperative commentaries on it. Among other things, the agitated critics targeted the Film Censor Board for their concerted attack.

Parambi Lonappan—whose letterhead introduced him as 'Ex-High Court Judge and Ex-minister of Cochin State; President, Catholic Indian Association, Coimbatore; Advocate of the High Courts of Madras and Travancore-Cochin States'—sent a letter to Rajaji on *Parasakthi*. The letter, marked 'Absolutely Confidential', exuded an air of high intrigue. He wrote:

I write this in my own hand to avoid leakage of information to my typist clerk even.

For the last few days the film *Parasakthi* is staged in the Diamond Talkies in Coimbatore town. The building is situated in a very important locality in the town *surrounded by mill labourers also.* I heard rumours that the government intend banning the show. Others represented to me that it is a good picture. And so yesterday (29-10-1952) I had the *misfortune* to see the picture.

It appears to me that is a *communist propaganda picture,* ridiculing Hindu religion, 'pujas' in and of temples, that it is no offence to attempt at number of murders on account of hardship due to poverty, etc., and that it is righteous to kill innocent children on account of difficulty to feed them, that the society, as at present constituted, is cruel to the poor people, that the government is callous towards the sufferings of the poor and the beggars, etc. The outrageous attempt of a brother to offend the modesty of his own sister is . . . depressing to the mind, filthy for public exhibition, etc. I think it is advisable for the government to examine the film whether its *obnoxious* impression upon the minds of the people should be allowed to continue (emphasis mine).[4]

Lonappan sought to assure Rajaji that his opposition to the film was not due to any personal reason, but in public interest: 'My intention in writing this letter is purely in public interest. For I am an absolute stranger to the producers of the film or the proprietor of 'the Diamond Talkies' in Coimbatore.' Lonappan's reading of godless communist propaganda in this explicit DMK film may seem surprising. But it makes perfect sense to one who is aware of the political milieu in the Tamil-speaking areas of the Madras Presidency during the late 1940s and early 1950s. During 1948–51, when the Communist Party was banned and its cadres were either languishing in prisons or forced to function from underground, it was the DK and the DMK which took up their beleaguered cause. Karunanidhi's role in this pro-Communist campaign was quite active. V.P.Chintan, a veteran trade unionist belonging to the Communist Party of India (Marxist), reminisced, '. . . We cannot but mention that Karunanidhi spoke throughout Tamil Nadu condemning the . . . prison atrocities [faced by the communists] and some youths, emotionally kindled by his speech, went to attack a police station . . .' (Illayabarathi 1989: 49–50). Also, during the early 1950s, C.N.Annadurai repeatedly emphasized that the DMK was genuinely Communist in its political tenets (Hardgrave Jr. 1965;

40). Given this, the spectre of communism could have genuinely haunted Lonappan in the precincts of the Diamond Talkies. In fact, worried reference to communism appeared from time to time in the campaign against *Parasakthi*.

If Lonappan belonged to one stratum of the social elite which opposed the film, S. Chinnasamy belonged to another. He was a salt and oil merchant and a truck owner. His trading firm was big enough in 1952 to have a telegraphic code of its own. Expressing his anger against *Parasakthi*, he complained,

At present, a film named *Parasakthi* is being screened in Salem. In that, the mental attitude and culture of women are degradingly portrayed. Moreover, denying theism completely, [the film is] filled with heaps of angry alliterative atheistic propaganda. Again, [it] contains compact *communist* slogans. [The film is used as] a propaganda instrument of a [particular] party (emphasis mine).

He also expressed his amazement at the Censor Board allowing the film for public screening.[5] Another trader, P.S. Subbaraman, proprietor of Kamadhenu Fertilizers and Distributors of Chemical Fertilizers to Madras Government, sent a concise letter typed out in English to Rajaji. It read,

Suffice it to say that the venomous propaganda that is directly made through this film against religion, idol worship, government and society in general is too powerful to be mistaken for mere entertainment. I, as a patriotic citizen, consider your government would be failing in *its fundamental duty if the exhibition of the above film is allowed for a day more* (emphasis mine).

This fertilizer merchant's uncompromising patriotism did not permit him to grant even a quarter of approval for the fledgeling DMK and he, exhibiting his familiarity with the Chief Minister, continued:

Rajaji, I dare say, you are not fully posted with the details of the content of a particular movement which is recently masquerading in Tamilnad as purporting to be social and reformist. You belong to a generation, which knew not the deeper hatreds that this 'movement' has nurtured in the minds and hearts of young Tamilians. I knew it fully . . . . This film *Parasakthi* is a product of that movement.[6]

K.R. Doraisamy, a cloth merchant from Chittode, was equally

worried. His worry was about what would happen to the illiterate commonfolk because of the film. In his petition to Rajaji, he claimed, 'By watching this film, atheism will find a place in the minds of the commonfolk who cannot read and understand newspapers.'[7]

As one would expect, the majority of the representations against *Parasakthi* came from Congress activists and sympathizers. P.E. Murugeasan, the Vice-President of Choolai Seva Sangam, a Congress-inspired association, sent a protest letter typed out in Tamil to the editor of *Bharata Devi*, a 'nationalist' Tamil daily, whose managing editor was M. Bhaktavatsalam, a future Chief Minister of Tamil Nadu, better remembered for his police brutality during the anti-Hindi agitation of 1965. *Bharata Devi*, in turn, marked the letter as 'confidential' and forwarded it to the Madras government.[8] It was after all 'their' government. The letter, which began with the mandatory 'nationalist' invocations of *Vande Mataram* and *Jai Hind*, carried long passages glorifying Rajaji's government and even claimed how his rule enjoyed divine sanction from the gods in the remote heavens. Turning to the issue of *Parasakthi*, it attacked the film for 'strengthening the Dravidanadu problem' and for running down the Congress government as well as the goddess Parasakthi. Not merely that he thought of the film as capable of taking the gullible people to the dangerous stage of 'carrying out a revolution' and unleashing a 'revolutionary river of blood', he also felt that those rationalists who made the film had no right to live. In unsuppressed anger, he wrote, '[Let us] build . . . a sacrificial platform and sacrifice these rationalists who wrote the conspiratorial story of *Parasakthi*.' He gave one month's ultimatum to Rajaji to ban the film and threatened to go on fast— in the so-called Gandhian fashion—in front of Rajaji's house if the ban was not imposed.[9]

 G. Umapathi, a Corporation Councillor belonging to the Congress Party and owner of a printing press and a cinema hall, organized a signature campaign in the Seven Well area of Madras city against the film, and sent a memorandum to the government charging the film with being derogatory to the Madras government and with ridiculing ancient *Puranas* and *Ithihasas*. The memorandum, which contained sixty-two signatures in English and only five in Tamil, was signed by the representatives of such Congress-inspired local-level organizations as *Gandhiji Desiya Valibar Sangam* (Gandhiji National Youth Association), *Rajaji Kalai Kazhagam* (Rajaji Cultural Association), *Vu Vu Ci Munnetra Kazhagam* (V.O. Chidamparam Pillai Progressive Association), *Netaji Valibar Sangam* (Netaji Youth Association), and *Namakkal Kavingrar Mantram* (Poet Namakkal Association).[10] Subramaniam, another Councillor from Tiruchi, sent a telegram seeking a ban on the film.[11] Arunachalam and Palanimalai, secretaries of *Desiya Seva Sangam* operating from the well-known Keezha Masi street in Madurai, informed the government—through a letter written on the letterhead of the Sangam carrying profiles of Gandhi and Nehru—that the City Cinema in Madurai had circulated handbills claiming that the central government had asked the National Pictures not to screen the film after 14 February 1953. They enclosed a copy of the handbill which asked the movie-goers of Madurai to watch the film before that imagniary 14 February.[12]

In addition, there were a number of petitions from the Congressites who were not organizationally associated with the party as well as from those whose political identities were not quite evident. A memorandum signed by 325 people from Rajapalayam town in southern Tamil Nadu, written in irregular hand and with signatures mostly in Tamil, presented a threatening scenario about the political potential of *Parasakthi*:

the film *Parasakthi* which has been released now is a revolutionary film which will do great harm to the country. Given the present state of affairs in Madras presidency, it will create a revolution. . . . In each frame of the film, dialogues attacking the government, gods, Brahmins and yourself have been thrust upon.

They sought the government's intervention to ban the film in a week's or ten days' time.[13] The religious faith of these petitioners occasionally exhibited strong streaks of fanaticism. For instance, one Lakshmanaswamy from Mannady, Madras, expressed in his letter great indignation against the film's anti-Hindu stance:

The film runs in several places so as to destroy Hindu religion . . . the man who rapes the women inside the temple is a Muslim. Nobody can tolerate this injustice. [This is a] film produced by those who take bribe from the Muslims . . . [I]n a film relating to Islam, would they give a good role to a Hindu. Even if he [a Hindu] acts [in such a role], think [of the possibility] whether such a film will be screened . . . Please go and watch the film and immediately take action to restore dharma in the country. It doesn't matter if it is your personal problem. It is a public problem.[14]

But the facts were contrary to the claims of this angry letter writer. It was K.P.Kamakshi—not a Muslim—who enacted the role of the controversial *poojari* in the film.

This vitriolic campaign against *Parasakthi* was strengthened with the so-called nationalist press joining it. *Dinamani Kadir*, a Tamil weekly belonging to the Indian Express group with a substantial middle-class readership, took the lead role in attacking the film. It carried an unusually long review of *Parasakthi*, running into three closely printed pages. The review was given a cynical title, 'Kandarva Mandalam' (The Abode of Kandarvas) and it began with a small box-item which read, 'Parasakthi: This goddess is abused in a Tamil film with her name.' The review opined: 'The main aim of the film is to attack the gods. Along with that, the government and society are overtly and covertly attacked.' The embittered and agitated reviewer further claimed,

He [the hero of the film], acting as a mad man, threatens and beats the people on the street and grabs whatever they have and eats it. Then he goes on to give repeatedly all those economics lectures, rationalist lectures and anti-god lectures. When we see the hero doing all that, it seems as if he is portraying the lives of those who are trying to force such ideas in the . . . film.

For the reviewer, thus, the DMK men were living on others' sweat and preaching unacceptable subversive ideas. The review also subtly attempted to evoke communal passions. It presented to its readers two possible scenarios: (i) Instead of Gunasekaran, Manickampillai, Kalyani and Vimala, [assume that] the characters in the film are Joseph, Arulanandam, Mary and Lily; and a Christian priest rapes Lily in the church: and (ii) Abdul Khadar, Said Hussain and Fathima Bibi are the characters in the film and a Muslim priest tries to rape her in a mosque. After describing these imaginary scenarios in some detail, the reviewer posed,

[I] ask the ones who made the film, the ones who provided the studio to make the film and those who censored the film, do you have the courage even to dream of introducing these sequences in the film? If [these sequences] were introduced [in the film], riots would have started and blood would have spilt.

Appropriately, this provocative film review was accompanied by pictures of goddess Parasakthi, Jesus Christ and a mosque.[15] Also, writing in *Dinamani Kadir*, Tumilan, a Tamil writer, criticized Karunanidhi's alliteration as 'Kadamuda Tamil', which roughly translates into English as 'coarse uneven Tamil' (Thirunavukarasu 1990: 57).

Recalling *Dinamani Kadir's* attack on *Parasakthi*, Karunanidhi (1975: 191), once an incorrigible relisher of controversies, wrote in his biography:

When *Parasakthi*, the film, scripted by me, was . . . running for over a hundred days in Tamil Nadu, a long review severely attacking the ideas and dialogues of . . . the film was published in *Dinamani Kadir*. In that review which ran for no less than ten pages, I was attacked from line to line.

The Congress Party conducted several meetings condemning me and *Parasakthi*. On the cover of *Dinamani Kadir*. . . there was a cartoon ridiculing *Parasakthi*: [it was in the form of] an advertisement showing a woman in dishevelled clothes! The caption of the advertisement was [given as] 'Parabrahmam'. It was written below, 'Story: Vasavu Thayanidhi.'

'Parabrahmam' is a word of reprimand used in Brahmin households, popularly meaning 'one who is unnecessarily confused'. 'Vasavu Thayanidhi' is, of course, a play on Karunanidhi's own name, meaning 'one who is generous with abuses'!

As we have seen, most of the representation attacked the film for its atheism and anti-Congress content. However, some critics made pointed reference to the manner in which women were portrayed in the film. Surprisingly, they found fault with the film for presenting women in a non-traditional mould. The review of the film in *Dinamani Kadir* recorded in exasperation, 'One woman [in the film], seeing her husband attempting to rape someone, tells that she will also rape a man and goes out for that.' Commenting on the Self-Respect Marriage at the closure of the film, the review subtly identified such marriages with a sort of barbarity:

[The film] speaks about tying a thread smeared with turmeric around the neck of the woman who is in love with the hero. At that point, the hero remarks, 'All this is not needed now. The cost [for the marriage] is two garlands alone.' Why even that difficulty of exchanging garlands? Did those who lived in caves and forests in ancient times exchange garlands?[16]

S.Muthukrishnan of Jyothi Sanmarga Sangam, Madurai, objected in his petition to the government that at one place in the film, a woman spoke contrary to the tradition of Indian women.[17] The reference was obviously to Kantha who threatened to rape a man. Tamilan, who as we have seen, has made the most elaborate analysis of the film, also remarked about the women characters in the film:

In the first song, they sing that among the women in the world, women of the Dravidanadu are the best in beauty, chastity and character. But the heroine, once married, runs around and dances in the park with her husband in a way which is worse than that of prostitutes.

He also objected to the Self-Respect Marriage: 'At the end [they] say, "Tying of 'tali' in marriage is old superstition. Exchanging of rings is the best." Is this a Dravidian tradition? Isn't it a copy of the West?'[18] In short, though the film affirmed traditional values about women to a very large extent, it was still not sufficient for its critics. The film should have gone even further!

As much as the authors of *Parasakthi* and its content, the Censor Board also came under remorseless attack. Most opponents of the film accused the members of the Censor Board of suffering from some kind of blindness and deafness. The memorandum from the people of Rajapalayam noted,

Even if [a] blind man was in this Censor Board, he wouldn't have allowed this film. It is not known whether the Censor Board members were dozing off or had taken bribe to allow such a film which will do harm to the country . . . see the film once. You will understand whether the members of your Censor Board are Dravidar Kazhagam comrades [or not].[19]

This speculation about the political leaning of the Censor Board members might not have been totally baseless. According to one source, *Parasakthi* could survive the censorship because of P. Balasubramanian, editor of the now-defunct *Sunday Observer* and a committed supporter of Dravidian politics, who was on the Censor Board (Thirunavukarasu 1990: 58). *Dinamani Kadir* was equally strong in its views on the Censor Board. It rather stridently commented,

What did the censors see in the film? Did they see again and again only which woman wore sari of what length and blouse of how many inches? Did nothing else appear to their eyes, fall on their ears? Were they specifically chosen from the blind and deaf school as censors for this film?[20]

Interestingly, the critics even pointed out that the film had carefully deployed ingeniously devised techniques to bypass the scissors of the censors. One of them reasoned that the makers of the film were deliberately showing a mad man abusing the gods and the government so as to escape censorship. The critic claimed that the film converted a normal man into a mad one because the Censor Board would not pass the film if the abuses were delivered by a normal person.[21] Another petitioner, the by-now-familiar Tamilan, made reference to why the story of the film was located in pre-Independence 1942:

At the beginning it is shown that all that has happened in the story occurred in 1942. But the later dialogues and scenes, from the beginning to the end, relate to the present times. [They have] showered abuses on the government at several places. It is because if someone questions this, [they can] escape [by saying], '[we are] speaking all about the British government of 1942 only. Who is abusing the present government?' This is evident even to a fool like me. Why didn't this reach the heads of the intelligent ones on the Censor Board?[22]

To sum up, the critics of *Parasakthi*, who were mostly drawn from the social elite and from the members and sympathizers of the ruling Congress Party, found this DMK film transgressing and occasionally subverting the socially given values with regard to religion, politics and woman, and they also thought the Censor Board to be hand-in-glove with the iconoclastic film-makers. They sought the Congress government's intervention to eliminate the threat posed by *Parasakthi* by banning it.

And the Madras government was none too reluctant to intervene.

## V

On 27 October 1952, just ten days after *Parasakthi* was released, the Home Department of the Madras government began exploring ways of getting the film into trouble. The man who pursued the matter with enormous perseverance was O. Pulla Reddy of the

Indian Civil Service, then Home Secretary to the Madras government. On 27 October, he requested J. Devasahayam, the Commissioner of Police, Madras, to 'depute an intelligence officer to see the picture and report the substance of the picture and whether there is anything objectionable about it.'[23]

The officer from the intelligence section of the Madras police, who watched *Parasakthi* and wrote a detailed confidential report on it, was, however, extremely sympathetic to the film. It may not even be surprising if his unstated political allegiance was with the DMK itself. He wrote with unconcealed admiration,

The dialogues for the film have been specially written in a *forceful manner* by Sri M. Karunanidhi, *the well-known leader* of the Dravidian Progressive Federation. . . . The film *graphically* describes the sufferings and hardships that a young widow with her babe in arms has to face due to poverty and how cruelly society treats her, or ill-itreats her (emphasis mine).

As we shall see soon, Rajaji, in contrast to this officer who introduced Karunanidhi as 'the well-known leader' of the DMK, found the makers of *Parasakathi* to be 'wicked persons'. The intelligence officer, in a kind of persuasive prose, further recorded,

The substance of the story by itself is *not at all objectionable.* The plot is *interesting* and story has a *powerful moral appeal*, namely that there will be ups and downs in a man's life and that chastity is the most precious jewel of womanhood (emphasis mine).

An intelligence officer could not, however, be all praise for a film that had landed itself in a bitterly acrimonious public controversy. That would invalidate his very report and inscribe it as being explicitly partisan. Perhaps because of this, he concluded his report with two long paragraphs pointing out some of the 'objectionable' features of *Parasakthi*:

The dialogues for the story written by Sri M. Karunanithi, however, is full of *subtle satire.* There are in the dialogues cleverly veiled criticism of the government, the exploitation of the Tamilians by the North Indians and chicanery of persons who dupe people in the name of religion, god, etc. The famine and poverty in the country is attributed to the indifference and lack of proper handling by the government. The one scene that *appears* to be out of place and rather strange is that of the 'poojari' trying to *seduce* the helpless girl in the precincts of the

Parasakthi Temple. *A section of the public* feels that such alleged rascality by a poojari is only in a thousand and that giving prominence to such a scene is likely to reflect generally on places of worship, temples, and the priests in-charge. *The scene appears to be essential and it does not appear as though any such conclusion could be derived.* The film contains a lot of Dravida Kazhagam ideals and sentiments in a cleverly camouflaged manner which *may not easily strike a casual filmgoer.* There appears to be no anti-Gandhian propaganda except Gunasekaran taking the law into his own hands and attacking the poojari and the statement by him alleging that Gandhiji himself has recommended 'mercy killing' in the case of certain incurable ailments in animals.

The other veiled criticisms against North Indians are (1) the scene depicting the north Indian camp officer refusing admission to maimed Tamilian refugees while he admits hale and healthy refugees from Delhi. (2) A north Indian dealer in second-hand clothes running his own business in Madras offering only eight annas for a good pair of tweed pants, and (3) A north Indian using harsh words to Kalyani to collect money due to him for provision supplied to her (emphasis mine).

This carefully worded and cleverly argued description of the 'objectionable' features of *Parasakthi* is indeed loaded in favour of the film. What was subversion, rape and Dravida Kazhagam propaganda for the opponents of the film were only 'subtle satire', 'seduction' and 'Dravida Kazhagam ideals and sentiments' for this officer. He disagreed with the opponents' reading of the controversial sequence showing a rape attempt within the Parasakthi temple and claimed it to be essential and also as harmless; and argued that the political message of the film was sufficiently veiled not to be deciphered by the 'casual filmgoer'. The fact that the 'casual cinegoer' did in reality decipher the political message of the film is, however, another matter.

In short, the intelligence officer's report denied the Home Department sufficient basis to proceed against *Parasakthi*. This forced a determined Pulla Reddy to explore other possibilities for his intended action against the film. On 10 November 1952, he proposed with much hope,

I have heard several persons complaining against this film and I think it should be seen by some *responsible* persons before we come to a finding. M[inister] (agriculture) also mentioned this to me. The Commissioner of Police might be asked to arrange a private show in consultation with the exhibitors and this could be seen amongst others by a few m[inister]s, the officers of publicity and information department, the I[nspector] G[general] of P[olice], select editors of newspapers and we can accept their general verdict (emphasis mine).

He could have legitimately hoped that the 'responsible persons' would definitely opine against the film—was not the film after all proving an incredible success because of the so-called irresponsible riff-raff who constituted the DMK and the DK cadres? But the chief minister, Rajaji, took a different line, which rather unexpectedly stalled this proposed preview of the film by 'responsible persons'. In a long rambling comment, which was a pot-pourri of his ideas about literature, cinema, democracy and the ubiquitous people, Rajaji noted,

I do not think we should honour this cheap attempt to destroy the faith of people by elaborate review by high personages. The position is clear enough. It is the introduction of a fictitious incident to show that rascality is practised in high places and by 'holy' men. People write cheap stories, long and short, how lawyers cheat, how doctors practice fraud and how men and women poison and kill. These incidents are not true but on them literature is built. Reading does not impress so much on readers as pictures do on picture-seers. This is what makes people object. There is nothing to be gained by our seeing the picture. . . . That it is designed by wicked people is obvious, but the course of freedom cannot be dammed now. These things must go on, until people themselves learn that these are worthless. . . .

Along with this confusing jotting, Rajaji suggested that the Madras government should ask the Central Board of Film Censors to re-examine *Parasakthi* and suggest what action needed to be taken. He also specifically asked the Home Department to inform the Central Board that 'the case is important enough [for re-examination].'

By the time the Madras government got in touch with the Central Board with the request for re-examining *Parasakthi*,[24] K. Srinivasan, the Regional Officer of the Board of Film Censors in Madras, had come out with fresh news about the film. He informed the Chairman of the Central Board that three additional scenes had been added to the original version of *Parasakthi* by the producers without getting prior permission of the Board:

I saw the film again and found that actually there were three additional scenes. I pointed them out to the producers and told that they had committed a serious breach of the rules. They said that the scenes were entirely unobjectionable. I told them that the explanation was unacceptable and that, if the practice of altering a picture after certification was allowed without check the whole idea of censorship would collapse.

But Srinivasan found it legally tricky and troublesome to prosecute the exhibitors of the film. He claimed,

In this instance, it would have meant prosecution against some 30–40 exhibitors and the only evidence to prove the additions would have been the testimony in each case of the examining committee members who saw the picture. Even against such testimony, it was open to the exhibitors to plead that they were under the bona fide impression that the copy given to them was one duly passed by the Board.

Given these difficulties, it was suggested, '. . . as the added scenes had nothing objectionable in them, the position could be met by issuing a severe warning to the producers that no such breach of the rules would be tolerated in the future.'[25]

The Union Ministry of Information and Broadcasting forwarded a copy of K. Srinivasan's letter to the Madras government and asked it to proceed legally against the producers and exhibitors of the film.[26] This suggestion understandably put the Madras government in a quandary. A Home Department note helplessly reasoned,

First of all this government has no information on the details of three additional scenes unauthorizedly exhibited, where and when they were exhibited and whether the members of the examining committee will testify that these additional portions were not in the film when it was examined by them.

The Home Department was also not quite sure whether the committee members should be responsive to the request of the state government:

The films are examined by the committee appointed by the Central Board of Censors the members of which are responsible to the Central government. The State governments are not even consulted when members of the advisory panel are selected by the Chairman, Central Board of Film Censors. In fact when the panel was first constituted in . . . [19]51, some of the members suggested by the State government were not appointed and some others, who were not considered by this government as suitable were appointed to the committee.

The Regional Examining Committee's cooperation was of key importance to gather and present evidence against the film. As a Madras government official noted in the file, 'It will be necessary for the members who examined the film to see the film as exhibited in the various centres and to make out a list of (a) portions ordered to be cut, but not actually cut and (b) portions added without proper authority.' Pulla Reddy was much peeved and his impatience with all these cumbersome procedures came out quite openly when he wrote,

The first mistake was for [the government of] India to have centralized these minor matters. Where the State government were in charge we were acting very quickly. Secondly the regional board *should have not at all certified this film*. Now they have landed themselves in a mess. When we requested them to review they are still examining *as though time is immaterial*. On the top of all these they want us to launch prosecution against unscrupulous producers and exhibitors. I consider the whole thing utterly futile (emphasis mine).

The Home Department finally suggested to the Central Board that its regional officer himself should initiate action against the exhibitors for showing the film with unauthorized additions. Without giving up hope, Pulla Reddy also requested the Central government that 'necessary action is taken . . . *very urgently* to see that the review of the film by the reviewing committee is expedited' (emphasis mine).[27]

Meanwhile the National Pictures, Madras, sent a letter to the Union Ministry of Information and Broadcasting profusely apologizing for adding unauthorized scenes in the film. It claimed,

In obedience to the directions of the panel, the portions specified by them were removed from the film as a consequence of which the continuity of the picture suffered in a few places. As the picture was scheduled to be released on 17 October 1952, Deepavali Day, purely in order to secure continuity, certain additions were made to the picture, . . . of an inoffensive character.

Their argument was perfectly plausible because the added scenes were not found to be objectionable, even by the regional officer of the Censor Board. Emphasizing this point, the letter argued, 'It was not our intention to bring in surreptitiously any of the portions cut or to insert any lewd or vulgar scenes to attract cheap popularity nor we did so.'[28]

The Ministry of Information and Broadcasting accepted the explanation of the National Pictures and dropped the plan for taking legal action against the exhibitors of the film. When the Ministry informed the Madras government of this decision,[29] the latter felt thoroughly let down and helpless. One Madras government official noted on the file,

It is unfortunate that [the government of] India have been so lenient as to allow the producers to go scot free with a mere expression of regret for their violation of rules. [The government of] India did not even invite our views in the matter before they decided on this course. The subject under reference is the concern of [the government of] India and there is nothing that can be done to retrieve the position except by way of protest pointing out our view. . . .

An exasperated Pulla Reddy was even more vocal:

The attitude of [the government of] India including their Madras B[oar]d from the beginning has been amazing. A *film which should never have been passed was certified* and then the producers and exhibitors made unauthorized addition. We brought the whole thing to the notice of [the government of] India. They seem to be in no mood to take any action. Meanwhile, I have heard from several respectable people that the film is doing *endless harm*. But it seems to be all a waste of time and effort. I agree that no further action is necessary on our part (emphasis mine).

However, the Madras government once again wrote to the Central government asking 'When the decision of the Central government on the report of the reviewing committee set up for the re-examination of the film entitled *Parasakthi* may be expected by this government.'[30]

Over six months after the Madras government started its move to get *Parasakthi* banned, the Central government informed the former that two sequences in the film required to be excised as recommended by the reviewing committee of the Central Board of Film Censors.[31] These sequences were (1) Gunasekaran knocking down the stone which he placed on the wall saying it had no supernatural power; and (2) The 'poojari' of the temple of *Parasakthi* assaulting heroine Kalyani in the sanctum sanctorum of the temple. The re-examination of *Parasakthi* was done by a Board consisting of Rajagopalan, V. Raghavan Manjubashini and C.R. Srinivasan. Rajaji immediately ordered for speedy action 'to communicate the order to all concerned so that the excised portions may not be any longer exhibited.'

Thus, for six months the fate of *Parasakthi* hung in the balance. The rather well-propagated possibility of it disappearing from the cinema halls due to state intervention only served to fuel popular enthusiasm for this film. It ran to packed houses for over a hundred days and proved a box-office bonanza.

## VI

This rather long story of the opposition to *Parasakthi* and the social and political force which sustained that opposition underscore the fact that the film definitely had a subversive edge. But that is only one way of assessing *Parasakthi*'s politics. *Parasakthi* appeared on the screen during a period when the Dravidian Movement, in its new incarnation as the DMK, gave up its character as a movement functioning outside the realm of electoral politics and became a political party exhibiting strong electoral ambitions. Given this, one needs to place the ideological attributes of *Parasakthi* in the Dravidian Movement's history and understand what sort of political *tendency* it represented.

To begin with, let us recall here that *Parasakthi* valorized chastity and deployed it as a sign for Dravidanadu. References to chastity, inauspicious widowhood and the literary figure, Kannagi abound in the film. Even the progressive Vimala, who absolves a vamp-like Jolly, compares herself only to Kannagi. In fact, the notion of chastity has been and is an important cultural given in Tamil society. As Jacob Pandian (1987: 49) puts it,

From ancient times to the present, purity or chastity has been associated with sacredness or spirituality which is in turn linked with Tamil language and Tamil womanhood. Just as Tamil language must retain its purity or chastity to retain its sacredness or spirituality, Tamil women should retain the purity or chastity to retain their sacredness or spirituality.

The film, thus, appropriates or rather works within, an element of the cultural given in the Tamil society which reproduces patriarchy.

Turning back to the pre-history of the DMK, that is, the Self-Respect Movement (and to a lesser extent the Dravidar Kazhagam) phase of the Dravidian Movement, what one finds is the reverse of this gender politics of the DMK. The early Dravidian Movement, in its all-out thrust to challenge the patriarchal ideology in Tamil society, campaigned against chastity, monogamy, and its associated symbol of *tali*. The most progressive trend within the movement was encapsulated in the founder and the most colourful figure of the Self-Respect Movement (as well as of the Dravidar Kazhagam), Periyar E.V. Ramasami. A befitting obituary of Periyar, published in the *Economic and Political Weekly*, neatly captures the politics of the early Dravidian Movement.

Another element in his [Periyar's] rationalist message was his campaign against the oppression of women. He championed the causes of widow-remarriage, of marriage based on consent, and of women's right to divorce. Pointing out that there was no Tamil word for the male counterpart of an adulteress he fumed: 'The word adulteress implies man's concept of woman as a slave, a commodity to be sold and to be hired.' Periyar's demand at a conference two years ago, that no odium should be attached to a woman who desired a man other than her husband (which the press so avidly vulgarised) as well as Periyar's advocacy of the abolition of marriage as the only way of freeing women from enslavement, were about as radical as the views of any women's liberationist.[32]

Within the parameters of this anti-patriarchal discourse, the early Dravidian Movement launched a concerted attack on classical Tamil texts such as *Chilapathikaram* (in which, as we have noted earlier, Kannagi was a central character) and *Thirukural*, for emphasizing chastity. It also relentlessly criticized Hindu religious text and ritual practices for once again celebrating chastity. The movement, moreover, organized Self-Respect Marriages which insisted upon equality between men and women, and liberated the institution of marriage from rituals (like tying of *tali*), which prescribed for women chastity as well as subordination to men.[33] Compared to this politics of the early Dravidian Movement, *Parasakthi*, inasmuch as it reflects the ideological tendencies of the DMK, stands as a sign of political regression—from challenges to the cultural givens of the Tamil society to a compromise with them.

The same tendency is discernible in *Parasakthi*'s attack on religion too. While *Parasakthi* did attack religion in definitive terms, it also exhibited a certain ambivalence about religion. This ambivalence comes out candidly in Gunasekaran's vituperative monologue in the court almost at the end of the film. As we have seen earlier, he says,

I created trouble in the temple; not because there should not be temples, but because temples should not become the den of dangerous men. [I] attacked the 'poojari'. Not because he is a devotee, but because devotion has become a day time disguise.

This is of course only a muted criticism of the religious order—it absolves religion and religious devotion, but criticizes their misuse only. In fact, the film was passed by the Censor Board because some of the members thought that it had a hidden message of faith and belief. The sequence that gave them this feeling was the following: Kuppan hearing the cries of Kalyani from within the Parasakthi temple rings the bell frantically. As if in answer to the cries of Kalyani, help comes in time, from behind the idol . . . from the sanctum. On the screen, the images of Parasakthi are super-imposed on the ringing bell.[34] With the passage of time, the DMK ironed out this ambivalence and affirmed its faith in religion. Soon after the DMK captured power in 1967, C.N.Annadurai claimed in the course of an interview:

I was always pleading for real faith in god. I mean by real faith, prayer to god through service and work which will be related to the generation of faith in society. I have always tried to see that our people do not lose faith in god. At the same time I have been anxious that they do not become hypocritical in their lives.

Of course, I am a rationalist who wants to end unreason and blind faith. . . . But genuine belief and true faith in god should be there amongst the people so that it helps them to become more and more aware and conscious of their duties and responsibilities to their fellow human beings. (Ramanujam 1967: 250, 251)

This too, as much as the question of gender in Dravidian politcs, stands in sharp contrast to the position of the early Dravidian Movement, which launched an uncompromising attack on religion as an irrational institution in itself and as an institution sustaining Brahmanical hegemony. Referring to this spirit of the movement, Irschick (1969: 340) writes,

. . . One pamphlet [of the Self-Respect Movement], typical of many, which appeared in 1929 was called *Visittiratevarkal korttu* ('Wonderful Court of Deities'). It used the device of a trial of all the gods of the

Hindu pantheon, in which a court of law subjected them to severe cross-examination of all the sexual and violent crimes they had committed. Shiva, Vishnu, and many other deities were convicted and given harsh sentences. In this way the entire basis of Puranic Hinduism was questioned and religion itself attacked as a superstition.

In those days, the movement did not provide much space for compromises with religion. The popular war cry of the movement was 'He who created god is a fool, he who propagated god is a scoundrel, and he who worships god is a barbarian.' Seen against this history of the Dravidian Movement/prehistory of the DMK, *Parasakthi*'s position on religion is again an affirmation of the received traditional values.

The reasons for this transformation of opposition to cultural givens into an affirmation of them in the politics of the Dravidian Movement (and hence in *Parasakthi*) can be traced, at least in parts, to the logic of electoral politics. Perhaps the best illustration of this is the so-called 'Salem Incident' and its aftermath. In January 1971, the Dravidar Kazhagam led by Periyar organized a 'Superstition Eradication Conference' at Salem. In the course of the conference, several posters depicting the obscenities of Hindu mythologies were taken out in procession; an effigy of Rama was beaten with chappals and burned in public too.[35] There was nothing unusual about this conference, as it was part of the tradition of DK politics. This event was stridently utilized by the Democratic Front (Congress (O) and its allies) to evoke pan-Hindu and anti-DMK sympathies during the 1971 election campaign. The Democratic Front printed thousands of leaflets carrying photographs of the posters of the DK procession at Salem and the message below read: 'These are the photos of the anti-god procession held in Salem under the protection of the DMK government. Should we still trust the atheist DMK? Must we cast our sacred votes for them?' (Pandian 1990).

With the election round the corner, the DMK did not waste much time. The DMK party functionaries, including M. Karunanidhi, repeated in public meeting after public meeting, that they were a party of believers. The spirit of the DMK's campaign was thus reported,

There will never again be any unseemly controversy as to whether the ruling DMK believes in god or not . . . this particular issue is fully and finally settled, and there need be no more any doubts over this. For, anxious to assuage the feelings of millions of Tamils who felt deeply hurt over the Salem incident of open denigration of Hindu gods, chief minister Karunanidhi and the DMK party treasurer and popular matinee idol M.G. Ramachandran have been assuring the Tamil people that they are not non-believers. They have been asserting in every one of their election meetings that it was wrong to condemn them as atheists. The DMK quickly followed this up by issuing thousands of posters and newspaper advertisements claiming that it was only during the DMK rule of the last four years that every religious festival had received great attention at the hands of the government (Ramanujam 1971: 175).

The logic of short-term political gains, based on electoral politics, thus, did not provide the DMK with enough elbow room to contest the pre-existing belief systems and cultural givens.[36] But, the early Dravidian Movement and its later variant of Dravidar Kazhagam could do so, given their politics as a movement working outside the parameters of elections, and hence immediate political gains.

Placed in this context, *Parasakthi* stood in 1952 as a sign of the coming days of a parliamentary Dravidian Movement. While the film still carried some of the radical tendencies found in the early Dravidian Movement, it was at once a signboard in the historical course of the Dravidian Movement, pointing to the consensual politics the DMK was destined to play in Tamil Nadu.

## NOTES

1. Tamilan to Rajaji, n.d., in Home, G.O. no. 1775 (ms.) (conf.), 29 May 1953 (hereafter G.O. no. 1775).
2. For a brief history of the Dravidian Movement, see Hardgrave 1965. The book deals with different phases of the movement—Justice Party, Self-Respect Movement, Dravidar Kazhagam and the DMK—separately.
3. All the details in this section are drawn from Tamilan to Rajaji.
4. Parambi Lonappan to Rajaji, 30 October 1952, in G.O. no. 1775. The film does not contain any sequences of a brother trying to offend the modesty of his sister, as alleged by Lonappan.
5. S. Chinnasamy to Rajaji, 18 October 1952, in G.O. no. 1775.
6. P.S.Subbaraman to Rajaji, 31 October 1952, in ibid.
7. K.R. Doraisamy to Rajaji, 11 November 1952, in ibid.
8 Editor, *Bharata Devi*, to the private secretary to the Chief Minister, 24 October 1952, in ibid.
9. P.E. Murugeasan to Rajaji, 23 October 1952, in ibid.

10. G. Umapathi to Chief Minister, 24 October 1952, in ibid.
11. Telegram from Subramaniam to Chief Minister, 20 October 1952, in ibid.
12. Arunachalam and Palanimalai to Chief Minister, 2 January 1953, in ibid.
13. Memorandum from the people of Rajapalayam to Chief Minister, n.d., in ibid.
14. Lakshmanaswamy to Rajaji, 7 November 1952, in ibid.
15. *Dinamani Kadir*, 2 November 1952.
16. Ibid.
17. S. Muthukrishnan to Rajaji, 6 November 1952, in G.O. no. 1775.
18. Tamilan to Rajaji.
19. Memorandum from the people of Rajapalayam to Chief Minister.
20. *Dinamani Kadir*, 2 November 1952.
21. Anonymous postcard to Rajaji, 22 October 1952, in G.O. no. 1775.
22. Tamilan to Rajaji.
23. Home Secretary, Madras, to Commissioner of Police, Madras, 27 October 1952, in G.O. no. 1775. All the information in this section is drawn from this G.O.
24. Home Secretary, Madras, to Chairman, Central Board of Film Censors, Bombay (lt. no. 195923 Pol V/52-1), 26 November 1952, in G.O. no. 1775.
25. Regional Officer, Central Board of Film Censors, Madras, to Chairman, Central Board of Film Censors, Bombay (lt. no. M-642/2511), 22 November 1952, in ibid.
26. Deputy Secretary, Central Ministry of Information and Broadcasting, New Delhi, to Home Secretary, Madras (lt. no. 4 (20) 52-F II), 17 December 1952, in ibid.
27. Home Secretary, Madras, to Secretary, Central Ministry of Information and Broadcasting, New Delhi (lt. no. 195923-Pol V/52-3), 3 January 1953, in ibid.
28. National Pictures, Madras, to Secretary, Central Ministry of Information and Broadcasting, New Delhi, 11 February 1953, in ibid.
29. Deputy Secretary, Central Ministry of Information and Broadcasting, New Delhi, to Home Secretary, Madras (lt. no. 4/2052-F II), 21 February 1953, in ibid.
30. Home Secretary, Madras, to Secretary, Central Ministry of Information and Broadcasting, New Delhi (lt. no. 195923-Pol V/52-4), 10 March 1953, in ibid.
31. Deputy Secretary, Central Ministry of Information and Broadcasting, New Delhi, to Home Secretary, Madras (lt. no. 4/20/52-F II), 4 May 1953, in ibid.
32. 'Passing of the Periyar', *Economics and Political Weekly*, 12 January 1974.
33. For details of the Self-Respect Movement's position on the women's question, see Anandhi, 1991; Pandian et al., 1991.
34. Theodore Baskaran's interview with Stalin K. Srinivasan, the Regional Officer of the Central Board of Film Censors, Madras, on 5 May 1975. (I am grateful to Baskaran for providing me with these details.)

35. A description of the posters exhibited during the Salem conference runs: Murugan, in the forms of Siva's son Skanda or Kartikkeya, is said in the *'Puranas'* to have been produced by Siva's 'seed' which was cast into fire. A Salem poster portrayed Brahmin priests standing around Siva, looking as though they were masturbating him while Parvathi, Siva's wife, held her hand out. Aiyappan, the growing popular deity to whose hill temple thousands of Tamils and Malayalis flock every year, is seen in the *Puranas* as being born from Vishnu and Siva, after Vishnu assumes the form of the goddess Mohini. The DK poster showed a lusty Siva preparing to have sexual intercourse with an eager and clinging Mohini. A third poster, drawing from a story in the *Satapatha Brahmana*, depicted Vishnu in his *avatar* of the boar having sexual relations with a very feminine Earth. . . . (Ryerson 1988: 179).

36. Even the parliamentary left parties are no exception to this tendency. For the case of the Communist Party of India (Marxist), see Sarkar 1991; Pati 1991.

# REFERENCES

Anandhi, S., 1991. 'Women's Question and the Dravidian Movement, c 1925–1948', *Social Scientist*, May–June.

Hardgrave Jr, Robert L., 1965. *The Dravidian Movement*, Bombay.

————,1979, 'When Stars Displace the Gods: The Folk Culture of Cinema in Tamil Nadu', in his *Essays in the Political Sociology of South India*, New Delhi.

———— and Anthony C. Neidhart, 1975, 'Film and Political Consciousness in Tamil Nadu', *Economic and Political Weekly*, 1 January.

Illayabarathi (ed.), 1989. *V.P. Chintan: Naan Yeppadi Communist Aaneyen*, Madras (in Tamil).

Irschick, Eugene F., 1969. *Politics and Social Conflict in South India: The Non-Brahman Movement and Tamil Separatism, 1916–1929*, Berkeley and Los Angeles.

Karunanidhi, M., 1975. *Nenchukku Needhi*, vol. II, Madras (in Tamil).

Pandian, M.S.S., 1989. 'Culture and Subaltern Consciousness: An Aspect of MGR Phenomenon', Review of Political Economy, *Economic and Political Weekly*, 29 July.

————, 1990. 'From Exclusion to Inclusion: Brahminism's New Face in Tamil Nadu', *Economic and Political Weekly*, 1 September.

————, S. Anandhi and A.R. Venkatachalapathi, 1991. 'Of Maltova Mothers and Others Stories: Women and the Self-Respect Movement', *Economic and Political Weekly*, 20 April 1991.

Pati, Biswamoy, 1991, 'Women, Rape and the Left', *Economic and Political Weekly*, 2 February.

Ramanujam, K.S., 1967. *The Big Change: Success Story of the DMK in Tamil Nadu in 1967*, Madras.

————, 1971. *Challenge and Response: An Intimate Report on Tamil Nadu Politics (1967–1971)*, Madras.

Ryerson, Charles, 1988. *Regionalism and Religion: The Tamil Renaissance and Popular Hinduism*, Madras.

Sarkar, Tanika, 1991. 'Reflections on Birati Rape Cases: Gender Ideology in Bengal', *Economic and Political Weekly*, 2 February.

Sivathamby, Karthigesu, 1981. *The Tamil Film as a Medium of Political Communication*, Madras.

Thirunavukarasu, K., 1990. *Dravidar Iyakkamum Thiraippada Ulagamum* (Tamil), Madras.

# II

*The 1950s: Melodrama and the Paradigms of Cinematic Modernity*

# 3

# Shifting Codes, Dissolving Identities: The Hindi Social Film of the 1950s as Popular Culture

RAVI S. VASUDEVAN

IN THIS ESSAY I wish to focus on certain aspects of Hindi commercial films from the 1950s to draw out a certain logic of the popular cinema. I start with how notions of the popular were produced within a critical discussion of the cinema of the 1940s and 1950s. This discussion elevated notions of realism, psychological characterization and restrained performance and, in an unexpected fashion, was echoed in the apologies offered by commercial film-makers for their product. A dominant intellectual discourse about the cinema seemed to be well in place; at the same time, I will not call it a hegemonic discourse, as we can hardly assume that the audience for the commercial cinema accepted its terms of reference. Even the standard film magazines pandering to an English-reading middle class, *Filmindia* and *Filmfare*, do not subscribe to these criteria of judgement in a consistent way.

I will then shift to an analysis of the formal and narrative strategies of the commercial cinema in this period to suggest the ways in which diverse systems of visual representation were brought into relationship with each other. I argue that this phenomenon, together with a narrative manipulation of characters' social positions, offered a certain mobility to the spectator's imaginary

Earlier published in *Journal of Arts and Ideas* pp. 23–4, 1992 and *Third Text* 34, 1996. These provide illustrations for the textual analysis. I would like to thank Radhika Singha for her comments on this article, and Shri Bhuwan Chandra for typing the manuscript.

identity. Finally, I will reframe the problem of popular modes of narration in relation to questions of melodrama, realism and the idiosyncratic articulation of democratic, nationalist points of view.[1]

## CONTEMPORARY DISCUSSIONS OF THE COMMERCIAL CINEMA

My basic premise about the dominant critical discussion of the cinema in this period was that it was related to the formation of an art cinema, that it addressed a (potential) art cinema audience and, in turn, was premised on a notion of social difference. The pertinent first reference here is to Ray who, when introducing his essays on cinema from the 1940s through the 1970s, noted that the formation of the Calcutta Film Society was related 'willingly to the task of disseminating film culture amongst the intelligentsia'.[2] In his 1948 essay on the drawbacks of the commercial film, he noted his dissatisfaction in the following way:

. . . once the all-important function of the cinema—e.g., movement—was grasped, the sophistication of style and content, and refinement of technique were only a matter of time. In India it would seem that the fundamental concept of a coherent dramatic pattern existing in time was generally misunderstood.

Often by a queer process of reasoning, movement was equated with action and action with melodrama. . . .[3]

Ray was therefore outlining, for a middle-class intelligentsia, a formal opposition between the contemporary cinema with its external, melodramatic modes of fictional representation, and an ideal cinema which would develop an internalized, character-oriented 'movement' and drama. Some thirty years later Ray implied that the norms for such an ideal cinema had already been met in the West, despite periodic discoveries and changes.[4] Whatever its adequacy for explaining Ray's own work, clearly Hollywood, or a refined version of the Hollywood norm, was being projected in Ray's advice that Indian film-makers should look to the 'strong, simple unidirectional narrative' rather than 'convolutions of plot and counterplot'.[5]

I will come back to these distinctions, especially the opposition between movement and stasis, in the next section. For the moment I will pass on to certain writings in 1957–8 of the *Indian Film*

*Quarterly* and *Indian Film Review*, journals of the Calcutta Film Society, which are in a direct line of descent from Ray's 1948 essay. Kobita Sarkar's 'Influences on the Indian Film'[6] and 'Black and White'[7] develop, at a more literary and thematic rather than aesthetic level, the discourse set in train by Ray's essay and the release of *Pather Panchali* in 1956.

Sarkar characterizes commercial cinema in terms which have now become familiar: as theatrical, tending towards a 'markedly melodramatic strain and exacerbation of sentiment and accumulation of coincidence',[8] and as failing in the analysis of individual character and psychological make-up.[9] What may be called the disaggregated features of the commercial film, performance-foregrounding song and dance sequences, were criticized for being 'infused arbitrarily into most varieties of film with a fine disregard for their appositeness'.[10] These criticisms were coloured by the image of a critic dealing with an infantile culture which needed to grow up. Thus, signs of greater character complexity in post-war cinema were welcomed as more 'adult',[11] what she perceived to be the tedious, moralizing aspects of film narratives were opposed to a more 'mature'[12] approach; and acting 'styles' were rejected as being more appropriate to a form considered the most child-oriented of entertainments: 'even . . . our more serious actors are frequently found cavorting in a manner more appropriate to the circus than the cinema'.[13]

A negative, pejoratively defined outline of the commercial cinema emerges from these accounts. Its negative features are: a tendency to *stasis* at the level of narrative and character development; an emphasis on externality, whether of action or character representation; melodramatic (florid, excessive) sentimentality; crude or naive plot mechanisms such as coincidence; narrative dispersion through arbitrary performance sequences; and unrestrained and over-emotive acting styles.

But Kobita Sarkar saw hope yet for the commercial cinema in that thematically at least a realist element seemed to be taking shape:

. . . drama is provided by the conflict of the individual against social and economic encumbrance rather than by inner complexities. . . . This emphasis . . . is not to be lightly derided, for though the preoccupation with a larger framework might diminish the importance of the human character, it makes for greater social realism.[14]

Evidently, that realist framework would not carry such weight with the critic unless it was given substance at the level of *mise en scène*. The decisive historical influence here was the International Film Festival of 1952. Sarkar argued that a certain depiction of social reality in Indian commercial films, whether through location shooting or the more 'fabricated' realism of the studio-set, reflected features of the Italian neo-realist work exhibited at the festival.[15]

However, for this critic, these positive features, of realist observation and theme, were clearly limited by melodramatic characterization and narrative. Achievement was ultimately measured against the model of *Pather Panchali*, seen to represent a 'logical progression'[16] in the development of such realist imperatives.

The commercial cinema audience was evidently being measured against an ideal social subjectivity. Pointing to the gross moral oppositions and simplified conflicts of the commercial cinema, Sarkar hazarded that 'perhaps . . . this element . . . is dictated by the *type* of audience—for unless it is sophisticated enough, it is difficult for them to appreciate the significance and nuances of characterization. For a less sensitive audience, this exaggerated disparity is morally justifiable. . . .'[17] She went on to note that 'till there is a radical change of approach on the part of the audience . . . rather meaningless turgidity seems to be an attendant evil'.[18]

I would suggest that there is a definite project underway here, in which the commercial cinema is seen to represent a significant failure at the level of social subjectivity. To counter this, critics and film-makers began to take it upon themselves to formulate an alternative order of cinema conceptualizing a different, more sensitive, psychological, humanist and 'adult' order of personality. What is surprising, however, is that these very attitudes were also apparent in the opinions of certain commercial film-makers of the time.

In 1956, M.A. Parthasarathy, head of Gemini International, noted of the Indian commercial film that the barriers to its achievement in the western market did not spring from the constraints of language but were due to the 'method of expression . . . not only the gestures and movements of our artists, but also the entire psychological approach of the construction of scenes and themes in our films'.[19] Again, Parthasarathy tied the imperative of reorienting the cinema to a redefining of the character of the audience. He noted that the economic headway that would be achieved through

state policies such as planning would increase the domestic demand
for films. However, in consonance with these new developments,
a new type of film would have to be envisaged: 'a type which is
more in line with the changes in social attitude that will go hand
in hand with economic prosperity. This will mean a more realistic
Indian film, where the method of telling the story is more like
that of films made in the West.'[20] Just the year before, S.S. Vasan
too had drawn out a connection between the economic situation
of the audience and its viewing inclinations:

Film artistry is, unfortunately, compelled to compromise with the
people's standards in living and life. . . . The mass audiences are generally
not so well equipped to appreciate artistic subtleties. . . . The great
majority of cinema audiences tend to favour melodrama and other easier
forms of emotional expression. . . . The prevalent low standards in art
are due, in a large measure, to our economic standards.[21]

There is an echo-chamber effect here, with the insensitivity of
Sarkar's audience being reprised as the incapacity of Vasan's audience to 'appreciate artistic subtleties'. Of course, the first view is
an explanation related to the need to change matters while Vasan's
is an apologia for why he makes the films he does.

In Vasan's and Parthasarathy's accounts an economic explanation
is proffered. Once economic circumstances were altered, the citizen-
spectator would be more attuned to humanist-realist cinema; exactly
the terms of Kobita Sarkar's definition of her ideal spectator.
Although Parthasarathy's exercise was also a prognosis about what
would go down well with a foreign audience accustomed to
American norms, it is possible to argue that these different views
were in fact complementary and sprang from the ideology of the
domestic context: that of the Nehruvian state, with its emphasis
on economic transformation and a critically founded individualism.

These lines of convergence should not suggest that discussion of
the cinema was entirely monolithic. In this connection, one
curiosity of this period is Chidananda Das Gupta's 'In Defence of
the Box Office',[22] a 1958 essay which tried to envisage an adjustment
of the cinema to the popular perceptions of its clientele: 'The starting point must be not one's own mind, but that of the audience.'[23]
In trying to evaluate audience dispositions, Das Gupta referred to
the aesthetics of representation, the 'two-dimensional, linear quality
which distinguishes almost all forms of Indian art' and the 'flatness

of Indian painting, its lack of perspective'.[24] In his argument, 'The vast unlettered audience of the East are yet a long way from acquiring the bourgeois prejudices. . . . It is only the urban middle class which . . . will question the distortions of the human figure in painting. . . .'[25] He believed this fact left the film-maker and artist freer to experiment with form and to rediscover his indigenous traditions.[26] Finally, he also tried to address the peculiarities of story-telling observable in the commercial film, and the significance it gives to the performative sequence.[27] The Indian audience, he argued, was oriented to an epic tradition 'which you can read from anywhere to anywhere, as long as you like . . . the Indian film audience . . . delights more in the present than in the past or future'.[28] He urged Indian film-makers to look to these traditions of narrative and aesthetics rather than rely on 'too many preconceived notions derived from the form of the film as seen in the West'.[29]

Das Gupta was not underwriting the investment which Indian audiences made in the contemporary commercial cinema as it existed. He was pointing to the potential this audience held for experimentation with forms of representation and narrative. Thus, while folk paintings of the Krishna legend were valued, the mythological film was condemned as the very worst expression of Indian cinema.[30] 'Film moghuls', he wrote, 'have fully sensed these traits of the audience. . . . In answer they have produced Bradshaws of entertainment, vulgar in taste and low in level but appealing all the same to the man for whom it is meant.'[31] Ironically, even the realist *mise en scène* and thematic content, regarded by Sarkar as signs of achievement in the commercial film, are dismissed in Das Gupta's analysis for derivativeness (from the International Festival) and an essential incapacity to rise above the more conventional cinematic entertainment.[32]

Although Das Gupta focused in his article on the epic and formal qualities of popular traditions, his underlying emphasis appears to have been on the film-makers and intellectuals rather than the audience. Indeed, the article appears to be a case of an Indian intellectual rediscovering the traditions of his country through an abstraction, 'the audience', rather than making a radical political investment in that wider society. To suggest a pertinent contrast, the 'Third Cinema' also writes of aesthetic recovery and reinvention, but relates this project to an intense political and historical analysis of social exploitation and resistance,[33] an engagement singularly lacking in Das Gupta's reference to the 'unlettered masses of the East'. Nevertheless, while his observations about aesthetic and narrative forms tend to be essentialist, they remain insightful in the critical context of their time.[34]

## FORMAL AND NARRATIVE ASPECTS OF THE COMMERCIAL CINEMA

I wish to draw upon this contemporary discussion insofar as it registered certain dissonances within a clear-cut model of the commercial film. I consider Sarkar's pinpointing of realism as one such complication, as also Das Gupta's identification of aesthetic and narrative dispositions in the audience's mental make-up. Contrary to their point of view, I suggest that these features were not exceptions to the norm but were part of a cultural form which was more complex than these contemporary critics would allow.

## Modes of Representation

In the Bombay cinema of the 1950s the 'social' film, from which I take the illustrations in this article, was the genre which the industry understood to address the issues of modern life.[35] Within these films, and much more widely in the cinema of that time, a number of modes of staging and narrating story events are in evidence. There is the iconic framing, an organization of the image in which stable meaning is achieved,[36] whether of an archaic or contemporary nature. This could range from the mythic articulations of woman, whether by herself or in relation to a man, to mythic formations stemming from contemporary iconography, such as Monroe in American culture or the Raj Kapoor–Nargis emblem of romantic love emblazoned on the R.K. banner.

Another arrangement is that of the tableau which, unlike the icon, presumes an underlying narrative structure: '. . . characters' attitudes and gestures, compositionally arranged for a moment, give, like an illustrative painting, a visual summary of the emotional situation.'[37] The tableau represents a moment caught between past and future, 'a pregnant moment', to quote Barthes.[38] Both the iconic and tableau modes are often presented frontally, at a 180° plane to the camera and seem to verge on stasis, enclosing meaning within their frame, and ignoring the off-screen as a site of reference, potential disturbance and reorganization.[39] Perhaps this was what Ray was reacting against when he complained of the static features of the commercial film.

However, the codes of American continuity cinema are also used in the Hindi cinema of the period. These codes—the eyeline match, point-of-view shot, 'correct' screen direction, match-on-action cuts[40]—generate the illusion of spatial and temporal continuity and a systematic relation between on- and off-screen in their generation of narrative flow. In doing this, they centre and re-centre the human body for our view, thus presenting us with a mirroring sense of our own bodily centrality and coherence.[41]

It is this American system which has defined ways of representing character subjectivity in a 'universal', almost hegemonic sense in world cinema, and it is the absence of this which Kobita Sarkar appeared to regret in the commercial film. In fact, these codes are not absent, but they are unsystematically deployed and are often combined with the other modes of visual representation I have described.

To illustrate this combination of codes, I will analyse a segment from Mehboob Khan's *Andaz* (1949). The story of the film details the troubles which engulf an upper-class young woman Neena (Nargis), when she risks a friendship with an attractive bachelor Dilip (Dilip Kumar), although she is engaged to another man. The particular sequence which I refer to, recounting Neena's birthday celebrations, is made up of nine shots, and begins and ends with a top-angled shot on the birthday cake. The first shot shows Neena's friend Shiela lighting the candles on the cake; the camera cranes down, as if paralleling Neena's movement down the hillside steps, and we see her father looking back at her as he moves foreground right. Shot 2 dissects the first, and shows Neena entering the space of the father, where she is introduced to Shanta, a family friend they have hardly met since the death of Neena's mother. The framing of this shot shows Neena standing next to her father, and in front of Shanta. Neena greets Shanta, moves on to greet a doctor and then another woman guest. At this point there is a match-on-action cut from Neena's movement of greeting in shot 2 to her touching this un-named woman's feet in shot 3a. The woman's back remains turned to the camera.

I suggest that shot 3 has the structure of an iconic representation. This woman is an unidentified, unseen figure; it is her very lack of identification which is suggestive. For the father has just mentioned the absence of the mother, the first time any reference has been made to her. Neena's introduction to an anonymous woman at this very moment can be said to reiterate and emphasize the absent figure. The woman's invitation that Neena sit next to her seems to be issued from the position of the absent mother, and is like an act of nomination: Neena is invited to enter the space of the mother.

This space is subverted by the deployment of a look away from the absent mother, to a position off-screen right (shot 3b). The iconic possibilities of the arrangement are then scattered, diffused. And yet, instead of a straightforward integration of Neena into the exchange with Dilip, the figure whom she sees off-screen, the next shot, 4, arranges a tableau against which this exchange takes on portentous dimensions. Neena and Dilip meet in the mid-ground of the frame; the father stands to the left in the background; and Shiela begins to move forward. The tableau-like characteristics of this repositioning are underlined when the next shot, 5, is not bound to shot 4 through a match-on-action cut on Shiela's movement. For, at the beginning of shot 5 she is *already stationary*, having been placed at the appropriate position, next to Neena's father. Shiela's placement with the father signals the commentary-like implications of the tableau shot. The arrangement of the frame bristles with contradictions. The look of the father at the couple indicates that they enact a spectacle of transgression. In the logic of the narrative it is Shiela, standing with the father, who should be with Dilip, while Neena should be where Shiela stands, in the space of the absent mother. However, as the narrative requires the temporary suspension of this illegitimate arrangement, the father's reprimanding look is effaced when Shiela moves towards the couple, to stand at Neena's left (shot 5b). Shiela's presence sets up a buffer, as it were, between Neena and Dilip, allowing the father to move away. The rest of the sequence follows this logic, with a series of shot-reverse-shots (shots 6-8) which do not allow the couple to be isolated again. But traces of the transgression remain in the final shot of the sequence, 9, when Dilip is positioned next to Neena, amidst the larger crowd, as he cuts the cake.

In this sequence there is a diegetic flow tracking Neena's

movement, glancing off her possible iconic placement and moving on to focus her (apparent) desire. That flow is brought to a halt with the frontal tableau frame, in which society exercises a censuring gaze through the look of the father. The flow is then resumed, through the shot-reverse-shot arrangement. While this procedure makes it possible 'to implicate the spectator in the eye contacts of the actors ... to *include* him or her in the mental and "physical" space of the diegesis',[42] in this segment, Shiela's intrusion functions as a residual trace of the tableau's social commentary, setting up a buffer within the transgressive intimacy of the scene.

The intrusion of the tableau is quite significant in the formulation of the spectator's subjectivity. While we have shared the movement and awareness of Neena, we are suddenly asked to situate that awareness within the space of the social code. That this is represented through an integral narrative space rather than a dissected one— Neena's father's awareness could as well have been registered through a close-up—indicates that it is not through a play of individual subjectivities that we are being asked to register the space of the social code, but as a structural field with definite points of authority and notions of convention. This does not prevent us from empathizing with the 'object' position within this field, but the *address* has an encompassing, normative aspect to it which momentarily throws us out of the flow of individual awareness.

## Appropriations and Transformations

It is my suggestion that this relay through different visual modes is also a rhetorical strategy which makes the cinema both attractive as something new in the field of the visual, and culturally intelligible because it incorporates a familiar visual address. I have argued elsewhere that both *Andaz*'s narrative strategy and the elements of its publicity campaign were oriented to generate an image of modernity for the Indian audience.[43] In terms of narrative strategy the film employs Barthes' 'hermeneutic code', the mechanism whereby information is deferred in order to engage spectatorial curiosity.[44] Although there are allusions to Neena's being involved with a man other than Dilip, they are elliptical, placing us very much within Dilip's field of knowledge, and his desire for Neena. As a number of writers have pointed out, Indian popular cinema is singularly indifferent to mechanisms of suspense and surprise;[45] the moral universe of the fiction, the figuration of guilt and innocence, is always already known. The induction of codes associated with American cinema into *Andaz* may be seen in combination with the publicity strategy used by Liberty, the cinema hall which showed *Andaz* as its inaugural film. The exhibitors drew attention to the modern projection equipment and elegant auditorium, suggesting that the viewing conditions met the standards of an audience used to viewing western films. The experience of seeing *Andaz* was therefore meant to generate a modern self-image through an appropriation of the symbolic social space occupied by watching American films. And yet, at the same time, the experience would not merely reproduce that of the American film. The film uses its woman character to set limits to the image of modernity. Through her, the narrative negotiates a notion of 'Indian' social codes and a larger, 'national' identity for the spectator of the film.

The controlled mobilization of American cinematic spectatorship into the commercial cinema is not untypical. The much maligned imitativeness of the Hindi film may be seen to set up a relay of appropriated and adapted narrative modes and spectatorial dispositions: as an organizing premise, as in the induction of codes of continuity and character subjectivity; but also as attraction, in the sense that Tom Gunning has used the term, where narrative is less significant than an amalgam of views, sensations and performances.[46] Works of the 1950s such as *Aar Paar* (Guru Dutt, 1954), *Taxi Driver* (Chetan Anand, 1954) and *CID* (Raj Khosla, 1956), deploy bank heist and car-chase sequences, but in ways which are not properly integral to the narrative development, nor wrought with a strong rhythm of alternations.

Along with the appropriation of narrative codes and sensationalist attractions from the American cinema, the Hindi social film also appropriated elements of American genre films in structuring the imaginary social space of its narrative. In the American *film noir* of the 1940s, the hero exhibits ambiguous characteristics, an ambiguity reinforced or engendered by a duplicitous woman whose attractions are explicitly sexual. As a result the heterosexual project of familial reproduction is jeopardized. As Sylvia Harvey has noted, 'the point about *film noir* . . . is that it is structured around the destruction or absence of romantic love and the family. . . .'[47] This repetitive narrative trajectory has been accompanied by stylistic features of a much more variable nature, from a constrained, distortive framing, to low-key lighting and chiaroscuro effects, these strategies being oriented to generating a sense of instability in character perception and moral situation.[48]

These generic elements, which American film-viewing audiences would have been familiar with from the 1940s, are reproduced in the cycle of crime melodramas of the 1950s, particulary *Baazi* (Guru Dutt, 1951), *Awara* (Raj Kapoor, 1951), *Aar Paar* and *CID*; but the elements are restructured into a melodramatic bipolarity, the stylistic and iconographic elements siphoned off into the world of vamp and villain, counter-pointed to the realm of morality and romantic love.

## The Dissolution of Social Identity

Nevertheless the hero's moral attributes are in jeopardy, and it is the narrative's work to move him through this bipolar world before recovering him under the sign of virtue, an objective often publicly and legally gained.[49] For my analysis of the popular ramifications of the commercial film narrative, what is of significance here is the way in which this melodramatic routing complicates his social identity.[50]

It is the hero's very mobility between spaces, spaces of virtue (the 'mother's' domain), villainy and respectability (the 'father's' domain) which problematizes social identity. Often the street, the space of physical and social mobility, is also the space of the dissolution of social identity, or the marking out of an identity which is unstable. In *Baazi*, Ranjani's villainous father espies Madan's tryst with his daughter on the street, causing him to conspire against the hero; in *Awara*, the glistening rain-drenched streets so familiar from the American *film noir* are the site of the uprooted Raj's birth, his subsequent tormented encounter with street toughs, the place where the villain Jagga plants the seeds of criminality in his mind, and the terrain on which he is involved in car thefts, bank heist preparations and murderous assaults. The taxi-driver hero Kalu of *Aar Paar* is by definition associated with this unstable space, one which draws him unwittingly into a criminal plot. Even the respected Inspector of Police of *CID*, Shekhar, framed for a murder rap, loses all social anchorage and is precipitated into the street.

This is a drama of downward social mobility. Most of the

characters identified here originate in respectable middle-class families. But the upheaval in the hero's circumstances is never so irreversible as to prevent the recovery of his virtue and of the possibilities of social renewal. Very rarely does the transformation of identity extend as far as a specifically working-class moment in the trajectory of loss. Loss and uprootment are contained by a moral opposition between the proper middle-class image of respected householdership and its other, the thief, who battens on that which is not his.[51] Narratives state and complicate these oppositions, suggesting how a respectable position is anchored in illicit gain, a bigoted social exclusiveness and, repeatedly, as a basic aspect of narrative structure, how its strictures and exclusions articulate an oedipal contest, a problem of generational transaction, between 'father' and 'son'.

## THE NARRATIVE OF THE FAMILY: CONFLICT AND CLOSURE

The family is the remarkable symbolic, if not literal, locus of the narrative's organization of both conflict and resolution. At its centre lies the iconic presence of the mother, stable in her virtue and her place, a moral orientation for her son but also a figuration of the past; for the space of the mother must give way to the changes introduced by the shift of authority from father to son. The family binds the son back into its space, securing him from the perils of the social void by restoring his name, his right to an inheritance and his social place. But it is a transformed family, one over which he must now exercise authority. The nucleated space of this new formation often emerges under the benign agency of the law, suggesting a complicity between state and personality in the development of a new society.

There is a remarkable instance of the mother's iconic presence, the kind of gravitational pull she exercises over the narrative's progression, and indeed over the very process of narration, in a sequence from *Awara*. This sequence again provides us with an example of the interplay between iconic modes of visual representation and the drives of continuity narration.

Raj, who has been working for the bandit Jagga, without his mother Leela's knowledge, returns home. His look is arrested by a photograph of his childhood friend, Rita (shot 1). Feeling that the photograph's 'look' upbraids him for his moral duplicity, he turns the photo to the wall (shot 2b), but Leela turns it over again (shot 4b). Raj declares that childhood friends can never be recovered (shot 4c) and leaves the house for an assignation with Jagga (shot 5). Leela, unpacking for Raj, is shocked to find a gun in his case (shots 7a, 7b). The camera tracks in from Leela (shot 8a) to the photograph (8b), and there is a dissolve which takes us to a cabaret performer (8c) dancing before Jagga and his gang. At the end of two short sequences, that of the dance performance witnessed by Jagga, Raj and the gang, and that relating to a discussion between Jagga and Raj, we return to Leela as she now turns the photograph to the wall (shots 9a, 9b, 9c).

The crucial feature of this sequence is of how the look of the female figure is relayed between the mother and the photographic image of Rita and how, quite unusually, this relay is used to elaborate the sequence as a macro-sequence, one which authorizes a moral perspective on the sequences in between.

The mother is the original repository of this moral look: the Rita-image reiterates or 'doubles' her function. Shot 3 shows how the look which Raj evades in shot 2 returns in his mother's look at him. Two looks focus on the hero then, and the reinstatement of Leela's recovers the other for Leela turns the photograph up again (shot 4b). The reframing which follows Raj's movement blocks our view of Leela, and Raj's body blocks Rita's photograph (shot 4c). Raj's trajectory in shot 4c therefore erases both female figures from our view, because he is about to enter an immoral terrain, that of the villain and vamp. With Raj's movement out of frame, the photograph regains possession of this space (shot 4d), but through a combination of character movement right and camera movement left Leela now blocks Rita's image (shot 4e). The mother's involuntary effacement of the photograph's idealized moral view foreshadows her knowledge of what Raj's 'business' actually is, with her discovery of the gun in shot 7. The dissolve of the Rita-image onto the 'tainted' dancer in shot 8c suggests that the image seems to 'look' and see its 'other', and, mirrored in that 'other', the figure of the male subject who would ideally be constituted within its own moral gaze.[52]

The completion of this circuit of looking two sequences later, with the return to the photograph in shot 9, indicates that the photo-icon has participated in a remarkable macro-narration. Aligned in Raj's perception to a moral gaze whose scrutiny he cannot bear, the photograph's 'gaze' oversees the transgressive sexual and criminal instances of the sequences in between. Leela then turns this 'gaze' away from such scenes, as if it may from now on only oversee the moral renewal of the protagonist; and this, indeed, is how it functions throughout the rest of the film.[53]

Young Rita's photograph is without depth, pure surface, a frozen moment of the past which, ironically, also represents a future state of grace for the protagonist. But it does not represent Rita, a figure whose narrative functions are bound up, from her introduction into the film, with sexuality. It represents, in fact, a time of innocence, before the advent of the oedipal contest with the father and the drives of desire and aggression. In this invocation of a past moment in the psychic trajectory of the subject, there is a strong correspondence between the image and the mother. And, indeed, the sequence plays upon the interchangeability of the gaze of image and mother, the latter reintroducing its look, substituting for it, and associating her censure with its withdrawal.[54]

But that authoritative moral function must be displaced, or at least subordinated, before the onward trajectory—which is also, of course, one of return—whereby Raj will recover his familial identity. This is an objective in which the character Rita will be decisive. The mother, the still centre of the narrative, must be moved, her place dissolved and her functions eliminated or transferred to the appropriate figure of the heroine.

The mixture of codes, generic and sensational elements, and a narrative undermining of social identity, makes the social film of the 1950s an imaginary space in which a popular audience of mixed social background were offered a rather fluid system of signs, modes of address and social positions. Industry observers had their particular explanation for this mixture. They believed that the 'social', initially conceived of as a conventionally middle-class genre, had become an omnibus form in which different social groups were being catered to by different elements of the film. One observer noted that, whereas in the 1930s dramatic and story values appealed to the middle and upper middle classes, and stunts and action dramas appealed to workers, in the 1950s 'a new type of social realism also came to occupy the screen. Actions, thrills, magic and stunts were introduced into the stories to attract the masses.'[55]

I would like to suggest, however, that the different modes do not necessarily correspond, by some reductionist sociological aesthetic, to particular social segments of the audience. Aesthetically, continuity codes mingle with, give way to and even take over the functions of codes more widely observable in the visual culture of society. An iconic construction is often observable in the arrangement of the new bearer of patriarchal authority in the story; and point-of-view structures formulated in a classical Hollywood way are used to shore up this quite 'traditional' framing.[56] Conversely, the tableau framing, while in some sense communicating an ordered, socially coded view for the audience, does not necessarily determine their perception of the narrative situation. In this sense, it is difficult to separate out 'traditional' from 'modern' address, or to suggest that such addresses correspond to distinct audiences. Even the sensational action sequences can hardly be regarded as attractive only to a lower class audience. I have argued elsewhere that a *masculine* culture was being addressed through such elements, one not restricted by class, and perhaps contributive to a new, more sharply differentiated sexual image for the male subject.[57]

However, there is a strong tendency to subordinate movement and vision toward a stable organization of meaning, in an iconic articulation. This has a parallel in the way in which the narrative reorganizes the family so as to secure a stable position for the middle-class hero. To my mind, this feature brings the complexities of the popular cultural form into alignment with a certain normalizing discourse and hegemonic closure.

## Redefining the Popular: Melodrama and Realism

The formal complexities of the 1950s' social film had, in a sense, been acknowledged in Kobita Sarkar's and Chidananda Das Gupta's pronouncements on its narrative and stylistic features. But they insisted on seeing these elements as constrained or unrealized. By subjecting the cinema to a certain purist criticism, they failed to grasp the complexity of popular forms such as melodrama. Recent work shows that, along with stereotypical, morally bipolar characters, melodramatic narratives have been known to deploy narration through the awareness of a single character.[58] Further, as Peter Brooks has noted, melodrama as a form has, from the nineteenth century, been associated with realism.[59]

In changing the way in which fiction organizes meaning, melodrama marks the transition from the prevalence of sacred and hierarchical notions to a post-sacred situation in which the sacred is striven for but meaning comes increasingly to reside in the personality.[60] The terrain of the personality is a social and familial matrix in which the reality of everyday life becomes an inevitable reference point. In the Hindi social film such a *mise en scène* is vividly in evidence. Whatever the degree of fabrication, the street scene of the 1940s and 1950s is animated by the activity of newspaper hawkers, vegetable peddlers, construction workers, mechanics, urchins and shoe-shine boys, petty thieves, pedestrians going about their business. Vehicles—cycles, trucks, cars, trolleys, buses, and significant places—railway stations, cafes, the red light area, are also deployed in the semantics of the street and of movement. Above all there is, the street lamp, signifier of both street and of night and therefore, of a physical, social and sexual drive.[61]

But the melodramatic narrative's invocation of the 'real' is merely one level of its work. As Brooks notes, melodrama uses

the things and gestures of the real world, of social life, as kinds of metaphors that refer us to the realm of spiritual reality and latent moral meanings. Things cease to be merely themselves, gestures cease to be merely tokens of social intercourse whose meaning is assigned by a social code; they become the vehicles of metaphors whose tenor suggests another kind of reality.[62]

Routing itself through the 'real', melodrama then penetrates to repressed features of the psychic life and into the type of family dramas I have referred to. Certain dramaturgical features, such as that of coincidence, are central to this process of making meaning, especially for relaying the significance of the social level to the audience. For coincidence insistently anchors figures who have a definite social function to relationships of an intimate and often familial, generational order.[63] In this sense cinematic narratives address the spectator in psychic terms, mirroring the most primal conflicts and desires and refracting all other levels of experience through that prism.

The conceptual separation of melodrama from realism which occurred through the formation of bourgeois canons of high art in late nineteenth-century Europe and America[64] was echoed in the discourses on popular commercial cinema of late 1940s and 1950s

India. This strand of criticism, associated with the formation of the art cinema in Bengal, could not comprehend the peculiarities of a form which had its own complex mechanisms of articulation. In the process, the critics contributed to an obfuscating hierarchization of culture with which we are still contending.

## THE POPULAR CULTURAL POLITICS OF THE SOCIAL FILM

As a result of this obfuscation, perhaps we have not quite understood the particular political articulation of the popular cinema of the 1950s. Nationalist discourses of that time about social justice and the formation of a new personality were then routed through familiar, if modified, cultural and narrational reference points. These were family dramas, iconic and tableau modes of representation. I would suggest that the cinema of that time communicated a popular democratic perception which worked through some of the rationalist and egalitarian approaches of the liberal-radical intelligentsia, but on its own terms. Of popular modes of representation and thought in late medieval Europe, Ginzburg has suggested that they 'recall a series of motifs worked out by humanistically educated heretical groups'. But such representations are original, they were not derivative from a high rationalist culture. He thus urges that despite divergences of form and articulation (e.g. literate/oral) he is investigating 'a unified culture within which it was impossible to make clear-cut distinctions'.[65] Mutualities of influence and features of common participation break down simplistic notions of cultural difference and hierarchization. When the intelligentsia started firmly associating popular forms with 'the common people', such stances were related to an active process of their dissociation from forms in which they had previously participated.[66]

However, once these distinctions are crystallized, it would be foolhardy not to pinpoint the ideological implications of the formal and narrational distinctions which emerge between art and commercial cinema; peculiarities which are quite central to the ways in which perceptions of change find expression in popular forms. I will not go into this at length, but both the deployment of the icon, and the narrative transaction around generational conflict, are centrally founded on the manipulation of women. In particular, with rare exceptions, such a manipulation actively divests women characters of the modern, professional attributes which they exhibit, placing them as objects of exchange within the generational trans-action. Further, the social film of the 1950s also tends to split the woman in terms of the figuration of her desire. Legitimate figures are held close to patriarchal hearth and diktat in terms of narrative space and symbolic articulation, and a more overt sexuality is displaced to another figure.[67]

Having said this, perhaps we should conclude by remembering that the art cinema is perfectly capable of such a subordination of women characters. This is so of the way Ray's *Ganashatru* (1989), for example, reduces the woman to a 'moral voice' and sexually threatened figure. Of course, psychological nuance and realist acting styles are evidently meant to prevent such a reduction of character to narrative function. However, not only does the commercial cinema exhibit such acting styles, as in the work of Nutan (for example, in *Sujata*, Bimal Roy, 1959, and *Bandini*, Bimal Roy, 1963); perhaps, as in song sequences such as 'Aaj sajan mohe ang laga lo' in *Pyaasa* (Guru Dutt, 1957) and 'O, Majhi' in *Bandini*, it has richer resources to express a desiring and divided subjectivity than naturalist canons would allow for.

## NOTES

1. I will not be analysing the place of performance sequences in this article, although they are central to an understanding of the popular aspects of the commercial film. For a preliminary attempt to evaluate their status, cf. Ravi Vasudevan, 'The Melodramatic Mode and the Commercial Hindi Cinema: Notes on Film History, Narrative and Performance', *Screen* 30(3), 1989: 29–50.

2. Satyajit Ray, *Our Films, Their Films*, New Delhi: Orient Longman, 1976, p. 6.

3. Ibid., p. 21.

4. Ibid., p. 13.

5. Ibid., p. 23.

6. *Indian Film Quarterly*, January–March 1957: 9–14.

7. *Indian Film Review*, December 1958: 6–11.

8. Kobita Sarkar, 'Influences on the Indian Film', *Indian Film Quarterly*, January–March 1957: 10. Marie Seton also remarked that the commercial film 'never entirely freed itself from the influence of the theatre. . . .', 'National Idiom in Film Technique', in *Indian Talkie, 1931–56*, Bombay: Film Federation of India, 1956, p. 58.

9. Kobita Sarkar, ibid., p. 10; '. . . the greatest potential weakness of our

cinema is the general lack of characterization . . .', idem, 'Black and White', ibid., p. 6.

10. Idem, 'Influences', p. 13.

11. Idem, 'Black and White', p. 6.

12. Ibid., p. 7.

13. Ibid., p. 8.

14. Idem, 'Influences', p. 10.

15. Ibid., p. 12.

16. Ibid.

17. Idem, 'Black and White', p. 7.

18. Idem, 'Influences', p. 13. Kobita Sarkar allows the occasional flicker of doubt about absolute standards of taste in art: '(The Indian film) . . . is derided by the more sophisticated largely because they have accepted more sophisticated standards of judgement. As it is not yet possible to set any absolute values as to what constitutes good cinema, perhaps it is rash to pass final judgement.' See ibid., p. 14.

19. M.A. Parthasarathy, 'India in the Film Map of the World', *Indian Talkie 1931–56*, p. 66.

20. Ibid.

21. R.M. Roy (ed.), *Film Seminar Report*, New Delhi: Sangeet Natak Akademi, 1956, pp. 29–30.

22. *Indian Film Review*, January 1958: 9–14.

23. Ibid., 10.

24. Ibid., 14.

25. Ibid., 11.

26. Ibid., 13.

27. Ibid.

28. Ibid., 14.

29. Ibid., 13.

30. Ibid., 12.

31. Ibid., 14.

32. Ibid.

33. Jim Pines and Paul Willemen (eds), *Questions of Third Cinema*, London British Film Institute, 1989.

34. These references are quite unelaborated, and the study of Indian cinema has only recently started investigating these issues seriously. Cf. Geeta Kapur 'Mythic Material in Indian Cinema', *Journal of Arts and Ideas* 14–15, 1987: 79–107; Ashish Rajadhyaksha, 'The Phalke Era: Conflict of Traditional Form and Modern Technology', ibid., 47–78, and 'Neo-traditionalism: Film as Popular Art in India', *Framework* 32–33, 1987: 20–67.

35. To quote a contemporary publicity release, a social film was 'based no on historical tales, but on life as it is lived at the present time'. *Bombay Chronicle* 27 October 1951: 3.

36. I draw upon Geeta Kapur's usage here: 'an image into which symbolic meanings converge and in which moreover they achieve stasis'. 'Mythic Material in Indian Cinema', p. 82.

37. Peter Brooks, *The Melodramatic Imagination: Balzac, Henry James*

*Melodrama and the Mode of Excess,* 1976, reprinted, New York: Columbia University Press, 1988, p. 48

38. Roland Barthes, 'Diderot, Brecht, Eisenstein', in *Image, Music, Text,* selected and translated by Stephen Heath, London: Fontana Paperbacks, 1982, p. 70.

39. As Barthes notes of the tableau, it is 'a pure cut-out segment with clearly defined edges, irreversible and incorruptible; everything that surrounds it is banished into nothingness, remains unnamed, while everything that it admits within its field is promoted into essence, into light, into view ... (it) is intellectual, it has something to say (something moral, social) but it also says it knows how this must be done.' Ibid.

40. For an outline of the classical system, see Kristin Thompson, 'The Formulation of the Classical Style, 1909–28', in *The Classical Hollywood Cinema,* pp. 155–240.

41. Stephen Heath, 'Narrative Space', in idem, *Questions of Cinema,* London: Macmillan, 1981, p. 30.

42. Noel Burch, *To the Distant Observer: Form and Meaning in the Japanese Cinema,* London: Scolar Press, 1979, p. 158.

43. See Ravi Vasudevan, 'You cannot live in society and ignore it: Nationhood and Female Modernity in *Andaz* (1949)', in *Contributions to Indian Sociology* 29 (1&2), 1995.

44. Roland Barthes, *S/Z,* London: Jonathan Cape, 1975.

45. Ashis Nandy, 'The Hindi Film: Ideology and First Principles', *India International Center Quarterly* 8(1), 1981: 89–96; Rosie Thomas, 'Indian Cinema: Pleasures and Popularity', *Screen* 26 (3–4), 1985: 116–32; Ravi Vasudevan, 'The Melodramatic Mode and the Commercial Hindi Cinema'.

46. Tom Gunning, 'The Cinema of Attraction: Early Film, Its Spectator and the Avant-Garde', *Wide Angle* 8 (3–4), 1986: 63–70.

47. Sylvia Harvey, 'Woman's Place: The Absent Family of *Film Noir*', in E. Anne Kaplan (ed.), *Women in Film Noir,* London: British Film Institute, 1980, pp. 22–34 (25).

48. For a summary of analyses of *film noir* in terms of narrative structure, sexual economy and stylistic features, see David Bordwell's remarks in *The Classical Hollywood Cinema,* p. 76.

49. This is characteristic of the way melodrama moves between familial and public registers. Peter Brooks, *The Melodramatic Imagination,* pp. 31–2; and below, under sub-head 'Redefining the Popular: Melodrama and Realism'.

50. The following analysis of relations between family and society in narrative structure is summarized from my 'Dislocations: The Cinematic Imagining of a New Society in 1950s India', *Oxford Literary Review* 16, 1994; and R. Vasudevan, 'Errant Males and the Divided Woman', Ph.D thesis, University of East Anglia, 1991, ch. 3.

51. Ravi Vasudevan, 'The Cultural Space of a Film Narrative: Interpreting *Kismet* (Bombay Talkies, 1943)', *Indian Economic and Social History Review* 28(2), April–June 1991: 171–85.

52. The apparently paradoxical phenomenon of an image which has power is quite a common one within Hindu visual culture. Lawrence Babb has noted

that whether the gods are represented as idols in the temple or the domestic space, or in the more pervasive phenomenon of photographs, the devotees desire the *darsan* (sight) of the God or religious preceptor (guru), a sight 'he grants to his devotees as a sign of his favour and grace'. Babb emphasizes that this is a question not only of the devotee seeing but being seen; and that such a constitution of the devotional subject may afford him not only the grace and favour of the deity, but may also empower him. Lawrence A. Babb, 'Glancing: Visual Interaction in Hinduism', *Journal of Anthropological Research* 37(4), 1981: 47–64. The subordinate position of the devotee in this relation has also been emphasized by Diana Eck: the deity *'gives darsan' (darsan dena)*, the people *'take darsan' (darsan lena)* and so 'seeing' in this religious sense is not an act initiated by the worshipper. Diana L. Eck, *Seeing the Divine Image in India*, Chambersurg, Pa: Anima Books, 1981, p. 5. Raj's evasion of this visual field stems from his transgression of its moral boundaries.

53. Ravi Vasudevan, 'Errant Males and the Divided Woman', p. 114.

54. There is a fetishistic aspect to the photograph here, a disavowal of lack in the psychoanalytical sense; but the lack involved or feared here is not that of the phallus, but that of the mother. As Kaja Silverman has noted: 'the equation of woman with lack (is) a *secondary construction*, one which covers over *earlier sacrifices* . . . the loss of the object is also a castration . . . the male subject is already structured by absence prior to the moment at which he registers anatomical difference.' Kaja Silverman, *The Acoustic Mirror: The Female Voice in Psychoanalysis and the Cinema*, Bloomington: Indiana University Press, 1988, pp. 14–5.

In this sense the photograph in *Awara* bears distinctly fetishistic features, covering over as it does a masculine lack of the maternal. In narrational terms, too, in the opposition between photo-icon and cinematic movement, the invocation of the photograph has the fetishistic aspect of denying movement, and thereby loss, and seeking a return to stasis. As Gilles Deleuze has noted, the fetish in this case is a 'frozen, arrested, two-dimensional image, a photograph to which one returns repeatedly to exorcise the dangerous consequences of movement, the harmful discoveries that result from exploration. . . .' Gilles Deleuze, *Sacher-Masoch: An Interpretation*, translated by Jean McNeill, London: Faber and Faber, 1971, p. 28.

55. 'The Hindi Film', p. 81.

56. Ravi Vasudevan, 'Dislocations' and 'Errant Males and the Divided Woman', especially ch. 2, in the analysis of *Devdas* (Bimal Roy, 1956) and *Pyaasa* (Guru Dutt, 1957).

57. Ravi Vasudevan, 'Glancing Off Reality: Contemporary Cinema and Mass Culture in India', in *Cinemaya* 16, Summer 1992: 4–9.

58. Rick Altman, 'Dickens, Griffith and Film Theory Today', *South Atlantic Quarterly* 88(2), Spring 1989: 321–59.

59. Peter Brooks, *The Melodramatic Imagination*, ch. 1.

60. Ibid., p. 16.

61. The street lamp is also a recurrent, metonymic element in songbook illustrations and movie posters of this period. The National Film Archives of India, Pune, has a substantial collection of both.

62. Peter Brooks, *The Melodramatic Imagination*, p. 9.

63. Coincidence also has an important temporal function: 'the apparently arbitrary separation and coincidental reunion of characters is actually motivated by the narrative requiring a certain time to lapse. These durations are related to the evolution of a set of substitutable functions (whether between characters, or within a character) in which the timing of the substitution depends on the exhaustion of one figure, and a maturation and acquisition of lacking functions in another.' Vasudevan, 'The Melodramatic Mode and the Commercial Hindi Cinema'.

64. Christine Gledhill, 'The Melodramatic Field: An Investigation', in Christine Gledhill (ed.), *Home Is Where the Heart Is: Studies in Melodrama and the Women's Film*, London: British Film Institute, 1987, pp. 33–6.

65. Carlo Ginzburg, *The Cheese and the Worms*, London: Routledge and Kegan Paul, 1976, pp. 22–3.

66. Peter Burke, *Popular Culture in Early Modern Europe*, p. 27.

67. Ravi Vasudevan, 'Dislocations' and 'Errant Males and the Divided Woman', especially 86–9, 169–70.

# 4

# *The Couple and Their Spaces:* Harano Sur *as Melodrama Now*

MOINAK BISWAS

IN THIS ESSAY we shall take a close, if partial, look at a representative film from the Uttam Kumar–Suchitra Sen melodrama, a cycle that started in 1953 and continued into the late 1960s,[1] creating the most enduring star-duo as well as a series of films that have had unprecedented success and persistence. One should speak of the broader genre it belonged to—the popular melodrama of the 1950s and '60s—but it is mostly the Uttam–Suchitra films, with what we have called a persistence, that have come to emblematize the entire period in question from the history of Bengali cinema. The Uttam–Suchitra duo has lent its name to the era and can be used as a sign for a large number of films that did not actually feature the stars together.

These films are currently enjoying a great resurgence through television, and consequently, through video circulation and popular film discourse. Set against the abject condition of the current Tolly-gunge fare, their values have become all the more apparent to the viewers. Even the critical eye trained in the categories of Art Cinema that began simultaneously in Bengal with a programmatic disavowal of this genre has been made to discover some of these values. The genre, particularly in the hands of directors like Ajoy Kar, Asit Sen, Agradoot, Tapan Sinha, Jatrik or Hiren Nag, was able to attain a stability of form through a rapport amongst institutions,

I am grateful to my friends and colleagues at Jadavpur University, Calcutta and Ravi Vasudevan, Madhava Prasad and Bhaswati Chakrabarty for their comments on the earlier draft of this essay.

material and technique that is unique in the industry's history. It successfully exploited a literary liaison established since the inception of sound cinema to draw a sustained charm of words, to create characters anchored in speech-idioms and narrative conventions supported by tradition. Besides the formidable talent of its prime star Uttam Kumar as an actor, it made use of an exceptionally able troupe of supporting actors creating a memorable repertory of character-types. And perhaps more than anything else for us, distanced viewers, it arrived in its best films at a certain style of black and white cinematography, a defined mode of lighting, framing and camerawork which has proved to be able to fix both a time and a yearning. It could articulate amongst a limited set of spatial choices or frames of action with great ease and negotiate a set of formal influences that this genre as a whole imbibed from Hollywood (for example, the blend of realism and expressionism that Hollywood cultivated from the 1930s). Rather than using a free tonality akin to post-1955 realist cinema, this cinematography schematized tones to create a polarized,' morally legible' universe that melodrama essentially needs and also, when necessary, an aura of psychological motivations and drives. This tonal system, perfected by cinematographers like Ajoy Kar, Asit Sen or Dinen Gupta, could negotiate amongst other things a fit amongst propensities and institutions like Star and Author, frontality and linearization (or picture and movement, as Martin Meisel has called it in relation to the larger context of melodrama in nineteenth-century Europe[2]), character and icon etc. In short, it embodied in a local context certain global signs of film melodrama, where a lot of energy from the narrative, in the absence of interior depths, flows into the 'body' of the film.

# I

Talking about the films now one has to, of course, acknowledge the distance, the resurfacing and the framing anew of this material. This acknowledgement should be a constitutive element of historical criticism and should distinguish itself from the facile nostalgia that the situation also produces, from the logic of what is called the 'nostalgia industry'. Before considering the text in hand, the 1957 film *Harano Sur*, an all-time favourite Uttam-Suchitra starrer directed by Ajoy Kar, we should talk about the specific context within which we are discovering these films. The great success of their reappearance on television (they have not found any substantial parallel redistribution through the theatres though) should prompt us, I feel, to consider reception as a paradigm in a specific way: to start on the point of charm, work through a media-cultural site to reach the text. I do not hope to map this path clearly in this paper and shall be mainly asking some relevant questions about the route.

I would like to argue, that the 'charm', even the 'spell', as it spreads across three decades, has roots in a process of continuity in discontinuity. It has to do as much with how and where the film is received as with what is in the film. It has to do with questions of recognition and reclaim; with questions of space in a special way for us, with desire and femininity.

Television, out of sheer necessity, has to use the films of the past, to reissue and reframe them, assigning particular current values to the generic elements. Television becomes a sequential flow of various generic modes with entirely novel means of embedding the past within the present. A film like *Harano Sur* cannot be seen today outside the slot it has found in the media-cultural site. Nostalgia is no longer a simple or experiential phenomenon in this situation, but is a constitutive, productive element in culture, an essential part of dissemination, reception and even production.

As a part of this excavation, and supported by the audio industry boom in the 1980s and '90s, the songs from the 1950s and '60s have had a strong resurgence. A whole host of television programmes and a large part of the music-cassette industry survive on this. The phenomenon serves as a simple illustration of how it is a matter of investment not only in the economic sense but in the field of desire and meaning-making. Through remembered songs by Hemanta Mukherjee, Shyamal Mitra, Manna De, Sandhya Mukherjee, Geeta Dutt—but most emblematically through Hemanta's voice—a powerful reinvestment in the films from the spectator's side is made possible. It is possible for him/her, moreover, to name an epoch, to bring under a single aura a cluster of signs of the Bengali middle-class cultural identity in its modern-popular phase, the latter having already been delivered from the post-Independence years to us for nostalgic contemplation. The songs as they were, of course, had strong affinities with the melo-dramatic structure itself. They played an important part in forming the specific generic substance in question, by helping to put 'melos into drama'.[3] Through an aural economy, they signified reflective moments in the absence of a proper reflective apparatus in the form. They signified a very important aura of loneliness in the films and, conversely, also embodied communicative trajectories between individuals when other pathways were blocked or prohibited.

But nostalgia brings to mind another, perhaps more important aspect of the image-world—the valorization of the black and white image in the new media space. The texture rather than the content of a past is invoked in such doubling of representation. Fredric Jameson, in his essays on postmodernism termed this process the 'mode-retro',[4] a phenomenon we are witnessing through the extensive use of black and white images in expensive advertisements, music-video, book and poster designing and even in some modes of painting in India—a postmodern situation even if not a postmodern condition. It is not only a question of deploying the ''50s look' as a mode of image-making, but is more fundamentally a question of finding a new way of looking at the films of the 1950s. We no longer have a direct access to these films, and as we look at them, we try to recreate the gaze of the spectator of the 1950s. We see a gaze, the look of the 'other' in a sense. We do not need to believe or identify with what we see in the film, rather the distance from the world it portrays becomes a necessary condition for viewing the gaze of the imaginary spectator of the 1950s who believed and identified with all this. In terms of the psychoanalytic theory of the gaze, this nostalgic looking can be seen as a denial of the essential antinomy of the eye and the gaze, a denial of the fact that the gaze cannot be owned exclusively by 'me'. We have the illusory pleasure of 'seeing ourselves seeing' here, of keeping the Cartesian subject of self-reflection in place and blinding ourselves to the fact that 'the other is already gazing at us'.[5]

For our argument, the dimension of reclaim involved here is perhaps more important. We see ourselves seeing, we retrieve our past seeing selves. Certain periods from the past and a certain selfhood is more necessary for the present spectator to retrieve. A certain kind of film provides the privileged site for this activity, not all kinds. We would tentatively suggest that the 1950s melodrama as a form, space as a cinematic substance and femininity as a condition are three basic issues at stake here. Besides reinvocations, then, we should also look at some 'organic' relations. For example, the relation between the black and white distribution within the image and the melodramatic work of translating psychological/emotional content into spatial/pictorial terms. We shall come back to this in a moment.

Encounters with the past or historical awareness of any kind are necessarily tied up for us with realistic modes of culture. It is essential to remember melodrama's troubled relations with realism when we are thinking of recollecting lost times or selves through films. Peter Brooks, in his authoritative study of melodrama, has shown how melodrama and realism have been closely interlinked since the nineteenth century. Rather than being two essentially antithetical modes, as our art-cinema criticism has usually held, in our context too one has shaped and deflected the other. The question is basically about melodrama being present as a condition across various modes of culture, including the realist one. This is particularly true about the period under review when a classic, Hollywood-inspired definition of melodrama emerged in Indian cinema simultaneously with modern realism. The melodramatic mode in *Harano Sur* displaces social reality and, at the same time, uses elements of realist narration so that representational identifications are also possible, making way, thereby, for the perception of a remembered world in a strangely concrete and sensuous manner. An acknowledgement of desire is perhaps what is involved in the concrete here which conventional historical modes fail to deliver.

What is seen as a denial of reality in melodrama by our conventional criticism has been explained by recent critics as a displacement of the social/political into the familial (this should not mean, of course, that denial never takes place). An upheaval in the family, for example, can stage in absence a crucial dilemma about the shift of authority in the political order; a crisis in the triad of lovers, likewise, can take the place of the conundrums of a society in transition. A fuller understanding of melodrama should, of course, look into the particularly fraught relation it has had with the history of realism in our context. The realist social novel in Bengal, for example, from Bankimchandra through Tagore, has often sought to figure momentous political and social upheavals through the familial.

When we are dealing with material of the kind we have, we cannot think about our encounter with the past cultural artifacts exactly the same way that Fredric Jameson does. This encounter will not necessarily be built upon a representational surplus as his argument would imply but will take place in a media-cultural site where the melodramatic text will now be embedded in a new representational flow. So we are thinking of two levels of embedment here: realism as sequentially employed within melodrama alongside other conventions, and the latter itself as a mode placed alongside other kinds of media-texts where realism or representationalism is much more in evidence.

In his subsequent book on postmodernism,[6] Jameson discusses how a post-nostalgic trend has come to negotiate a problematic historicity in American films of the mid-80s. He extends his arguments on mode-retro and pastiche into what he sees as an allegorical encounter with the past. This periodization cannot be applied to our context, but his idea of allegory can illuminate two basic things we have in mind: (1) the heavily mediated nature of our appropriation of a world through melodrama now, and (2) the way a film like *Harano Sur* embodies desire by creating figures of space.

The guarded, domestic world of melodrama faced a threat of dissolution in the 1970s with the introduction of the criminal hero and the revenge theme. The anti-social's world brought about a new configuration of the social. The necessary liaison between violence and realism—violence turns the world real—eventually gave rise to entirely new visual and narrative conventions in the late 1980s. The new breed of realism, making use of the technical wherewithal of the TV age, has, among other things, released a certain flow of commodities in the image and has effected a dynamization of the narrative itself under the aegis of this 'flow'. There is a new density of objects and bodies within the image. This, coupled with the multilayered, digitalized soundtrack, lend the texture its violence as much as the acts of violence within the film. In the 1950s melodrama, the realism of the *mise en scène* had to be articulated as one register among others of the space. The decor still depends heavily on the 'artificialities' borrowed from popular visual arts and theatre, but to invoke the social and familial matrix of the everyday, it uses reality effects of locality, character, etc. This lends the space a notational character totally ignored by those who take artificiality of the decor as an irredeemable fault. The essentially sparse spaces of melodrama could give the limited objects a special effect; something that happens in *Harano Sur* with a bunch of tube-roses, a fountain-pen, a purse or a ball of knitting wool in the context of a loss of memory. Whereas, a vividly realistic scene in the film, the one where the hero goes out into the streets of a mofussil town, meets with an accident and becomes the object of the collective gaze of a crowd, appears to be the most dreamlike. Certain signs of real life became, through circulation in many films, strangely concretized. A particularly sensuous example is the street lamp.[7]

The notational space has its roots in the basic quality of the melodramatic universe. Besides the internalizing process (the displacement of the social/political into the familial), there is also a process of externalization in evidence in the form. What is essentially interior or subjective in realist fiction gets translated into external polarities of character and action in melodrama. A Manichean schema of good and evil, of essential embodiments, has to be created. Peter Brooks has argued that as a bourgeois form, melodrama emerges in a post-sacred world, it has to take up the functions hitherto performed by allegory or tragedy, and its immediate historical task was to reinvent the 'moral occult' as the realm of 'meaning and value'. This happens even as the 'person' becomes the last source of morality and ethics in the melodramatic world.[8] The world has to become morally legible, so to speak, and must infuse ordinary human actions with larger significances.[9]

Recent researches into the history of the melodramatic form have shown that since its birth in the Minor House, non-legitimate theatres of the eighteenth century, a spectaclisation of its address took place. There were some contingent reasons too, one being the actual prohibition on spoken words. The melodramatic *mise en scène*, to various degrees, has translated character into action and action into spatial characteristics (earlier examples of which lie in the pre-Jamesian novel, ballet, opera etc.).[10] Freudian ideas about hysteria as a kind of 'body-writing' have also been evoked to explain how the emotion that remains undischarged in the patriarchal moral world of the text is siphoned off to the elements of the *mise en scène*, to songs, dances, costumes or hyperbolic expression.[11]

We could come back to the black and white image here—the

tonal schematization of light that we have talked about. It would be worthwhile to note its special rapport with the polarization and externalization mentioned above. I am reminded here, among others, of Martin Meisel who, studying how a special fit between visuality itself as a drive and the melodramatic mode emerged historically through the nineteenth century, has observed that the association of melodrama with elemental contrasts of darkness and light goes back to certain modes of painting and to the time of its inception in the late eighteenth century when new lighting technologies were being introduced in the theatre.[12]

To give an example from *Harano Sur*—a typical yet elegant one— of how a black and white scheme 'embodies' mental states in animation, let us remember the sequence where Aloke and Roma make the vow to stay together forever: Aloke goes to sleep in Roma's house in Palashpur where she is trying to cure him of his amnesia. A bunch of tube-roses, already introduced as a motif, lies at the head of the bed. Aloke has told her that their aroma in the darkness is one of the things that comes back to him. There is a highlight on the bunch of flowers and a prevailing darkness in the room. Roma turns off the light, the camera pans over the darkness as she exits the room, and only the outlines of the characters' faces and the flowers are visible. She crosses the corridor to her room, and in the process is made to traverse alternating zones of light and darkness. She reaches her room, the theme music floats in, she looks lost in thought, and lies on her bed. The light scheme there is exactly of the same value as in Aloke's room before the light there was switched off. There is a table-lamp in her room, which she turns off, and the second stage of lighting in Aloke's room is repeated. Voice off, we hear Aloke's words about the aroma in the darkness. The storm starts. The pattern that has been established with the two states of light and darkness distributed over phases of action, now appears in quick succession, on the same face or object. The window in Roma's room and the one in Aloke's room start flashing with lightning. Aloke's face and the flowers flash on and off in the same manner. We hear the sound of the alarm, a memory from the moment when Aloke fled the asylum. He looks almost demented, an ultimate victim of nature and society. A hand rests on his head. It is Roma's. He clutches her and says, "Don't leave me, 'Daktarbabu'." Her face flashes too—light, darkness, light—she says she never will. The lighting pattern creates a system of alternation within the frame, between frames, and then, as a shorthand of what has already been done, within the frame again. In short, it creates a musical formula, combines with sound and performs a narration. To narrate through alternation is a familiar compulsion of films, but it is interesting to note how this sequence translates a whole exchange between characters in terms of the basic and polarized elements of the *mise en scène*.

We will have occasion to get back to the terrain of space again, but at this point let me broach the question of femininity. We are thinking in terms of allegory once again—allegories of femininity—not only of direct encounters. I suggest that a tryst with the feminine is at stake in the recovery of the lost time or self. Or else one cannot comprehend the fascination of finding these films again. Once again we relate the issue to the two dimensions: the textual material, and the sequencing/positioning of it in a media-cultural site.

The sequential placement with other media texts has, among other things, helped reveal the generic skeleton of the films. This makes possible perhaps, a conscious appropriation of a certain time-space through a named marker—through a visibility of the 'chronotope'—though the time-space in its social reality may have been blocked or displaced in the film. One can perhaps argue that for the Bengali audience the function of this mode ties up with a shift from an appropriation of the national real (with which realism has been historically linked) to an appropriation of the regional real. It would not be far-fetched to suggest that, for historically contingent reasons, to recollect a Bengaliness from these films, in contrast to the search for a national essence, means also to retrieve a femininity for the self.

One strand in Bengali popular cinema now, represented by Anjan Choudhury, Sujit Guha, Swapan Saha and others, has set upon a vengeful regression into the feudal family romance of a particularly crude variety. These films are consciously targeted at rural and female audiences, as the industry people often say. The truth that this advocacy reveals is that there is an articulation of a 'female', or a 'rural' domain in the cultural site, emerging in the face of the all-India Hindi film, or the up-market television products. Both terms are relatively feminized—the female and the rural—and they denote a condition rather than always an actual status of the audience. It is one thing to note the desire of women to see certain kinds of films and quite another to make that synonymous with the actual films that meet that desire. It is by viewing the two as synonymous that we have often come to uncritically judge not only certain tendencies in culture as invariably low, but have also ascribed a certain low spiritual status to the feminine, or the peasant-like. It becomes necessary for historical criticism to investigate the domains addressed or vied for, by a genre like melodrama, and to make distinctions within the genre: to see where the films come to respond to the more democratic, affirmative and nuanced aspects of its audience's desires and where not.

For our argument, then, it is important to note how in the site of media a feminine space has been opened up, how the 1950s melodrama can sometimes lay a special claim to that space, and also how the spectator has to adopt or even recover a certain femininity to rediscover these movies, to submit to their charm.

We shall note a world in *Harano Sur* that is feminine and also now, historically 'feminized': an articulate female presence, the feminized quality of its emotional content, the positively feminized quality of its male protagonist and even, I would argue, its now feminized/ruralized cityscapes captured in notation like the naive and peaceful comic-book locations. We shall suggest that the film produces a feminine subjectivity independent of the female subject in the story.

*Harano Sur* belongs to that variety of melodrama which has been termed the woman's film. By placing the woman at the centre of the story, these films can often open up a whole field of experience and desire that cannot be entirely accommodated within the patriarchal ideological framework of the film. Examples from Mehboob, Guru Dutt or Kamal Amrohi also come to mind. The issue has been investigated in detail by a host of feminist critics in the last two decades. Laura Mulvey, for example, has argued in her 'Afterthoughts on "Visual Pleasure and Narrative Cinema" ' that in such films the woman might for a moment stop being only a male projection of drives and values and can project her own divided subjectivity into the contrasting male characters of the story. Thus she might finally embrace the legitimate and reject or (as she did often) kill the illegitimate man in her life, but in the process she might have to stand at the core of a staging of her inner tensions. An unknown range of choices for subject-positions is opened up for her through all this. Mulvey invokes Freud's concept of a regression into masculinity of the woman to suggest that not only in such films but even in a 'male' genre like the Western, the female spectator can derive pleasure from the possibility of a rediscovery of the forgotten masculine phase within her. Our argument, in a sense, runs in an opposite direction to Mulvey's: it is possible—when we keep in focus not only a text but its cultural repositioning—to activate a feminization of both the male and the female spectator by films like *Harano Sur.*

What role does the star play in all this ? What resides in the black and white face of Suchitra Sen ? The substance is not only nostalgic, but has relation to a promise of individuation and independence, of a modernity which is yet to be fulfilled. The star phenomenon of the mature sound era in America has a close parallel with the star-phenomenon that post-Independence popular cinema in India produced. And in both cases it had a deep affinity with the principles of melodrama. The way melodrama valorises the 'person', for example, and yet externalizes psychology, thereby making the person an embodiment of psychic or moral qualities, is very similar to how the star persona operates in the signifying process of the film, how it embodies a set of values which it carries from film to film.[13] It is important to note how in our context a personality has to be organized around a star like Suchitra Sen in films where the woman otherwise would not lay claim to 'personality' in the modern sense of the term. One can compare a Pramathesh Barua film like *Mukti* (1937) with *Harano Sur* to find out the difference in question.

We have talked about the loneliness about these films. It stems finally from the isolation and the sovereignty of the couple, but in order that the couple be formed, an individuation of the male and female protagonists gets underway, enveloping them with the aura of loneliness. In *Harano Sur* the crowd appear only in the few scenes where conjugality is absent or momentarily dissolved. It is interesting to note how the cinematographers of the period developed a lighting and composition style that seemed to take the Suchitra Sen figure into spaces where she appears at times to be occupying a place outside social and even familial boundaries. This fantasy and its style have become entirely unknown to the Tollygunge melodrama after the mid-1970s.

Heterosexual couple formation, the goal of coming together of the man and the woman, lies at the heart of conventional film narrativity almost globally. It can be shown that the dominant model of narration in cinema has developed to a large extent in elaboration of this basic motivation. The absolute autonomy of the couple can be seen as a negation of the social dimensions, as a social-political destitution, but if one takes into consideration the generic imperatives of melodrama, a different aspect of this isolation can emerge in certain cases. If the social is already imploded into the familial, what the couple tries to conditionally negate is the family framework itself. From the familial to the conjugal space is a journey that is completed in Hollywood films but remains largely unfulfilled in Indian popular cinema. It is a migration from an older patriarchy to a bourgeois one and it often comes to emblematize a desire for modernity itself for the audience as well as for the characters. We should keep the same desire in mind when observing how post-Independence popular cinema for a while tried to emulate the Hollywood style of film-making itself. It is no longer a case of simple imitation then, but a question of resignification, of making Hollywood signify something else—let us say a modernity which does not have the same meaning as in the West. I borrow the expression 'desire for modernity' from Madhava Prasad who has argued in a recent essay that since the migration from the familial to the conjugal has remained incomplete in the social reality of our films, the very gaze itself, as produced in our cinema, should be considered in a different manner. Certain areas in the characters' lives are not visible at all because the 'private' space of the couple does not exist in the modern sense.[14]

What still fascinates us about a film like *Harano Sur* is how it acknowledges this desire, how it finds a way of 'articulating' the absent space of the couple. Space in *Harano Sur* stores the possibility of absent spaces. In the following description of the film we shall move between various denominations of the term 'space': we shall mean by it purely the location; we shall use it figuratively as a site carved out by a character or an event and also, as that which cannot be simply presented and hence is articulated between various strata of what is present as spaces.

## II

*Harano Sur* can afford a degree of reflexivity and become symptomatic of its genre to us because it deals with the age-old concerns of recognition, loss and gathering of identity and memory as its very subject. The crucial question is: whose identity is at stake? The affinity between the 'scenarization' of subjectivity found in the moments of complexes in psychoanalysis and the family-drama has been pointed out. The latter has been compared with what Freud has called *Familienroman* or family romance.[15] The ego enters into a scenarization—a melodramatic plot—in a situation like the oedipus complex, whereas in the family romance it creates fantasy and makes imaginary 'corrections' of all kinds of sexual relationships. Both in such discourses of ego formation and in actual melodramatic plots, the subjectivity of the romancer is predominantly a male subjectivity. The romance gives a strong symbolic function to the woman in the process of the identity formation of the man, but a film like *Harano Sur* places so much emphasis on the vision and agency of the woman, takes her through so many shifts of identity, and she mirrors so much of the man, plays so many roles to him in the romance process, that the film has to wrench a space away from these sites of struggle. The space that is figured for the woman is the necessary mediation before the couple can claim its own chimerical space.

Ajoy Kar, the director and cinematographer, takes the story from *Random Harvest*, a 1942 MGM melodrama starring Ronald Colman and Greer Garson, directed by Mervyn LeRoy, but changes it substantially. There is also little resemblance in narrative structure and visual style. *Harano Sur* opens in a mental asylum and states the enigma as Aloke's (Uttam Kumar) loss of memory in a train accident. A discourse on mental illness and psychiatry is introduced (a theme that has come down from the self-conscious 'Freudianism' of Hollywood melodrama after the War and carried into films like *Deep Jwele Jai* in the 1960s very successfully). The senior male doctor is found to be oppressing Aloke, the young female psychiatrist Roma (Suchitra Sen) intervenes on Aloke's behalf and has to resign from her job. Briefly, before her resignation, she is shown administering an electric shock to a patient, and being disturbed by the experience. We also see Aloke's mother in the asylum whom he cannot recognize, and she vanishes from the story for a long time. When Roma is leaving the hospital, an alarm is raised; a storm scene ensues, in the midst of which Aloke escapes.

Back in her bungalow, Roma finds Aloke lying on a couch, using her house as a refuge from the police and the storm. She protects the miserable, traumatized man from the clutches of doctors and the police, and takes him along with her to her father's home in Palashpur. With the help of an extremely mild and supportive father, Roma sets about treating Aloke to bring him out of the amnesia. He is presented as childlike, lost and delicate, at times mildly tormented. This torment gets converted into its conventional signified, the experience of love, soon after. From a doctor Roma becomes a mother-figure which makes it possible for her, on the other hand, to articulate her love gradually, to play around with the affect love on more than one register. Aloke, one might add, keeps calling her 'Mr Doctor' (*daktarbabu*).

In a moment of helplessness, in the storm scene that we have already talked about, Roma promises Aloke she will never abandon him and turns her promise into a vow of marriage. She tells her father that a wife can do what a doctor cannot. In this love scene an outdoor spot under a tree plays a rather important role. It is the place where they spend the wedding night also, with Roma singing a song that becomes the dramatic clue in the recovery of memory later. A moment of domestic bliss follows which presents Aloke in the age-old Bengali ideal of Bholanath, a lovable combination of the absent-minded Shiva and the child. He keeps putting away objects—a pen, a purse, a ball of knitting wool—belonging to Roma in his pocket. There is a moment when they plan to build a little house for themselves, and Roma cherishes with extreme affection the thought that the forgetful Aloke might mistake another home for his some day and might lose his way. But throughout this passage, Aloke also keeps looking away from her constant gaze and appears a little disturbed about his own passivity and her overbearing love. Aloke meets with an accident on the street, recovers his lost memory but loses the memory of his time with Roma. For the first time we see a real outdoor location, a crowd, distinct faces. We shall see how this distinction lends this space the status of a bridge.

Aloke goes back to Calcutta, to a huge mansion where he lives with his mother and a young niece. Roma also goes to the city to seek him out. She begins this episode by narrating the events to her father in letters (referring to the knitting-wool ball and an unfinished jumper she was knitting for Aloke, she says she has to start 'weaving' again). She controls the narrative point of view while gesturally she changes into a demure, docile woman. Aloke, the owner of a company, is changed into an authoritative, even rude figure in his words and gestures. Roma finds work in his household as a governess to his niece Mala. What begins is, interestingly, a new genre of domestic melodrama, a genre which has its roots in the earliest English novels (e.g. Richardson's *Pamela*), among other things, and has been cycled in countless plays, novels and films—the story of a subordinate woman winning her male boss's heart, mellowing him into domesticity often by presenting a good-mother image to the children in the house. The other condition is also met, for there is a non-domestic fiancee of Aloke—Lata, rich and arrogant, tormenting Roma with the aid of her slightly villainous brother Mihir.

Roma initiates the process of remembrance for Aloke but fails at crucial moments, including the final one when Aloke is on the verge of dissolving into his previous identity with the shadow of madness again looming over him, and asks her, 'Who are you?' This indecision, while highlighting a certain femininity, actually works as a cover for her other agency to effect a move of genre-crossing. She goes on serving the child and the mother and watching Aloke who clearly feels uncomfortable under the pressure of her gaze. A bunch of tube-roses and burning incense are introduced as tools of remembrance from the past and then comes the major clue—the song from the wedding night. The song has to work both on the thematic (belonging to expressive content) and functional (of structural significance) levels as Thomas Elsaesser would put it, and it is introduced in bits and parts, first as a tune, then in disembodied singing, and finally as presented by Roma directly. It will be relevant to note that there are only two songs in the film.

Aloke gradually loses his authoritative bearing before her, but through a typical trick, through a process of prohibition that actually functions as delay, it is not made clear whether he is only remembering a lost past, a lost wife through Roma or is falling in love with this other Roma. The prohibition is necessary to keep intact his sexual purity, but in the most crucial moments in the episode it is utterly tenuous. It also serves to keep away from stating love as love, to maintain it as a transcendental signified. He says to Roma he is 'endangered'. After a climactic encounter between them, Roma is driven out of the house by Aloke's mother. Aloke begins to resemble his earlier incarnation in appearance. He learns from his manager that Roma has gone back to Palashpur. Then he remembers hearing her name from the people on the street when he regained consciousness after the accident. He moves out in a scene which looks like renunciation, turning away from a series of calls, goes to Palashpur, and finds his way to the spot under the tree. He comes to remember the tune of the song sung there and arrives at the final recognition. We should note that his cry 'Roma' takes on a melodramatic-musical function: he is only shown mutely uttering the name, then a disembodied cry floats over to Roma's house, and as he at last whispers her name, we hear it on the face of Roma, voice-off (Hemanta Mukherjee said in an interview that this cry was dubbed in his voice). The film ends with Aloke and Roma in the proverbial embrace. The place is Roma's courtyard, which has now become a space of tenuous, half-mythical status.

## III

I would briefly comment on only a few aspects of the film as a melodrama, as there is no scope for a comprehensive analysis.

By making loss, substitution and displacement its theme, the film makes desire itself somewhat foregrounded, and consequently underlines its own longing for form. It has to hang on to an illusory autonomy of love, has to acknowledge an overspill of longing by crossing sites of the actualization of love, it must locate the couple in relation to patriarchies old and new, but then, it also must stop in a transitional space between the last two and mythically make the couple free. It works, therefore, through allegories of space and transition, and I think, the genre-split in the film is central to this.

The film is not only about memory, it is also about the affect which comes as a supplement to it. The recovery is also a form of loss, and the film tries to attain resolution by recurrently moving from loss to recovery. But this last reconciliation is also left incomplete. It is so because not only does Aloke (and Roma) come out of his house ( he almost renounces it and, unlike most other films, no parents from either side follow the characters to the site of the reunion ) but also because he has to take leave of a certain genre to make this scene 'figurable'. He moves in body and through locations away from its iconographic and formal distinctions and is not recovered by his family.

It was necessary to shift the story from the first to the second genre to establish the high-rank and patriarchal solidity of the unknown hero (something that usually comes as the final revelation), to compensate for the lack of patriarchal authority that we find in Roma's home. But it was also necessary to complete Roma as a character by completing her as a woman, by having her play a range of woman's roles. The function of the star is also of importance here, the star often has to become him- or herself in the course of narrative unfolding. As they move from one role to another, the star personae of Uttam Kumar or Suchitra Sen are gradually brought to completion.

But this generic split is overseen by a larger narrative of loss and gain/recovery which makes these two sites incompletely complementary, even brings them into contest and makes a linear maturation of the woman (or man) impossible. It also asks the generic sites to articulate between them an absent term, a third place for the couple.

This larger story of loss and gain/recovery constitutes Aloke/Uttam Kumar as an object, setting a feminine determination in operation (one has to think of the star-phenomenon particularly in relation to a gendered spectatorship that is activated here—Uttam Kumar as an object of feminine gaze). A great tenderness and sensuousness accumulate along the path that makes *Harano Sur* a love story in the way they are no longer made. Aloke does not know how, like a treasure, he is lost to his family, then lost by the doctor-authorities, gained by Roma, claimed by Roma his wife again, lost to her, gained by his mother, lost to her, and recovered by Roma. His oblivious tucking away of objects belonging to Roma mirrors this tenderness. Let us also remember the immortal Geeta Dutt song on which much of the action hinges. It says, 'You are mine'.

David N. Rodowick, commenting on the domestic Hollywood melodrama of the 1950s, noted how an absence of a legitimating father-figure through death, desertion or weakness produced themes and signs of madness in the films, which was itself a sign of the disjunction between a general ideology and the established social, sexual and formal economies of the melodramatic genre.[16] As the story of *Harano Sur* changes sites from the asylum to Roma's house to Aloke's house, there is a constant process of loss and substitution of authority. The signs of madness Aloke shows, on the other hand, have two signifieds: one is the loss of memory, the other his being in love. The two possibilities are played with often, one coming as a cover for the other, and they are linked through the universal sign of sickness.

Memory is a theme as well as a narrative agency in the film which has a typical structure of delayed recognition. I will mention two scenes in which there is a constitutive link between memory as a theme and love. Interestingly, in both cases there is an overlapping of the former and the latter as the utterance of love has to be covered and delayed in the first instance, and has to be revealed through prohibition in the second. The first scene is where Aloke and Roma come to the tree spot for the first time. He looks intently at her and says, 'I think'; she is about to come out of her role as a doctor, but we cannot be sure; she says, 'What do you think?' as if it is a question about his remembrance. After the marriage there is no longer any query from Roma about his past, as if she knows she has to uproot him from his bearings for the sake of love. The second episode is in Aloke's house towards the end when Aloke says he has not fallen in love with Roma as she would think, he is looking for a woman he has forgotten—a statement that tries to say 'no' to what has been visualized in earlier scenes. In these one has already found Aloke unsettled by the attraction he feels for Roma.We know she is Roma but Aloke does not, a morally fuzzy area is created, and the imperative of monogamous and 'pure' sexuality is thus dispersed by the work of narrative. He has to fall in love, but with whom? The love object has to be kept in suspension as well as the utterance of love now. Love's transcendence is thus a function of various forces at work, it is not just given.

Roma brings in her wake an iconographic memory of the first part into the second generic location. Her close-ups abound while Aloke is mostly seen in mid-long- and mid-shots. He continues to be watched by Roma and often turns away from her look. Her close-ups, as we have said, carry strong visual memories from the early part of the film and these signs spread out as the moment of recognition draws near. There is an early moment in the episode when she is snubbed by Aloke for prying into his privacy; she is architecturally 'framed' as she appears through a door. This is often done with grille-work, mirrors, door and window frames in domestic melodrama to isolate and polarize figures, but here she is framed with an accent as a sign from another life and another genre.

There is also a distinct division of spatial characteristics which makes it possible for one generic space to contradict, remember and renew the other. This process of inter-spatial articulation takes on sharper contours when we remember the other minor spaces. These are of two kinds: one stylized and synthetic, the other realistic.

The courtyard of Roma's house and the tree in the outdoor landscape fall under the first category. The courtyard is only used in quick transitions a few times until the final scene. Till then, it is like the intermediary space between the asylum and Roma's house which becomes indistinct in the storm. But the tree is an important site where they fall in love and spend their wedding night. It is an idyll tucked away beyond the confines of even the ideal home. These locations are studio built and done in a style that looks incredibly effete, appearing almost like a 'fault' in the total *mise en scène*. They are definitely a residue from the 1930s and 40s studio-styles, increasingly abandoned in this melodrama. (These stylistic mixtures of decor are a sign of development of the other contemporary trend in Bengali cinema also, witness the examples of *Udayer Pathe*, *Chhinnamul* and *Nagarik*). The popular film-text becomes a combination of idioms assigning particular functions to particular generic or stylistic units. In *Harano Sur* the 'artificial' spaces in question play host to scenes of love and singing which are rendered in a heightened, sentimental, remote style. This is how the earlier section of the film also figures another genre of space within it in an allegorical fashion.

It is precisely at the moment of transition between two major sites that memory is visualized as a process. It is when the road accident occurs that a realistic kind of space is established for the first time. We see a small-town road, railway station, bits of landscape and, most important, faces of local people (before that the local people are represented by a completely artificial Santhal family). In Calcutta this style is only briefly evoked before we are confined into another space—Aloke's house, which is stylistically as distant from this sharp realism as Roma's house. As if a brief moment of realism was needed to effect a passage between spaces which belonged to a more psychic order. To me this moment appears to be the most dream-like as a consequence.

When the courtyard appears in the final scene in its effete, and generically parenthetic cast, it appears to be a function of the transitions between sites (and genres) we have been talking about. It is the location where Aloke and Roma consummate the embrace: the disembodied cry 'Roma' has already traced a path, covered the distance between the two spots; he arrives at the gate, Roma comes out of the house at the call and runs through the courtyard into his arms. Not only the decor, there are then, other positive factors contributing to the unreality of the location—it is a space arrived at through the editing with the help of a sound that tries to connect, without following the logic of spatial unfolding. One cannot forget, moreover, the overlapping cuts on Roma when she comes out of the house—she is made to cover the same area more than once in the process, prolonging her journey and disturbing the rationality of the space.

The embrace in these films was a ritual sign of ending. One could hardly have found a more native one for the genre, of a more ready means of elision—from the 'closing' of the couple to the closing of the film. Space implodes in an embrace as the couple is finally formed in *Harano Sur;* it collapses into a non-space between them and a nowhere for them. The courtyard now 'holds' the absent term that is articulated amongst all the sites including itself, namely, the space of the couple. The lasting fascination of *Harano Sur* lies more than anything else in its ability to stop at a transitory point in a migration when what is present as physical location becomes an embodiment of a desire—desire for the private, the autonomous, the modern.

## NOTES

1. Uttam Kumar and Suchitra Sen did their last film together in 1972 but we are thinking of a generic phase here which culminates in the late 1960s.

2. Martin Meisel, 'Scattered Chiaroscuro: Melodrama as a Matter of Seeing',

in Jacky Bratton, Jim Cook, Christine Gledhill (eds), *Melodrama: Stage Picture Screen*, London: 1994.

3. Thomas Elsaesser, 'Tales of Sound and Fury: Observations on the Family Melodrama', in Christine Gledhill (ed.), *Home is Where the Heart Is: Studies in Melodrama and the Woman's Film*, London: 1987.

4. Fredric Jameson, 'The Politics of Theory: Ideological Positions in the Postmodernism Debate', in David Lodge (ed.), *Modern Criticism and Theory*, New York: 1988. Also Jameson, 'Postmodernism and Consumer Society', in Hal Foster (ed.), *Postmodern Culture*, London: 1983.

5. See, for a discussion of this problem, 'Pornography, Nostalgia, Montage: A Triad of the Gaze'; in Slavoj Zizek, *Looking Awry, An Introduction to Jacques Lacan through Popular Culture*, Cambridge, MA: 1992.

6. Fredric Jameson, *Postmodernism, or, The Cultural Logic of Late Capitalism*, London: 1991.

7. See Ravi Vasudevan, 'Shifting Codes, Dissolving Identities: The Hindi Social Film of the 1950s as Popular Culture', *Journal of Arts & Ideas* 23–24, 1993.

8. Peter Brooks, *The Melodramatic Imagination*; quoted in Christine Gledhill, 'Signs of Melodrama', in Gledhill (ed.), *Stardom: Industry of Desire*, London: 1991.

9. See Gledhill, ibid.

10. See Gledhill, 'The Melodramatic Field: An Investigation', in Gledhill (ed.), *Home is Where the Heart is*.

11. See Geoffrey Nowell-Smith, 'Minelli and Melodrama'; in Gledhill (ed.), ibid.

12. Martin Meisel, 'Scattered Chiaroscuro'.

13. See Gledhill, 'Signs of Melodrama'.

14. Madhava Prasad, 'Cinema and the Desire for Modernity', *Journal of Arts & Ideas* 25–26, 1993.

15. See Geoffrey Nowell-Smith, 'Minelli and Melodrama'. In fact, melodrama seems to be doing here what has been discredited as a mode of criticism, namely, reducing other orders of phenomena to an underlying structure of family romance.

16. David N. Rodowick, 'Madness, Authority and Ideology: The Domestic Melodrama of the 1950s', in C. Gledhill (ed.) *Home is Where the Heart is*.

# III

## *The Politics of Film Form in the Contemporary Era*

# 5

## Signs of Ideological Re-form in Two Recent Films: Towards Real Subsumption?

### M. MADHAVA PRASAD

THE PRESENT MOMENT in the history of Indian cinema is a moment of transformation. In the midst of the ongoing 'liberalization' campaign, cinema is acquiring new skills and technologies, new ideological tasks, and facing challenges to its established modes of representation.[1] Some cracks in the consensual ideology of the Bombay film are widening and new entrants into the field are bringing new skills and ambitions into play. One of the signs of this changing field of force is the sudden vanguard position achieved by one or two southern film-makers who, unlike their predecessors, have become nationally popular without making films directly in Hindi. A new capital base, the adoption of management techniques, Hollywood styles, and new aesthetic strategies have played a part in this transformation. This emerging segment of the industry promises (or threatens, depending on your viewpoint) to establish the industry on a new basis. A nexus between directors of repute, cultural corporations, managers and other agents is emerging to shore up the achievements of the past few years.

Although behind the new developments, the vast majority of films continue to be made in the old style, the emerging formation is growing in strength and has achieved national visibility. It is bound to have a central role in shaping the future of the industry nationally.

From this complex, multi-faceted, changing field, two films from the early 1990s are considered in this chapter, as instances of an ideological shift attempted by the emerging formation as a complement to its still evolving mode of production. They are subjected here to a symptomatic reading, to reveal processes of ideological reform underway in contemporary Indian cinema. The change in question is not in content, but in form, or the content *of* the form. The intention is not to suggest that the work of re-form in these two films is emblematic of the current transition. They represent only one of several different directions taken by the current flurry of experimentation in Indian commercial cinema.[2] However, they are of special interest to students of cinema in that they try to constitute a new representational space which includes and overcomes the dominant form. As such they provide a glimpse into a process of transformation that, instead of coming in with *alternative* modes, and trying to establish parallel, competing segments, works on and appropriates the existing mode, bidding to replace the dominant rather than to wrest a space beside it.

We have noted elsewhere,[3] how a redundancy of resolutions in the feudal family romance can be read as a symptom of the ideology of formal subsumption at work. To recapitulate, in the 'classical' Hindi film, two resolutions to the narrative crisis would follow in quick succession, one enforced by the traditionally given authority of the exemplary subject(s) of the narrative; the other, following immediately after, and comically redundant in appearance, enforced by the agents of modern law. At the climax of such films, as everybody knows, 'the police always arrive late', just after the hero has decisively defeated the villains. The laughter evoked by this redundancy should not distract us from the ideological necessity of this doubling. If the first resolution was dictated by long-established narrative conventions, which emerged in a different social context than ours, the second one was necessary in order to assert the final (though not pre-eminent) authority of the law. Here the law has the 'last word' but this is as yet only a formality, an observance of form. The terms and relations of the preceding narrative are not reconstructed in anticipation of the finality of the word of the law; rather, the terms and relations and their modes of combination as already established are merely supplemented by the law's gesture of recognition.

This relationship of complicitous supplementarity was seriously disrupted in the early 1970s when, in the midst of a national crisis, the cultural economy of cinema underwent something of a transformation. After much groping and fumbling, a new dominant form emerged in which the law was no longer a supplement but the most important stake of narrative conflict and resolution. Whether as agents of the law or as its enemies, the characters around whom these narratives turned were initially defined by their expulsion from the familial utopia of the earlier dominant form. Disinherited, marginalized, and thrown into the world of law and criminality, their stories brought the state to the centre of the narrative, and while not eliminating the feudal family romance, relegated it to a subordinate status, where it sometimes served as an object of nostalgia, a lost object, the desire for whose repossession is the driving force behind the action. In spite of the dramatic entry and consolidation of this new form, however, there was no decisive turn away from the previous form. Rather, they co-existed as irreconcilable or very weakly reconciled forms.

We will have occasion to return to these instances later on, but for the time being the point of this brief recounting is to call attention to the existence of a problematic of form that is at least tendentially independent of the particular narrative content of individual texts. It is now time to turn to the two films in question, to see what kind of work of narrative re-formation they undertake. What follows is not meant to be taken as suggesting some kind of unique and irreversible turn. Indeed, it is possible to identify, throughout the history of post-Independence cinema, similar instances of formal innovation which may or may not have proved to be significant. My purpose is to make a case for the existence of the formal problematic as a real and significant issue and to demonstrate that the critique of the ideology of form can give us insights into cultural processes that might otherwise go unnoticed.

Fredric Jameson and, more recently, Slavoj Zizek are among the few critics who have dealt with the question of the ideology of form. Jameson (1981), in his book on the 'political unconscious' has offered one of the most comprehensive accounts of the possibilities held out by Marxist cultural analysis. His theory of interpretation distinguishes between three related horizons or 'concentric frameworks' of textual analysis, each with its own specific object. These three horizons are identified by reference to their field of pertinence, the ground in which the interpretative as specific to these horizons places the textual object. The first, and narrowest, is the ground of political history, the yearly turnover of events; the second horizon is society, in its appearance as 'a constitutive tension and struggle between social classes'; and the third, and most comprehensive, is the ground of history, 'conceived in its vastest sense of the sequences of modes of production and the succession and destiny of the various human social formations' (Jameson 1981:75). These semantic horizons are not just different contexts in which 'the same' textual object is to be placed—they differ from each other in the way they construe their object, the text.

Of these the third—historical—horizon, is where the idea of the content of the form is elaborated. Transcending the other two horizons, on the historical plane the analytical focus is on the historicity of the unity—the appearance of coherence—effected by a master code whose terms determine the discursive form taken by ideological conflict. It is the concept of mode of production that provides the 'organizing unity' of this horizon. Jameson does not employ this concept in order to develop a typology of cultural forms in which any text can be placed in one or another 'stage' of historical evolution. Such a permanent solution is ruled out by the fact that a mode of production is, strictly speaking, a theoretical rather than an empirical object. In other words, any social formation, as Poulantzas (1978: 22) has argued, is characterized by the structured co-existence in specific combinations, of several modes of production.

Thus, situating the textual object in the ground of mode of production need not result in a typology, since every social formation will have its own specific combination which will have to be discovered, and every text will be 'crisscrossed and intersected by a variety of impulses from contradictory modes of cultural production all at once' (Jameson 1981: 95). The same combination of modes also argues against the assumption of a homogeneous synchronicity or the permanence of the features of a social formation since the interaction of the elements of the combination is always open to change. The point finds support in the Althusserian argument against the empiricist notion of the synchronicity of the present and in favour of a structure where time is itself divided up into a combination of temporalities with a distinct and changeable character of its (the *combination's*) own.

What would be the object of study in such a horizon? In the second horizon, class contradiction was the object, understood in its relational aspect and not class as a group. Here, similarly, we cannot take any particular mode of production as the object. Jameson then proposes 'cultural revolution' as the object and defines it as 'that moment in which the co-existence of various modes of production becomes visibly antagonistic, their contradictions moving to the centre of political, social, and historical life' (ibid: 95). However, the task of analysis under this programme will be the study not only of moments of crisis when contradictions attain visibility, but also the 'normal' time when such contradictions are dormant.

Having thus identified the horizon as consisting of the cultural revolution, the next step involves specification of the 'textual object', the equivalent, in this horizon, of the 'symbolic act' in the first and the 'ideologeme' in the second. The text here is conceived as 'a field of force in which the dynamics of sign systems of several distinct modes of production can be registered and apprehended' and this dynamics is termed 'the ideology of form' (ibid.: 98). In this horizon, form itself undergoes a re-conceptualization, appearing not as the bearer of content but as itself content. The formal processes, when found in combination, can be understood as 'sedimented content'.

The primacy of form has also been asserted by Slavoj Zizek (1989) in his study of the discovery of the symptom by Marx and Freud. Parallel to the triple division of interpretative labour proposed by Jameson, we find in Freud the distinction between three elements of the dream: the manifest dream-text, the latent dream-content or thought, and unconscious desire. Of these, the third is the most difficult to discover because it is 'on the surface' rather than hidden from view, serving as the mode of articulation of the latent dream-content into the manifest text: the work of the unconscious lies in 'the *form* of the "dream"' (Zizek 1989: 13). Similarly, Marx goes beyond the classical political economists when he focuses not on some 'secret' hidden behind the commodity form but on the 'secret of this form itself' (ibid: 15). However, Zizek's understanding of the relation between social reality and what he calls the 'ideological fantasy' differs from Jameson's in one important respect. On his reading, it is the fantasy that supports and organizes social reality and gives it coherence. Structured in this way by ideological fantasy, reality itself is a shield against any direct encounter with the Real—the antagonism that resists symbolization. The different social formations, the modes of production, etc. are on this reading, so many ways of organizing reality against the threat of the Real— the fundamental, irresolvable antagonism.

It is against this horizon that I propose to situate the following analysis of two recent films, Rajkumar Santoshi's *Damini* (1993) and Mani Ratnam's *Roja* (1992). It stands to reason that these texts can also be reconstituted as objects within the other two horizons, or even, indeed, approached through a combination of these and other theoretical tools. In fact one of them, *Roja*, has been the object of a number of interpretations which can be construed as employing, either separately or in conjunction, approaches specific to the first two horizons.[4] The ideological analysis I undertake here takes the 'content of the form' as its primary focus. The aim is to discover a new object, a different level of semiosis, with very different, and perhaps more durable, cultural consequences.

The reason for bringing together these films, from two traditions of film-making (Hindi and Tamil) which, while sharing a common history, have also developed along fairly independent trajectories, is simply that they both manifest the same global formal construction which can be represented as follows:

$$/ \underline{\quad} / \underline{\qquad} / \underline{\qquad\qquad} /$$
$$fB \qquad A \qquad\qquad B$$

where $A$ and $B$ represent the two principal narrative segments, and $fB$ a fragment that is metonymically linked to $B$ but separated from it by segment $A$; or, to put it differently, segment $A$ is sandwiched between segment $B$ and its brief, enigmatic premonition.

What are the effects produced by this formal organization of the text?

Let us note, first of all, that the transition from $fB$ to $A$ comes as rupture, a sharp discursive break which leaves something unexplained until segment $B$ retroactively absorbs the enigmatic fragment into its order of narration and thereby infuses it with meaning. Secondly, it is only because of the isolation of fragment $B$ from its proper narrative habitat that we are at all able to identify a second break in the narrative, since the transition from $A$ to $B$ is *relatively* smoother. Thus the fragment serves, in the overall organization of narrative flow, as (1) an enigma which hovers over the action of segment $A$, a premonition of things to come, of which the figures of the narrative are themselves blissfully ignorant; and (2) a cue which enables us to identify the second break.

It should be obvious by now that this segmental analysis bears little resemblance to the more famous one that is associated with Christian Metz's construction of the 'grande syntagmatique' of the units of film language in his search for the master code of cinematic narration, as well as its variants, notably that of Raymond Bellour (Bellour 1986). The Metzian segmentation is intended to provide a general table of all possible units of filmic narration. As such, beyond the basic filmic unit of the *shot* (recognized by the cut that separates one shot from another), the identification of syntagma depends upon the coincidence of shot changes with other indications of shifts in time, space, motif, theme, etc. that form part of the narrative content. As Metz himself put it, 'all the units I have isolated are located *in* the film but in *relation* to the plot' (Metz 1986: 58). In our examples, however, the segmentation is discovered not by scanning the units of narration from the smallest upwards or the other way round, but through a narrative device whose function is to signal the division. As such it has an ideological function that far exceeds its convenience as a way of breaking up the narrative. The segments discovered here signal a *formal* break, the insertion of an 'alien' body into the larger body of the film text, rather than a categorical separation or grammatical punctuation.

As mentioned above, the fragment serves as a warning about the future and enables us to identify the second break. But its narrative function is not limited to these two effects. This becomes clear if we speculate for a moment about the change that might come about if the initial fragment is removed altogether. In terms of narrative content, hardly anything is lost since in both cases, the informational content of the fragment is (i.e. will be) already contained in $B$. What will be lost, however, is the *masking effect* that conceals the break between two narrative trajectories that each have their own resolution. At the threshold that separates $A$ from $B$, there is every possibility that the spectator will perceive, not the transition to a new stage of the same narrative, but the cessation of one plot and the beginning of another, entirely different one. Two stories instead of one, which would mean a fragmentation of the narrative. But the fragment, whose meaning remains a mystery until the beginning of *B*, has already served to redefine the action in segment *A* as a *prologue* to what will follow. It has already served to subordinate the action in segment *A* to that of segment *B*.

Thus (3), the organization of the textual sequence, while enabling the recognition of the break, also serves to mask the fragmentation that this would imply. It would then appear that *B* is the dominant segment, the main concern of these films (this is confirmed by the primacy accorded to segment *B* in discussions of *Roja*), but that they are nevertheless dependent on the subordinate segment *A* for . . . what? Why do these texts reject the easier solution for achieving unity, that is to say the exclusive concentration on the action of segment *B*, or even the subsumption of all narrative elements into the spatio-temporal framework of narrative *B* ? (Mani Ratnam has been asked this question, in a slightly different form, by an interviewer.) Why, instead, do they put the very possibility of narrative unity at risk and *then* try to reunify the text by deploying *fB* as a sort of 'secret agent'?

On first glance this textual organization may seem no different from other familiar instances where a part or all of the narrative is recollected in flashback. But in those instances, continuity is established by the flashback device itself, with an individual character's memory serving as the link. In the two films in question, the juxtaposition of segments, lacking any such diegetic motivation, brings into play an authorial intention, an act of deliberate separation and reorganization of segments that produces effects beyond those deriving from the plot itself. This is important not because authorial intention is itself new or unprecedented but because it makes visible the absence of such a disjuncture, such a supplementary work of signification, in the dominant narrative film. Not only does it bring such absence into focus, it also indicates that that dominant form cannot be re-formed internally, through the substitution or supplementation of its content by a reflexive layer of meaning. Instead, the method adopted here can be described as an act of laying siege to the dominant form, of harnessing its pleasures to another narrative project and staging, in the process, an ideological rehabilitation of its narrative elements. The delegation of a fragment to an outer zone, its separation from its proper metonymic chain, enables the constitution of a syntagmatic chain marked by arbitrary juxtaposition, which is its true function. Thus, the potentially metaphoric relation between the two segments is pre-empted and the first segment is integrated into a new syntagmatic order as a subordinate element.

Let us take a closer look at the segments themselves. In *Damini*, the opening fragment shows a woman in a state of absolute terror, in a nightmarish sequence in which we see her running away from unseen pursuers and finding herself trapped. Her predicament is highlighted by the interrogation that a doctor conducts. At first the questions are hurled at her by a voice located somewhere behind the camera—the voice of the Other—while the terror-stricken woman is trapped in a paralysed state in front of the camera, as if by the camera. For a moment it looks as if we in the audience are the collective interrogator. Then tension created by the invisibility of the interrogator approaches breaking point before we get relief in the form of a reverse shot of the doctor, who now looks benign, and appears to be doing no more than his duty. When the next cut brings the woman back into the frame, her terror has already been redefined as the result of her own unstable mental condition, a hallucination. Our spontaneous identification with her has been deprived of its rationality. The transition from this fragment to segment *A* is startling: from paranoid hallucination and terror we cut to a close-up of the same woman's face whence the camera pulls back to reveal a stage on which she is dancing. From madness to the innocence and romance of youth. The *mise en scène* in particular conveys a strong suggestion that the whole sequence *fB* is a nightmare, in which case it would fall within the diegetic framework of the narrative delineation of character psychology. Such an instance can be found in *Rajnigandha* where the heroine has a nightmare in which she dreams of being 'left behind'. However, the difference between these two sequences is that in the latter, we see the dreamer wake up and acknowledge the preceding sequence as an element of her own subjectivity, whereas in *Damini* the contrast between the woman's state of terror and the matter-of-fact look of the doctor and other indications argue against the reading of the sequence as a nightmare. And in any case, subsequent events prove that the fragment was not a representation of a psychic event. The change of scene also, in its abruptness, does not allow any scope for reading a subjective link, since in *A* the woman is introduced to us in a stylized space where her performance is emptied of subjectivity. In both these films, the psychic dimension is far removed from the 'psychological' approach of the middle-class cinema and is inscribed in the objective formal features of the text.

The same contrast between terror and innocence is conveyed by the parallel transition in *Roja*. Here, however, there is no scope for even the suspicion of a subjective link since the two scenes are completely different from each other in content, the only link between them being that they (presumably) succeed each other in time, since the dawn that breaks on the capture of the Kashmiri militant also illuminates the Tamil Nadu countryside. Fragment *B* in *Roja* shows the capture of the militant by troops combing the forests of Kashmir just before daybreak and cuts to the Tamil Nadu village, as the sun rises on a beautiful landscape and the heroine is introduced, singing a song about her 'small desires'.

Beginning thus, with a conventional representation of feminine innocence, suggestive of the anticipation of romance and conjugality, segment *A* reaches its own local (and of course, 'incomplete') resolution well before the midway point in the text. In *Damini*, the 'hero' Shekhar (played by Rishi Kapoor) watches the eponymous heroine performing a dance number with Aamir Khan (playing himself and serving as a reminder of the proximity of the 'romance' to follow to the conventions of the world of Bombay cinema) and falls in love, this event witnessed, again in keeping with conventions of film romance, by a male assistant/friend. He meets her again near her home, when she is out shopping, in order to pursue the romance. Here we get a glimpse into the distinction of Damini's character: she is a compulsive truth-teller. A quotation from Gandhi which serves as the epigraph has prepared us to expect an 'experimenter with truth' but at this point in the narrative, Damini, after publicly exposing the dishonesty of a merchant, is shown talking aloud to herself, as Shekhar follows her. This scene pathologizes the truth-telling subject, at least for the moment locating the origin of this compulsive honesty in her hysteria. This is because while in segment *B* her honesty will acquire a central role in the movement of the narrative, in segment *A* the independence of character that this implies would work against the requirements of the conventional family romance. As they walk together, they encounter Damini's father. On the spot, Shekhar asks him for permission to marry his daughter, and Damini expresses surprise but does not resist this abrupt turn. Shekhar leaves, to inform his family of his decision.

Damini's family, consisting of parents and an elder sister, is in crisis. Just before Shekhar's family arrives to 'see' Damini, her sister runs away with a boyfriend. In front of the guests, Damini, against her parents' wishes, reveals this incident and wins Shekhar's father's heart with her honesty. The wedding takes place quickly. In her husband's home, Damini resides in splendour, but as if in captivity until a reconciliation takes place between her and Shekhar. The segment concludes with the symbolic freeing of a caged bird, a present from Shekhar. What we get in segment *A* can be described as a highly compressed version of the feudal family romance which typically ends with the integration of the romantic pair into the politically autonomous order of the propertied joint family.

In *Roja*, the resolution of segment *A* is similar in so far as it also concerns the reconciliation of a couple bound together in matrimony in great haste, but the movement towards this conclusion takes a different route. Roja's marriage to Rishi Kumar (Arvind Swamy) in this segment occurs as a result of an unexpected hitch in an earlier plan by which Rishi was to marry Roja's sister. Rishi's declaration of his liking for Roja is received by the diegetic audience (except the sister) as a serious transgression and Roja is unforgiving even after she has moved to the city with her husband. But when he discloses the fact that it was her sister who rejected him because she wanted to marry another man in order to bring about a reconciliation between their feuding families, Roja is finally reconciled to her marriage.

To turn now briefly to the level of the 'latent content': In both films, the couple has already gone through two stages; first, a conventional union, legitimate in the eyes of society but as yet lacking its own internal unity; second, a moment of clearing of doubts and exchange of assurances which seems to fill the vacuum. But even after this second moment, in spite of the appearance of fullness and harmony, something is left over, an excess that provides the principal motivation for the continuation of the narrative drive. The movement into segment *B* and *its* specific resolution can be described as a movement from reconciliation (a local event) to *rehabilitation* or re-grounding of the couple (a global change). To anticipate one of the conclusions of this analysis, the reconciliation is a sufficient resolution for the narrative movement of segment *A* but its 'insufficiency' has been ensured in advance by the arbitrary— and once introduced, compelling, unsettling—glimpse of another world, an alien threat, in fragment *B*.

As segment *B* unfolds, however, it becomes clear that the very self-sufficiency of the narrative of segment *A* is a threat to something else, to the existence of another ground. The closure that 'comes naturally' to the romance narrative cannot be breached, cannot be opened up to the experience of an alien reality (i.e. a reality alien to its conventions, to its congealed ideological discourse) except through the subterfuge of an unexpected juxtaposition which pro- duces for the spectator the effect of incompleteness that will justify the prolongation of the narrative. The difficulty made visible here is a measure of how deeply the conventions and ideology of the domi- nant film form are entrenched in culture. At the same time, we should remember that the aesthetic project of these films does not simply encounter the resistance of the dominant form in the world at large but itself produces the (foreshortened) image of that resist- ance and, in the interior of its own body, stages a confrontation with it. This is important to note because it is perfectly possible— and there are many instances of films that try to realize this possi- bility—to produce a new aesthetic as an *alternative,* occupying another site, addressed to another audience, where the conflict with the dominant is staged, if at all, not inside the limits of the narrative but outside, in a segment of the industry. The desired result of this latter approach is a segmentation of audiences, since such films appeal to the audience's desire for distinction, and promise a pleasure that only the discerning can enjoy.

In *Damini,* it is the Holi celebration scene that clearly marks the beginning of segment *B,* while in *Roja* this is signalled by the transfer of the Kashmir assignment to Rishi in the hospital scene. During the Holi celebrations, the hero's brother and his friends rape the servant-maid Urmi. Damini and later Shekhar are both witnesses to the rape but as an autonomous political unit, the feudal family resolves to administer its own form of justice, which would consist of bailing out the family member by compensating the victim and her family for the loss. Shekhar, in spite of being a witness, goes along with this, but Damini refuses to hide the truth. She insists that the law of the Indian state alone has the legitimate power to render justice in the case. Although she goes along with the family's wishes for a while when they falsely assure her that Urmi is well and being looked after, this compromise is represented as a temporary suspension of her truth-telling character. Telling the truth thus acquires here a very precise definition. In the epigraph, Gandhi speaks of the conscience as an authority that transcends all human laws. The question underlying the truth-teller's dilemma is: tell the truth *to whom*? Who must listen in order for the truth *to have been told*? If honesty is merely a compulsion, then it would be satisfied by any telling, any declaration, anywhere, before anybody. The Gandhian dictum is that the conscience is the authority that insists on the telling of the truth. But who is the addressee of the truth? Unless the addressee is specified, the injunction loses all meaning. And if conscience itself (or God as its objective form), is the addressee, the truth need never be declared in public. For the truth involved in *Damini*, however, the issue is clear: it will not have been told until it is told to the state. Damini's honesty is a hysterical symptom because the problem that it represents for the narrative will not have been solved until the Other who listens to her truth and the demand implied in it, does not appear: 'what is hysteria if not precisely the effect and testimony of a failed interpellation?' (Zizek 1989: 113). It is through the invocation of this larger entity that the narrative succeeds in subverting and delegitimizing the moral-political authority of the state-within-the-state, the politically autonomous *khandaan*.[5] Within this framework, the process of rehabilitation of the nuclear couple is also set in motion, which ends with the couple's relation re-grounded in the state's range of vision, with Shekhar's public declaration of his love for his wife, under the aegis of the law. It is only now that the relation achieves full closure and permanence.

On the formal plane, this segment achieves its effects through a process of combination of filmic genres which ends in a new synthesis. In a Hegelian perspective, *Damini* can be read, on this level, as a synthesis that subsumes the feudal family romance and the post-1970s narratives of disidentification with the state. Through the agency of the 'unhoused' female subject, the film breaks open the closed economy of the feudal romance and invokes the state as the sole legitimate authority. The state, however, is itself rotten, as the films of the 1970s showed time and again. Like the innumerable rebels who walked out of the system, confronted it as criminals or militant transgressors of the code (in the service of the code), the lawyer Govind (Sunny Deol) lives as a recluse, having quit his profession after the law failed to render justice in a case relating to his wife's death. The casting also reflects the generic combination: Meenakshi Seshadri and Rishi Kapoor as the romantic couple and Sunny Deol (known for his action-hero roles in the genre inaugurated by the Bachchan films) as the disillusioned lawyer. In the 1970s' films, these heroes pursued their own desires, nostalgic for a lost harmony. Here Govind, who has abandoned all his own battles, enters the picture as a distinterested agent through whom the state will be reformed in order to produce the space where the romantic couple can be rehabilitated. As such on his very first appearance, there is a complete transfer of agency from Damini to Govind. Before this scene, Damini's honesty has led to a situation where she has been confined to a mental hospital by court order. Overhearing a plot to kill her, she runs from hospital and is pursued by the group of killers. The entire scene conveys an overwhelming sense of helplessness, complete exhaustion, physical as well as subjective, before the relay of agency to Govind is accomplished (and visually represented) when Damini grabs him by the shoulder and pleads for help. (As if to compensate in advance for this impending loss of agency, the chase is preceded by a dance—again of ambiguous status: dream or extra-diegetic interpolation?—in which Damini is transformed into the all-powerful Kali.)

Having invoked the Hegelian dialectic, we should note that the synthesis accomplished here is not without remainder. At the end of the narrative, Govind remains excessive. At the same time this surplus leaves no trace of disruption in the closure achieved by the narrative. His role has been that of what Jameson calls the 'vanishing mediator' whose agency enables a transformation that destroys its own grounds for existence.

Turning to *Roja*, we find, not surprisingly, a similar narrative movement. This film has come to be received by the public as a film 'about Kashmiri separatism'. But this aspiration to 'about-ness', i.e. an aesthetic of topicality, is still only tendential, subordinated to the film's preoccupation with the allegory of transpatriarchal migration. One of the stakes of the struggle in which the film is engaged is precisely to wrest a space for staging the present, to break out of the timeless frame of conventional narrative.

Unlike *Damini, Roja* does not stage its narrative within the terms and terrain of the history of film genres, although it is possible to read the village segment as a reprise of narrative films set in the countryside, of which there is a steady output in the cinemas of the south, and which often reaffirm the autonomy and self-sufficiency of the village as a social unit.[6] As we have seen, the village segment ends with the reinforcement of the conventional union by a union of hearts made possible by the late revelation of Rishi's innocence in the matter of Roja's sister's 'betrayal'. That some obstacle nevertheless remains is made clear in the scene following the reconciliation when Rishi, as he prepares to leave for Kashmir, tells Roja to go back to her village even as she insists on accompanying him.

The story that unfolds subsequently is well-known: arriving in Kashmir, Rishi gets down to the work he has been sent there to do, deciphering the enemy's intercepted communications and, in his free time, showing Roja the sights of Kashmir. At the very moment when Roja is sending a message of thanks to her personal village deity through divine courier, her husband is kidnapped by militants. The plot then weaves together the parallel stories of Roja's encounter with the state and Rishi's with the militants. Finally, when the state agrees, at the risk of losing its advantage in the fight against secessionist militancy, to submit to Roja's demand that her husband's freedom should be purchased by releasing the arrested militant, Rishi, in a parallel move, saves the state's honour by escaping from captivity and, with the help of a reformed militant, returns to Roja, thus preventing the return of the captured leader.

At the conclusion of the second segment, the couple has been rehabilitated, rescued from a situation of terror and re-settled under the aegis of a new patriarchal authority, the state. In both the films, the couples move out of a pastoral world—the village and the genre of family romance—only to encounter terror. From the perspective of this overarching narrative, the perils of the outside world signify above all, the acutely felt absence or suspension of Authority. In *Damini*, before the moment of transfer of narrative agency to Govind the lawyer, the terror of the moment derives precisely from the impending encounter with the trauma of what psychoanalysis terms 'the hole in the Symbolic' (Zizek, *For They Know Not*, 1991), the terrifying encounter with the truth that there is no Other guaranteeing the consistency of the Symbolic order and the meaningfulness of the world. The image of the woman hounded by merciless killers intensifies the anticipation of the traumatic glimpse into the Real and then, at the very last moment of this intolerable tension, produces (not out of nowhere but precisely from that one place where bodies have pre-assigned meaning: the star system) a male Rescuer whose provisional function is to fill the hole in the Symbolic until the law is ready to take over. Indeed, the entire scene of the chase can be read as a tendentially tableau-like representation of woman's state of in-betweenness, in a 'no-man's' land between the representatives of a discredited traditional phallic power and an emergent alternative, the patriarchal authority of the modern state. Now the scene of Damini's apotheosis, when she assumes the form of the phallic mother-goddess, which preceded the chase, can be retrospectively read, not only as a compensatory gesture to pave the way for the transfer of narrative agency, but also as a forewarning of the (terrifying) alternative prospect that might arise if the transfer of phallic authority from one patriarchy to another is not accomplished swiftly.

In *Roja*, such a glimpse into an unpleasant alternative to patri-archal authority is woven into the village segment itself. Apart from the hierarchical relation between two formally autonomous units of narrative that is common to both these films, *Roja* is distinguished by the repetition of key narrative and thematic features across the two segments. These two segments can in fact be read as mirror images of each other. A close reading of the first segment is required in order to reveal this parallelism. The comic episode of the man who wanders through the village in search of his lost goats and is ridiculed by a group of women is linked, by the mentonymic relay of the goats' cries, to the scene in which, having commandeered the goats, Roja sets up an ambush at a spot that calls to mind similar scenes in dacoit films: a bend in the road, a cluster of rocks providing natural cover. The overt purpose of this trap is to catch a glimpse of the man who is arriving by car to 'see' Roja's sister. Roja's declared intentions are altruistic but for the spectator, the entire scene is so constructed as to invest her glance with a desire of which she herself is as yet unaware or which she is unwilling to acknowl-edge. The split here between conscious purpose and unconscious desire defines Roja too as a hysteric, creating the space for the narrative of reinterpellation to follow in segment *B*. It is not by coincidence that beginning with this incident, until the moment of his declaration of preference for Roja, Rishi finds himself besieged, a captive of the collective will of the village. Key elements of the second segment are prefigured in the first: abduction (by Roja), captivity, the 'exchange' proposal (Roja's sister wants Rishi to be an object of exchange in an operation that will restore to the family its greater unity by bringing an alienated branch back into the fold), the pre-emption of exchange by a counter-move: escape with another captive (Roja in the first segment, and the 'humanized' militant in the second). As for the last feature, there is, of course, a difference: what Rishi pre-empts is not the reunion desired by the sister, but his own neutralization as a pure object of exchange. His abrupt and scandalous declaration of interest in Roja makes possible the reunification of the family but at the same time successfully breaches its will to autonomy from another flank.

Through these parallels, the film establishes a strong connection between two kinds of resistance to the national-modern project: the anti-national and the pre-modern. The village's autonomy is not the result of a conscious disidentification with the modern state, unlike the separatism of the militants. Nevertheless, the modern state encounters both the pre-modern enclave and the separatist movement as challenges to its will to hegemony. The village threatens Rishi's and the modern state's project (his desire to marry a(ny) village woman symbolizes the state's need to subordinate the village/region/clan, in short the pre-modern, to itself) by imposing its own laws on him—first by attempting to absorb him into independent social circuit, and again by trying to use him as an instrument for its own purposes. The women of the village are thus figured as castrating, as phallic mothers who jealously guard their domain. Roja demonstrates that she participates in this collective protection of phallic authority when she stages the ambush.

From the detour, this film 'about Kashmir' equips itself with a 'voice'. The autonomous village is a threat because it will not legitimize the state by demanding its existence. It is a structure that enforces its own laws on those who enter its domain. It is not in a dependent position vis-à-vis the state. The wedding and the second-stage reconciliation, however, change everything. Henceforth, the village figures as a voice, expressing a demand that only the state can respond to. Voices emerge from the ruins of a structure. This process is completed only when the demanding subject participates in elevating the state to absolute dominance by surrendering her own personal source of phallic power. In the case of *Damini*, this is accomplished when the Gandhian conscience is dissolved into the objective apparatuses of the state and truth-telling is equated with telling the truth to the state. For Roja, this shift involves a transfer of loyalties from her personal village deity (with whom she has a secret liaison, to whom she confesses and who grants her all her wishes) to the state: this is accomplished when she explicitly names the state as her saviour during her meeting with the central minister. This scandalous subordination of religious authority to the secular authority of the state is only one element of a long process: by making unreasonable demands, by fully assuming the position of a hysteric, Roja actively provokes the state to respond to her call. The state, figured as a neutral place of pure altruism, obliges and even indulges the demanding subject.

The gulf between two patriarchal zones is bridged in both films by the figure of the woman. It is through her agency that it becomes possible to allegorize historic transformations. The 'homeless' woman is the bearer of the phallus, which she must pass on to the emerging power. The doubling of the plot in *Roja* enables the allegorization by importing Roja from one domain into the other. The

## Master Antinomy:
### State vs Autonomous Segments

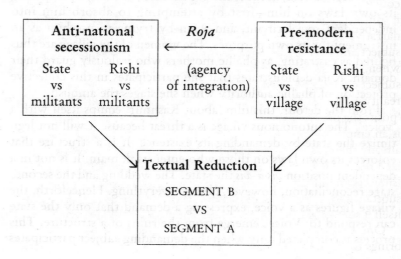

primary antinomy of the plot is subdivided into a series of oppositions, as shown below.

The call that Roja addresses to the state is its most important source of legitimacy. As a demanding woman, her role is to provoke the state into existence, to free her of the unbearable narrative function of phallic authority. The relief attendant upon the transfer of this authority to an agent of the law is much more vividly represented in *Damini* but it is there in *Roja* too. In *Damini,* the split that we have noted in *Roja* is neither necessary nor possible. However, both texts manifest the anxiety created by the phallus-in-transit, and in both, the object of the female figures' crusade, not capable of narrative resolution in itself, is subsumed under the more manageable resolution by which their individual desires are fulfilled. Thus Damini's concern for justice, which seemed to exceed her personal interest, is redefined within the terms of her desire for conjugal rehabilitation. Whereas in *Roja* the hysteric's demands are deployed in another scenario of hegemony vs autonomy, in *Damini* the hysteric's demands focus back on the world she left behind. In one, the siege of the pastoral enables the invention of the topical film with a window to reality; in the other, the same assault on the pastoral romance leads to the invention of the modern women's melodrama.

The narrative process thus achieves its completion only when the subject *posits* the state as the external emodiment of its Self. Of course, the state in its objectivity pre-exists the subject's positing of it. But this state of affairs is intolerable, it provokes a movement of narrative resolution precisely because there is a gap between the subject and this external substance, a disjuncture which only arises when, having exited another structure and become 'voice', the subject comes face to face with what Zizek terms the 'pre-Symbolic reality'. The resolution of this crisis is arrived at when the subject 'posits the big Other, makes it exist' (Zizek 1989: 230). This positing is an empty gesture, a purely formal act which transforms what is already there, as external reality, into a subjectively posited, symbolized reality. It is this act that completes the subject's re-grounding: 'subjects are subjects only in so far as they presuppose that the social substance, opposed to them in the form of the State, is already in itself a subject (Monarch) to whom they are subjected' (ibid: 229).

One of the problems that the formal structure of these films brings to the fore is that of narrative enunciation. The fragment *B* causes unease in part by displacing the enunciative function of the narrative, putting this function into crisis precisely by emphasizing it, by foregrounding it as a problem through the conflicting and unexplained juxtaposition of sequences. The fragment hovers menacingly over the patstoral segment $A$, inscribing a lack at its centre, robbing it of its customary naturalness and self-identity. The spectator's attention is thus divided, so that it is impossible to fully identify with the pastoral narrative. In both films, the pastoral segment reinforces this distraction in scenes that demonstrate the split between the principal character's conscious assertions and unconscious desire: Roja directs an altruistc gaze at Rishi but we know that there is more to it; Damini always tells the truth but there is something else that speaks another truth: her hysteria. The narrative stages a 'war of position' (P. Chatterjee 1986: 48–9), robbing the pastoral discourse of its fullness and self-identity, creating the need and the space for another agency that will take on (indeed, has already taken on) the function of enunciation and narrative control. Segment $B$ thus appropriates the position of subjective pre-eminence by demonstrating its capacity to commensurate the seemingly incommensurable content of fragment $B$ and segment $A$. The resolution of the thematic conflicts—between the state and the militants, between Damini and a bunch of criminals—is secondary to the more important resolution that tackles the dissonance of incommensurate worlds co-existing in the same narrative/national space.

Everything depends on fragment $B$. What exactly does it do? We have seen how it helps to embed the feudal family romance in a new syntagmatic order, a symbolic register in which the principal figure of the romance enters and becomes Subject. Thus in both these films, the imaginary relation between husband and wife as represented at the end of segment $A$ is subjected to a disruption in order to break the imaginary fullness and force the subject to enter the Symbolic network, where a final resolution will have to be achieved. This precise allegory of real subsumption has, however, proposed at the very beginning a solution to the disruption that it will enforce. Fragment $B$, as noted above, brings to the fore the question of narrative enunciation. Indeed, in a field (of popular cinema) where the enunciative function was non-existent as a problem, the wilful juxtaposition of $fB$ and $A$ abruptly produces the problem. In the process, it also posits an enunciator, invisible but not insignificant. The fragment that menaces the pastoral segment thus also contains the supreme ideological reassurance: that there is an Other who directs the unfolding of the new order. Not just the director, Santoshi or Mani Ratnam; nor even the efficient army which captures the terrorist in *Roja's fB* or the benign doctor of *Damini*—but one for whom they are surrogates: the Other in whom we trust when we trust in captitalism.

It would be premature to say that a new popular film aesthetic is signalled by the work of ideological reform that these films manifest. Nevertheless, one can speculate on the significance of the strategic deployment of form, the struggle waged, within the framework of the text for enunciative pre-eminence: the imperative for this struggle arises from the ambition to occupy the same place that is now occupied by an older dominant form. In this effort, these films may deploy the resources of alternative/middle cinema, but they aspire, not to take the place of the alternative, but to conquer the larger market.

For a more comprehensive picture of the nature of ongoing transformations to emerge, we shall need to examine several other dimensions of the process, such as the emergence of culture corporations, signs of monopolistic tendencies, the new bid by Hollywood to expand its market beyond Anglophone frontiers, etc. (Of these one of the most visible, and for speculations about the future of native film form, extremely important dimensions is that which concerns the film song as a sub-commodity. In this segment of the cultural market, the emergence of music video as an autonomous form, supported by a vast televisual system that is still expanding and experimenting with old and new materials and formats, can be expected to challenge the narrative film's role as the pre-eminent host of musical spectacle, forcing it towards new experiments as a means of survival.) This process can be defined as constituting a re-commodification, or re-invention of the cultural commodity.

Until these processes are clarified, we can only speculate on the significance of stray events like the coincidence of a formal structure in the two films we have chosen for analysis. One speculative proposition of this essay is that the formal structure of these texts is a trace of the work of the 'political unconscious'. In the moment of arrival of real subsumption (that we are living through), capital is breaking out of the impasse of the ruling coalition, emerging into complete dominance. It is no longer necessary to artificially prolong the life of 'tradition', that alleged entity which was modernity's own invention, its preferred rendering of the adversary's profile. The ideology of formal subsumption, which insisted on the difference between the modern and the traditional, and the need to protect that difference, resulted in the protection given to the feudal family romance as the appropriate form of entertainment for the masses. This difference and the apparatuses that are meant to preserve it are no longer sustainable. While the ideologues of formal subsumption stubbornly cling to their superannuated posts, the remaking of Indian ideology goes on apace.

It would nevertheless be a mistake to see these films as simply reflecting the changes that are underway, of being superstructural representations of what is happening in reality. These texts are works of ideology, not mirrors of reality. The changing realities are, no doubt, one of the conditions that make these films possible and necessary, not in order to reflect these conditions, but to construct ideological resolutions for the contradictions that accompany these changes.

## Notes

1. For a detailed discussion of the history preceding this moment, see M. Madhava Prasad, *Ideology of the Hindi Film: A Historical Construction*, New Delhi, Oxford University Press, 1998.

2. Another significant trend has been discussed in Dhareshwar and Niranjana (*JAI* 1996).

3. See Madhava Prasad, *Ideology of the Hindi Film . . .*, pp. 95–6.

4. See Niranjana (1994), Chakravarthy and Pandian (1994), Bharucha (1994), and Vasudevan (1994).

5. See Pathak and Sundar Rajan (1989) for a discussion of the state-within-the-state as a structural of modern India.

6. See Ravichandran (1997) for a discussion of this genre, known in the industry.

## References

Bharucha, Rustom, 1994. 'On the Border of Fascism: Manufacture of Consent in *Roja*', *Economic and Political Weekly*.

Chakravarthy and Pandian, 1994. 'More on *Roja*', *Economic and Political Weekly*.

Dhareshwar and Niranjana, 1996. '*Kaadalan* and the politics of re-signification: Fashion, Violence and the Body', *Journal of Arts and Ideas* 29, rpt. in this volume.

Niranjana, 1996. 'Integrating whose nation? Tourists and Terrorists in *Roja*', · *Economic and Political Weekly*.

Pathak and Sundar Rajan, 1989. 'Shahbano', *Signs: Journal of Women in Culture and Society* 14(3).

Ravichandra, 'Karma Yoga and the Middle Class: Recasting Identities in *Thevar Magan*', 1997. Paper presented at Cultural Studies Workshop, Gwalior, 1–5 February 1997, organized by the Centre for Studies in Social Sciences, Calcutta.

Vasudevan , 1994. 'Other Voices: *Roja* against the Grain', *Seminar* 423.

# 6

## Narrating Seduction: Vicissitudes of the Sexed Subject in Tamil Nativity Film

SUNDAR KAALI

I

THE 1970S WERE a period of profound crisis for Tamil cinema. Early in the decade, M.G. Ramachandran left the DMK to launch his own party and turned to active politics. Later, on the occasion of his victory in the 1977 elections, he announced that he would give up his career in films. Sivaji Ganesan, another mega-star of Tamil cinema, continued to act in films, but, starting in the mid-1970s, his films failed at the box-office despite the inflated budgets and ever-newer actresses. Apprehensions about an erosion in the star image of Sivaji were raised, and the ensuing debate attracted a wide variety of viewer-opinions, aside from a good amount of arguments from actors and actresses, producers and film-makers, and film journalists of different persuasions.[1] While fan loyalties still continued to remain unshaken, most other views emphasized that youthful roles simply did not fit Sivaji's ageing looks. It was argued that he had always been known for his compe-tence as an actor and not as an 'ever-young hero', the image that MGR, for instance, fostered. Sivaji had acted as elderly characters early in his career and need not look for youthful roles now; he

I wish to thank J. Vasanthan, K. Ravi Srinivas and K. Ravichandran for com-menting on a first draft; and V. Aravindan, K. Babu, Venkatesh Chakravarthy, K. Govindan, M.S.S. Pandian, Suresh Paul, R. Prabakar, M. Saravanan, and R. Ulaganathan for help in other ways.

should take up roles befitting his age and looks. Whatever the pros and cons of this argument, and its value in terms of audience opinion, it brought to the fore certain grim realities of the 1970s: a star system founded in the 1950s and thriving unabatedly in the 1960s was no longer on firm ground.

This crisis manifested itself at the economic level too. Film-making activity went down considerably, as the leading production companies experienced considerable setbacks and opted either to close down business or to cease active work temporarily. An industry for so long heavily reliant on the star system found that things no longer worked the way they used to (Chakravarthy 1996: 115). When MGR announced his return to films in the late 1970s, though he still had the lustre of chief-ministership, the whole situation had changed so drastically that he had to review his decision and give up his acting profession for good. Never again were either MGR or Sivaji to recover the dominance over the industry which they had acquired over the years, through careers—including acting styles, star personae and political persuasions—that at once contradicted and complemented each other.

It was in this context of a deep crisis that certain new modes of representation emerged in Tamil film. And these modes themselves employed narrational strategies that significantly addressed and problematized certain elements of the crisis. In what follows, I will attempt to chart the trajectories of this development, and in particular, discuss the emergence of the generic grouping known as Neo-nativity Film.[2] In doing so, I shall be largely leaving out of my consideration the alternative cinema of the late 1970s. Mainly an outgrowth of the film society movement and part of the pan-Indian New Indian Cinema, the films of this category differed in many ways from the corpus I am discussing. Further, I shall limit my discussion to the period from 1976, the year in which the path-breaking work *Annakkili* was released, to 1981, a period of transition that allowed for recoding of conventions on a very large scale. By the early 1980s, a great degree of generic formalization was noticeable, though changes continued to occur at a slower pace. In delineating the prehistory of the genre, let me first discuss certain texts of the pre-1976 period to show how the Neo-nativity Film draws upon earlier narrative structures and yet recodes them in significant ways.[3]

## II

The class of films that I term as Old Nativity Film was characterized by an ideological investment centred on the rurality of its plot-events and roles. Examples of this category can be found as early as the 1950s and continue to appear well into the 1970s. The hero of the film is usually a rustic tenant farmer or peasant and is placed in opposition to a local landlord-villain. In an MGR film he might marry the landlord's city-bred daughter as well. Alternatively, in a Sivaji starrer, he will be the sacrificing hero who gives up everything to his brothers and/or sisters. If the narrative complication proceeds to show the breaking of the extended family and the concomitant tragedy that sets in, a family reunion would be the fitting closure to this kind of plot. In either case, the film is usually framed by melodramatic codes. Also, in both cases, though the film is primarily set in the village, the hero often moves to the city and wins his woman. The taming of the educated, urbane woman is the means by which male lack is liquidated, or rather, projected onto the female. Male insufficiency—in terms of caste, class, and/or education—is, thus, disavowed and displaced onto the figure of the woman. A reaffirmation of the phallus is engendered by such a narrational move, and the whole plot hinges upon this reaffirmation as the phallus is not just a 'privileged signifier' but a 'signifier of privilege', its status being 'the marker of a complex of psychic, social, political, and economic differences' (Silverman 1990: 113).[4]

This recurrent patterning of the narrative can be seen in films like *Raman Ettanai Ramanati* (Rama O, How Many Ramas, P. Madhavan, 1970), *Pattikkata Pattanama* (The Rural vs. the Urban, P. Madhavan, 1972), *Pattikkattup Ponnaiya* (Ponnaiya the Rustic, 1973), *Ponnukkut Tanka Manacu* (Woman with the Golden Heart, Devaraj-Mohan, 1973), and *Pattikkattu Raja* (The King of the Village, 1975) in the pre-1976 period. Elements of it return in the subsequent period also, in films like *Rataikkerra Kannan* (The Krishna of Radha's Dreams, 1978) and the recent *Maman Makal* (Uncle's Daughter/Cross-cousin, 1995). In *Pattikkattup Ponnaiya* MGR plays the twin roles of a peasant and his brother, a college student in the city. The peasant supports the college-going brother (who marries a city-bred woman), but he has to leave the village due to the vicious schemes of the villain. In the city he becomes a professional wrestler and uses his earnings to pay his family's debts to the villainous landlord. In the wrestling-ring he wears a mask to conceal his face. In one tournament, he meets another masked figure, and, after knocking his opponent out, tears away the mask to see the face of his educated brother. This is a classic instance of disavowal of the rustic hero's lack. While the family reunion later in the narrative signals a resolution of the contradiction embodied in the split image of the hero, the outcome of the wrestling bout itself clearly points to the phallic affirmation of the rustic upon which the reunion is to be predicated. In *Raman Ettanai Ramanati,* we similarly see a good-for-nothing rustic hero leaving the village to become a film star in the city and win his girl. Elements of the kind of mental inadequacy found in the portrayal of the hero in the later Neo-nativity genre are noticeable in this film, but they miraculously disappear in the course of the hero's journey to master the city. In a more realistic vein, *Ponnukkut Tanka Manacu* depicts the hard struggle of a rustic hero making his way up from the humble position of a clerk to a peasant leader and then to the office of Minister of Agriculture. His classmate, the district collector whom he initially served as peon, becomes his subordinate toward the end of the film.

The exemplary text of this class is, however, the film *Pattikkata Pattanama.* A huge box-office success of the early 1970s, this film traces in vivid detail the mythic ascent of the rustic hero. Mukkaiyan, the hero of the film, is a farmer living in the village of Colavantan. The heroine Kalpana, his cross-cousin, is a London-educated modern woman. At the beginning of the film, she arrives home and happens to visit her rustic cousin and his family on the occasion of the village festival. Her initial fascination with village-life in general and the rustic cousin in particular persuades her to accept him in marriage. While her father and the hero think of the marriage as a customary right, and the hero, in fact, resorts to abduction to marry her, the city-bred mother of the heroine disapproves of the match from the beginning. Once placed in the rural household, the heroine feels terribly disturbed and disturbs it in her turn. The initial problem arises when she leaves the bathroom in a state of undress, providing a stunning spectacle for others in the household. But the actual polarization of opinion between husband and wife is structured around two later events: the remodelling of the traditional house and the birthday celebration of the heroine. On the consent of the hero to remodel the house to suit her tastes, the heroine engages in a complete restructuring of the place, aspects of which turn out to threaten the fundamentals of the rustic hero's existence. The heroine's act of replacing two objects, the photographs of the hero's parents and an ancestral plough, points to the nature of this threat. She exchanges the parental images with a modern painting and puts a potted cactus plant in the place of the plough. The modern tastes of the urban woman are symbolically opposed to the values of genealogical continuity and agrarian values. The replacement of the plough by the cactus would carry connotations of the non-fertility of land in agrarian sensibilities. The venerated plough, more than just signifying fertility, is a phallic substitute, a sign of the phallic power that flows in and through genealogical formations.

The heroine's symbolic assault on the hero's universe of values extends into an active disruption of village normalcy when her friends arrive to celebrate her birthday. They drink a lot, dance wildly and have a real spree, embarrassing other household members into leaving the place. Learning of the utterly shameless acts of his wife, the hero enters the house to witness the spectacle, and, enraged, whips his wife's friends and later whips the heroine too. Here, the phallus returns in the form of the whip (see Mulvey 1989: 6–13), and is expressly used for the task of disciplining the female body.

Immediately after, the heroine decides to leave her husband's place for her parental home in neighbouring Madurai. Her mother takes her to live in Madras, where she runs into the hero again. Looking very different, he speaks good English, and sings and dances in the most modern manner. At one point, he stealthily enters the heroine's bedroom and forces sex on her at knife-point. From the generative symbol of the plough, through the punitive and murderous functions of whip and knife, this phallic trajectory of the film indicates the depth of violence in the relationship between men and women in *Pattikkata Pattanama*. Ironically enough, it is under the threat of phallic murderousness that the hero 'implants his seed', the real tamer of the resistant woman, the ultimate cure when every other remedy has failed.

The heroine gives birth to a child, which her mother takes away and leaves in an orphanage. Already distressed by the social stigma of her single-woman status, the heroine now emerges as the 'loving mother' denied her child, the ultimate image of the 'good woman' within popular film narratives. Here the maternal image serves to make the woman 'natural', even 'biological'. This is noticeable in the manner of the heroine's longing for her child. She experiences unbearable pain in her breasts due to their engorgement and passionately craves for the child to suck and give her release.

The heroine learns that her husband has taken the child away from the orphanage. Her distress is compounded when she hears that he is about to remarry. She rushes to the village, only to find everything set for the marriage at the hero's house, begs to breast-feed her child, and attempts to reclaim her husband. As it turns out, the marriage is actually between the hero's cousin, a 'traditional' woman, and another man. The reunion takes place of a now fully disciplined heroine who accepts the phallic authority of the rustic hero, her femininity restored to her in her fusing with the child. Not satisfied, the narrative reiterates its objective in the final scene, where the hitherto submissive father of the heroine whips his recalcitrant wife into submission and forcibly takes her to the village. The trajectory of the female subjects' return to the domain of the phallus, already mapped for the heroine, is thus re-stated.[5]

The phallic affirmation of the rustic is, then, a clear marker of the Old Nativity Film. Locating this marker, however, hardly aids us in either isolating a generic corpus or delineating the primary ingredients of the genre. In other words, delimiting the generic boundaries of this class of films is highly problematic. As I have noted, these films share many a feature with the genre of family melodrama as well as the action film of the MGR-variety. While serving as the focus on which the entire plot pivots, the triumph of the rustic hardly ever manages to cohere other compositional elements to its logic, an operation that would have allowed for the evolution of a relatively stable and consistent generic frame. Stated in Russian Formalist terms, this marker fails to function as a *dominant*, a unifying element around which other components gather to form a genre (See Tomashevsky 1978: 52–5 and Neale 1990: 59–60). My grouping of certain films under the head Old Nativity Film is, therefore, inherently problematic and arbitrary to some extent. But if the notion of genre is understood as a process, rather than as being defined solely by repetition and consistency of properties, there emerges another way of looking at this problem. As Neale (1990: 56) argues,

It may at first seem as though repetition and sameness are the primary

hallmarkers of genres: as though, therefore, genres are above all
inherently static. But . . . genres are, nevertheless, best understood as
processes. These processes may, for sure, be dominated by repetition,
but they are also marked fundamentally by difference, variation, and
change . . . (T)he elements and conventions of a genre are always *in*
play rather than being, simply, *re*-played . . . .

Seen in this manner, generic trajectories will consist not just in
moments of regular evolution, but also occasional outbursts of revolutionary transformation. (Tomashevsky 1978: 52–5). Embedded
as they are in the (textual histories of) generic formations as well
as the wider sociocultural formations (Neale 1990: 59), these changes
in individual genres have profound ideological significance and
implications for those formations as well. More often than not,
generic revolutions are characterized by a marked shift in the canon-
ized forms: a 'prevailing canon is overturned and power passes to
the devices that have previously been subordinate' (Tomashevsky
1978: 54). Marginalities are foregrounded, or move to occupy core
positions, even as the dominance of previously central elements is
displaced.

This view of genre as process enables us to see the evolution of
the Tamil Nativity Film as a long historical trajectory, characterized
nonetheless by a radical transformation or break in the late 1970s.
In adopting this position, rather than the other view whereby
disparate elements of the pre-1976 period were put together in the
formation of a genre that actually came into existence only in the
late 1970s, we have the analytical advantage of coming to grips with
the ideological thrust of the generic moment: a moment that, in
many ways, refers back to filmic discourses of the earlier period in
particular, and cultural discourses in general. In what follows, I
will be arguing that the ideological thrust is cast fundamentally in
phallic terms, a definitive continuity with the Old Nativity Film,
and the generic recoding that occurs in the late 1970s amounts,
above all, to a radical refiguring of the phallus.

## III

One of the most salient features of the Nativity Film in its post-
1976 form is a certain displacement of narrational agency from the
hero to that of the village as collective actant.[6] In film after film, a

narrative move to locate the *native* or the *rustic* as the *inside* is discernible. But, rather than upholding the authenticity of the native as it figures in the text, and thus posit an absolute opposition between the inside and the outside, the narrative usually tends to problematize the transaction or exchange between the two. While in the Old Nativity Film the city, coded as the modern, is, in some sense, quite removed from the village, and the hero's phallic triumph over the urbanity of the modern woman seems almost mythical in character on account of this remoteness, in the transformed genre the modern and the urban flow quite easily into the everyday of the village. A set of characters rather than just the heroine represent the outsiders.[7] These include the doctor/health worker, the teacher, and the military man. There is now a profound sense of ambivalence in the manner in which these outsider-figures are characterized. While the teacher and the militaryman are mostly seen as bene-factors, and, in some cases, as even liberators, the doctor is always viewed with a bit of suspicion. Further, whereas the doctor and the teacher are, for the most part, *pure outsiders*, the militaryman is basically a *quasi-outsider* who mediates between the village and the outside. He represents an *in-between,* a position which, by defini-tion, belongs neither to the inside nor to the outside. He is seen at once to stand guard for the legitimate interests of the village, on the one hand, and to aid the transgression of its norms when they become oppressive, on the other. These characters apart, the hero might also leave the village temporarily, seeking his fortune in the city. In extreme cases, the hero and the heroine might even permanently leave the village. This happens when the village as a collectivity is placed in a position of active villainy and forces the hero and the heroine into deciding to leave for good. In the former case, the hero's journey to the city and his later return to the village are seldom characterized as constitutive of a phallic affirmation. Quite the contrary, the journey and return are frequently associated with loss and despair.

The portrayal of the village is also, in many ways, different from older depictions. A care for detail is markedly visible and forms part of the general look to verisimilitude in the representational modes of the transformed genre. It should be noted in this connection that shooting in actual exterior locations became a dominant film-making practice beginning with the film *Annakkili* in 1976. It produced concomitant changes in conventions of camera-work, editing, and *mise en scène*. The emergence of screenwriters like R. Selvaraj and composers like Ilaiyaraja, whose work was inflected with ruralized song, speech, and aural motifs, coupled with a 'realistic' picturization of landscapes and living spaces, helped create a distinctly new filmic ambience and altered viewing experience in a very fundamental way.[8]

Not only is there a significant displacement of actantial energy/agency from the figure of the hero to that of the village collective, there is also a sense in which the village is portrayed as bounded, an entity isolable from the outside world.[9] While the village is by no means valorized unconditionally, and, in certain instances, might even be characterized as villainous, autonomy remains an inalienable property. In *Ponnu Urukkup Putucu* (The Woman is New to the Place, R. Selvaraj, 1979), this guarded and bounded discreteness finds expression in the image of a fortification that surrounds the village. Traditional belief and custom hold that not more than 999 persons can live in the village at any one time, and, in an ironic narrative move, this proves to be true; towards the end of the film the heroine qua outsider in the role of a family planning worker marries the rustic hero and settles down in the village, whereas the hero himself has to leave the place after committing a murder. The number remains unaltered, restoring the community to a perfect equilibrium. The film, in fact, ends by posing the spectator with a question about this irony, in the form of a voice-over and a written title-card. This is clearly a question about the boundedness of the village community, and the nature of the disturbance and change that the heroine qua outsider bring to it.

Similarly, in *Kallukkul Iram* (Moistness within the Rock, Niwaz, 1980), the seemingly unchanging character of the village prevails in the end even after the massive intrusion of the urban-modern in the form of a film-shooting crew. Early in the film, the community is depicted as a series of faces in freeze-frame close-up, suggesting a certain timelessness and resistance to change. These images first occur at the moment of the film crew's arrival in the village and later recur at crucial narrative junctures. At the beginning of the film, the film crew's entry is shown as a procession of cars and vans that evokes surprise and amazement in the villagers. The fascination offered by the cinema draws the villagers to the shooting spot in large numbers, and during the extended stay of the crew in the village, relationships develop between crew-members and the villagers, such as the one between the star Sudhakar and the village girl Katti, and director Bharatiraja and another girl Colai. While Katti is expressive of her desire for the star (which the latter rejects as he is engaged to a girl in the city), Colai is reticent, largely keeping her wishes and fantasies to herself; expression is minimal, conveyed through silent gestures, a little note, anonymous graffiti on a wall. These, then, are two feminine faces of the village, two different ways in which the village responds with a certain fascination to the outside world. Others are hostile. A madman who brings Colai small gifts and is received with warmth and pity, is, in many ways, her watchful guardian. Representing the community's conscience, he spears and kills both Colai's cousin, who attempts to rape her, and the director Bharatiraja, when he changes his mind about leaving the village and comes back to Colai. The village itself turns hostile to the film crew. In the climax, a midnight sacrificial rite occasioned by the annual festival is cross-cut with two other events, a play and the attempted rape of Colai. The play featuring Katti as the heroine ends in Katti's real death by suicide, and the rape attempt is punctuated by the madman's killing of the offender. The deity's rejection of ritual offerings, considered a bad omen, occurs at the same time. Traditional belief and custom hold that offerings thrown up into the sky to propitiate the deity are not to be seen by the offerer afterwards; on this occasion, a small boy sees the food fall to the ground. The forbidden look, now exercised by a child who fails to abide by custom and norm, proves threatening. ('Why did you see?' is the first response to the boy's discovery.) A shaman is possessed by the deity shortly afterwards, and orders the film crew, believed to be the source of the evil omen, to leave the village. On the visual register we see images of the empty stage, temple bells ringing, a worried and thoughtful film crew, while, aurally, the single voice of the shaman flows and merges into a multitude of voices. The disembodied sound is used here to underscore the actantial quality of the village collective, a characteristic device of the genre.[10] The subsequent shot shows the film crew packing up and leaving amidst a violent storm. Later, when the director comes back to Colai, his death at the hands of the madman is an attempt to effectively wipe away any trace of the film crew's intrusion, and secure the community in its former equilibrium. But the depiction of the village's fascinated engagement with the filmic image and apparatus haunts any such drives to gain hermetic closure. I shall have occasion to return to this point later.

If the two heroic figures of *Kallukkul Iram* barely qualify as regular heroes (despite the fact that they are both 'real heroes' of the 'real film world'), the focalizers of the narrative primarily being the female figures, a film like *Utirip Pukkal* (Unwoven Flowers, Mahendran, 1979) dispenses with the heroic role altogether. Instead, the central actantial position is that of a villainous character whose vices and sadistic dispositions impel him to his own destruction. Towards the end of the narrative, in a rather unusual move in popular film, the entire village gathers to punish him by forcing him to drown in the river. As the crowd awaits the enactment of this almost ritualistic event, the villain notes the displacement of villainy from his own person to that of the collective body of the community. This classic instance sums up the profoundly ambivalent role of the village collective in the Neo-nativity Film.

I will now turn to *Rocappu Ravikkaikkari* (Woman with the Rose-coloured Blouse, Devaraj-Mohan, 1979) to extend my analysis of the intrusion of the modern qua exterior into the village and its implications for the changed figuration of the rustic hero. The film opens with an extreme long shot, offering a panoramic view of the village and a narrator's voice-over that characterizes the place as distinctly remote and isolated from everything modern. The film introduces its hero Cempattai sleeping late in the morning, his niece lying next to him on a cot. His mother is annoyed and wakes him up to work. Cempattai sells goods brought from the neighbouring town and he has, on this day, the additional responsibility of inviting friends and relatives to his forthcoming marriage to Nandhini, an educated girl and daughter of his maternal uncle, a teacher. Fixed by the elders when the boy and the girl were very young, the marriage is very much in the manner of any such arranged marriage. The heroine of the film is, thus, not the valued object that the rustic hero wins toward the end of his valiant phallic journey, but is part of a culturally given arrangement whose basis the film examines. The hero is uncouth, wears shorts and occasionally, even flowers in his ears, a sign in Tamil culture of immaturity and mental inadequacy. Note how the introductory shots shows him in a position of infantile dependence. The hero's sidekicks who work with him accentuate this image, both of them being even more immature, one limping and stuttering to boot. The hero's elder brother is also depicted as rather innocent. Having said this, it should not be forgotten that the hero articulates the village with the outer world. More than just a purveyor of goods—which initially are mostly the regular groceries available only in 'town' shops, but later include such things as items of dress and make-up—he serves as an intermediary, a go-between who mediates the modern into the village. After reading newspapers in the town tea-shops, he also brings news of the outer world into the village, about Gandhi's Salt March and the public meeting addressed by Periyar and Rajaji in Salem.

But it is the coming of the heroine which signals modernity's direct intrusion.[11] Many of the signs of modernity familiar to the heroine, such as her dress and make-up codes, are totally unknown in the village. This creates a series of disturbances in the hero's household and the community at large (when, for example, the village women try to emulate the heroine by wearing undergarments and make-up), ultimately leading to the collective anger of the village against the hero. The tragedy of the hero arises from his position as mediator. Torn between a domineering mother who epitomizes the traditional, and a wife inclined to the modern, he is unable to make a decisive move until the end, when he finally thinks perhaps his mother was right. Further, his experience of the modern wife is overwhelming, even as it seems infantile. His memory, or rather fantasy, of the heroine as a child is shown in flashback before the marriage takes place, the children vying with each other to assume the role of husband in a game of husband-and-wife. Again there are freeze-frames of the heroine as she starts to undress in the sequence showing his intimacies with her on the marriage night. The wife's figure overwhelms him, particularly her hitherto-unknown use of undergarments and make-up in a place where women are not even used to wearing a blouse. The heroine is an exuberant woman who takes most of the initiative, introducing her husband to a mutual perfuming of bodies that brings uncouth hero and modern heroine into bed. This serves as an olfactory bridge that indexes, at the moment of its bridging, a gap, an insurmountable hiatus, a distance that ultimately offers no point of arrival. But in the aftermath of their love-making she seems unsatisfied as, disturbed by the hero's noisy snore, she lies wide awake.

The image of a fascinating but alienating modernity is augmented in various objects the heroine brings to the village: a gramophone, a gaslight, and metallic kitchenware. Of these the gramophone often functions intrusively, offsetting the hero's own functions as singer and story-teller; the gramaphonic voice as sign of a techno-modernity at once distant and seductive contrasts with the folkloric inflections of the hero's performance. This line of seduction continues into the heroine's succumbing to Manikkam, an outsider who works for a white plantation-owner. Significantly, his initial appearance occurs on the occasion of a house-warming ceremony that celebrates the hero and heroine's entry into their newly built house, after breaking with the extended family household. Later, while the hero himself refuses to leave the village to work in the factory, he helps the white man and his deputy recruit workers. The recruited villagers unwittingly sign a three-year agreement which binds them to indentured labour in Burma. The line of seduction thus extends through Manikkam and the white plantation-owner into wider mechanisms of colonial power. The film's invocation of the Salt March becomes significant as a political move in which the national is positioned as native in opposition to an intrusive imperial design.

The hero, as an intermediary of this seductive modernity meets with the collective wrath of the village. He is charged with corrupting the women's minds through his trade, and for aiding the plantation-owner in his vicious designs. He is severely beaten up and fined in the village panchayat. A lone person, sympathetic to his good intentions and acts, raises his voice arguing for a more 'realistic' assessment of the advent of modernity and of the changes it is likely to produce in the community. This man secures the hero's release by paying a heavy fine. In a state of desperation the hero returns home to find his wife and Manikkam together in bed. Later he commits suicide, and there is a suggestion that the heroine does the same. The final shots of the film echo the opening panoramic shots of the village and the surrounding wilderness, the hero's voice selling his wares still reverberating on the soundtrack.

But the rustic voice has already been overlaid or intersected by other external voices. The intrusion of the heroine as outsider is profoundly unsettling of the hero's subjectivity. An examination of narrative and song-sequences suggest that whatever the apparent gestures of containment, a decisive shift in the subjective economy of popular film has occurred and a fundamental recoding of the phallus. This new figure of the hero is quite remote from the heroic template of the Old Nativity Film where the heroic trajectory assumes mythic proportions in the omnipotent hero's mastering of the modern. In the new image of the hero, his development seems instead to be arrested. The Neo-Nativity Film of the transition period here transfers mental inadequacy, normally reserved for comedians or minor characters, to the figure of the hero, and so precludes the hero's moving away from infantile maternal fusion and immature sexuality to adult male status, culminating in his getting married and assuming the role of the father (see Mulvey 1989). It also functions as a sign of social insufficiency, or, to put it in Silverman's terms (1990: 114), *social castration*, a representation of the hero's deficiencies in terms of education, class, and/or caste. Grounded in his rurality, the perceived locus of such lack, this mental condition of the hero is never completely cured in the Neo-nativity Film, despite the heroine's unrelenting attempts.

Alongside the theme of mental inadequacy is that of physical failure. *Patinaru Vayatinile* (At the Age of Sixteen, Bharatiraja, 1977) dramatizes in vivid detail this theme of the male wound and the touch of the desperate female that seeks to heal. The protagonist of the film, Cappani, belongs to the general kind of the uncouth, immature hero, one associated with a certain animality, and suffers a further disability in being lame. In fact, lameness marks his personality, as is evident from his name, meaning cripple. The heroine, Mayil, at first scornful of Cappani, slowly comes to realize the value of the simpleton's devotion after suffering at the hands of a visiting city man. Then begins her enterprise to reform not only Cappani's attire and appearance, but to infuse him with a sense of dignity and self-respect. In short, it is a project of re-phallicizing the rustic hero, one that is aimed at his passage to manhood, but destined, on that very account, to be doomed in the film.

Portrayals of other kinds of mutilated male subjects are found in films such as *Mullum Malarum* (The Thorn and the Flower, Mahendran, 1978), *Oru Kai Ocai* (One-handed Clap, Bhagyaraj,

1980), *Kannip Paruvattile* (The Tender Years, Balaguru, 1979) and *Puttata Puttukkal* (Dysfunctional Locks, Mahendran, 1980). *Puttata Puttukkal* is perhaps the finest example of this class of films, both for its dramatization of male lack and its stylistics of narration. The hero, Uppili, is actually infertile, not impotent. Running a small tea-shop-cum-restaurant in the village, he is a strong, good-looking man, a successful Casanova who flirts with many a village girl, including married women. His wife Kanniyamma, a calm, reticent person, craves a child, and performs a variety of austerities to get one. Uppili tries many remedies, including folk medication. When he brings home a small boy with a view to adoption, his wife shows disapproval. Later, he has to force the boy out on discovering him too sexually inquisitive for his age. Images of the couple in bed carry signs of extreme distress and unpleasure.

Generic expectations of the arrival of the outsider here are fulfilled in the person of the forest ranger Thyagarajan. Kanniyamma gradually yields to Thyagarajan's overtures, and there are indications that the affair is deeply pleasurable to her. When she leaves home for the first time to have sexual intercourse with the outsider, there is the sound of a child crying over the shot of a cat. The next shot shows the crying child attended by its mother. This shot then zooms out to show the housemaid looking with curiosity at the departing heroine. There follows a close-up of Kanniyamma's legs over a drum-sound that stresses the moment's significance as a crossover. The cat, sitting on the steps in this shot is absent from this position in the next one. Clearly anticipating the enjoyment of escaping the confines of conjugality, this image of the cat's disappearance is joined to certain other auditory signs from early in the sequence. These are the sounds of children playing and a temple-bell ringing when the heroine is shown at the threshold of the house, on the verge of stepping out.

Uppili comes to know of his wife's affair, and when he questions her about her infidelity, in an insistently reticent move, the heroine refuses to answer. When Uppili finally forces her to speak, she turns furious and, in spiteful rage, points to his unmanliness. Uppili, dismayed and angry, takes a stick to beat her but drops it. The heroine now exposes her body, fully naked underneath the sari, saying, 'Kill, kill me. What pleasure did I find living with you? Let me die.' The desperate hero raises his hand to slap her, but the frame freezes, the raised arm of the hero stuck midway. The male subject's paralysis in making a decisively aggressive move is followed by expressions of regret for his violent gestures, and his seeking of forgiveness from his wife.

Kanniyamma leaves home in the middle of the night for Thyagu's place. Not accepted by Thyagu's folks and urged even by him to leave, she leaves for some faraway place. Meanwhile Uppili is reduced to utter hopelessness. He loses all he earned, and even closes down the business. No longer the proud Casanova, he is the butt of vicious gossip about his wife's affair. When all efforts to trace Kanniyamma's whereabouts have failed, there arrives news of his wife. She now works in a brick-kiln as a labourer and is brought to Uppili by one of his acquaintances. Reticent about the intervening period, Kanniyamma urges Uppili to agree that they separate. The only moment she expresses intense feelings is when Thyagu comes to advise her to live with Uppili. In a sudden outburst of aggression, she turns uncontrollably violent and vents her spiteful fury on Thyagu, hitting him with a broom and pouring cow-dung water on him.

Later, the village censures Uppili for taking Kanniyamma back. At first defiant, the hero later decides to send Kanniyamma away. In the final shots of the film Uppili joins a departing Kanniyamma saying, 'Take me along with you'. A moment underlining the hero's helplessness, this is a fitting closure to the dramatization of male lack, a drama which '(f)ar from obliging the female subject to display her lack to the gaze of her sexual other, repeatedly calls upon her to look acceptingly at his lack—to acknowledge and embrace male castration' (Silverman 1990: 119–20). This is a radical restructuring of the libidinal economy of earlier cinema by demythologizing the phallus; a tale in which the male subject is not only picturized in his phallic injury, but offered no means of rehabilitation.

## IV

The transformation of the functions of the heroine that occurs within this revision of genre is expressed in several ways. Central is a libidinal infraction, the mobilization of ungovernable amounts of libidinal energy that refuses to be channelled into conjugality and motherhood, or what Mulvey calls *married femininity*. The

heroine then evokes a series of alternative images. There is the
*Eternal Spinster*, who passionately waits for the ideal husband to
arrive and take her in marriage, a dream eventually doomed to
unfulfilment; the *Strong Woman*, constituting a shift in focalization
and narrational control, who is masculinized to the extent of serving
as phallic support for the utterly de-phallicized hero;[12] to take this
re-focalization further, there is the *Castrator par excellence*, who
epitomizes an anti-phallicism in its extreme and functions in the last
instance as the community's guarding spirit. Annam, the heroine
of the film *Annakkili* (Annam, the Parrot, Devaraj-Mohan, 1976),
is perhaps exemplary in combining in her character aspects of all
three types in a very imaginative way. The credit sequence at the
beginning of the film shows various places in the village Colaiyur,
culminating in a temple where we see certain of the guardian deities
of the village. The camera cuts to a panoramic view of the village
to emphasize the properties of its landscape. It then moves on to a
cinema-house in which the heroine Annam is seated in the audience,
watching the devotional film *Sri Andal* (1948). In this film the saint-
poet Andal makes offerings to Vishnu and sings songs from her
work *Nacciyar Tirumoli*.[13] Annam's spectatorial pleasure is interrupted by a message calling her to help a woman give birth. An
accomplished midwife, regarded as highly auspicious in the community, Annam is the main breadwinner of a family composed of
her sister, the sister's drunkard husband and daughter. Annam's
cross-cousin, the rustic Makutapati, wants to marry her, but Annam
herself dreams, like Andal, of an outsider who would miraculously
appear and take her in marriage. The arrival of Thyagarajan, a
teacher who comes to work in the village school, seems to presage
fulfilment.

Annam is portrayed as a woman confident enough to take the
initiative in her relationship with Thyagarajan. Imaged as part of
the wilderness that surrounds the village, hers is an untamed femininity accentuated by economic and familial independence. She is
associated with a swing that hangs suspended in the wilderness,
signalling, as in Satyajit Ray's *Charulata* (1964), connotations of
freedom, sensuality and instability. Again echoing *Charulata* and
films of the neo-nativity genre like *Patinaru Vayatinile* and *Enka
Uru Racatti* (The Queen of Our Village, 1980), the sensation of
the heroine's swinging is augmented by the camera swaying at the

moment of distress. After Thyagarajan sees Annam on the swing, he tries to mount it and falls down and hurts himself. Annam not only tends the wound but also teaches him how to swing. She teaches him other things unknown to the urbane hero, such as swimming in the river. Further, she is generous, parting with a sizeable portion of her savings when he needs money to obtain a job in the city. That he loses this in a swindle matters little to Annam, who now regards the teacher as her much-awaited lover. While Thyagarajan reciprocates her love, Sumathi, daughter of the village headman and an educated girl from the city, falls in love with Thyagarajan and wants to marry him. The headman promises to support Thyagarajan's family in arranging the much-delayed marriage of his elder sister, a gesture of patronage which makes his mother and sister extremely happy, and leaves Thyagarajan barely any choice in the matter. Initially dismayed, Annam soon recovers her self-effacing generosity: she wants from Thyagarajan and Sumati only the favour of delivering their child.

Meanwhile, Alagappan, the villainous proprietor of the village cinema-house and a Casanova character, attempts to seduce Annam. He calls for her in the middle of the night on the pretext of his wife's expected delivery. Once aware of his intentions, Annam talks to him enticingly, fondles his arm, and then pins him in a painful grip. The villain, overpowered and reduced to utter helplessness, is forced to flee. This is the moment of the Castrator par excellence, the aggressive, anti-phallic face of Annam's femininity, one that is confirmed at the story's conclusion.

Years later Thyagarajan and Sumathi visit the village with their son to whom Annam becomes very attached. While Thyagarajan feels terribly guilty for what he has done, Annam has a different view, invoking the life of Andal to observe that for her pleasure is achieved through pain. An image of Andal is superimposed over Annam, a conflation of the mythical and the everyday that culminates in the film's climax. Here the villain Alagappan abducts Thyagarajan's son and demands Annam in exchange. The villain's attempts to rape Annam are intercut with climactic moments in the film *Kannagi* (1942) which is running in the cinema. Annam fights back with the lamp she carries and escapes. The lamp sets the entire theatre ablaze, a scene interwoven with images of Kannagi in the film within the film cursing the city of Madurai to be destroyed by fire[14]. A stampede ensues, and while Annam manages to save the boy, she herself is fatally injured and dies in Thyagarajan's lap saying, 'I will not leave this place. I will roam this village, the river and the wilderness. I will sing for the well-being of you all.' The last few shots refer back to and revise the beginning of the film: images of the village are intercut with those of the cinemahouse in towering flames, with a final image of the guardian deity and a title-card underlining Annam's identity with Andal.

Sandwiched between excerpts from two quasi-mythologicals of an earlier period, *Sri Andal* and *Kannagi*, the narration of *Annakkili* assimilates mythical semes arising from these films, Annam cast within a narrative axis deriving from Andal, Kannagi, and the guardian deities of the village. Of the wilderness even when living within the community, Annam is now integrated to the wilderness, while continuing to infuse the community with her ambivalent presence—solitary and spinsterish, yet a midwife to the community, at once passionate lover and destroyer of manhood. *Annakkili* is not just a tale of devotion and sainthood in any conventional sense; and Annam is not merely a martyr-saint whose devotion to the gods elevates her to godliness. Placed within the genre of neo-nativity, the film is primarily about seduction, the seduction of the female subject by the modern, of the inside by the outside. As in *Kallukkul Iram*, the cinema itself is central to the constitution of this modern exteriority. Given the nexus between film and politics in the Tamil context, and apprehensions that the spectator over-identifies with the filmic image,[15] this figuring of the seductive relation in Tamil Nativity Film takes on profound significance, both within filmic discourse and cultural discourse in general. It raises fundamental questions about spectatorial identification and the processes by which not only individual subjectivities are constituted, but entire communities are made and unmade. Recent work in psychoanalytic and feminist film theory has gone beyond simple equations by positing models of multiple and shifting identifications. (See, for instance, Neale 1983; Mulvey 1989; Stacey 1991; and Hansen 1991.) These studies also show that identification with ego-ideals on the screen need not inevitably entail 'misrecognitions of self', but, in many cases, could involve elements of empowerment. As Stacey argues, 'Many forms of identification involve processes of transformation and the production of new identities, combining the

spectator's existing identity with her desired identity . . .' (1991:160).
Put in Lacanian terms, 'although the subject has no identity without
an alienating image, that image may be put in place either *by the
subject* or *by the other*' (Silverman: 76).

The narratives of seduction offered by Tamil Nativity Film are
then tales not merely of passive devotion but of erotic contest. Films
like *Kallukkul Iram* and *Annakkili*, operating at a meta-cinematic
level, draw this generic scenario into an exploration of the vexed
problem of identificatory excess in the process of cinematic viewing.
In *Kallukkul Iram*, the filmic apparatus is at the outset posited as
the modern intruder exercising a seductive fascination over the two
village women. While Katti is an ardent fan of the star Sudhakar
(she keeps an image of the star amongst her personal things), Colai
characterizes the film-maker as a *kuttattukku vattiyar* ('a guru of
the crowds') in graffiti which the hero Bharatiraja sees through his
viewfinder. Here the film-maker is distinguished from other
*vattiyars* represented in the film, the theatre director (*kuttu vattiyar*)
and the school teacher (*pallikkuta vattiyar*), and is placed alongside
MGR, popularly known as the exemplary *vattiyar* of Tamil
cinema.[16] Another instance reflecting a cinematic self-consciousness
amongst the characters is when Katti, Colai, and some village children enact a mock-shooting situation. This represents a reworking
into a theatrical modality of the techno-semantic load that the
apparatus and experience of cinema instantiate.[17]

The flow between the cinema and media like theatre and graffiti
is also found in *Annakkili*. In an important sequence Annam talks
about her identification with the image of Andal and refers to the
*Harikathakalakshepam*, a traditional performance mode of narrating
puranic stories as the source of such identification, not the cinema.
Far from disavowing cinematic experience, this account underlines
the elementary, yet significant, fact of the female subject's ability
'to put the image in place': the capacity to fashion a visuality at the
moment of the forbidden look under patriarchy, as in the ritual
context of *Kallukul Iram*, and to draw upon disparate images, both
from the cinema and elsewhere, to structure and restructure her
subjective location in a very fundamental way. This female subject
is then very different from the image of the passive spectator, a
conventional picture of the spectating subject who revels in her
wholesale subjection as devotion. The narrational move in

*Annakkili's* climax when Annam's fire dismantles or, rather, displaces the apparatus of the magic lantern—much like the fire of Kannagi's breasts—is a moment that points toward further subversion: an invocation of the filmic image only to subvert the apparatus that sustains it.

## NOTES

1. See Narayanan (1981: 685–94) on the issues raised in the debate.

2. The term Nativity Film is widely used within the Madras film industry and within journalistic discourse on cinema. However, the distinction I make between the Old Nativity Film and the Neo-Nativity Film is theoretical.

3. For some later developments in the genre, see Srinivas and Kaali (forthcoming).

4. As is obvious, I am heavily indebted to Silverman for the theoretical frame of this paper, particularly her extended use of the psychoanalytical notion of castration.

5. Interestingly enough, the comedy-track of this film has a tough, rustic woman going to the city and taming her husband who disavows his rustic origins to become urbane.

6. On the notion of *collective actant*, see Greimas (1989: 615–26).

7. On the significance of the outsider in Bharatiraja's films, see Chakravarthy (1986). See also Vasanthan (1978) for an interesting comparison of outsider-figures in Hollywood and Indian cinemas.

8. It is interesting to note that a massive 'regionalization' also occurred in the Tamil literary world around this time. For instance, the label *Karical Ilakkiyam* (Black Soil Literature) came into use during the late 1970s, and a considerable number of writers identified themselves with the idea of forming a group.

9. Cf. the portrayal of the community-as-actant in Jean Gabin's films (Vincendeau 1985).

10. A variant of this device would be to feature the visual stripped of sound. In either case, the disengagement of sound from the visual, and the consequent non-synchronization, tend to lay bare the characterological significance of the village community.

11. The narratorial voice anchors Nandhini's status at two significant moments in the narrative: first when she enters the village immediately after the marriage, and again when she and the hero's mother quarrel with each other. In both these instances, a freeze-frame shot and the narrator's voice-over stress the heroine's location as that of the modern.

12. Manga, the wife of the hero Kali in *Mullum Malarum*, exemplifies this kind of strong woman. When the hero loses his arm and thus is unable to win in a sport he used to excel in, Manga contests on his behalf and emerges victorious. That she is indeed the hero's phallic support is unmistakably attested to when she helps him button his pants, something that he himself cannot do.

13. Andal is a Tamil saint-poet who loved Vishnu passionately, rejected any mortal man as her husband, and was finally taken by the god in marriage.

14. Kannagi is the archetypal angry woman who in the fury of being violated cursed the city of Madurai to destruction by fire, and tears apart and hurls a breast on it. The subject of veneration in numerous narrative and cultic traditions in south India and Sri Lanka, Kannagi represents an extreme version of an angry femininity.

15. See, for instance, Jayakantan's novel *Cinimavukkup Pona Cittalu* (1972) which portrays the life of a proletarian woman who, as a result of such identificatory excess, first commits adultery, then turns to prostitution, and finally ends up insane. In another example, the film *Cinimap Paittiyam* (The Craze for Cinema, 1975), a remake of the Hindi film *Guddi* (Hrishikesh Mukherji, 1971), depicts a case of identificatory excess in a young middle-class girl which is similarly problematic. Interestingly, this film invokes Periyar and Annadurai in connection with the notion of 'good cinema'. In both these instances the lives of woman saints are also invoked to talk about the infringement of conjugal bounds that over-identification seems to entail. In his preface to his novel Jayakantan writes: 'When as a boy I first saw the film *Bhakta Mira*, my sympathies were all with that Rana who married Mira. My heart bled for him. But later when I came to know the spiritual implications, like the relationship between the great soul and the little soul and so on, I was able to reconcile myself to the event. But for the immense spiritual and philosophical background associated with Krishna, Mira's desertion of her husband and rejection of his love would have appeared cruel and immoral. But Mira's story has the ring of universal truth since it is like the life going out of a body in a natural act of death. When family life and conjugal love are forsaken for something more meaningful and of a greater value, then the resultant sadness gives place to a certain elation. This will not be the fall or betrayal or moral transgression of the people concerned. It takes them to a higher plane of human existence. But we cannot accord the status of Mira to the gulls who fall for those masquerading in Krishna's robes to make some money out of it. To do so would be an indication of the decline of our society. Such a fall contributes nothing to the welfare either of art, people or life'. The film *Cinimap Paittiyam* similarly invokes the life of Andal. The heroine of the film has doubts about the legitimacy of her love for a married man, the film star. At this instance, she happens to listen to a *Harikathakalakshepam* on the life of Andal in which the narrator justifies Andal's love for Krishna as *bhakti*, a devotion that knows no conjugal bounds and which is readily accepted by the god. Upon this, the heroine feels reassured of her devotion to the celluloid god.

16. The following is the complete text of the graffiti: Yellow shirt/Yellow pants/Curly hair/Angry man/A guru of the crowds/Coffee-coloured hat/I'm in love with this.

The pronoun at the end (the Tamil equivalent is *itu*) suggests that it is the image of the diegetic director-hero that Colai is writing about.

17. Note that while Katti plays the heroine, Colai takes up the directorial position.

REFERENCES

Chakravarthy, Venkatesh, 1986. 'Bharatirajavin Cinima', *Ini,* October.
———————, 1996. 'Maniratnamum Cinima Araciyalam', *Dinamani,* Pongal Malar, January.
Greimas, Algirdas Julien, 1989. 'Description and Narrativity', *New Literary History* 20(3).
Hansen, Miriam, 1991. 'Pleasure, Ambivalence, Identification: Valentino and Female Spectatorship', in Christine Gledhill (ed.), *Stardom: Industry of Desire,* London: Routledge.
Jayakantan, 1972. *Cinimavukkup Pona Cittalu,* Madurai: Meenakshi Puthaka Nilayam.
Mulvey, Laura, 1989. *Visual and Other Pleasures,* London: Macmillan.
Narayanan, Arantai, 1981. *Tamil Cinimavin Katai,* Madras: New Century Book House.
Neale, Steve, 1983. Masculinity as Spectacle, *Screen* 24(6), November–December.
———————, 1990. 'Questions of Genre', *Screen* 31(1), Spring.
Silverman, Kaja, 1989 'Fassbinder and Lacan: A Reconsideration of Gaze, Look and Image', *Camera Obscura* 19.
———————, 1990. 'Historical Trauma and Male Subjectivity' in E.Ann Kaplan (ed.), *Psychoanalysis and Cinema,* New York: Routledge.
Srinivas, Ravi and Sundar Kaali, forthcoming. 'On Castes and Comedians: Discourses of Power in Recent Tamil Cinema.'
Stacey, Jackie, 1991. 'Feminine Fascinations: Forms of Identification in Star-Audience Relations', in Gledhill (ed.), *Stardom.*
Tomashevsky, Boris, 1978. 'Literary Genres', in L.M. O'Toole and Ann Shukman (eds), *Formalism: History, Comparison, Genre,* Russian Poetics in Translation, no. 5, Oxford: Holdan Books.
Vasanthan, J., 1978. 'Leave the Outsider Alone', *Filmfare* 27(20).
Vincendeau, Ginette, 1985. 'Community, Nostalgia and the Spectacle of Masculinity', *Screen* 26(6).

# 7

# Kaadalan *and the Politics of Resignification: Fashion, Violence and the Body*

VIVEK DHARESHWAR
TEJASWINI NIRANJANA

THE SONG 'MUKKAALA MUQABLA', from the Tamil film *Kaadalan* (Loverboy), has been, perhaps, the biggest hit of the 1990s.[1] The peculiar voice of Mano has been resonating in cinema halls, living-rooms, streets, and video coaches across the nation. The visual sequence of the song—which dominated various TV count-down shows such as *Superhit Muqabla*, *BPL Oye* and *Philips Top Ten*—is quite fantastic, even bizarre. A pastiche on spaghetti Westerns, the sequence opens with the hero, his hair and beard bleached blond, straddling a horse with a noose around his neck and the bad guys about to shoot the horse. The heroine gallops into the frame with a gun and shoots off the rope to liberate the hero. Then begins the dance, performed with great élan by Prabhudeva. The sequence itself is a strip of narrative very much in the MTV genre, and has no apparent link to the larger narrative of the film. The song/dance sequence in Indian films has always been a relatively autonomous block, one of the requirements of the dominant form of manufacture rather than a diegetic necessity. This tendency of the song/dance sequence toward autonomy has been

We must thank Ashish Rajadhyaksha for urging us to publish an earlier version of this paper in the *Journal of Arts and Ideas* (29), January 1996. Venkatesh Chakravarthy, Mary John, M.S.S. Pandian, A.S. Panneerselvan, K. Satyanarayana and Madan Gopal Singh discussed with us earlier drafts of this paper. We are particularly grateful to Ravi Vasudevan for his detailed and thoughtful editorial comments. Thanks also to Mohan Krishna for helping us to re-view *Kaadalan*.

intensified in recent years by the competition of television and the
MTV genre as well as by the market opened up by them. So
elaborately orchestrated dance sequences, each representing an autonomous strip of narrative, have become an imperative for the
survival of the film industry.

At first sight, therefore, the 'Mukkaala . . .' dance sequence seems
to instantiate this logic and respond to its imperative, its link to
the filmic narrative seeming to be only a loosely metaphoric one.
The hero has been in police custody undergoing elaborate torture.
The heroine embarrasses her father, who had ordered the confine-
ment, into releasing the hero. Then follows the song/dance we
described above; clearly a celebration, an expression of liberation.
But why the peculiar form and 'Western' theme?

The narrative action within the song has a bizarre moment where
the hero, now dancing with a hip MTV-type baggy suit, hat and
shoes, has the visible parts of his body—the face, hands, ankles—
shot off. And, with only a moment's pause, the garb continues to
dance, perform and signify. This moment, and this song sequence,
synecdochically foregrounds both the 'theme' of the film and the
complex enunciative folding or layering of its filmitude; its formal
enunciative complexity placed at the service of its attempt to elaborate a cultural politics of resignification.[2] As we will try to show
below, almost all the song-sequences in the film do that, some more
spectacularly and successfully than the others. However, before
analysing the politics of resignification attempted by the film, or,
rather as a prelude to it, let us repeat the synecdochic structure of
the film and analyse briefly the 'Mukkaala . . .' sequence.

As an independent block, with its own narrative, it can be seen
as competing with the MTV genre. Inserted into the film, but still
taken as an autonomous block, it can be seen as the film's attempt to
assert its superiority over other media and other media-genres.[3] As
an enunciation orchestrated by the film, it is also a comment on the
circulation and consumption of spaghetti Westerns (but we should
not forget the even longer history of the fictions of Oliver Strange
and Louis l'Amour) by the urban middle class, on our ability to
register that genre. We could then take it as an attempt to draw
upon and comment on the perceptual habit formed by various
'foreign' elements—Western novels, films, the pastiche-use of them
in MTV. And the high-tech aesthetic staging of the dance to

highlight Prabhudeva's stunning dancing body superimposes and resignifies the previous enunciative elements both formally and thematically. The MTV culture, as well as more generally the global televisual culture, is here and we have to negotiate it. Film as an industry has to negotiate it in order to survive; culturally we have to negotiate it, again in order to survive. Let us for convenience use 'fashion' as a signifier for the onslaught of 'globalized' culture. So the hero/Prabhudeva takes on rap, MTV, the high-tech audio-visual apparatus—but also, as we shall see, Bharatanatyam and Tradition—and resignifies them. The body, then, is the site of this negotiation; the source and target of violence, of stimulation. The body, that most material of signifiers, must cope, mediate, transform the various forces—globalizing economy and culture, the state and its violence, 'tradition' and its demands—that make it their target. The bizarre moment we described above—of the body dancing, performing, signifying even after the 'referent', the material body is destroyed—that moment registers the politics of resignification, with the body foregrounded as the site and agency of that politics. The song then reconnects with the theme/form of the film; or, better still, it synecdochically re-articulates what the film attempts to enunciate: resignification as a cultural politics.

It is the burden of this essay to show how *Kaadalan* engages, and forces us to engage, in a politics of resignification that centres around the body—the caste body, the class body, and the body politic; body embedded in the modalities of class and caste, caught in and engaging with the different forms of violence. The film orchestrates very different, heterogeneous enunciative or signifying systems by spatializing the conflict or antagonism between them: MTV, saturation of the visual field of urban spaces by all kinds of objects, liberalized political spaces, and traditional spaces. We hope to explore how as a film it is able to do that, and what intertextual field emerges from that orchestration. In exploring this process, we will be forced to confront or interrogate issues of politics, not merely or only of the politics of culture in our time, but more fundamentally, what can be the shape of politics in the emerging cultural economy that seems to be redrawing and covering up the economic and social dislocations caused by its own incursion. For the purposes of this essay, then, to use a predictable if convenient pun, *Kaadalan* is both a pretext and an intertext. In fact, the film stages itself as such, that is, as a pretext and an intertext for engaging in a politics of resignification, although what might surprise us are the elements or traces that make up its intertextuality, that it opens up for resignification. Signification presupposes codes that are grounded in stable structures and institutions; this is true as much of political and social signification as it is of cultural institutions such as cinema. Just as *Kaadalan* re-examines and re-deploys structures of identification and misrecognition which make cinematic viewing possible, it enables us to re-assign different meanings to contemporary political and cultural phenomena. The very audacity of the film, however, makes all the more evident its limitations and its blindnesses (to use 'blindness' in the Paul de Manian sense, as that necessary moment which produces what he calls an 'insight') regarding certain areas, notably that of gender. We have attempted to read *Kaadalan* through certain interpretative structures derived from our understanding of contemporary politics, most significantly the different strands of dalit cultural politics that have emerged in the post-Mandal years. The 'validity' of such a reading can be measured, it seems to us, only by whether or not it illuminates some facets of the present-day political scenario, and not by its 'faithfulness' to the filmic text. What we as audience bring to the theatre, which is what informs our response to the film, seems to have everything to do with a political space that has been formative for us, that has in a sense generated our questions, questions we do not leave behind us when we watch a film like *Kaadalan*.

The film, as we shall show, represents the state and the law as attempting to arrest, block and even destroy the process of resignification that is already underway. Again, the body is the site and agency of political signification too. The two signifiers (violence and the body) and their complex enunciations that the film tries to represent, enfold and resignify, cross one another within the film as they do outside it. The hero is confined and tortured by the police on the orders of the state's governor because he has fallen in love with the heroine, who is the governor's daughter. That torture sequence too foregrounds the body in all its nakedness and vulnerability. And yet the terroristic attempt by the state to destroy his body is shown by the film to be futile. Indeed, terrorist politics— if the state's actions can be described as such—is shown to be caught in the referential illusion. Terrorism attempts to get hold of and destroy the 'reference', the materiality of body, in the hope of arresting or abolishing signification. That attempt has to fail—even if the violence it engenders wreaks havoc—insofar as reference itself is the effect of signification. Along with processing the signifier 'fashion'—which stands in for the apparatus, the institution, and the culture of television, advertising and other parts of the media industry—*Kaadalan* also processes and encrypts the political system of contemporary India and its enunciation. 'Violence' is the signifier of this system of enunciations, its institutions and practices. The film's reflexivity about its filmitude consists not merely in formal gestures but in its attempt to resignify that filmitude itself in so far as the film seeks to index the political culture in which it is embedded, namely, the political culture of Tamil Nadu where the filmic idiom and filmic iconicity are inseparable from politics. A similar situation obtains in the political culture of Andhra Pradesh, where the authors of this essay live. Here we would like to add that while acknowledging the importance of locating *Kaadalan* in a specifically Tamil political and cinematic history, we would also like to claim that the film's 'effects' are not confined to a Tamil space alone. The film, called *Kaadalan* in Tamil Nadu, circulates in Andhra Pradesh as *Kaadalan*, a Telugu film. It circulates in Karnataka as a 'south Indian' or even Tamil film. It is now circulating in northern India as *Hamse Hai Muqabla*. Although the phenomenon of dubbed films is not new, *Kaadalan*—like the Mani Ratnam films—is creating a new space of signification which may depend on (may not be unrelated to) its feeding into or converging with local situations, whether in Andhra Pradesh or Uttar Pradesh.

What first strikes one about this film is its verve, energy and style. Its use of colour—each sequence is a veritable riot of colour—its use of fashion, its orchestration of violence, make us euphoric. And this euphoria is consumerist—the film itself stages it as such. As though to make sure we don't miss this point, the first song-sequence choreographed to showcase the dancing talent of Prabhudeva, uses a Charms cigarette hoarding with the message, 'Taste the Spirit of Freedom'. The body is the site that unites the two signifiers, 'fashion' and 'violence'—the body mediating, and being *mediatized* by, the global televisual junk through its response to the MTV culture and to the kung fu films; the body enacting

Tradition, the body, as we have already said, as the source and target of violence.

The trope that governs this cinema of the body is synecdoche.[4] One could in fact argue that the film attempts the impossible— namely, to present each shot, indeed each frame, as a synecdoche (it being understood that the relationship between part and whole is reversible). This accounts, we feel, for the predominance of the spatialized shots, lacking in depth, displaying as it were what we might call, after Ashish Rajadhyaksha, 'neo-frontality'.[5] Spatialization and synecdoche are obviously related in more than a casual sense, one implication of this being that the relationship between the shots are less important, or are subordinate to the relationship within the image. The most productive link between the synecdochic representation and spatialization are established in those shots in which, to put it in Deleuzian terms, the 'sheets of past' and moments or 'peaks of present' are made to inhere in the image. The film in fact aims, as we shall show, to spatialize conflicts that are temporal, this in order to heighten the intensity of the time-image and thereby to open up the past, insofar as it inheres in the present, for resignification. The spatialization and the synecdochic trope that governs it are evident most clearly in the song/dance sequences, although they structure other scenes too.

*Kaadalan* employs a banal plot: poor boy falls in love with rich girl, and the two negotiate a happy ending through numerous narrative twists; the main obstacle to the couple's union is the girl's father (played, coincidentally, by major modernist icon Girish Karnad), the governor of the state who turns out to be engaging in a series of terrorist acts. The critique of the indigenist-modernist celebration of the Indian peasant begins in the very first sequence of the film, in which a farmboy wearing a dhoti with a towel over his shoulder, dives into a haystack and emerges as the suave, jeans-clad high-tech bomb-expert Malli (who is the governor's hired hand, played with great panache by Raghuvaran). Malli proceeds to the city to set up an explosive device, disposing of a guard who tries to stop him; this device will go off in the next sequence, which introduces us to Kakarla Satyanarayana,[6] associating the representative of the state from the beginning with violence, although his complicity, even initiative, in the acts of violence is established for the spectator only somewhat later. The governor, therefore, appears throughout the film as the embodiment of the law. Interestingly, the film constantly represents violence as being generated *within* the established political system itself, its main agents shown as the governor and his mercenary, or the police who capture and torture the hero. In this, *Kaadalan* differs considerably from Mani Ratnam's *Roja* (1992) and *Bombay* (1995), with which it engages in a kind of intertextual polemics, and which portray the perpetrators of violence as anti-national terrorists or communalists (*Roja*), or as misguided fundamentalists (*Bombay*). The significance of such a portrayal in *Roja* and *Bombay* lies in their understanding of violence as existing outside of signification, or as disruptive of signification. Violence in this scheme is seen as senseless, outside reason or the rule of law.[7] In *Kaadalan*, however, violence is internal to the signifying system and integral to the rule of law (in Lacanian/Zizekian terms, the obscenity of law), to the maintenance of the state, just as it is integral to the processes of liberalization and globalization which are helping to fashion the new Indian citizen-consumer. The figure of the governor and his actions also show the links between law, state and sexuality: the state embodies the terrifying patriarchal law, the law that provokes/forbids/dissimulates violence, as well as the obscene law of enjoyment, which is the inseparable superegoic underside of the public law.[8]

To understand the specific ways in which *Kaadalan* reorganizes the idiom of cinema in India, and popular cinema in particular, we could contrast it with the films of Mani Ratnam, who, especially since *Roja* and *Bombay*, has contributed so significantly to the articulation of a near-hegemonic middle-class neo-nationalism. The achievement of a film-maker like Mani Ratnam lies in his ability to draw on the representational idioms of the 1970s modernist-realist cinema as well as the Hindi and south Indian popular cinema, in fusing the naturalism of the former with the song-and-dance entertainment afforded by the latter, producing this fusion of idioms through a highly sophisticated technical apparatus. What emerges in Mani Ratnam's films, therefore, is an aesthetic that is post-national-modern (that seems to revel in displaying and drawing attention to its technical virtuosity, especially in its camera-work, unlike the earlier realist cinema) and a politics of (upper caste/middle class) neo-nationalism. We shall have occasion to return to Mani Ratnam in the course of our argument.

Clearly, a film like *Kaadalan* is made possible by the techno-aesthetic space created by the Mani Ratnam team, but it seems to signal a different set of political possibilities. Most importantly, these possibilities have to do with the way in which an urban popular culture, mediated by a global televisual culture but implicitly marked as dalit, is contrasted time and again in the film with the upper class/caste cultural space. This contrast, we argue, displaces on the one hand the modernist opposition of 'folk' to upper caste which has been so culturally thematic in India, and on the other hand creates the possibility for the imbrication, and resignification, of dalit and upper-caste cultural spaces. The congruence of dalit and the urban popular points here, it would seem, to the unmistakable modernity of urban dalit cultural politics today, a recognition of which should confound attempts to relegate caste to the immutable realm of 'tradition'. Coming as it does after Mani Ratnam's political melodrama, *Roja*, and as it were coming into the signifying space created by him, *Kaadalan* nevertheless overturns Mani Ratnam's neo-nationalism and transforms his space and modes of signification. What, then, could we describe as the specific 'work' of *Kaadalan*? It consists of bringing together the signifying systems of fashion and violence in a sustained exploration of the body as both site and signifier of a larger process of resignification that is underway in the space of contemporary politics. The fixity and stability of existing referents and codes—whether they belong to the social, e.g. caste, or to the aesthetic—are being dissolved today; the re-elaboration or even re-embedding of these codes and referents do not necessarily indicate one direction or one political possibility. Thus caste today is undergoing a process of re-elaboration in such a way that 'dalit' is not so much the name for a fixed social identity but a signifying space for a new politics. Again, the question is not one of endorsing, in the old fashion, the 'good' object (proletariat, women, subaltern), but of creating spaces for inscribing new desires and generating new actions—a more critical and risky task than endorsing an *a priori* political correctness (protect the environment, support feminist 'issues,' uncover the popular as resistance, etc.).

Violence, therefore, is seen as part of the signifying process narrativized by the film, rather than something that cannot be represented. Thus, the contemporary despair about the inability to represent, expressed in particular with regard to communalism or 'communal riots' (these phenomena being an index of the 'sense-lessness' of our time), and manifested not only in filmic practice but in areas such as historiography, is nowhere to be found in *Kaadalan*, which explicitly thematizes the body as the very site on which violence of different kinds can be represented. The neo-modernist—which includes the left as well as the liberal response today—outrage (we almost hear the voice of Conrad/Kurtz saying 'The horror, the horror') at the unutterability of violence—more often than not coded as 'communal' violence—detracts attention, it seems to us, from two crucial contemporary forms of violence that *Kaadalan* is able to address, and negotiate: around the question of caste, and the question of liberalization/globalization. Import-antly, therefore, violence also gets resignified here. Not only does the film do this, it actually inscribes on the bodies of its protagonists the intersections of these two questions. And the inscription, we would like to suggest, is made possible by the film's refusal of a 'natural' body, by its holding a part of body as referent from body as signifier, by its dramatization of the processes by which the body signifies. The most striking illustration of this refusal is in the 'Mukkaala Muqabla' song-sequence which we have already analysed, where the hero's face, hands and ankles are shot away but he (or more accurately, his clothes) can continue to dance.

*Kaadalan*'s ability to draw attention to its modes of enunciation shows the film-maker's awareness that the cinematic process of signification, as Christian Metz would have it, is reflexive rather than deictic.[9] Here, too, this film is markedly different from those made by Mani Ratnam, who short-circuits the signified by collaps-ing the referent and the signifier in such a way as to naturalize his protagonists. Nowhere is this more clearly seen, and nowhere more explicitly comparable, as in Mani Ratnam's production of the consumer-citizen (*Geetanjali, Roja*) or of the patriot-lover (*Roja, Bombay*). As argued elsewhere, these films present their protagonists precisely in their 'garb' as consumers, so that they appear to us as 'real' and 'natural', the historical processes that fed into their formation becoming invisible in the asserted and assertive contem-poraneity of the filmic narrative.[10] The techno-aesthetic in Mani Ratnam thus contributes to the reification of social life. The process of signification is given fixity so that the suturing effect can come about more effectively. One of the attractions of Mani Ratnam's films for the urban middle-classes—yuppies—is precisely those 'cinematic moments' and diegesis that resemble Hollywood realist melodramas, as for example in the deployment of the newsroom, the TV, and the newspaper in *Roja* and *Bombay*.

In contrast, *Kaadalan* deploys a striking self-reflexivity. Even while presenting to us the euphoria of consumerism, as in the 'Take it Easy, Urvasi' song sequence, the film points to the explicit fashioning of the new consumer by staging the song like an advertisement, and posing its protagonists against advertising hoardings. Where Mani Ratnam's films naturalize upper-caste, middle-class privilege, *Kaadalan* renders the markers of such privilege mobile, making them available for interrogation and resignification. One example of such mobility is the wearing of blue jeans by the hero's sidekick Vasant (played by the comedian Vadivelu); the film focuses on Vasant's jeans during the 'Urvasi' song, part of the significance of this apparel being that Vasant is wearing his jeans on top of a 'traditional' loincloth, a matter of great humiliation for him when the governor's security guards make him strip to establish that he is not hiding anything under his trousers.[11] Blue jeans before the era of liberalization in India have been a marker of westernized modernity and a privilege of upper-class-caste youth, and part of the present-day transformation of the south Indian urban landscape can be seen in the appropriation of blue denim by young lower-caste-class men. The male dalit body is fashioned in the film as a 'modern' body, and our attention is sought to be drawn to the process of its fashioning. In contrast, the modern body in Mani Ratnam's films is naturalized as the middle-class, upper-caste body (as in the representation of the body of the actor Arvind Swamy in *Roja* and *Bombay*, for instance, where one sees the convergence of the MTV body and the anti-Mandal body) whereas in *Kaadalan* this naturalness is prised apart, and the MTV body is foregrounded as the actor Prabhudeva's dalit body.[12] In a short sequence on the beach where Prabhu and his friends are talking about Shruti, one of the young men says to Prabhu that the (upper-caste) heroine will not be interested in him because he doesn't look like Mani Ratnam's hero Arvind Swamy. Towards the end of the film, there is a moment of wicked humour when the dark-complexioned, slender and bearded Prabhu in dark glasses and baseball cap is passed off to the villagers (by Shruti's grandparents who are trying to reunite ti : lovers against their son, the governor's wishes) as the fair, plump, clean-shaven archetypal south Indian film hero of the 1960s, N.T. Rama Rao, whose film *Lava-Kusha* is then shown to them by Vasant posing as a producer.

The banality of the plot of *Kaadalan* is one of its important features. The film's deployment of the spatialized synecdochic representations subordinates the diegetic temporality to the dynamic temporality of the time-image. The unfolding of the plot takes place almost as a succession of time-images and these images are constructed around spaces or sites. Spaces of very different kinds dominate almost all the important scenes, especially those that construct a synecdochic representation of the film's themes: streets, college, dance-school, stadium, temple, forest, interiors of homes, the governor's residence. It is at first sight puzzling why the camera frames these sites sometimes lingeringly but often relentlessly—even when an action is taking place, the background stands out in bold relief—until we realize that these are all sites of potential conflict. The only exception to this is the home/the interior of the hero, which is a place where the hero's desire and phantasy are nurtured, where his relationship with his father is presented as a bantering, playful, supportive friendship. In a sense, the father is complicit in his son's desire, as demonstrated in the 'hook' song-sequence or in his urging the young man to learn classical dance in order to win the heroine's love.

It is indeed the hero's desire for his phantasy woman that sets the narrative going. The scene where that desire is first presented takes place in the hero's study, where his friend Vasant is presenting his typology of women. The camera lingers on this interior, lit in luminous yellow, reddish brown and red—in which we see a poster of Chaplin above the table, and a table-lamp shaped like an old phonogram, the lamp calling attention to its own luminosity as Vasant keeps playing with the switch. The hero outlines the phantasy features of his ideal woman; he has in fact outlined those features in his sketch-book. The framing of this shot clearly illustrates the functioning of what we have been calling the spatialized synecdoche and its ability to draw in different or heterogeneous modes of enunciation: by setting the Chaplin-figure—the semiotic body *par excellence* in the history of cinema—in a relationship with the table-lamp shaped as a phonogram, the film both folds in the temporality of cinematic enunciation within itself and signals its own preoccupation with the semiotics of the body; and the luminosity of the phonogram signalling its restaging of the relationship between sight and sound. The auditory signifier is here subordinate to the visual signifier. So the 'before-present' in this time-image refers not obviously to the previous scene or shot but to the cinematic past; it is as though the film is audaciously returning to the bodily semiotics of the silent era with the sound and colour added, both as attitudes of the body itself.

Superimposed on this enunciation, which draws in the past of the cinema itself, is the genesis of the hero's desire or phantasy. This, then, is the real beginning of the film, although already the college has been marked as the site of conflict and political mobilization, the hero being the president of the students' union. The next site—the site of political power—is the governor's residence, in which the hero makes his entry, accompanied by Vasant and a professor of physics from the college. And from here onwards all the spaces that the hero enters turn into sites of conflict or struggle. It is during this visit to the governor's residence that the hero sets eyes on his phantasy figure, Shruti.

The very first song-sequence in the film, 'Urvasi, Urvasi . . .', demonstrates clearly both the problematic of spatialization and the synecdochic structure that governs the film. The hero, Prabhu, and his sidekick, Vasant, disguised under *burqa*s, get into a 'ladies' special' bus filled with girl-students. They are discovered and slapped around; then they break into 'Urvasi, Urvasi, . . . take it easy policy'. As the bus traverses the cityscape of Madras, the dancing provides the camera an opportunity to revel in its cinemascope spatializing shots and to encompass the landmarks, such as buildings—both colonial and contemporary—and objects such as other modes of transportation, for example, the bullock-cart. Halfway through the sequence, there comes about a fantastic and phantasmatic transformation: the already vivid colours and upbeat music take on a different hue and timbre, and the ordinary bus turns into a veritable post-modern one made of transparent glass. This almost phantasmagoric change is registered through the stunned faces of an old man and a child, and through the sound of a wailing voice which is distinctly middle-eastern. If we see this 'phantasi' (*sic*) scene as again synecdochically spatializing the different signifiers—in this case, the urban space as we have known it with its sturdy buses ('modernity') coexisting with the bullock-carts ('tradition') against colonial buildings, slums, and modern structures—we can then reinterpret what appears as phantasmagoric as precisely our perceptions of the rapid changes occurring before our eyes (or the eyes of the old man and the child), exemplified, especially in the southern cities (Madras, Bangalore, Hyderabad) by the profusion of what are indeed called 'high-tech' buses, with their stylish architecture—huge inclining windshields, collapsible doors, back-engines, and pulsating colours. Even as the body is being transformed by the rhythms of rap or Michael Jackson's dancing or Jackie Chan's kung fu, and as the perceptual apparatus is assaulted, mediatized and retrained by Cable TV, Hollywood films (the hero has just seen *Jurassic Park*), so is the phenomenology of objects, sights and sounds in space, a space which is itself undergoing vast mutations. The song-sequence begins with the shot of a Muslim man selling birds in cages and the sound of the *azaan*. It develops into a dance which is Prabhudeva's version of rap, and a song which is the composer A.R. Rahman's special blend of techno-pop. Each frame of the song, in its characteristic spatialized shot that foregrounds the whole frame as it were, represents what we might now feel justified in calling the mediatized body against a background (which might accurately be termed the foreground!) of 'liberalized', or 'structurally adjusted', space.

The complex hermeneutic situation that the film mobilizes through its synecdochic representational structure negotiates, not surprisingly, the dominant idioms of cinema in India. How does one characterize the institution of Indian cinema? Madhava Prasad has argued persuasively that it is 'an institution that is part of the continuing struggle within India over the form of the state.'[13] In this fundamental sense, Indian cinema is 'about' imagining the conflicts and contestation over that form as well as an attempt to shape the form itself. The dominant textual form of Indian cinema, then, is structured by the allegory of the state. The production of this form, Madhava Prasad argues further, is marked by 'the heterogeneous form of manufacture' (SCH: 17). That is to say, various elements in any given film tend to be more or less autonomous, for example, lyric/music, the song-sequence, fight-sequence, subplot involving comedians, etc., with the story-line itself having the status of a component, rather than being a centralizing force as in the classical Hollywood form of manufacture. With the post-Independence emergence of film-makers like Satyajit Ray and the imbrication of their filmic practice with Nehruvian nationalism,[14] the 'good' Indian film, or the 'art' film comes into being in the late 1950s, funded by the state-owned Film Finance Corporation. By the 1970s, the realist film is modulated into what Madhava Prasad calls the 'developmentalist aesthetic' of the films of Shyam Benegal and others, which serve the crucial function of distancing for their urban audience the feudal set-up which is now realistically 'othered' as the rural, the folk, etc. While on the one hand, the 1970s are marked by the rise of the new realist Indian cinema, the period also sees, on the other hand, the emergence of the avant-garde film-makers like Kumar Shahani or Mani Kaul who innovate in terms of film-form. The two currents appear to converge in a director like Mani Ratnam in the 1990s, who combines them with the idiom of commercial cinema. Certain avant-garde techniques such as the frontality of framing seem to reappear in Mani Ratnam via his training in advertising, bearing out the validity of Andreas Huyssen's suggestion that the modernist avant-garde's formal innovations are taken up by and become part of the vocabulary 'of the culture industry.[15]

One of the most remarkable things about *Kaadalan* is the major shift it negotiates in filmic idiom. This is not to say that the shift is solely accomplished by this film and none other, but only to draw attention to its achievement in working through the technical and referential possibilities of cinema itself even as it represents, or rather interprets for us, our new cultural-political landscape. In the post-Independence cinema and theatre scene, we have on the one hand the modernist Benegals and Karnads who dramatize the dichotomy between upper class/caste and 'folk' (suggesting a revitalization of the former by the latter, as in the play *Hayavadana*, or the film *Ankur*),[16] and on the other hand a figure like the popular Kannada hero Rajkumar, whose most commercially successful films (like *Bangaarada Manushya*) represent the good rustic triumphing over the villains from the city. Both sorts of films, it can now be seen, contribute to the shaping of a national(ist) aesthetic, especially in setting up the crucial opposition between urban and rural, privileging the latter in a compensatory and patronizing gesture, all the more striking since it is produced by the enormous urban technical apparatus of the movie industry. The gesture, as Madhava Prasad has argued, is a necessary one for the consolidation of the nation-state, which creates the hierarchy between modern and feudal, or urban and rural, by the act of distancing (SCH: 350). This hierarchy, we suggest, is one that is disturbed by a film like *Kaadalan*.

One area the film fails to problematize, or make available for major resignification, is that of gender. It is almost as though the film's destabilization of the male markers of caste-class privilege centrally depends on the representation of the upper-class-caste woman. As cinematic desired object, the body of the actress Nagma, who plays Shruti, signals the characteristics (light skin, brownish hair, light eyes, well-nourished arms and legs) of the typical Hindi movie heroine. One of the tasks of the film seems to be to present the dalit male as culturally desirable to the upper-caste woman, a process in which the dalit woman as romantic partner becomes quite invisible. She can appear only parodically, as in Vasant's drag attire during the peta-rap sequence when she pretends to be a shy village maiden; or appear (as in the motorbike chase sequence) in her cotton sari as the bearer of rustic ethnicity, only to have her sari appropriated by the heroine who exchanges for it her denim skirt. Clearly, *Kaadalan* like the Mani Ratnam films is a post-Mandal phenomenon, but whereas the latter produce the effect of what we may call after Madhava Prasad class-caste endogamy, this film sets out to resignify the upper-caste, anti-Mandal, anti-dalit woman so that her antagonism turns into acceptance, even romantic love. We use 'anti-Mandal' as a shorthand term to refer to the sort of middle-class, upper-caste female subjectivity that emerged during the anti-Mandal agitation of 1990. It was a subjectivity that formed itself in opposition to the dalit male who was the pro-reservationist imaged as taking away the jobs of the upper-caste men who were the rightful partners of the women of their class-caste. We see Shruti in *Kaadalan* as the anti-Mandalite college girl who is the visual representation of the women who took to the streets against the Mandal Commission's recommendations. Although there may be no direct mention of Mandal in *Kaadalan*, in our opinion the film cannot be read without the interpretative frame of caste politics that has thrown up some of the most significant political questions of our time. To read the film solely in terms of the auteur's intention

and ideological predispositions may severely limit our understanding of what we have called the 'effects' or 'work' of *Kaadalan*.
The desirability of the dalit male is produced by the dress codes
of globalization (Prabhu's craving for a new pair of sneakers, his
trendy clothes) as well as by the male's demonstrated cultural
prowess, represented by the film as his ability to dance, whether it
is 'peta-rap' or Bharatanatyam. In fact, the film's focus on dance is
an important component of its resignification of the body in terms
of the politics of caste. Observe the representations of 'Indian
classical dance', here Bharatanatyam, in the film. The heroine Shruti
is urban, westernized, ostensibly deracinated. But she is shown as
claiming the space of 'tradition' through her dancing skill. The
depiction of her dance school, Natyalaya, bears a close resemblance
to the famous Kalakshetra in Madras, suggesting *Kaadalan*'s attempt
to interrogate the formation of a nationalist dance tradition in the
1930s (the figure of Rukmini Devi Arundale is central here, as is
the theosophist Annie Besant and the Indian National Congress)
when the lower-caste, *devadasi* dance form *sadir* was transformed
into the brahminical Bharatanatyam, the practitioners of the latter
inventing a suitably upper-caste genealogy for the dance which then
became imbricated with the nationalist conception of Indian
womanhood as chaste, pure and genteel.[17] Interestingly, even as this
nationalist upper-caste aesthetic emerges in southern India, in particular in Madras Presidency, the Self-Respect Movement of Periyar
Ramasami Naicker is not only creating a space for the assertion of
lower-caste identities but also challenging the nationalist conception
of the nation in terms of caste, region and language. It is tempting,
then, to look at the contest over Bharatanatyam in *Kaadalan* as
not being unrelated to these specific historical moments, as suggesting in synecdochic fashion the historical conflicts that are being
rearticulated in the present. The peta-rap sequence is a vivid presentation of the Deleuzian time-image which spatializes temporal
conflicts, and shows the past inhering in the present. The peta-rap
is introduced into the Natyalaya lessons by Vasant and Prabhu to
alleviate their boredom and attract Shruti's attention. Vasant glosses
it for an American student in the dance school as a combination of
'American rap' and 'our local drum'. It is indeed a combination of
southern Indian 'folk' singing and globalized rap music, and Prabhu
and Vasant's bawdy dance evokes astonishment, embarrassment,

some participation, and finally Shruti's outraged injunction to 'Stop it!'.

Like the other sites Prabhu enters, the dance school too is turned into a site of conflict when the hero arrives there in pursuit of his object of desire. This is also the site of Past as Tradition, and conflict erupts here almost immediately, between the distinctions of Tradition embodied in the bodies of the dancers, especially Shruti, and the newly mediatized body which also carries with it the old lower-caste-class folk impulses exemplified in the peta-rap sequence. The synecdochic representations of the dance school then opens up the consensus embodied in its site as Tradition to contestation and new signification. The very presence of the inappropriate bodies of Prabhu and Vasant before the signifier of Tradition and its imperatives for the hero in the form of a demand from his love object that he respect Tradition, enables this particular representation to again synchronize the past into present conflict or antagonism. The temporality of the past as tradition is spatialized and the ground prepared for the next synecdochic representation of subsequent sites—forest ('nature') and the temple (sacred space, or tradition as eternalized present)—which now begin to draw in and explicate the conflicts marked in the earlier sites.

After the heroine has scolded Prabhu and Vasant for their display of 'peta-rap' which she says has spoiled the sanctity of Natyalaya, Prabhu on his father's advice sets out to learn Bharatanatyam. This he does almost entirely by himself, without a guru, without entering into a long period of apprenticeship, without the obeisance to the gods that is an integral part of the classical dance tradition. And when he has mastered the dance form, he gains entry to the heavily guarded mansion of the heroine and dances for her, his footwork creating her portrait on the flour-powder he has strewn on the floor. After this display, Prabhu seems to abandon his newly learned art, for we do not see him ever dancing Bharatanatyam in the rest of the film, as if to suggest that his achievement was meant to signify not a change of heart, or a change in artistic direction for him, but rather a demystification of classical dance, a delinking of it from its gender-caste connotations in the national imagery.

Thus the hero succeeds through the semiotic prowess of his body in responding to the imperative addressed to him through his love-object and assimilates—or more accurately perhaps, learns how to *signify*—Bharatanatyam, winning her love in the process. Now follows the escapade of the couple on Prabhu's motorbike, as they take the road to Chidambaram where Shruti and the Natyalaya students are to perform in the temple. En route, the hero and heroine are forced to spend a night in the forest. Here the hero turns out to be completely 'at home'; he deftly makes toys and dishes with leaves, rustles up a meal, teaches the heroine how to brush her teeth with a finger. Although the heroine embodies Tradition, she has no links with the ways of the past; the hero, on the other hand, despite his immersion in globalized mass culture, preserves in his body the skills of a past which is still the non-contemporaneous present. The body of the woman which has always been made to bear or carry tradition and past is here resignified: the tradition she claims to practise is a tradition she has appropriated; 'nature' is not a signifier with which her body is associated. These paradoxical inversions and displacements are foregrounded in the synecdochic representation of the night in the forest.

The dance scene in the temple never quite takes place—the governor has marked the place for one of his 'destabilizing' terroristic bombings, which is why he had forbidden Shruti from undertaking the trip with the Natyalaya students. Informed about Shruti's escapade with Prabhu, the governor has the temple suddenly swarming with helicopter, commandos, bomb-defusion squad and sniffer dogs. The dance is interrupted, the bomb 'found' and defused, and Prabhu's resistance brushed aside, Shruti is whisked off in the helicopter. If so far Prabhu's entry onto any site sets off a disturbance or conflict at that site, now the conflict becomes polarized: the law (public/patriarchal) on the one side, and on the other, the body of Prabhu as the source/agency/target of new signification as well as the violence of the state. The temple scene then retroactively reveals the governor's residence as a potential site of conflict—between the law—as the state as well as the patriarchal/brahminical order—and the agencies of new political/symbolic signification (let us remember that the hero first meets the governor as the president of the students' union); at the same time, the 'governor's residence' shows the resistance of the existing order—sites symbolizing institutions of all sorts—to the emergence of new signification, its attempt to block or arrest any attempt to make these sites resignify.

Although the governor is shown as involved in a despicable conspiracy to destabilize—another synecdochic framing of a site, this time the sacred banks of the Ganges at Kashi, the governor apparently appeasing his ancestors to the background sound of a Lata Mangeshkar devotional, but in fact conversing with a 'Swami' who has given money to the governor to precipitate destabilization. There are two ways of destabilizing a political situation—use the social power of money to arrest and silence political signification (a strategy which has obvious limitations) or destroy sites and agencies of signification, which according to the governor, is the cheaper, safer and more effective method. In a situation where, as the governor puts it, the Muslims are fighting the Hindus, Kannadigas are fighting the Tamils, and the Harijans are fighting the Brahmins, who will trace these terroristic acts of the state to the state?

The deeper significance of this, though, is that the state is shown to have withdrawn from its function of mediating the social conflicts and political antagonisms; no longer able to control the signifying space of its sovereign territory, it is bent on destroying the 'work' (colleges, temples, hospitals) of which it was part and guardian. What may appear as the opposition animating the narrative surface of the film—terroristic state and freedom from state—is in truth a desire for reconceptualizing the polity.

After Shruti's rescue from the temple, conflict erupts at the governor's residence: Shruti submits to but also defies the patriarchal/political law of the father, and wants to run away with the hero. The scene in which she meets Prabhu is set in a spectacular stadium—presumably indexing an agonistic space regulated by fair play. The hero, confused by the events he himself has initiated, barely has time to collect himself when the commandos set upon him. There unfolds a 'spectacle' against the background of the stadium—its shapes and colours as vividly present as the hero's martial arts skills. This confrontation with the state ends with the hero finally subdued and relegated to the police torture chamber and the heroine confined to her room. The torture scene again foregrounds the body—this time as the target of torture, the state's desperate and futile attempt to reduce body to its materiality and eliminate it as the source of signification. Interestingly, both the agents of the state—the doctor who performs the virginity test on the heroine, and Prabhu's chief torturer in jail—are women, perhaps indicative of the strength of patriarchy and the rule of law, a rule that deploys women as its visible enforcers. The two parallel female figures—Prabhu's mother and Shruti—are presented by and large as ineffectual, as having no real bond with their children. It is Prabhu's father who is the tender, loving parent (witness his bathing his adult son, dancing with him in the 'hook' song sequence, letting him cry on his shoulder), and the mother's customary role in the narrative is displaced.

Shruti forces her father to release the hero, by embarrassing the governor at a party he has hosted. This is followed by the 'Mukkaala Muqabla' sequence. The next sequence takes us to the village home of the governor in Andhra Pradesh where Shruti is left in the care of her grandparents. Again the hero and Vasant enter this space, and once again conflict surfaces, although with some unexpected turns. The grandparents, once without doubt powerful figures of traditional authority, are shown as clown-like figures; their power too has been absorbed by the state. Therefore these figures and spaces are again open to resignification; and indeed the grandparents enter into complicity with Prabhu and Shruti, taking them to ancient temple grounds, where the grandfather literally manipulates a statue to confirm the hero's love for Shruti. Once again, Prabhu's entry turns this space—the palatial ancient home, the vintage car, but in the outhouse high-tech equipment that Malli the villain uses to keep in touch with the governor—into one of conflict. The hero's entry into the village is orchestrated by the grandfather; Prabhu pretends to be the actor N.T. Rama Rao, and in fact a filming of NTR's old hit *Lava-Kusha* is arranged. Vasant organizes the screening, savouring his role as producer, and both we as well as the audience within the film, watch the shot framing NTR as Rama enunciating the law of just rule—the just rule does not take into account pride, friendship and love, we hear him utter. This shot again draws in, enfolds and ironizes a cinematic moment within its own synecdochic enunciative space, both justice and the legality of rule having been ironically articulated through the figure of the terrorist-governor.

It is in this ancestral village home of his lover that the hero, (playing a video-game!), accidentally discovers the governor's conspiracy. Prabhu swings into action and foils the attempted bombing of a hospital, mobilizing in the process students from the medical college to rescue the patients. Maintaining its concern with the body with gruesome consistency, the mutilated body of the terrorist Malli electrocutes the body of the governor; but the destruction of these bodies too cannot resolve the problem until the space occupied by them, by the law in both its aspects (obscene/punitive and respectable/benevolent), is transformed.

The hero's desire—synecdochically framed and enfolded in the temporality of cinema and media—and its trajectory then initiates the process of resignification and politicization. His love makes him enter spaces, sites and institutions that had excluded him and his entry opens up for contestation and interrogation, law, figures of authority, spaces of culture and tradition (the sites of ideological reproductions). The trope of love is drawn into processes and structures that do not remain external to it. In this *Kaadalan* explicitly positions itself against the dominant politics of piety that has come to govern the discourse of secularism: namely, how secularism of love can engender love of secularism. This piety is ultimately what a film like Mani Ratnam's *Bombay* sets out to secure.

The last scene unfolds under a hoarding with the message 'No Problem' with a freeze of the hero and heroine—a repeat shot of an earlier song-sequence—in a dancing gesture. It is, it seems to us, an ironic ending, and what is being ironized is precisely the enunciative message of the advertising industry. As our analysis so far should have made clear, this ironic gesture is meant to signal a distantiation and disidentification from the signifier 'fashion', in the same way as in an earlier sequence, the hero, who is also the president of the students' union, gets his class-mates to repaint the college walls which are covered over by the slogans and posters of his own election campaign. We are shown a couple of printed posters with Prabhu's face on them being torn down. And in a fleeting gesture, the hero himself paints over the slogan 'Vote for Prabhu'. This gesture too, one could argue, mobilizing as it does the collective energies of the students, indicates a politics of disidentification, disidentification from the politics of iconicity and the violence that it engenders. This is important because the effectivity of political signifiers depends on their ability to mobilize identification, which they do by promising unity and wholeness. The latter always prove to be temporary and phantasmatic, thereby setting in a process of disinvestment, disidentification and political paralysis.

(Think of the fate of the political signifier 'socialism' or, to take a recent example, 'Ayodhya'.) 'But', as Judith Butler asks, 'does politicization always need to overcome *dis*identification? What are the possibilities of politicizing *dis*identification, this experience of *misrecognition*, this uneasy sense of standing under a sign to which one does and does not belong?'[18] That is indeed the political question that *Kaadalan* leaves us with: the hero and heroine standing under the sign—enunciated by and standing in for the forces, the apparatus, the institutions that are dominating our visual/social/political space—which says 'No Problem'. Clearly all the problems, all the political problems, begin in this disjunctive, disidentificatory space that the film has helped clear for resignification.

## Notes

1. *Kaadalan* (Tamil) (1994), directed by Shankar, produced by K.T. Kunjumon, music by A.R. Rahman. Dubbed into Telugu as *Premikudu* and into Hindi as *Humse Hai Muqabla*.

2. As Christian Metz ['The Impersonal Enunciation, or the Site of the Film', *New Literary History*, 22 (1991)] argues: 'Enunciation is the semiological act by which some part of a text talks to us about this text as an act' (p. 754). Metz rightly claims that the cinematic enunciation is reflexive rather than deictic. 'All figures of enunciation consist in metadiscursive folds of cinematic instances piled on top of each other' (p. 769). And yet Metz seems confused about how to clarify the nature of cinematic enunciation without inheriting the anthropomorhpism of a linguistics of deictics. He inherits this confusion, or so it seems to us, from the linguistic monism of semiology. Gilles Deleuze, who opts for Peircean semiotics precisely to avoid this confusion, offers a diagnosis of the confusion inherited by a semiology of cinema: 'We . . . have to define, not semiology, but "semiotics", as the system of images and signs independent of language in general. When we recall that linguistics is only part of semiotics, we no longer mean, as for semiology, that there are languages without a language system, but that the language system only exists in its reaction to a *non-language-material* that it transforms. This is why utterances and narrations are not a given of visible images, but a consequence which flows from this reaction' (emphasis in the original). *Cinema 2: The Time-Image*, Minneapolis: Minnesota University Press, 1989, p. 29.

This has implications for how to read or theorize the film. The Metzian position tends to reduce the semiotic enunciation of cinema into an optics, on the one hand, and into quasi-linguistics narratology, on the other. On the former reduction, see Joan Copjec, *Read My Desire: Lacan against the Historicists*, Cambridge, MA: MIT Press, 1994, pp. 21–38.

Our approach here has been positioned against formalism: the punishing shot by shot analysis which describes the diegetic movement, the different kind of shots, editing, etc.—which is an attempt to recontain the political, antagonistic meaning of the film. It would be unfortunate indeed if the impasses of narratology in literary studies were to be replicated in film theory. We prefer Deleuze's conception of film-theory as 'interference', rather than as 'application'. See Deleuze, *Cinema 2*, p. 280.

3. See Fredric Jameson, *The Geopolitical Aesthetics*, London: British Film Institute, 1992.

4. Deleuze's remarks (*Cinema 2*, pp. 188–203, 276) on the cinema of the body and its link to time-image—the image that presents time directly as distinct from the movement-image which presents it indirectly—are especially illuminating in this context: 'But there is another pole to the body, to mount a camera on the body, takes on a different sense: it is no longer a matter of following and trailing everyday body, but of making it pass through a ceremony, of introducing it into a glass cage or a crystal, of imposing a carnival or a masquerade on it which makes it into a grotesque body, but also brings out of it a gracious and glorious body . . .' (p. 190).

'The attitude of the body is like a time-image, the one which puts the before and after in the body, the series of time . . .' (p. 195) '. . . there are now only attitudes of bodies, corporeal postures forming series, and a gest which connects them together as limit' (p. 276).

5. For a discussion of 'frontality', see Ashish Rajadhyaksha, 'The Phalke Era: Conflict of Traditional Form and Modern Technology', in T. Niranjana, P. Sudhir and V. Dhareshwar (eds), *Interrogating Modernity: Culture and Colonialism in India*, Calcutta: Seagull Books, 1993.

6. The name is an unmistakably Telugu one, and is common to both the Tamil and Telugu versions of the film. In the Tamil version, the Telugu Governor who is trying to destabilize the state is an obvious reference to how the AIADMK, which was in power until the 1996 elections, and to which producer Kunjumon is close, sees the Telugu Governor of Tamil Nadu, Chenna Reddy.

7. See for example, Gyanendra Pandey, 'In Defence of the Fragment: Writing About Hindu-Muslim Riots in India Today', *Economic and Political Weekly*, annual number, 26(11–12), March 1991: 559–72.

8. On the two sides of the law, see Slavoj Zizek, *The Metastases of Enjoyment*, London: Verso, 1994, ch. 3.

The scene where the heroine Shruti, after having spent the night in the forest with the hero, is subjected to a virginity test is clearly a scene of violation, and the agency of that violation is the father, who has ordered the doctor to conduct the test just as he has ordered the torture of the hero. Shruti resists her father's obscene injunction by throwing a slimy green chemical on his face, but eventually she is subdued and penetrated, an act portrayed in the gruesome cinematic tradition of depicting rape scenes, with only the heroine's face—up front—registering the violation.

9. See Metz, 'The Impersonal Enunciation . . .' .

10. See Tejaswini Niranjana, 'Cinema, Femininity and the Economy of Consumption', *Economic and Political Weekly* 26(43), 1991.

11. In this scene, Vasant, who is part of a delegation that has gone to invite the governor to participate in a college-day function, is wearing trousers and shirt, and a tie.

12. It might be worth re-emphasizing here that when we speak of the actor's 'dalit body' we do not refer to any 'natural' or 'self-evident' physiognomy, but instead draw attention to how the representational structures of the film continually *position* the character, and to how—given our present political conjuncture—these structures may be read.

13. Madhava Prasad, 'The State and Culture: Hindi Cinema in the Passive Revolution', Ph.D. dissertation, University of Pittsburgh, 1994 (unpublished), p. 3. Cited in the text as SCH.

14. See the articles on Ray by Geeta Kapur, 'Cultural Creativity in the First Decade: The Example of Satyajit Ray' (pp. 17–49), and Ashish Raja-dhyaksha, 'Satyajit Ray, Ray's Films, and Ray-movie' (pp. 7–16), in *Journal of Arts and Ideas,* nos. 23–4, January 1993.

15. Andreas Huyssen, *After the Great Divide: Modernism, Mass Culture, Postmodernism,* Bloomington: Indiana University Press, 1986, p. 170.

16. The 'folk' emerges in nationalist modernism, however, processed through an upper caste, urban aesthetic.

17. See Susie Tharu and K.Lalita, 'Empire, Nation and Literary Text', in Tejaswini Niranjana, P. Sudhir and Vivek Dhareshwar (eds), *Interrogating Modernity: Culture and Colonialism in India,* Calcutta: Seagull Books, 1993. Also the unpublished research of Srividya Natarajan, Department of English, University of Hyderabad.

18. Judith Butler, *Bodies That Matter,* London: Routledge, 1993, p. 219. The question of politicizing disidentification, raised so sharply by Judith Butler, is an important one in contemporary India. The dominant assumption is that political mobilization requires identification with a political signifier. We need to problematize this requirement, and not only in the case where disidenti-fication has set in.

# 8

# Avenging Women in Indian Cinema

## LALITHA GOPALAN

T HAT THERE HAS been an escalation of violence in contemporary Indian cinema is now a well-worn cliché. *The Illustrated Weekly of India* cashed in on this truism by publishing a roundtable discussion among film-makers, critics, and stars that explored the 'correlation between violence in films and violence in society and the various implications of the nexus.'[1] The discussion attentively dwells on film as a mass cultural product, but fails to offer any specific link between a particular film or genre and its effects on society. What also remains unacknowledged in this discussion is how these films feed off the crisis of legitimacy of the Indian state, a crisis that unleashed an open display of the state's coercive powers and precipitated most visibly after the state of emergency between 1975 and 1977. Even if it is debatable that the state of emergency is the origin for the crisis of legitimacy of the Indian state, at the very least we can speculate that it did set into motion contestations between power *and* authority which have pressed upon a more thorough exploration of hegemony, citizenship, community, nationalism, and democracy in India. In short, discussions of violence have to consider how films replete with avenging women, gangsters, brutal police force, and vigilante closures stage some of the most volatile struggles over representations that shape

A version of this paper was presented at the South Asia Regional Studies, University of Pennsylvania and I have greatly benefited from all the thoughtful comments and challenging questions raised on that occasion. I wish to thank Robert Schumann, Sandhya Shetty, and Nalini Natrajan for their generous comments on previous drafts. Finally, thanks to Itty Abraham who has been there at every turn, offering his critical eye and support.

our public and private fantasies of national, communal, regional, and sexual identities.

With less programmatic overtones but, with a cinephile's nitpicking taste, Firoze Rangoonwala definitively names the decade between 1981 and 1992 'the age of violence'.[2] Assembling Hindi films from both 'parallel' cinema—Govind Nihalani's *Ardh Satya* (Half Truth, 1984)—and the commercial industry with vigilante resolutions, he identifies a marked shift towards escalating violence in this period. Rangoonwala, however, does not comment on the social impact of these films as the roundtable discussion tended to do, but directs his sharpest criticism towards popular cinema for having 'succumbed to a hackneyed formula'. Arguably, dismissing formula-ridden popular cinema, however hackneyed it may be, unwittingly grants it processes of standardization of cinematic codes and narratives and in turn, exorcises a widely held view that Indian cinema randomly picks up story-lines only to finally deliver a *masala* film.

M. Rahman offers a less disparaging report of the Indian film industry in the 1980s by spotting the workings and consolidation of a new 'formula' in Hindi cinema inaugurated by N. Chandra's film *Pratighat* (Retribution) and soon followed by *Sherni, Khoon Bhari Mang, Khoon Bahaa Ganga Mein, Commando, Bhraschtachar,* and *Kali Ganga*. The common theme in these films, according to him, is their portrayal of women as 'hardened, cynical, vengeful creatures'.[3] Interviewing director N. Chandra and prominent actresses like Hema Malini, Dimple, and Rekha, who have all played avenging women, Rahman provides us alternative viewpoints from within the film industry. While director N. Chandra suggests that these violent films are generated in response to the voracious viewing habits of an audience that wishes to see something different from the stock male 'action' film, the actresses argue that screenplays with dominant and powerful women are a welcome break from stereotypical roles as submissive and dutiful mothers and wives.

Maithili Rao too, identifies an emerging trend in the industry, set off once again by N. Chandra's *Pratighat*, a trend that she calls the 'lady avengers'.[4] Arguing that they 'reflect the cultural schizophrenia in our society,' Rao reproaches these films for being 'hostile to female sexuality' and for passing themselves off as nothing more than 'victimization masquerading as female power'. This feminist spectator's critique neither figures in Rahman's interviews with directors and actresses nor does it address the tremendous box-office success of these films, however perverse they may be.

This essay assumes that these contradictory and diverse readings of aggressive women films are provocative enough to warrant another look at their visual and narrative goriness; another reading of these configurations of femininity and violence staged in these films, I argue, will uncover the contours of their appeal. My reading strategies employed in this essay are indelibly shaped by feminist film theory that argues for formal textual analysis as a means to grasp the articulation of sexual difference in cinema. Although it tends to focus heavily on Hollywood productions, feminist film theory remains useful for at least two reasons: first, deploying it for an analysis of Indian cinema interrogates a monolithic conception of 'national cinema' and opens the possibility of exploring points of contact with international film-making practices; secondly, its nuanced theorization of scopophilia and spectatorship holds up extremely well for the films discussed here. Despite a general move to place Indian cinema within international film-making practices, I do want to argue provisionally at this point that any Indianness we attribute to these cinemas lies in the various ways censorship regulations of the Indian state shape and influence cinematic representations; we must acknowledge and theorize the presence of the state when discussing the relationship between films and spectators.

Tailing the critical reception of these films is the frequent use of the term 'formula', which is bandied about to belittle the structures of repetition between films and only tangentially accounts for the viewer's pleasure. This essay explores how it may be equally possible that we are not only drawn to the visceral images in these films, but also the various circuits of inter-textual relays between and among them. Redrawn in these terms, I find it pertinent to call on the theoretically more viable concept of 'genre' which allow us to place both industry and spectator stereophonically: the industry's suggestion that these films are different from male action films, juxtaposed alongside critical evaluation which may condemn these films for cunningly representing female victims as vigilantes. In other words, only genre simultaneously addresses the industry's investment in standardized narratives for commercial success on the one hand,

and the spectator's pleasure in genre films with their stock narratives structured around repetition and difference on the other. While culling production details from the industry to verify the spawning of genres is a legitimate line of inquiry, I employ textual analysis of different films to unravel the structuring of repetition and difference and firmly demonstrate the workings of a genre.

Pruning Rahman's loose cluster of films around the figure of the 'dominant woman' where *Sherni* (The Lioness, 1988)—a film closer to the bandit genre—and *Zakmi Aurat* (Wounded Women, 1988)— a film closer to the police genre—are grouped together, we can isolate a genre of films I will call, following Maithili Rao, 'avenging women'. A standard narrative obtains in the following manner: Films open around family settings which appear 'happy' and 'normal' according to Hindi film conventions, but with a difference: there is a marked absence of dominant paternal figures. The female protagonist is always a working woman with a strong presence on screen. These initial conditions are upset when the female protagonist is raped. The raped woman files charges against her perpetrator, who is easily identifiable. Courtrooms play a signifi- cant role in these films, if only to demonstrate the state's inability to convict the rapist on the one hand and to precipitate a narrative crisis on the other. This miscarriage of justice constitutes a turning- point in the film—allowing for the passage of the protagonist from a sexual and judicial victim to an avenging woman.

The general features of this narrative and the production of horror in rape scenes point to its close similarity to rape–revenge narraives of Hollywood B films, especially horror films.[5] Critical writing on Hollywood rape–revenge films, particularly Carol Clover's work, suggests that the marginal status of these films, in contrast to mainstream Hollywood, permits them to address some of the unresolved and knotty problems on gender and spectatorship that are carefully regulated and managed by the mainstream. Clover turns to the sadistic and masochistic pleasures evoked by these horror films to suggest that B films are the 'return of the repressed' in mainstream Hollywood. Focusing on B horror films, where low production values couple with sex and violence, Clover argues that these films displace the woman as the sole site of scopophilic pleas- ure and opens possibilities of cross-gender identification through the sado-masochistic pleasures encouraged by these films. The most compelling aspect of her work is the classification of these rape–revenge films within the larger rubric of *horror* films, a move that retains the sadistic and masochistic pleasures—prerequisites for watching a standard horror film—staged in these rape–revenge narratives. Clover concludes in the following fashion:

I have argued that the center of gravity of these films lies more in the reaction (the revenge) than the act (the rape), but to the extent that the revenge fantasy derives its force from *some* degree of imaginary participation in the act itself, the victim position, these films are predicated on cross-gender identification of the most extreme, corporeal sort. (p. 154)

Instead of privileging the revenge narrative or the rape scenes as Rao does, it is more useful to explore how the narrative nuances of this genre are predicated on a cinematic logic that draws these two parts together. Rape scenes are not unusual in Indian cinema. They are, however, frequently subject to censorship rulings on grounds both of their irrelevance to the main narrative and the unseemly pleasure they evoke.[6] Yet rape scenes in avenging women films are indispensable to their narrative, repeatedly evoked as evidence in a courtroom sequence or repeated as a traumatic event experienced by the victim. In other words, the centrality of the rape scenes in the narrative heightens their intimate relationship to the subsequent revenge plot where once again there is a replay of negotiations between sex and violence.

While N. Chandra's *Pratighat* is frequently cited as an originary moment in the avenging women genre, the combination of rape and revenge was already secured in B.R. Chopra's *Insaaf Ka Tarazu* (Scales of Justice) produced in 1980.[7] The latter's initial box-office success can be partly attributed to the heroine of the film: Zeenat Aman. The *Encyclopaedia of Indian Cinema* describes the conditions of reception that shaped this film:

This notorious rape movie followed in the wake of growing feminist activism in India in the 1970s after the Mathura and Maya Tyagi rape cases, the amendment to the Rape Law and the impact of, e.g. the Forum Against Rape which offered legal assistance to rape victims.[8]

References to the feminist movement are obviously one of the determining features structuring the reception of this film, but its notoriety points towards a different route of analysis where we have to consider how this film relies on our knowledge of these rape cases as a point of entry into fantastical stagings of our anxieties about women, sexuality, and law, anxieties that in turn, are set into motion, but not resolved, by anti-rape campaigns.[9] Re-evaluated through generic details identifiable in later avenging women genre films, *Insaaf Ka Tarazu* unquestionably stands out as one of the early experiments in rape–revenge narratives.

*Insaaf Ka Tarazu* opens with a rape scene. A colour sequence showing us a medium shot of a screaming woman in a sari, rapidly changes into a black-and-white shadow play. The silhouette of a man first chases and then disrobes this woman. Another male figure enters the scene and a fight begins between them. The film returns to full colour when the potential rapist is fatally stabbed. The following credit sequence is a montage of stills from various religious and tourist sites in India with the soundtrack playing the title song of the film. These two sequences juxtapose rape against representations of India and this association with India is further played out in the film by naming the female protagonist Bharati—the feminine name in Hindi for India. These first scenes suggest considering female rape as an allegory of a beleaguered nation-state, a suggestion that however ceases to be developed further in the film.

The second rape sequence in the film is distinguished from the opening sequence by the continued use of colour footage and the absence of a male saviour. Using a calendar art print of a woman in bondage in the victim's (Arti's) bedroom as a reference point, the sequence provides glimpses of a rape scene that includes both coercion and bondage. Furthermore, the scene offers us another point of identification through the victim's younger sister, Nita, who accidentally walks into Arti's bedroom during the rape. Arti files charges against the rapist, Gupta. A number of social encounters between Gupta and Arti preceding the rape, combined with Nita's confused testimony, are employed in the courtroom to suggest that Arti was not raped but consented to have sex with Gupta. The court finds Gupta not guilty of rape.

The court's verdict in Arti's rape case comes as no surprise to he spectators, for the film mobilizes this doubt throughout the cene. For instance, Nita's testimony is crucial to this case but the lefence lawyer convincingly argues her inability to tell the difference between coerced and consenting sexual relationships. The film frames Nita very much in the mould of a horrified voyeur witnessing a primal scene, thus infusing the scene with both fear and pleasure of sexual knowledge—instead of recognizing it as sexual violation pure and simple. The sadistic-voyeuristic pleasure also surfaces here pointedly through the poster on the bedroom wall. The viewer might expect the poster's subject to be identified with the aggressor, a traditional strategy. Instead, the poster shores up a confusion between representations of rape and rape itself—thus eroticizing the scene of violation and escalating our masochistic identification with this scene. Privileging Nita's relationship to the scene, the film also exposes and depends on our inability as spectators to tell the cinematic difference between a scene of sexual consent and rape.

Notwithstanding the relationship between Nita's credibility as a witness and the court's verdict, Nita's ambivalence presses upon another aspect of the film's narrative—the unfolding of the revenge plot. Keeping pace with the ambivalence around the charge of rape in Arti's case, the film delays and reserves the revenge scenario until it can represent an unambiguous rape scene. It is only after Gupta proceeds to rape the virginal Nita in his office that Arti's revenge is allowed to unfold. In the film's climax Arti shoots Gupta, circumventing a judicial verdict on Nita's case. The film closes with another court scene where this time the judge abdicates his office for failing to deliver justice in earlier rape cases. Closing the rape-revenge narratives around a court scene or a figure of the state is now a standard feature of this genre and stands in sharp contrast to the male vigilante genre where the figure of the state is repeatedly undermined, for example, in *Nayakan* (Don, 1987). Although *Insaaf Ka Tarazu* did not have spin-offs for another seven years, the film established some of the basic conventions that squarely locate it as the inaugural moment in the avenging woman genre.

*Pratighat* is retroactively a classic of this genre because of the manner in which it consolidates some basic strains of the rape-revenge narrative.[10] The film revolves around corrupt politicians and the ongoing crisis over law and order in a small town. The female protagonist, Lakshmi, is a college teacher who lives with her lawyer husband and his parents. The film opens with several scenes of hooliganism orchestrated by Kali—a lumpen youth leader—in Lakshmi's town. These scenes are also strung together to lead us through Lakshmi's conversion from an ordinary, disinterested citizen to an active intervenor against Kali's reign of terror. Her complete conversion to an avenging woman hinges on a crucial scene when she openly confronts Kali by filing a criminal suit against him and refuses to withdraw it even when he threatens to harm her. As the stakes continue to rise in their confrontation, Kali finally resorts to a gendered resolution: he disrobes Lakshmi on the street in front of her house, with all her neighbours and family watching in silence. This violation establishes the primary conditions for Lakshmi's revenge against Kali and his gang and at the same time seals her estrangement from her husband. Lakshmi is rescued from this scene of public humiliation by Durga, whose own life has been scarred by Kali's violence—she was gang-raped by Kali's men and her husband tortured to death—but who nevertheless continues to galvanize support against Kali. Lakshmi moves into Durga's home, recovers, and receives support for her own revenge plan.

*Pratighat* displaces the conventional representation of rape by reconfiguring the rape scene as a disrobing sequence at both the visual and narrative registers. Ironically, while Kali declares that disrobing is a part of the Hindu tradition, evoking the *Mahabharata*, cinematically the film disengages with all the conventional representations of rape. The entire disrobing scene is spliced as a medium-length shot, and in the final moment of complete nudity, the film converts to colour negative conveying the full extent of this violation in Indian cinema. Moving away from the standard representations of rape scenes, *Pratighat* draws our attention to the visual proximity between scenes of rape and disrobing in Hindi cinema, and interrogates the ethics of a 'full view' circumscribing such scenes.

The scene of revenge where Lakshmi confronts Kali is also framed with narrative references to Hindu mythology and filmic gestures suggesting cross-overs with mythological films from the Madras film industry and the *Ramayana* and *Mahabharata* television serials. Clad in a red sari, Lakshmi garlands and anoints Kali at a public meeting and then repeatedly strikes him with an axe originally intended as a gift to him. The final killing scene is edited by juxtaposing shots of Kali's larger-than-life cardboard cut-out against the on-stage altercation between Lakshmi and Kali, fight scenes between Kali's men and Lakshmi's students, and colour negative stills from the original disrobing scene. The cardboard cut-out evokes an inter-textual relay from the poster in *Insaaf Ka Tarazu*, playing on the unrepresentativeness of rape in the former and suggesting that Lakshmi's aggressive attack in *Pratighat* is equally horrific. Moving the narrative focus away from a single killing scene to a general murderous chaos, replays the film's own pet themes where rape is located alongside other social crimes like hooliganism and corruption.

Two contradictions must be noted. Even as the film is critical of rape, rape scenes figure periodically in the narrative, signalling in each instance the consolidation of criminality and vigilantism with an increasing displacement of the state's law-and-order role. Similarly, criminalizing rape, the conceit employed in this film, appears to identify with a progressive legal position, but we find it cannot respond to the sadistic-voyeuristic pleasure prompted in the cinematic representations of rape. Kali's death may bear a formal resemblance to the disrobing scene, but is not subject to the same censorship regulations that underscore sexual representations in Indian cinema. *Pratighat* nevertheless, irks us with the limits and possibilities of equating rape and revenge scenes and thus coaxes us to reconsider the masochistic underpinnings of the rape scenes in this genre. While the film relies on our masochistic identification in the rape scene to fully play out its horrifying potential, the sadistic dimensions in this very scene propel the revenge plot and remind us retroactively that the ensemble of elements in the rape scene is always a volatile marriage between sex *and* violence.

There are several reasons for *Pratighat*'s success, but its ability to summon horror in the revenge sequences is one of them which, in turn, opened the gates for other permutations and combinations of rape and revenge. The full import of prompting horror in revenge scenes is further developed in Avatar Bhogal's *Zakmi Aurat* (Wounded Women) released in 1988.[11] Retaining the rule of targeting 'modern' women as victims, e.g. a fashion model in *Insaaf Ka Tarazu* and a college teacher in *Pratighat*, *Zakmi Aurat* picks a policewoman as its protagonist. With the rape scene occurring early in the narrative, the pivotal turning-point emerges when the judicial system refuses to convict the rapists, in spite of policewoman Kiran Dutt's own testimony. Abandoning legal recourse, Kiran Dutt now joins forces with other rape victims in the city. Together, the women come up with a fitting revenge plan: to snare the rapists and castrate them.

Kiran's gang-rape is edited as a fight sequence that closes around a conventional representation of rape. The rape scene returns to the bedroom familiar from *Insaaf Ka Tarazu*, but with a twist. Refusing to linger on Inspector Kiran Dutt's body as the rapists strip her, the film instead focuses on the rapists as they tear down her jeans and fling them on the ceiling fan. The unrepresentativeness of the actual sexual act in this rape scene climaxes through a series of shot-reverse-shots of fetishized objects—the ceiling fan and a medium close-up shot of Kiran's screaming face.

The shot sequence employed in the gang-rape of the female police officer creates the basic template for the castration revenge scenes. Again, details on the edge, like the doctor's operating gown, her mask, and the overhead lamp are excessively in focus and fetishized. The camera cuts off the entire abdominal region of the man, refusing to zoom in on a cloaked genital area. Rapid freeze shots of men's faces, and ninety-degree shots of the overhead lamp in the operating theatre signal the ongoing process of castration. This equivalence between the gang-rape and castration scenes, spliced by repeating shot/reverse-shots of a face and an overhead object cinematically, attempts to balance rape and revenge.

Critics have lambasted this film for offering an improbable resolution to rape. However, such a reading assumes that films have an indexical signification to political reality instead of examining how their narratives repeatedly stage various fantastical possibilities of these very same realities for the spectator.[12] One of the crucial constitutive features of this genre are its vociferous stagings of 'reality' through familiar references: shots of real newspapers, photographs of Gandhi on courtroom walls, footage of the Indian flag, etc. *Zakmi Aurat* relies on these elements more extensively than other films: the opening sequence shows us actual newspaper reports of various rape cases in India and the film draws an obvious link between the Kiran Dutt character and Kiran Bedi—a well-known woman police officer in Delhi. Inhabiting the *mise en scène*, these authenticating details appear to be strategically placed to heighten our viewing pleasure of the unravelling horror plot; reeling the spectator into scenes of escalating horror that culminate precisely at the very juncture when the film plays on an uncanny resemblance to extra-cinematic icons and events. These narratives in general may not directly respond to or satisfy demands of justice in particular rape cases, but they do unleash scenes of resolution that both extend beyond the law of the state and expose the spectator's complicity in the terrifying rape sequences.

Defending the spectatorial pleasures ensuing from *I Spit on Your Grave* (Meir Zarchi, 1977)—a film that bears an intimate relationship to *Zakmi Aurat*—Carol Clover writes: 'what disturbs about *I Spit on Your Grave* is its perverse simplicity, the way it closes all the intellectual doors and windows and leaves us staring at the *lex talionis* unadorned' (p. 151). Clover's comment is aimed at up-market films like *The Accused* (Jonathan Kaplan, 1988), where the legal process takes over the narrative, leaving little space for the rape victim to articulate her torment and substantially closes off the possibility of direct vigilante action. Her defence bears on my own reading of *Zakmi Aurat*, where, despite the film's narrative simplicity, it significantly precipitates the problems attending the visual representation of revenge in these films. As we have seen, films in this genre rely on convincingly meting out vigilante revenge that must equal, or even surpass, the horror of rape. While this equation produces ongoing narrative tensions, visual representations of rape in Indian cinema also remind us of the authority of censorship regulations and suggest the possibility of sado-masochistic pleasures structuring these rape scenes.

I have argued elsewhere that despite overt protests over film censorship, the Indian film industry is crucially dependent on the presence of the state at the register of cinematic materiality for generating sado-masochistic pleasure.[13] The female body is always the object in focus, and is repeatedly subject to a withdrawing camera that banks on an intimate relationship between the psychic law ruling taboos and the state overseeing censorship. The rape scenes in the avenging woman genre are not far from this formulation, where the narrative informs us that the horror of rape is in part motivated by the absence of the state, but attention to cinematic materiality suggests that the state, as censorship authority, is very much present as one of the crucial negotiating sites. Until the arrival of the revenge plot in these movies, rape scenes appear to be mere substitutes for sex, relentlessly eroticizing violence. It comes as no surprise that the criticism levelled against these films is sparked by a suspicion that violent sex is being flaunted as rape, a suspicion that also guides censorship regulations.

To mitigate and ward off such criticism, revenge scenes in these films have to be equally horrific in order to allow us to read the scenes of violent sex as rape *retroactively*. The narrative and visual machinations of this genre thus revolve around the problem of balancing rape and revenge: *Pratighat* settles rape by evoking figures of Hindu *shakti* goddesses and killing the rapist, whereas *Zakmi Aurat* resorts to an anatomical equation by suggesting castration as an act of revenge and escalates the horror of rape by visually locating the castrated male body in an analogous position to the raped female body. Settling rape through castration resonates with a feminist utopia, where, at least momentarily, the easy economic equation between the penis and phallus resolves the differences between gender and power that are constantly complicated by and subjected to the symbolic *difference* between the penis and phallus. The question is, while revenge narratives in this genre seek continuously to 'match' the horror of the rape, can they ever succeed?

*Zakmi Aurat* brings to a head the entire problem of visually and narratively, matching rape with revenge through its absurd logic of five rapes to fifteen castrations, a logic that heralds a moratorium on this genre in its current configuration. At the same time, *Zakmi Aurat* spawned films like *Aaj Ki Aurat* (Today's Woman) and *Damini* where the narratives not only wedge the difference between the raped woman and avenger, but also return to exhaust the possibilities of pleasure in violent rape scenes.[14] Even while revenge narratives, as Rahman informs us, provide female stars with more dominant roles, because women's access to avenging power in these films is intimately predicated on rape as a violent litmus test of gender identity, rape scenes are never so neatly cordoned off from Indian cinema's extensive use of the woman's body as a stand-in for sex, as a crucial site of scopophilic pleasure. Faced with these contradictory demands, the avenging woman genre surfaces as a giddy masculine concoction: the rape scenes provide the narrative ruse for the revenge plan while also providing the spectator a conventional regime of scopophilic pleasure. Revenge allows female stars to dominate the screen, but the genre demands that a violent assertion of masculine power in the form of rape is the price to exact for such power. Clearly, at the periphery of this genre where the interlocking narratives of rape and revenge are less than minimally finessed, gratuitously deploying rape does not sufficiently dislodge or displace conventional representations of women in Indian cinema or appease Maithili Rao's suspicions.

Located within the larger rubric of other violent action films produced in the same period, the more taunting feminist aspects of the rape–revenge films are most apparent in their narrative closures. Here the avenging woman's unhindered access to power is always limited by the arrival of the police; this finale differs markedly from the more assertive vigilante resolutions of the masculine genres like the gangster and bandit films. Coupled with the prolonged judicial sequences revolving around rape cases, the appeal of these rape–revenge narratives arguably rests on their ability to stage all the anxious points that attend the relationship between patriarchy and the state. If the social imagery promotes a unity between symbolic law and the state, rape cases inject a dissonance between these sites of authority to remind us that 'issues' of honour and shame are only provisionally resolved through legal proceedings. For the victim, the state's betrayal in rape cases is equally accompanied by patriarchal abandonment, and together they consolidate as the precipitating moment in the narrative that allows it to shift towards the revenge narrative. Faced with an orderless universe, the avenging woman narrative proceeds on a transgressive vigilante path, incites masculine anxiety about the phallic female, and opens the representational circuit for women on the Indian screen, but this unfettered power is undercut by finally reeling in the authority of the state and revealing the avenging woman's own overwhelming investment in the restoration of the social imagery. Casting women as embodying and sustaining tradition recycles an old stereotype from Indian films; however, the forced closure in this genre only provisionally irons out the anxieties between patriarchy and the state.

Although both the narrative closure accompanied by the very conventional reintegration of the woman into the social order and the precarious necessity of rape in these films weigh down the radical potential of the revenge narrative, they cannot completely regulate the series of unstable desires and identities set in motion through the ongoing dynamics between rape and revenge. Finding anything subversive about rape–revenge narratives both at the register of the cinematic form and spectator's pleasure, leads us to some tangled issues plaguing feminist film theory. Laura Mulvey's classic essay 'Visual Pleasure and Narrative Cinema' argues that 'Hollywood style at its best (and of all the cinema which fell within its sphere of influence)' offers pleasure by enacting a conventional heterosexual division of labour in its narrative structure between active/male and passive/female for the masculine spectator.[15] Challenges to Mulvey's essay besides her own revision through melodrama, have been mounted by feminist film theorists as they move into other genres of Hollywood, particularly to B films that include horror, slasher, and pornographic elements. Focusing on the less-than-best cinematic styles of B films that are directed to and have a loyal female audience and incorporate a heady combination of sex and violence, feminist film theory—Carol Clover's work on slasher films and Linda Williams's on pornographic films—has been forced to a reconsider the dynamics between identification and pleasure, particularly sado-masochistic pleasure.[16] Arguing for the presence of *sado-masochistic* pleasure in violent pornographic films, Williams writes:

. . . it seems to me preferable to employ the term *sado-masochistic* when describing the perverse fantasies that inform these films. While still problematic, the term at least keeps in play the oscillation between active and passive and male and female subject positions, rather than fixing one pole or the other as the essence of the viewer's experience. At the same time, it does not allow us to forget, as some celebrations of masochisms (e.g. Studlar or Samois) do forget, where ultimate power lies. (p. 217)

Drawing on Williams's economic articulation of sado-masochism, it appears that the rape–revenge scenes in the avenging women genre similarly rely on the generation of sado-masochistic pleasure, a pleasure that unwittingly challenges, however provisional it may be, the straightforward sadistic impulses of rape in Indian cinema. Because rape scenes are inextricably meshed with the revenge plot in this genre, the masochistic dimensions of the rape scenes far outweigh their conventional sadistic associations while at the same time the unfolding revenge plot leans on provoking the spectator's sadistic investments in revenge and punishment. Interweaving sadism and masochism through different filmic moments, this genre upsets the normalizing fetishistic economy with the fragmented woman's body as the central object but, complicating these generic pleasures is the ongoing tussle between every Indian film-maker and the state over censorship. As a result, it is precisely through overt submission to censorship regulations that the commercial film industry parodies the authority of the state, a relationship that is not unlike the masochist's relationship to patriarchal law; therefore, we may have to consider the possibility of the rape–revenge device as yet another ruse to circumvent censorship, resorting once again to the woman's body. At the same time, tightening the rape–revenge equation unwittingly opens possibilities for cross-gender identifications. Not resolving the gender imbalance prevalent in social power relations, the contradictory forces of Indian commercial cinema beg for a reconsideration of the other identifications available in this heady combination of sex and violence. Responding in part to the debates on violence in Indian cinema which cast these representations solely in terms of their regressive effects on society, I suggest instead that violent scenes circumscribed by cross-cutting genre features and pressures can in surprising ways challenge patriarchy's normalizing overtones on the issue of gender and constitute one of the crucial axes of spectator interest in these films.

Arguably rape–revenge narratives are not available as positive models for feminist utopias, but they do stage the aggressive and contradictory contours of sexual identity and pleasure that in turn throw up aggressive strands of feminism. I am not salvaging the film industry's regressive casting of female roles, but do want to suggest that cross-cutting pressures from both the female star system and feminist movement have colluded to stage some of our unacknowledged aggressiveness, both public and private, which also underscore our understanding and articulations of sexual identities.

Before we commit ourselves to the idea that all roads to female aggression inevitably lead us to rape scenes in Indian cinema, it is worth remembering that this tight relationship between rape and revenge is a recurrent feature in Hindi cinema. Whatever peculiar production rationale helps to fortify this link, the yoking of rape with revenge cannot be disconnected from the modes of address structuring Hindi cinema; a national audience is always already its imagined addressee. In other words, its desire to command a national audience severely shrinks Hindi cinema's ability to stray from a successful, yet conventional paradigm.

However, a preview of other regiōnal cinemas, particularly Telugu films with the actress Vijayshanti in the lead, demonstrate that there are other contours to aggression, without the routine rape scene. Dispensing with rape scenes, these films allow aggression to shadow desire. On another register, these films lend themselves to a rich reading of regional and global cinematic issues. For instance, as Telugu films they are in constant dialogue with political dramas—a *forte* of the Telugu film industry—challenging the masculine rule of this genre. As female-centred action films, they recall Nadia's stunt films from 1930s to the 1950s, and their agility reminds us of a slew of films and television shows from *Suzie Wong* to *Charlie's Angels*. In addition, as films initially made in Telugu and subsequently dubbed into Hindi and Tamil, they raise interesting issues about the new economics of dubbing that has gained a national market for regional cinemas.

Rumours and reports from the industry claim that Vijayshanti is one of India's highest paid female stars whose cache at the box-office is greater than most of her male counterparts. However, she too has had her share of rape–revenge narratives—N. Chandra's *Pratighat*, for instance, is a remake of a Telugu film *Pratighatan*, with Vijayshanti cast originally as the avenging woman—and is not altogether protected from playing the submissive wife in *Eashwar* (1992). Nevertheless she manages to corner some of the most spectacularly aggressive roles in Indian cinema. Vijayshanti's own self-representation does not rest on emulating other heroines, but as she puts it: 'I always have to kick and pound the villains to pulp. That's why I'm called the Amitabh Bachchan of Andhra Pradesh'.[17]

When examining rape–revenge narrative, I steered away from considering the influence of the female star economy, choosing instead to focus on textual analysis. But when faced with Vijayshanti's films, for example—*Tejaswini* (1991), *Auto Rani* (1992), *Rowdy Inspector* (1991), *Streetfighter* (1994) and *Superlady* (1991)— despite different directors, they hold together as if to constitute a genre and challenge my own marginalization of the female star economy in my previous readings of the avenging women films. Each of her films upturns several conventional associations between femininity and aggression, but all too often their narratives tend to characterize female aggressiveness as a feature belonging exclusively to the pre-Oedipal phase. Kodi Ramakrishnan's *Police Lock-up* (1992) on the other hand, refuses any narrow casting of female aggressiveness and in turn, allows for an intriguing relationship between law and desire.[18]

The narrative takes the following route: Vijaya—Vijayshanti—is an upright police officer who arrives in town—Visakhapatnam—to investigate a political assassination. She has to contend with corrupt policemen and a conniving and ambitious Chief Minister—Panjaraja—who we know is responsible for the assassination. Panjaraja accuses her of being a terrorist and Vijaya is thrown into jail. A second story line now unravels: Shanti—Vijayashanti's double role—is the wife of a zealous Police Inspector—Ashok—who is frequently transferred because of his honesty. Shanti is obviously cast as Vijaya's alter ego: meek, clad in a sari, devoted to her husband, and pining for a child. It is precisely her guilelessness that lands her in jail one curfew night. The police throw her into Vijaya's cell and the two see each other for the first time. Unlike stories of lost sisters and brothers that recur in Indian films, this scene does not drag in mothers and fathers to claim kinship between the two women. Instead, it moves quickly through the respective events that brought the two women to jail. The crucial detail that lends credibility to Vijaya's story of her capture is Shanti's encounter with a dying journalist, who, mistaking Shanti for Vijaya passes on details of yet another assassination scheme. Shanti suggests that they switch places so that Vijaya can complete her investigation and arrest the corrupt Chief Minister. Vijaya reluctantly agrees, and the following morning leaves with Ashok, now passing as his meek wife. The film now gallops along, plotting Vijaya's pursuit of the Chief Minister. We see her move effortlessly from sari to jeans, from submissive daughter-in-law to strong and masterful police official. Through various twists and turns that include the notorious international assassin John, the film ends in a temple courtyard where Vijaya and Ashok annihilate the villains. The wily politician is the last to go: Vijaya blows him up with his own bomb, strapped in a belt, reminding viewers of the way Rajiv Gandhi was killed. The film closes with Vijaya and Shanti embracing.

Departing radically from both the rape–revenge narratives and male action films, *Police Lock-up* reconfigures the relationship among power, authority, and gender; opening up a wide range of fantastical possibilities for feminist identifications. There are many obvious scenes of positive identification secured in the film. For instance, the film introduces Vijaya as a police officer driving her jeep through a series of slow-motion shots, thus breaking away from the routine logic of passage from victim to avenger in the rape–revenge genre. The film ungrudgingly celebrates her ability and success as a police officer by showing us elaborate details of her work: there are several fight scenes where both guns and kung-fu fighting styles are exhibited; her acumen and confidence with technology occur more than once. My own favourite is when Vijaya, dressed as Shanti, uses a video camera to shoot an exchange among Panjaraja's hoodlums. She then replays this scene in slow motion and decodes their conversation through lip-reading in order to discover where a kidnap victim is hidden. These scenes suggest the presence, possibility, and intervention of female control over modern sites of technology which are all too frequently represented as male prerogatives. Collectively, these details easily constitute the bedrock of any feminist primer on positive identifications, but they fit too neatly and are too far from the messy economies of identification and desire that cinematic spectatorship thrives on. What we do see in *Police Lock-up* is a woman's excessive investment in the law, a law that we often mistrust for the ways in which it gives feminism short shrift.

The cornerstone of this film's innovativeness, however, is its deployment of the double role. Indian cinema has long been fascinated with double roles and utilizes them both to recognize and bank on a star's popularity. When female double roles surface, for example in Ramesh Sippy's *Sita aur Gita* (Sita and Gita, 1972), the narrative revolves around separate lives and identities of twins, and conventionally closes on family romance: lost siblings, cast as opposites, find each other, find their parents, and so on. In sharp contrast, *Police Lock-up* refuses to recuperate the family: Vijaya and Shanti are not lost-and-found twins, and their resemblance is never resolved narratively in the film. Demonstrating that the two women effectively and easily pass for the other—Vijaya as the submissive wife and Shanti as an aggressive officer—the film mobilizes change in each woman and closes around a less polarized distinction between the two. Obviously the blurred distinction between them draws this film dangerously close to the horror film genre on twins.[19]

Rejecting a narrative closure around biological kinship, this film

Readers Wanted

# Readers Wanted

We know you value reading. Would you like to help thousands of blind and print impaired people throughout Massachusetts read daily newspapers, magazines or a good book over the radio? If you can read well aloud, if you're dependable, committed and can give as little as an hour a week, call the Talking Information Center (TIC) today to arrange to take our volunteer reader audition test. If you pass the audition, you could have a rewarding volunteer career helping others. Call TIC today at 781-834-4400 to schedule an appointment.

*"Reading maketh a man full"*
Francis Bacon

*Reading is to the mind what exercise is to the body"*
Edmond Hoyle

Talking Information Center
130 Enterprise Drive
PO Box 519
Marshfield, MA 02050
800-696-9505

general@ticnetwork.net

**LISTEN ON THE WEB:**
**www.ticnetwork.org**

wrings out the full effects of masquerade. Vijaya's competency is asserted through her ability to masquerade not only as Shanti, but also a telephone line repair man and the killer John, at various points in the film. Masquerade controls and mobilizes this film's narrative.

Joan Riviere's conceptualization of masquerade continues to abet theorizations of cross-gender identifications that attend the female spectator when viewing a masculine-ordered universe in Hollywood cinema.[20] Among all the available appropriations in film theory, John Fletcher's reworking stands out for returning to the signifying form of the film as a potential site of masquerade.[21] He writes:

The importance of Riviere's conception of the masquerade is that it constitutes a transgressive doubleness, an inscription of alternative wishes. The potential for a critical distance from the mythemes of femininity (passivity, responsiveness, deference, flattery, etc.) is lodged already within it and the narratives it might generate. (p. 55)

Reconsidered for the film on hand, it can be said that masquerade functions at different levels in *Police Lock-up*. The film is clearly located within the male action film genre where restoration of law and order dominates the narrative and always close on a conventional rearrangement of law and order. Usurping the standard male hero's role, that is, masquerading as a police officer, Vijayashanti plays this role to its full. The film supports this masculinization completely, for instance, by holding off song-and-dance sequences exclusively around her. Reeling Shanti into the narrative as an upright inspector's wife is a perfect foil for providing a feminine domestic space that both cushions and counterpoises Vijaya's aggressive public self, and together the two roles demonstrate Vijayashanti's ability to perform across different and competing terrains. Doubleness is further supported by naming the characters from parts of the star's full name thus 'assuring' the masculine subject, as proposed by Riviere, that behind the mask lies this powerful phallic figure that unites both halves of polar screen personalities.

The double role in this film also actuates a different fantastical staging of desire. The lack of parental origin as a reason for their resemblance unhinges the film from closing around a cosy sibling unity, while simultaneously unleashing a desire for the other. For instance, when Shanti suggests they switch places, the scope of this offer clearly extends to her spouse—we see Vijaya effortlessly passing for Shanti in her home, even masquerading her love for Ashok. It is only later in the film that Ashok reveals that he suspected Vijaya was not Shanti when she rejected his sexual demands. Of course, the film suspends all knowledge on the exact moment of his discovery, leaving open the possibility of a sexual interaction between Ashok and Vijaya. The switch thus opens the possibility of Ashok being exchanged as a sexual object between them.

We have seen the male version of this arrangement first proposed by Levi-Strauss and then ingeniously resurrected by Lacan and revised by feminists.[22] Eve Sedgwick's reformulation in *Between Men* shifts the exchange of women between men from a heterosexual matrix to homosexual.[23] Sedgwick proposes that women are exchanged between men to avert, ward off, and occlude the articulation of homosexual desire for each other while simultaneously oppressing women and producing homophobia. These terms seem uncannily reversed in *Police Lock-up*, raising the possibility that Vijaya and Shanti's full-scale switching is driven by a desire for the other, however narcissistic it may appear. This reading is further endorsed by the final moment of the film where we see them embracing, a closure that displaces and postpones heterosexual resolutions.

Although Vijaya has been the focus of most of the dramatic moments in the film, Shanti too provides enough dissonance in the plot despite her conventional representation of passive femininity: she not only initiates the idea of the switch but also remains extremely loyal to her role as Vijaya in spite of arduous conditions in the jail. But it is in a more eccentric detail that her location in the plot allows for displacements. The film elaborately informs us that Shanti's anxiety about having children has absurd effects on her behaviour: she daydreams about phantom children, upsets her husband's work routine by demanding his presence at various fertility rituals, and above all, she has a pathological attachment to a dog who she treats as her child.

I am reminded here of Edmund Leach's stimulating essay 'Animal Classification and Verbal Abuse', where he argues for an intimate relationship among human classification of animals, verbal abuse, and incest taboos.[24] There is an unrelated, yet similar take on domestic pets by Avital Ronell in an interview where she expounds on the Bush family and pets after Millie's 'autobiography' was published.[25] She comments: 'I remember telling people, "Watch their rapport to the dog, because here is where they articulate things that are taboo, that are unconscious".' (p. 142)

Shanti's attachment to Caesar, her attempts to anthromorphize, cast aspersions on the fertility of this heterosexual unit, particularly on her husband and his ability to reproduce. Furthermore, her incapacity to differentiate between dog and child in many scenes, a difference that conventionally marks so many sexual, dietary, and verbal taboos, throws asunder all normative images of a reproducing human family and even anticipates the remarkable switch suggested and promoted by her. The film encourages her attempts to humanize Caesar by providing it, on more than one occasion, subjective point-of-view shots. Notably, Caesar supports her switching places with Vijaya without a bark and unlike Ashok, he can spot the difference between the two women. Exchanging husbands and circulating fetishized objects such as dogs between them, allows us to read these movements as circuits of desire between Vijaya and Shanti, thwarting our expectations of a normative heterosexual closure to most tales about twins. Curiously, this intimate bond between Vijaya and Shanti permits representations of other kinds of transgressions: Ashok's uncle is indisputably cast a stereotypical homosexual and surfaces as a symptom of the film's nascent homophobia; and Panjaraja, the Chief Minister, schemes to have his own daughter kidnapped to gain political ground, a motive that violates most conventions of paternal affection.

The film galvanizes one of the most common signs of love we can procure in Indian cinema to stage desire—a song-and-dance sequence spliced together as a dream sequence from Shanti's point of view. Triggered by Vijaya's visit and finding herself pregnant, Shanti longs to go home, but instead lulls herself to sleep singing a song. This sequence is set around a pregnancy ritual, and she begins a duet with her husband, but soon substitutes him with Vijaya and the song closes around their embrace. Like the final embrace of the film, here too the heterosexual convention of these songs in Indian films is subverted. In the absence of any clear performative declaration of a lesbian identity in the film that may allow for a straightforward reading of a lesbian desire plot, I propose that *Police Lock-up* approximates a female buddy film genre that allows and encourages a staging of lesbian fantasies. As a police narrative, the film shadows and masquerades the male action genre to the hilt while surreptitiously displacing conventional expectations and resolutions attending its masculine counterpart.

In sharp contrast to the avenging-woman genre, where the inept law and order system allows for the avenging plot to unfold with a closure that reintegrates the woman into the social and civic order, *Police Lock-up* and other Vijayashanti films harbour a less antagonistic relationship to the law. Located directly within the law, most prominently played out in *Police Lock-up*, the female protagonist is constantly settling law and order problems produced by corrupt politicians and policemen, a relationship with the state that is unabashedly accommodational. Nevertheless, Vijayashanti films raise some of the most knotty and unresolved problems attending representational struggles around femininity, violence, and the state.

## NOTES

1. 'Imaging You', *The Illustrated Weekly of India*, 29 May–4 June 1993: 24–37. The discussants included N.Chandra, Prakash Jha, Javed Akhtar, Meenakshi Seshadri, and Maithili Rao.

2. Firoze Rangoonwala, 'The Age of Violence', *The Illustrated Weekly of India*, 4–10 September 1993: 27–9.

3. M. Rahman, 'Women Strike Back', *India Today*, 15 July 1988: 80–2.

4. Maithili Rao, 'Victims in Vigilante Clothing', *Cinema in India*, Oct–Dec. 1988: 24–6.

5. See Carol J. Clover, *Men, Women, and Chain Saws: Gender in the Modern Horror Film*, Princeton: Princeton University Press, 1992; Peter Lehman, '"Don't Blame This on a Girl": Female Rape-Revenge Films', in Steven Cohan and Ina Rae Hark (eds), *Screening the Male: Exploring Masculinities in Hollywood Cinema*, New York: Routledge, 1993.

This explicit resemblance to Hollywood B movies throws up a set of new issues: it draws limits to 'national' styles of cinema, forcing us to consider the exchange and appropriation of cinematic styles across national boundaries. Every 'national' cinema has, of course, to contend with Hollywood hegemony, but if the points of contact between Indian and Hollywood film are the much maligned, yet often experimental, B films, it raises a host of fascinating questions relating to taste and the distribution networks of B films in the Third World.

6. See Aruna Vasudev, *Liberty and License in Indian Cinema*, New Delhi: Vikas, 1978, on censorship regulations.

7. *Insaaf Ka Tarazu*, dir. B.R. Chopra, with Zeenat Aman, Padmini Kolhapure, Raj Babbar, and Deepak Parashar, B.R. Films, 1980.

8. Ashish Rajadhyaksha and Paul Willemen, *Encyclopaedia of Indian Cinema*, New Delhi: Oxford University Press, 1995, p. 416.

9. For a useful discussion on the public discussion of rape and the women's movement, see Ammu Joseph and Kalpana Sharma, 'Rape: A Campaign is Born', in Ammu Joseph and Kalpana Sharma (eds), *Whose News?: The Media and Women's Issues*, New Delhi: Sage Publications, 1994, pp. 43–50.

10. *Pratighat*, dir. N. Chandra, with Sujata Mehta, Arvind Kumar, Charan Raj, and Rohini Hattangady, Usha Kiron Movies, 1987.

11. *Zakmi Aurat*, dir. Avatar Bhogal, with Dimple Kapadia, 1988.

12. Farhad Malik, 'Fact and Fiction', *Cinema in India*, August 1981: 5–8.

13. 'Coitus Interruptus and the Love Story in Indian Cinema', Vidya Dehejia (ed.), *Gender and Art in India*, New Delhi: Kali for Women, 1997.

14. Other film productions include *Serai, Prema Pasa*, and *Khoon Bhari Mang*.

15. Laura Mulvey, 'Visual Pleasure and Narrative Cinema', in Constance Penley (ed.), *Feminism and Film Theory*, New York: Routledge, 1988, pp. 57–68.

16. Linda Williams, *Hard Core: Power, Pleasure, and the 'Frenzy of the Visible'*, Berkeley: University of California Press, 1989.

17. Interview with Vijayashanti, *Filmfare*, July 1993.

18. *Police Lock-up*, dir. Kodi Ramakrishnan, with Vijayashanti, Kumar Films, 1992

19. Horror films on twins similarly do not use the cushion of a family romance and play on all the horrific aspects of twin identities and the twinning reproductive process itself. The most competent film in this genre is David Cronenberg's *Dead Ringers* that takes on both Peter Greenaway's avant-garde film *Zed and Two Noughts* and Bette Davis's *Dead Ringer* to render a techno-horror film that borders on incest.

20. Joan Riviere, 'Womanliness as a Masquerade', in Victor Burgin, James Donald and Cora Kaplan (eds), *Formations of Fantasy*, London: Methuen, 1986, p. 35. Mary Ann Doane's essays are good examples of this kind of appropriation. See her 'Film and Masquerade: Theorizing the Female Spectator', in *Femmes Fatales*, New York: Routledge, 1991; and 'Masquerade Reconsidered: Further Thoughts on the Female Spectator', ibid., p. 33.

21. John Fletcher, 'Versions of Masquerade,' *Screen* 29(3), 1988: 43–70.

22. Claude Levi-Strauss, *The Elementary Structures of Kinship*, trans. James Harle Bell, John Richard con Sturner, and Rodney Needham, Boston: Beacon Press, 1969.

For a pithy elaboration of Levi-Strauss and Lacan see Jane Gallop, *The Daughter's Seduction: Feminism and Psychoanalysis*, London: Macmillan, 1982.

23. Eve Kosofsky Sedgwick, *Between Men: English Literature and Male Homosocial Desire*, New York: Columbia University Press, 1985.

24. Edmund Leach, 'Anthropological Aspects of Language: Animal Categories and Verbal Abuse', Eric H. Lenneberg (ed.), *New Directions in the Study of Language*, Cambridege, MA: MIT Press, 1964, 23.

25. Avital Ronell, interview, *Re/Search* 13, San Francisco: Re/Search Publications, 1991, 127.

# 9

# From Subjectification to Schizophrenia: The 'Angry Man' and the 'Psychotic' Hero of Bombay Cinema

RANJANI MAZUMDAR

The body is the inscribed surface of events (traced by language and dissolved by ideas), the locus of a dissociated self (adopting the illusion of a substantial unity), and a volume in perpetual disintegration. Genealogy as an analysis of descent, is thus situated within the articulation of the body and history. Its task is to expose a body totally imprinted by history and the processes of history's destruction of the body.                                                               —Michel Foucault

MEDIATING THE MARGINALIZED through the symbolically central figure of the 'angry man', Amitabh Bachchan became in many ways *the* most powerful and perhaps the last iconic hero that Hindi cinema has ever produced. Attempting the 'illusion' of unity through a complex process of performance and representational masking, Bachchan's body became the site of a magnified subjectification. The plurality of social, symbolic and discursive spaces that Bachchan occupied, enabled him to acquire a status that has been difficult to match after the eclipse of the 'angry man' image. Serious questions need to be asked whether the over-coded discourse of the 'angry man' (congealing in his iconic presence) can be re-produced in the current constellation[1]. Embarking on an investigation of the 'angry man' imaginary, we

Discussions with members of Mediastorm, Ravi Sundaram, Ravi Vasudevan, Ravi Kant, Ira Bhaskar and Deepu Sharan have helped in the writing of this paper.

attempt to analyse and yet go beyond the Bachchan phenomenon of the 1970s, culminating in the emergence of the 'psychotic' hero of contemporary cinema.[2] It is important not to historically relativize the Bachchan phenomenon as a phenomenon of the 1970s alone, but to theorize a series of discontinuities and ruptures in the narrative strategy of the 'formula' which allow for the articulation of new modes of representation. The new figure of the psychotic and the older 'angry man' can be posed as dialectical 'force fields' addressing each other in an attempt to rewrite the constellation of the 'formula'[3].

In his *Origin of German Tragic Drama*, Walter Benjamin offers a dialectical juxtaposition of the baroque mourning play (*Trauerspeil*) and tragedy (*Tragödie*). By posing Trauer and Tragedy as dialectical force fields, Benjamin shows how the allegorical form of the Trauer, expressing itself through fragments and ruin, poses a critique of the organicism and unity of Tragedy.[4] It seems to us that a dialectical juxtaposition of the 'angry man' of the Bachchan era and the psychotic persona of Shahrukh Khan can offer interesting insights into contemporary film practices. Appearing almost as the *other* of the Bachchan phenomenon, the psychotic hero seems to have no apparent relationship to social reality yet manages to explore hitherto unknown territories of desire, a deeper exploration of 'interiority'[5], generating a space in which a struggle occurs for the production of new meanings. Recognizing the 'other' within the 'self' of the Bachchan era, the psychotic becomes an *instance of intertextuality*, inviting an allegorical reading of its construction.

Locating the body of the two stars within a constellation of narratives, we explore the question of identity/subjectivity: the transformation of the body through performance and technological transformations, the deployment of a star system historically specific to the 'angry man', the discourse of pain experienced by the body on screen and the reinvention of the city of Bombay by the 1990s. This constellation is embedded in a political, historical transformation of an earlier imaging of the nation, its crisis resulting in the Emergency—and the long historical transition to a new phase in the 1990s.[6] This period witnesses the growing centrality of the city, both as a reference point and as a point of departure in cinematic representation. The cinematic explorations of the dichotomy between the country and the city, the 'rational' versus the disintegrating 'self', the utopian impulse of freedom versus the experience of inequality and loss, the promise of order versus the threat of anarchy—have all unleashed a new and dynamic discourse of the body. An understanding of this new discourse in the last three decades is to perhaps take a step towards raising new questions about the diminishing power of the hegemonic icon in contemporary cinema.

While nationalism and modernity remain reference points for this essay, a dissolution of the particularity and dynamic nature of film narrative within these broad themes will not help us to understand the *formal* mechanisms by which the national imagery gets allegorized, through the body/star/icon/figure. The hegemonic icon, whose magnified subjectivity was created in Bachchan's case through a complex form of masking, is perhaps, de-masked or re-masked in the image of the psychotic. Here lies the cultural politics of performance,

honoured with dismantling textual authority, illusionism, and the canonical actor in favour of the polymorphous body of the performer. Refusing the conventions of role-playing, the performer presents herself/himself as a sexual, permeable, tactile body, scourging audience narrativity along with the barrier between stage and actor.[7]

It is this practice that allows for the blurring of boundaries between the character and the actor, thus investing the body with a new mobility.

Operating within the interstices of private worlds and the turbulence of the public arenas of political citizenship, the crisis of legality, received notions of order and individual freedom, the films under discussion pose issues of subject-formation and an engagement with questions of memory. We hope to work at different levels of analysis: where the body exists and overlaps at both formal and discursive moments. Our discussion centres on three films made between 1973 and 1994, namely *Deewar, Darr* and *Baazigar.*[8] *Deewar* in many ways is the 'originary text' of the 'angry man' image, as such the film occupies a major part of this essay.

In conventional terms, the 'formula' sets the pattern for generating the symbolic presentation of binary oppositions that defined modernity, albeit in an Indian cast. The hero is usually confronted with the classic choices—tradition versus modernity, truth versus falsehood, rural innocence versus urban sophistication etc. The 'formula' film with its melodramatic narrative structure is also marked by the typical conventions of 'melodramatic acting'—an excess of expression. Christine Gledhill charts out the performative elements that make up the melodramatic imagination.

Notoriously, the production of melodramatic identities involves excess of expression: hyperbolic emotions, extravagant gesture, high-flown sentiments, declamatory speech, spectacular settings and so on.[9]

This deployment of excessive expression within the 'formula' underwent a significant turn with the emergence of the 'angry man' image. Bachchan's innovation was his control over *excess* and a calculated economy of motion[10]. The emergence of Shahrukh Khan's psychotic image seems to pose a radical discontinuity with the 'angry man' image. Shahrukh's deployment was in many ways the negation of Bachchan's control—*excess* was re-invented to challenge the moral codes of the 1970s 'formula'.

## MAPPING THE BODY

In contrast to the naturalized body, the historical body exists in a space of contingency, always mediated through a complex cultural system of signs.[11] Visuality and cinematic experience offer a unique vantage-point to deconstruct the body as the experience of watching the screen also involves pleasure in looking at the bodies of actors, their movements, performing skills and an interest in their real-life personalities.[12]

The historical body of the 'angry man' is also a register of *pain*. Pain in the 'angry man's' persona operates as the regulator of his action, the guarantor of his memory and a ritual affirmation of his marginality. Pain explicates the trauma of family division (*Deewar*), and exaggerated agency of the lone psychotic (*Darr, Baazigar*). Pain forms part of the male body's capacity to negotiate with history and the nation, with 'self' and the trauma of identity. As with the body, the discourses of pain in the 'angry man' are by no means discrete for each time period/actor—rather, they follow overlapping yet discontinuous trajectories.

In *Deewar*, pain in the body was defined by its outward economy and expressed as *tragic* pain. Here, there were little signs of external, self-inflicted disfigurement as in the later period, but periodic flashes in the form of the body scar/tattoo which serves as a repository of memory. Tragic pain—resolved by death, makes meaningful the 'angry man's' tragic-heroic resistance. The anticipation of death in the narrative goes hand in hand with a focus on the hero's ability to carry pain and his resistance to share it with all others except the Mother. Through the acknowledgement of death, *Deewar* seeks to undertake a mediation on the social—a process where the focus is on the control of the body and 'self'. Here tragedy does not entail complete loss—it is a means to undertake an examination of the 'self'.

In the psychotic films, the body moves towards a thoroughgoing sublation of the Bachchan era. The 'self' and the physical body seem separated, and pain externalized through voluntary/involuntary disfigurement. The space of the social appears to be erased, the city becomes an abstraction and the nation a crucial absence. The articulation of the body is increasingly schizophrenic. Pain for the psychotic seems to lack the ethical/visionary quality of his predecessors. For the psychotic, pain seems an organizing principle of movement, leading to the final destruction of the 'self'. What occurs thus is a process of reversal in which the particular problem of projecting 'interiority' articulates itself through a new kind of excess. As Elaine Scarry says when discussing the complexities of representing (projecting) inside and outside surfaces of the body,

. . . projection entails not simply an alteration in degree but a much more extraordinary form of revision in which the original given is utterly eliminated and replaced by something wholly other than itself. . . . What is wholly absent in the interior is made present, as conversely, what is wholly in that interior state (pain) is now made absent. Thus, the reversal of inside and outside surfaces ultimately suggests that by transporting the external object world into the sentient interior, that interior gains some small share of the blissful immunity of inert inanimate objecthood; and conversely, by transporting pain out onto the external world, that external environment is deprived of its immunity to, unmindfulness of, and indifference toward the problems of sentience.[13]

While the Bachchan phenomenon appears to conceive the body from the 'outside', the psychotic on the other hand is conceived as a 'desiring' or 'fearing' being whose experience of 'interiority' is presented through an inward movement of the narrative.

## Amitabh Bachchan, *Deewar* and the Economy of Desire

Amitabh Bachchan's rise to stardom was epitomized through his complex and varied portrayal of the formulaic 'angry man', a screen space occupied by the star for well over a decade. Bachchan's dialogue delivery, sense of timing and superbly crafted restraint in acting ushered in a new kind of anger on the screen, generated primarily through his physical gestures and movements. The brooding, inward-looking, yet outwardly searching, vulnerable anger of Bachchan was symptomatic of its time. His ability to absorb and transmit both the 'modern' and the 'traditional', the 'eastern' and the 'western' through a novel body language was perhaps the single most important reason for his unmatched star status in the history of Bombay cinema. Bachchan was neither completely 'Indian' nor totally 'western.' His own history as the son of a well-known Hindustani poet who grew up in Allahabad, as well as his exposure to western culture as part of the cultural intelligentsia, seems to have privileged Bachchan with a body language that would always get projected in his screen persona. As scriptwriter Javed Akhtar says,

Amitabh Bachchan cannot be compared with just another actor. Bachchan is an exceptional actor. He has been fortunate enough to be living in a kind of no man's land for a very long time, between the eastern oriental Indian and western culture. So that is how and that is where he has been able to imbibe from both sides and I suppose today in modern India, whether the writer or the actor, or the director, only those people will be effective who have the best of both worlds. If you are too westernized then you get alienated by the audience, you get too far—if you are too Indian then you cannot fulfil their aspirations because their aspirations are different. So you have to be the synthesis of Indian and western influences and I think fortunately Amitabh had the background and circumstances for that.[14]

What was unique about Bachchan when compared to his predecessors was a novel use of space, an economy of words in his dialogue, a restraint in his anger and an immense and total control on his body. The new language of control was in many ways operating against some of the existing melodramatic codes of the 'formula'. It was this resistant posturing through an evocation of a new set of codes that seemed to mark the 'beginning' of the 'angry man' image and a rupture with the romantic persona of the former superstar, Rajesh Khanna.[15]

Amitabh Bachchan was an angry hero, torn between a desired future and an unhappy and turbulent past. The historical meaningfulness of this image lay in allowing for plural forms of identification through a performative mode that enabled Bachchan's body to become the symbolic terrain for a multiplicity of narratives. In a sense this enabled Bachchan to evolve a style that seemed to mask the *other* within, mapping himself into the regulated spaces of the body and 'self'. As Pile and Thrift point out,

People map themselves into socially-sanctioned regulations of body and self—but they do so only imperfectly: people are not chameleons. . . . The mask/drag, that people use to get them through the day, is a veil which continually threatens to be torn away by the violence of the other.[16]

Masking/masquerade, while inherently fragile, nevertheless plays a crucial role in de-naturalizing the body, and generating in Bachchan's case, multiple signs of recognition/identification for the film public. The ability to generate a mode of address that could articulate and draw on a variety of social experiences, a range of human emotions and an easy handling of different forms of body attire—all within a single narrative, perhaps became crucial for Bachchan's iconic status. The interesting thing here is that all these different forms of emotion and feelings continued to be preserved in their distinctiveness, with Bachchan's performance providing an imaginary unity.

*Deewar* is in many senses the film that marks the acknowledgement of the crisis of post-colonial nationalism. The disenchantment with the settled categories of nationhood is mediated through the crisis of the family, fratricidal conflict and tragedy. It was this disenchantment that spoke (albeit complexly) to a society convulsed by social struggles culminating in the imposition of the Emergency. *Deewar* was a deeply contextualized text: there was an 'elective affinity' (Weber) between the 'moment' of the film and historical transformation.

The story of *Deewar* is of two brothers who follow different paths—one (Bachchan), becomes a dock-worker/smuggler, the other (Shashi Kapoor) a police officer. *Deewar* develops various strategies to confront the crisis—in acknowledging the widespread poverty, inequality and the ineffectiveness of the regime. In a further innovation, *Deewar* poses a striking acknowledgement of urban space. Thus the city loses its fundamentally diabolical character, becoming a space where the hopes and yearnings unleashed by the promise of nationalism are either fulfilled or even dashed. *Deewar* seems to generate initial viewer-identification with the smuggler, Bachchan. While the 'formulaic' death of Bachchan[17] is meant to resolve the problem of this identification, this strategy is largely unsuccessful, given the various disruptions within *Deewar* itself.

The entire story of *Deewar* is presented in a flashback mode as Shashi Kapoor is honoured by the state for performing 'exemplary' duties. The flashback narrates the story of a militant worker forced to betray his comrades in order to protect his family. The posing of the family versus the community of workers sets the tone of the film and resonates throughout the narrative unfolding of *Deewar*. As the father runs away in shame and humiliation, the older son, the young Bachchan is caught by the workers one day and taken to a man who tattoos the boy's arm with the phrase *Mera baap chor hai* (My father is a thief). This tattoo marks out the different paths taken by the two brothers and haunts the personality and character development of Bachchan throughout the film. I refer to this as the scarred body of Bachchan, physically, symbolically and metaphorically.[18] The scar now becomes a signifier for marginality and social displacement, soon taking Bachchan outside the pale of the family.

The transition from childhood to adulthood takes place within the next ten/fifteen minutes with the screenplay dwelling on different spaces of the city—construction sites, underbridges, hutments, high-rise buildings, schools, children working (the boot-polishing sequence with the young Bachchan) and so on. Having mapped out the cityscape of the urban poor of Bombay, the film proceeds to move towards the moral question central to the narrative of *Deewar*.

The first cut to adulthood takes place inside and outside the space of the temple. As the mother, with Shashi Kapoor, comes out into the open, the camera looks down at Bachchan sitting on the steps, slouched, distracted and waiting for his brother and mother to come down. As the three stand together within the space of a single frame, appearing like a tableau,[19] Bachchan's body gestures are contrasted with those of Shashi Kapoor. The contrast between gestures and acting styles not only shapes the emotional resonance of this scene, but also makes legible the fundamental conflicts and issues of the film. Bachchan is shown as sceptical of the rituals of the family/nation. The nation is metaphorically reproduced through the figure of the mother whose overarching presence underlines both morality and suffering, pain and determination, all of which made the family of *Deewar* an explosive site of contest.

The film now proceeds to narrate the lives of dock-workers and in the process builds on the character and personality of Bachchan. Here is a cynical man whose subsequent solidarity and anger after a worker is killed, leads him to an open confrontation with the mafia. Through a series of tableau images of the dockyard, Bachchan's personality is built as a man who creates his presence through a controlled regime of feelings rather than melodramatic excess. In the canteen when Bachchan makes his well-known statement '*Rahim Chacha kal se ek aur coolie in mavalion ko hafta nahin dega*' (Rahim uncle, from tomorrow, one more worker will refuse to pay money to the mafia), the camera begins a zoom that ends on his face. A major transition from other films, the protagonist's anger is still being expressed through his controlled posturing. The shot ends with Bachchan slowly standing up and the camera tilting to a close-up to capture his expression. An excessive use of static long shots and the zoom on to his face, is a running technique with the 'angry man' image. To my mind, this technique allowed for a spatial positioning of the actor, where the body's gestures and multiple signs are released externally in an outward movement in the long shot and the zoom on to the face, enabling a look into the 'interiority' and hidden inscriptions of memories, traumas and desires. As Barry King says,

It is generally accepted that film poses limits on the representation of interiority, inclining towards behaviourism, showing the surface of things. . . . Films tend to re-site the signification of interiority, away from the actor and on to the mechanism.[20]

Thus the projection of the 'angry man's' 'interiority' is also enhanced through a filmic strategy (long shot to zoom in), symbolizing an order of dialogue where the 'outside' and the 'inside' are interlocked. The transfer of subjectivity to the camera also occurs in Bachchan's case because the multiple articulation of the perceived body, operating as the mask required for a magnified subjectification, poses limits on the exploration of 'interiority'. Through the use of the zoom technique, Bachchan's subjectivity is explored from the 'point of view' of the world at large, attempting a dual objective of both identification and distance creating a diegetic strategy of positioning the protagonist.[21]

On the other hand, Bachchan's body seems to generate its own dynamic. Thus when we see him walking along the docks through a rival mafia gang leader's car window (actor Iftekar), a full shot shows Bachchan walking with the posture of an aristocrat. As Iftekar calls Bachchan to join him in the car, we see him turn his head, pause for a second, finally moving towards the car. In the conversation between the two across the window, we see Bachchan's face—cynical yet curious. He finally accepts Iftekar's invitation and gets into the car with the confidence of a man used to sitting in cars. This is what is so fascinating about the Bachchan phenomenon. The underdog always operated with the symbols of poverty visually inscribed on the body and the codes of an upper-class upbringing projected through his gestures and posturing. It is this combination of narratives that seems to have made Bachchan into such a popular star for so long: a combination of spectatorial desire, fantasy and images of the 'real' coming together in an amalgamation of multiple codes of performance. The fantasy of a rise in class status, is itself imbued with a desire that remains unfulfilled in the narrative, but strikingly apparent in the images. Through the performance of Bachchan, we sometimes see Clint Eastwood, sometimes Marlon Brando, sometimes the actor as a person and sometimes the character of Vijay himself. These narratives are not random but converge to assume particular historical forms. The dominance of these forms is achieved not through a conscious ideological manoeuvring by the film-makers but through 'multiple processes of different origins and scattered locations'.[22]

As the 'eastern' and the 'western', Hollywood and Bombay, on screen and off-screen, provide a multiplicity of signs, signals and narratives, the hero within the screen narrative must take recourse to a search for his 'origins'. Origins of an 'authentic' experience written and expressed through the body, as living memory. The notion of 'origins' as evoking a centralized force seems to allow for a movement of the fissured or dispersed gaze towards a unified and unidirectional one. The metaphor of pain as a universal yet intensely individual 'experience' allows the possibility of both sharing pain as well as acknowledging its location in difference. As the multiple articulation of Bachchan's body language evokes plural forms of identification, pain becomes the galvanizing force mobilized for a magnified subjectivity.[23]

Bachchan's scarred body is central to his negotiation within the codes of the 'formula'. The scar is an index of memory, a regulator of his practice, a constant intrusion into his life and a reminder of his marginality. The scar is introduced periodically to regulate the multiple narratives that inform Bachchan's discourse of the body—this is resolved by stressing the return to 'origins'—the shame of childhood. For example, following the conflict with the mafia at the dockyard, Bachchan replies to his mother saying, '*Tum chahte ho ki main bhi mu chupake bhag jaun?*' (Do you want me to also hide my face and run away?)—the reference to the failed/absent father. Bachchan justifies his act as part of a redemptive strategy dealing with historical pain—pain that has been inscribed in the body of the hero. At the close of the sequence, the camera dwells on the now sleeping Bachchan's arm with the scar/tattoo. This is the first re-emergence of the scar in Bachchan's adult life—its image here, through the gaze of the mother, paves way for a narrative transition in the hero's life. When confronted by his Inspector brother, Bachchan uses the tattoo to justify his transition to criminality. Another important moment is when Parveen Babi, unable to take Bachchan's anguish, asks him to remove the tattoo through plastic surgery. Bachchan replies that the tattoo had left deep marks on his body, soul and hand and no plastic surgery in the world could remove it. In a shot where both stars are in the frame, we see Parveen Babi bending her head to kiss the tattoo, an erotically charged moment where she proclaims her solidarity with his past/pain. During the funeral sequence where the long-lost father is cremated, the camera moves from the fire to Bachchan's arm which is lighting the fire. The scar/tattoo is highlighted: thereby focusing on Bachchan's burden of shame/revenge. Here the scar's symbolic status differs from other meaningful objects of family reunion dramas which are recalled to resolve the broken home. In *Deewar*, the scar is constant, and publicly exhibited to be carried by one of the protagonists until final redemption by death. The past, its history and shame are important regulators of Bachchan's trajectory in *Deewar*. A damaged past is the site of constant referral and the justification for criminality, a tragic death/sacrifice is the 'formula's' resolution of Bachchan's multiple coding of his body. In a sense, death is also Bachchan's return to his 'origins': his death in his mother's arms offers the possibility of partial redemption by re-entering the space of the family/nation.

The number 786—Bachchan's identification badge as a dock-worker—circulates throughout the narrative of *Deewar*, as a symbolic device, channelizing the evocation of memory through flashes. The badge assumes the status of a fetish object, whose phantasmic powers are summoned periodically through the film. The fetish/badge becomes the object of memory, evoking a multi-layered realm of meaning. The first invocation is a 1970s version of secularism (as 786 stands for *Bismillah-E-Rehmane Rahim*),[24] then the badge/image emerges as the bodyguard or protector from death as Samanth's (a mafia gang leader) men try to kill Bachchan—almost as though remembering the past is always beneficial for the present. Finally, the sliding away of the badge, the break with his past, is what ultimately brings about Bachchan's death. The status of the badge changes once Bachchan changes his proletarian clothing to become a smuggler—no longer worn on his arm, it rests uneasily in his pocket.

The status of the fetish is theoretically complicated, lacking a stable referent: its magical powers are exaggerated by its very ability to transcend its initial functionality in Bachchan's coolie stage. At one level the fetish seeks to inscribe Bachchan's identity as an adult, his class status as such by merging with his body. The badge/fetish also seeks to regulate Bachchan's transition to upward mobility (having joined a mafia gang) by acting as a magical guarantor of life. Having saved Bachchan's life twice, death comes when his body is separated from the badge. Michael Taussig says when describing the formal mechanism of fetishism, 'the signifier depends upon yet erases its signification'.[25] Operating as an emblem endowed with sacred meaning, the badge in *Deewar* evokes some of the moral discourses of the narrative. The emblem's fetish power emerges from its ability to erase the presence of the past that is concentrated and animated in the badge. This fluid process of inscription and erasure is precisely what allows the emblem/badge to become an important narrative device/strategy, symbolically addressing the complicated process of abstraction and figuration in representation.

At another level the fetish/badge may be contrasted with the scar/tattoo in organizing the narratives of the 'angry man's' body. While both serve as sites of memory and to some extent regulate identity, they operate at different levels of temporality and inscription. While the scar is posed as a historical given for the body, of Bachchan from childhood, the fetish/badge on the other hand maintains an uneasy relationship to the body, allowing Bachchan to move between different social spaces—notably his transition to a higher lifestyle. This displacement of the badge from the arm to the pocket evokes a desire for class ascendancy, at the same time drawing attention to his 'origins'.

Bachchan's power is also generated through a consolidation of his masculinity, a masculinity that acknowledges the object of desire yet fails to possess it. Take for example, Bachchan's relationship with Parveen Babi. In a remarkable departure from other films, they are shown to have a physical relationship out of wedlock. Bachchan's feelings and emotions towards Parveen Babi somehow seem to threaten his sense of masculine identity, since the denial of such feelings and desires is what constitutes his male identity.[26] This is also strengthened by a constant denial of 'femininity' or feminine qualities. The 'angry man's' subjectivity is maintained not through physical restraint or coercion, but through a gaze thrown back upon itself, generating a process of self-surveillance. The narrative logic of the 'formula' ultimately takes first Parveen Babi and then Bachchan to their death, their freedom, and redemption.

## THE PSYCHOTIC AS PROTAGONIST

The psychotic hero of contemporary cinema no longer speaks the broad social language of the earlier 'angry man' but remains within a world of seemingly unrelated individual obsessions. The psychotic is both desiring of a family as well as its ultimate destroyer, who kills even as he 'loves', evoking passionate emotions of love and hate through his obsession with a young woman in *Darr* and *Anjam* and the mother in *Baazigar* (where the mother's victimization creates the psychotic).

An interesting point to be noted here is the unself-conscious spirit of the psychotic's body. Shahrukh's movements on screen, his speed and spontaneity, allow him to experience a pleasure not through a display of his physicality, but through innovative and stylistic movements which ultimately become the site of destruction and extreme forms of cruelty. In almost all the three films mentioned, there is either a process of disfigurement or graphic violence inflicted on the body. Shahrukh's exaggerated movements on screen, through a new kind of body language, is the re-invention of *excess*, a mark of the body's controlled 'interiority' appearing externally. This expression of 'interiority' is taking place within a historical context where the 'external' world of social life, history, culture and politics have thrown into question the ability of the post-national citizen/subject to define and construct a vision of the nation. It seems to us that the image of the psychotic may be read as an allegorical comment on the representational limits of the 'formula', its inability to articulate the current crisis.

In *Origin of German Tragic Drama*, Benjamin shows how the *Trauerspeil* (the mourning play), was an allegorical intervention *vis-à-vis* the continuum of historical catastrophe (the Thirty Years War). The conventional form of Tragedy with its focus on the tragic-heroic resistance of the hero and what George Steiner calls an 'aesthetic of reticence', could not articulate the magnified pain and terror of the times.[27] An engaged response, says Benjamin, could not be but in the form of allegory—the *Trauerspeil* or the 'play of mourning'. Breaking with the conventions of Tragedy, the Trauer magnifies negativity, evil, lamentation, and gesture—here the central themes are decay, ruin and the personification of evil in the corpse. The *Trauerspeil* does not 'address' history but is the expression of historical crisis:

The *Trauerspeil* does not offer some manifest commentary on these historical events. Rather, the experience of historical catastrophe itself is incorporated into the structure and content of the work, becoming the controlling premise of dramatic action, the fixed metaphorical referent for the generation of dramatic language.[28]

Like the *Trauer*, the psychotic image seeks to generate a new discourse of pain, dispersed morality and a violent drive towards death—a response to our own catastrophe: the violence of 1992 after the demolition of the Babri Masjid and the pogroms in the city of Bombay. One is aware that this is a rather strong statement, but perhaps it is possible to draw such meanings if one consciously advances an allegorical reading of images. Such a process is possible, in my opinion, only during moments of 'historical catastrophe'. Like Benjamin's allegory, the psychotic image is a fragment in the current constellation of images present in Bombay cinema.[29] And like the *Trauer*, the image of the psychotic allows us entry into forbidden realms of desire, pain and subjectivity not accessible through given narrative structures.

By breaking the long-standing hold of the 'formula' and the star system, the psychotic's image seems to question the more 'rational', restrained and controlled anger of the Bachchan era. Bachchan's portrayal of the wronged man, unstable but always 'morally' bound, an outlaw but committed to the family and the 'honour' of the women in his life, seems a different image from that of the psychotic whose apparent retreat on screen from the values of social justice seems to embody the 'schizophrenia' that has possibly become part of public discourse today.

Schizophrenia as a metaphor for understanding the experience of contemporary society has been theorized by many. Jameson's use of the term refers to a stage in society where the past becomes unimportant and the present is celebrated.[30] Deleuze, on the other hand, has a more productive usage of the term where the flow of desire is seen to have the potential for a radical displacement of the repressive structures of late capitalism.[31] I would argue that while Deleuz's formulation enables an understanding of the ways in which dominant forms of representations can be displaced through transgressive images, Jameson's thesis shows us how these transgressions can sometimes erase the 'radical past'. However, it is perhaps possible for us to historicize the loss of history in the image of the psychotic through an allegorical reading of its construction (in the Benjaminian sense) as a new mode (not just a retreat from the past) that seems to challenge the 'formula's' imposition of a moral, ethical and legal order. Ironically this 'retreat' from the old imagery of the 1970s has opened up new possibilities, the least of which is the changed architecture of *desire*, where the psychotic's action holds out the utopian possibility of breaking all boundaries.

Shahrukh's attempt at destabilizing the terms of the 'angry man's' discourse is projected through a dangerous instability of desire, through a cinema of transgression that attempts to subvert the constraints of all other forms of discourse by situating itself in a position of difference. As the stable notion of the 'self' undergoes a transformation, the instability of schizophrenic desire is represented through various textual strategies, deployed to heighten the inward dialogue with the 'self'.

Darr is the story of three characters placed in a triangle, yet in a radically different mode from the earlier triangle films.[32] Sunny Deol is a naval officer whose romantic involvement with a college student (Juhi Chawla) is disrupted by the third character in the film, Shahrukh Khan, whose obsession with Juhi is the driving force of the narrative of Darr. Darr opens with the setting of a hill station with the female protagonist Juhi Chawla reading a letter from Sunny Deol. As it starts raining, Juhi is forced to run for shelter. As she starts untying her dress, the spectator's look overlaps with the look of an unknown voyeur/psychotic. This overlapping point of view also draws attention to the changing look of the camera, a look that may want to interpellate the audience in its gaze, to implicate the desire of the spectator with that of the voyeur. As the film's movement/vision emanates from a human body (via the camera), it seems to become an eye to that body. What emerges is something like a cyborg-like[33] experience where the spectator, the actor and the camera coincide in their point of view, their bodies overlapping and their vision synchronizing. As a strategy used in the opening section of the film and some other instances in the film, Darr evokes a narrative of 'interiority' that identifies quite clearly with the psychotic's gaze, implicating the spectator as a 'desiring machine'. As Javed Akhtar says,

I suppose we respect perfection. We respect freedom, there is an evil in all of us, there is a sadist hidden in each one of us, but our morality has imprisoned it and when we see somebody whose evil has broken all the moral norms and now he's a complete person in himself, even in his ill doing, we admire that person because he is a law unto himself, he's a morality in himself. We respect that power. We don't want to imitate him, but that power fascinates us.[34]

However, while spectatorial plurality may resist such a homogenizing position as Akhtar's, this statement reveals an assumption about spectatorship in the industry insofar as films of this nature are concerned.

In the next sequence, the space of the college, a song is played on the soundtrack, but the singer is not established throughout the song, except through fragmented disembodied shots of his hand, profile, etc. The song ends with Juhi coming face to face with 'I love you Kiran' written on the blackboard. The interesting point here is that Juhi still cannot differentiate between the lover and the voyeur. As she leaves Simla in a train, the film cuts to a voice saying 'I love you Kiran' and a hand holding a photograph of Juhi. The voice/body relationship and its cinematic negotiations in *Darr* are effectively deployed to evoke the 'inner' thoughts of the person, to seemingly privilege them over the exteriority of the perceived body as thoughts and utterances emerging from within, yet not as conscious speech but as unconscious desire. It is a textual process that has the ability to question the unitary effects of synchronized sound.

The disembodied voice of Shahrukh in *Darr* is cinematically effective in creating an uncanny aura for the development of the narrative. As Mary Ann Doanne says,

As soon as the sound is detached from its source, no longer anchored by a represented body, its potential work as a signifier is revealed. There is always something uncanny about a voice which emanates from a source outside the frame . . . the narrative film exploits the marginal anxiety connected with the voice off by incorporating its disturbing effects within the dramatic framework.[35]

As the title of the film itself reveals, the fear of the unknown face, an unexplainable anxiety is what marks the story and cinematic construction of *Darr*. The overlapping of the look of the camera with that of the spectator combined with the sound of the song whose source cannot be pinned on to anybody on screen, at some level implicates the audiences, constructing the imaginary spectator within the narrative disclosure of *Darr*. The open reference to off-screen space in both visual and aural terms, locates the spectator at the centre of this universe of moving images.

The voice/body dichotomy is also deployed interestingly through the use of telephonic conversations and the psychotic's recorded voice on a tape-recorder. The other characters trying to look for the psychotic cannot connect the voice to the body. The voice/body split occurs at another very interesting moment, where Juhi fixes a meeting with Shahrukh on the phone in an effort to nab him, while Sunny Deol is waiting, looking down from a building.

Shahrukh is shown sitting in a chair talking to Juhi—in his imagination. We only hear his voice, but do not see his lips moving. Shahrukh's voice appears like what Doanne calls an

interior monologue, where the voice and body are represented simultaneously, but the voice far from being an extension of that body, manifests its inner lining. The voice displays what is inaccessible to the image, what exceeds the visible: the inner life of the character. The voice here is the privileged mark of interiority, turning the body inside out.[36]

The disembodied voice of Shahrukh in *Darr* seems to question the unity of the speaking 'self', a profound turning-point in the representation of the 'angry man'. The stuttering speech and stammer deployed by Shahrukh, the madness in his acting style, are also evocative of the nervous, uncontrolled 'self'.

*Darr* underlines a recurring theme in the psychotic films—the *inability to name evil*. Evil is ubiquitous—very similar to Benjamin's mourning play. In a significant sequence, Sunny Deol is established as a dedicated soldier fighting terrorists who are trying to 'destabilize' the nation. With neither location nor time revealed, the patriotism of Deol is evoked in abstract terms. In an amazing departure from earlier depictions of patriotic zeal, *Darr* shows an entire rescue operation led by Deol with only music and visuals—no dialogue, no speech, no real encounter with the enemy. The significance of this abstract patriotism, fighting abstract, unnamed terrorists in the name of an abstract nation, sets the ambiguous tone of the events to unfold.

*Baazigar* is the story of a boy who grows up with vivid memories of his father and sister dying in tragic circumstances instigated by the villain (Dalip Tahil) and Shahrukh's mother losing her sanity as a result. While the child Shahrukh has these memories entrenched in his mind, the interesting thing about the narrative of *Baazigar* is that those memories are revealed to the audience through two very important flashback sequences *much* later in the film. The family's destruction turns the protagonist of this film into a ruthless killer, with a single-minded obsession for revenge. The living mother played by Rakhee provides the legitimacy and motivation for Shahrukh to emerge as a psychotic.

The two younger women in the film are daughters of Dalip Tahil, the original instigator of Shahrukh's family tragedy. The narrative proceeds to show Shahrukh becoming romantically involved with both the sisters, first killing one of them (Shilpa Shetty) and then killing other witnesses to wipe out any trace of evidence against him. Shahrukh is then set for a marriage with the second sister (Kajol) until the chain of unfolding events leads to Shahrukh's exposure. The film ends again like *Darr*, with the psychotic's brutal death.

As Shahrukh makes his entry from childhood to adulthood in a cut that seems like an exact copy of *Zanjeer*,[37] the transition takes place via negative images of childhood memories of his family's destruction. In *Zanjeer*, the transition is a haunting dream, a fragment of Bachchan's childhood memory and thus an unclear image, since the child witnesses his parents' murder through the gap between cupboard doors behind which he is hidden. His frame of vision is limited. However, the spectator is allowed the privilege of knowing what Bachchan's dream actually refers to. In *Baazigar* interestingly, the psychotic controls the narrative unfolding in its totality. The negative film images are meant to mask the audience's look into the child's memories. The audience is allowed entry into his past only when Shahrukh wants them to, through two very important flashback sequences. As the audience is taken to the past that bears a direct relationship to the present, one is reminded of Maureen Turim's ideological analysis of the flashback:

One of the ideological implications of this narration of history, through a subjective focalization is to create history as an essentially individual and emotional experience. Another is to establish a certain view of historical causality and linkage. By presenting the result before the cause, a logic of inevitability is implied, certain types of events are shown to have certain types of results without ever allowing for other outcomes than the one given in advance. . . . This fatalism presents a cynical view of history, cyclical, guaranteed to repeat that which we have already seen.[38]

The structuring of these flashback sequences as following the brutal actions of the psychotic within the narrative of the film, makes the character of Shahrukh in terms of his lack of behavioural consistency with the structuring codes of the 'formula' appear to be strange, unmotivated and frightening. Shahrukh's action 'constructs' the past through selective, episodic filters, in contrast to Bachchan in *Deewar* where the flashback from Shashi Kapoor's point of view appears more as a functional strategy of story-telling, creating the temporal continuum of past/present/future which is overwhelming and almost external to the inner psyche of the hero.

The first flashback takes place after Shahrukh takes charge of Dalip Tahil's empire. As the chair on which Shahrukh is about to sit starts rotating, we are taken into the character's past. Since Shahrukh is sitting in this room alone, the flashback is directly addressed to the spectator in narrative terms. The psychotic hero conducts an internal dialogue with the past and his psyche while simultaneously addressing the spectator. Since the re-enactment of the past via the flashback shows the child witnessing the gradual disintegration of his family because of a crooked relative, the child as the spectator of all the events, imbues the flashback with the notion of a perceived past. The recounting of the flashback sequences at crucial moments within the narrative again constructs the imagined spectator, by narrating a series of traumatic events emerging from childhood fixation, making possible the pleasure of loss and suffering, all of which takes place within the diegesis of *Baazigar*. The second major flashback takes place towards the end of the film as Shahrukh completes the story of his past for Kajol. Through this process *Baazigar* resolves the dilemma of both Kajol, the daughter of the villain, and the spectators for whom the jigsaw puzzle is finally completed. But again through this second recounting of a *perceived past* (a subjectively focalized narrative, to use Turim's words) *Baazigar* finally moves on to the gruesome climax whose causal inevitability is now available to us.

In occupying the traditional space of the villain within the 'formula', the psychotic seeks to explode the regulated desires of the iconic hero on whom the codes of morality imposed by the 'formula' are at play. This complex interplay of a social morality and a rewritten geography of desire is taking place within a new configuration of the 'formula'. The pain and pleasure that the psychotic experiences can be read as both the externalization of an agonized subjectivity and a schizoid movement towards 'non-rational' fulfilment .

Although the 'recovery' of a subterranean 'interior' in the case of the psychotic is projected through an explosion of desire, I am not trying to suggest that the emergence of this 'self' is an authentic projection of 'interiority'. Rather, in the techniques and practices of the 'self' as they configure to work on the body, there emerges a space which cannot be brushed aside simply on moral grounds. What the psychotic manages to achieve is the creation of a third space that has not been articulated within the 'formula' before. It is in the creation of this zone of desire and emotion that the binary forces within which the 'formula' is structured get challenged both in formal and historical terms. The mirror sequences in both *Baazigar* and *Darr* where the protagonist talks to his own image, draw attention to the role of the fuzzy, unmapped region between 'self' and 'other'. As Stam says in his commentary on Bakhtin,

Even when looking within oneself, one looks in and through the eyes of the other, one needs the other's gaze to constitute oneself as self. Even the apparently simple act of looking in the mirror is complexly dialogical, implying an intricate intersection of perspectives and consciousness.[39]

In giving vent to what can perhaps be called schizoid desire, the psychotic aspires for a freedom that is elusive within the codified nature of the 'formula'. As the expression of an 'interiority' fights for a public space, visuality and the process of filmic constructions exaggerate this movement through a politics of *excess*. It is only in relation to the Bachchan phenomenon that one can understand and see the loss of control over the body, a control that was in the former's case premised on a politics of limits, of containment and of boundaries.

As the mirror sequences, the flashback sequences and other forms of personal dialogues suggest, the psychotic is given ample opportunity within the narrative to provide the causal links required to justify his actions. Structured as they are at crucial moments within the films, the psychotic's dialogue, the style and mood of the *mise en scène* acquire the aura of a confession almost directed at the audience for extracting sympathy. As the psychotic stretches the limits of narrative possibilities, there emerges a character—frightening, yet attractive, illusory as well as 'real', a character who both defies and yet encourages identification. In creating this third zone for the interplay of desire and fantasy, *excess* is reinvented yet in a radically new form. Here schizophrenia opens up the possibilities and potentialities of desire, disrupting, challenging and reinventing some of the master codes of Bombay cinema.

The psychotic experiences a freedom in death. The torture that leads to death, the pain inflicted on the body is both pleasurable and painful. In a sense the psychotic embodies the pain of a scarred and torn city expressing an agony that needs to be shared. As Elaine Scarry says,

It is through this movement out into the world that the extreme privacy of the occurrence (both pain and imaginary are invisible to anyone outside the boundaries of the person's body) begins to be shareable, that sentience becomes social and thus acquires its distinctly human form.[40]

## TIME/SPACE AND THE ALLEGORIZATION OF THE CITY

From *Deewar* to *Baazigar* and *Darr*, the city of Bombay undergoes transformations registering a process of both erasure and reinvention. In *Deewar*, as was significant of many films of that period, the city is constructed as a site of hope and loss, mapping Bachchan through the urban space in the form of analytical time, time that carves out a space to evoke the crisis of the 1970s. The spatial construction of Bachchan's body in relation to the city, privileges the spectator with the complete knowledge of the individual. *Deewar* seems to contextualize the processes of rendering visible the manner in which a variety of discursive practices map the grounds from within which the protagonist *must* speak. In doing this, *Deewar* creates a social reality that seems to define the frames through which the 'angry man' is rendered legitimately visible. A series of tableau sequences map out the causal chain of narrative events, enabling an understanding of the 'angry man's' behaviour. *Deewar* offers a multi-layered explanatory screenplay situating the protagonist in ways that turns Bachchan into a powerful iconic image, an image whose power is rendered through a heightened form of subjectification.

The city in the psychotic films is allegorized through a shrinking of the cosmos. This process of turning inward is also enabled through technological transformations, transformations that reshape and rework the narrative organization of space in time. For example, there is a privileging of time/movement over space in the psychotic films which positions the body of the two actors (Bachchan/Shahrukh) quite differently. As the technique of the long shot and the zoom make clear in *Deewar*, Bachchan's body is hardly ever fragmented into close-ups. The long shot and the zoom seem to have an interlocked relationship where Bachchan always gets positioned within the spatial dimensions of the city. The temple sequence, the underbridge, the five-star hotel, the bar, the dockyard—in all these places, the body is tall, straight and controlled. Bachchan's subjectivity is guided within the screenplay through a series of narrative events structured around the city of Bombay. Bachchan is also situated at a low angle in relation to the high-rise buildings, the camera always showing him looming large, but the buildings being even higher. Bachchan is always shown looking up at the buildings.

In the case of the psychotic there is a shift. In both *Baazigar* and *Darr* Shahrukh in certain crucial scenes is placed on a height from where the streets of Bombay are neither visible nor important. The city of Bombay seems to suffer from a collective amnesia, with the logic of the narrative moving inwards, towards the internal psyche of the scarred hero. In *Darr*, only after Shahrukh's look and speech have been introduced, do we get to see his entire body in the frame. The disembodied voice gives way to the full-bodied image, against the backdrop of Bombay. As Shahrukh walks on the railing of a high terrace—the city appears below him as an empty space shorn of any utopian drives. In *Baazigar* the act of killing the woman is accomplished from the top floor of a skyscraper: the space above the city is the site typically favoured by the psychotic. The spatial and temporal shifts are also heightened for instance through the use of the steady cam[41] to capture Shahrukh Khan's energy in the two chase sequences in the city. The steady cam movement privileges speed/movement over the spatial dimensions of the frame. The result of the chase is that the city appears as a blur rather than the space so crucial to the construction of the Bachchan phenomenon. In *Deewar* for example, the narrative disrupts the final chase with the badge (786) falling down and Bachchan's final attempt to hold on to his past. The camera stays on this sequence for a few minutes before the chase is renewed. The city of Bombay, whose social signifiers disrupt the chase through the use of the fetish/badge, simply have no equivalent in *Darr* or *Baazigar*. The effort seems more to present the city as a functional backdrop, rather than a space invested with diverse histories and utopian hopes. Even the fragmented body, the claustrophobic monologues and the rapid cutting of shots, succeed in turning the narrative inward into the psyche of the psychotic hero. The city is present in the psychotic films by its absence. Through a process of textual amnesia, we move away from the city of *Deewar* into the claustrophobic world of the psychotic.

Fredric Jameson writes in *Marxism and Form* that the utopian impulse, while not being able to abolish death, may 'rob it of its sting'. Death cannot abolish life 'fully realized' in a 'perpetual present'.[42] In the case of the 'angry man' the city was the canvas that provided a utopian counter to the tragic-heroic death. The city retains its character as a site of the unrealized utopian impulse of the hero despite the redemptive death of the protagonist in *Deewar*. For the psychotic, death is stripped of its mythic qualities, lacking the beauty of tragic martyrdom. For the psychotic, death is unrelated to the utopian impulse of the city: the act of dying seems emptied of meaning and fulfilment. Yet even in the image of the psychotic a weak utopian urge shines through, perhaps in an allegorical allusion to the possibility of freedom in schizoid action. While in *Deewar* the hyper-subjectification of the hero leads us through a well-defined journey of redemption, the psychotic in *Darr* and *Baazigar* fleetingly poses the unimaginable during a moment of historical ruin, destruction and death in the city.

## NOTES

1. By 'current constellation', I refer to the existence of a variety of new icons that have emerged in recent years in Bombay cinema but have not been able to match the powerful iconic status of Amitabh Bachchan. In many ways the iconic image has undergone a process of disintegration, embodied most explicitly in the schizophrenic imagery of the psychotic hero under discussion.

2. While many actors today are playing the role of the psychotic, thereby establishing it as a fairly popular trend, this essay looks primarily at the first appearance of the psychotic played by the popular actor Shahrukh Khan.

3. Bombay cinema's narratives are usually structured around a set of social and cultural codes or signs loosely put together to form what is colloquially referred to as the 'formula'. These codes repeat themselves within specific historical configurations. In other words, the 'formula' is in a dynamic relationship with historical codes of representation at any given time. The use of the word 'formula' here is deliberate as the phrase is part of the film public's perception of film texts. Though the term 'formula' film has been subjected to pejorative comments by critics of 'commercial' cinema, we find it a useful term to negotiate the discursive space between the film-public, the industry and representation.

4. London: Verso, 1977.

5. The notion of 'interiority' and its projection is always rather complicated in the case of visual representation. How do we define 'interiority'? Foucault contests the inner/outer distinction by drawing attention to how regulatory practices working on the 'inner', hidden space of the body get manifested on the surface of the body. While in agreement with Foucault that the inner/outer dichotomy is only a 'construction' that helps in creating the illusion of a rational, coherent subject, I would argue that visual images are still constantly trying to struggle with the representation of an imagined 'interiority', however unstable that may be. In this essay I use the term frequently only as a problem of cinematic representation.

6. Earlier imaging of the nation refers to the complicated ways in which representations of the nation were worked out around the country/city relationship. However one must shy away from sociological analysis where representation is *functional* to historical transformations, however mediated. Even a thinker of such insights as Jameson falls victim to such an account. See his historicist juxtaposition: modernism-industrial capitalism, postmodernism-late capitalism in *Postmodernism or the Cultural Logic of Late Capitalism*, London: Verso, 1992. The effect of Jameson's schema is to miss the breaks and ruptures both at the level of representation *and* history. For a brilliant critique of Jameson see Mike Davis, 'Urban Renaissance and the Spirit of Post-Modernism', in E. Ann Kaplan (ed.), *Postmodernism and its Discontents*, London: Verso, 1990, pp. 79–87.

7. Elin Diamond (ed.), *Performance and Cultural Politics*, London: Routledge, 1996, p. 3.

8. While the discourse on the two actors have been shaped by a plurality of images, the 'angry man' and the psychotic image are examined here through their specific textual constructions in the three films.

9. 'Signs of Melodrama' in Christine Gledhill (ed.), *Stardom: Industry of Desire*, London: Routledge, p. 212. Also see Ravi Vasudevan 'The Melodramatic Mode and the Commercial Hindi Cinema: Notes on Film History, Narrative and Performance in the 1950s', *Screen* (London) 30(3), 1989 and 'Shifting Codes, Dissolving Identities: The Hindi Social Film of the 1950's as Popular Culture', *Journal of Arts and Ideas* 23–24, 1993.

10. Peter Brooks talks about *excess* as an important feature of melodrama. Excess here is a reference to the expression of 'interiority' as it articulates itself in the structure or the realm of emotions that make up the melodramatic imagination. As such excess has no stable referent, but operates as a mode of performance. See *The Melodramatic Imagination: Balzac, Henry James, Melodrama and the Mode of Excess*, New York: Columbia University Press, 1985.

11. For an interesting article that develops this notion using and amending Foucault's classic pronouncements, see John Fiske, 'Cultural Studies and the Culture of Everyday Life' in Lawrence Grossberg et al. (eds), *Cultural Studies and the Culture of Everyday Life*, New York: Routledge, 1992. Also see Susan Bordo, 'Feminism, Foucault and the Politics of the Body' and M.E. Bailey, 'Foucauldian Feminism: Contesting Bodies, Sexuality and Identity' in Caroline Ramazanoglu (ed.), *Up Against Foucault*, London: Routledge, 1993.

12. James Naremore, *Acting in the Cinema*, Berkeley: University of California Press, 1988, p. 2.

13. *The Body in Pain*, New York: Oxford University Press, 1985, p. 285.

14. In an interview with Shikha Jhingan and Ranjani Mazumdar, *The Power of the Image: Themes from Popular Hindi Cinema*, a documentary series under production. Javed Akhtar along with his co-script writer Salim Khan, were the originators of the 'angry man' image.

15. The 'angry many' image did not, of course mean the end of romance in Bombay cinema, nor was it limited to Bachchan alone. In fact, Dharmendra in *Yaadon Ki Baraat*, seems to anticipate Amitabh's later persona, but lacks the multiple, trans-class persona of Bachchan. Thus while Bachchan performed other roles in addition to his 'angry man' image, his iconic presence was defined by the latter.

16. *Mapping the Subject*, London: Routledge, 1995, p. 49. As we shall see, the entry of the psychotic creates a crack or a 'fold' (Deleuze) in the angry man's mask, to pave way for a third zone of subjectivity and action.

17. Here 'formulaic' death refers to the construction of an event through which the rule of law and 'assumed' notions of public and private morality are retained within the narrative, despite the existence of counter-narratives within the film.

18. These signs become particularly important for the representational strategies of Hindi cinema, acquiring fetishistic powers of signification. The tattoo in this case becomes symbolic for the metanarrative of the 'angry man' phenomenon, thus lending itself for a metaphoric interpretation.

19. A tableau is a structured and well-defined frame that appears self-contained in its organization and dispersion of meaning, almost like a painting. For more detailed discussions on the tableau, see Roland Barthes, 'Diderot, Brecht, Eisenstein' in *Image Music Text*, New York: Hills and Wang, 1997, pp. 69–78 and Peter Brooks, *The Melodramatic Imagination*.

20. 'Articulating Stardom' in *Stardom: Industry of Desire*, London: Routledge, 1991, p. 177.

21. For a discussion on focalization see Edward Brannigan, *Narrative Comprehension and Film*, London: Routledge, 1992, pp. 100–7.

22. Sumita Chakravarty in her section on Bachchan, talks about the importance of Bachchan's own class background providing an important extra-textual discourse, whose 'knowledge is used to judge how he measured up to the expected behaviour patterns associated with each group that are themselves textually constructed and lodged in the popular mind through repetition'. See *National Identity in Indian Popular Cinema*, Austin, Texas: University of Texas Press, 1993, p. 201.

23. For a detailed discussion on pain see Elaine Scarry, *The Body in Pain*, New York: Oxford University Press, 1985.

24. In *Deewar*, there is a significant discussion around the badge when Bachchan in his coolie stage, talks to a Muslim worker (Rahim Chacha), who informs the former about the sacred power of the number in Islam (786 is the numerical total of the chant *'Bismillah-E-Rahmane Rahim'*). This sacred meaning of 786, combined with its everyday functionality as an identification number

for Bachchan, enhances the role that the badge plays throughout the film. Interestingly, the same number was used by Bachchan in Manmohan Desai's film, *Coolie*, where the former plays the role of a Muslim worker.

25. Michael Taussig, *The Nervous System*, New York: Routledge, 1992, p. 118. Taussig elaborates on a historical genealogy of the word 'fetish', linking it to totems and taboos in certain cultures. The 'origins' of the word 'fetish' are grounded through Bill Pietz's genealogy 'in a western history of *making*, rooted in strategic social relationships of trade, religion, slaving, and modern science' (118). This anthropological exposition is relevant for our discussion of the badge in *Deewar*.

26. For a more detailed description, see Sudhir Kakar, *Intimate Relations: Exploring Indian Sexuality*, New Delhi: Penguin India, 1989, p. 40.

27. In the Introduction to Walter Benjamin, *The Origin of German Tragic Drama*, London: Verso, 1977, p. 18.

28. Max Pensky, *Melancholy Dialectics: Benjamin and the Play of Mourning*, Amherst: University of Massachusetts Press, 1993, p. 75.

29. The psychotic image co-exists with other images in Bombay cinema today. Unlike the Bachchan era where the 'angry man' narrative was dominating and overwhelming in its power, this older iconic image has imploded into various fragments, out of which the psychotic is only one. It is, therefore, the critic's task to provide an allegorical reading of this new constellation.

30. See Jameson, *Postmodernism or the Cultural Logic of Late Capitalism*.

31. *Anti Oedipus: Capitalism and Schizophrenia*, London: Athlone Press, 1983.

32. While earlier films of such a nature resolved the triangle by the tragic death/sacrifice of one of the two male protagonists, in *Darr*, Shahrukh's hero/villain status robs his ultimate 'death' of the usual sacrificial/teleological status.

33. See Donna Haraway, *Simians, Cyborgs and Women: The Reinvention of Nature*, London: Free Association Books, 1991.

34. Jhingan and Mazumdar, *The Power of the Image*.

35. 'The Voice in the Cinema: The Articulation of Body and Space' in Bill Nichols (ed.), *Movies and Methods*, Berkeley: University of California Press, p. 571.

36. Ibid., p. 572.

37. *Zanjeer* (Chain) is the first of Bachchan's vendetta films. In this film however, Bachchan is part of the establishment (police inspector). With *Deewar*, Bachchan crosses over to the other side and becomes a law-breaker/criminal.

38. *Flashbacks in Film: Memory and History*, London: Routledge, 1989, p. 17.

39. *Subversive Pleasures: Bakhtin, Cultural Criticism, and Film*, Baltimore: Johns Hopkins University Press, p. 5.

40. Scarry, *The Body in Pain*, p. 170.

41. The steady cam is a brace used to fix the camera on the shoulder of the camera person to capture speedy movements without the jerks normally associated with hand-held shots. The steady cam was also used to capture chase sequences in *Roja, Bombay*, etc.

42. *Marxism and Form*, Princeton: Princeton University Press, 1971, p. 142.

IV | *Indian Film, Film Theory and Democracy*

# 10

## Viewership and Democracy in the Cinema

ASHISH RAJADHYAKSHA

### THE 'INSTITUTION' OF INDIAN CINEMA

PICK UP ANY account of the Indian cinema and you usually face a phrase about it being the 'world's largest film-making nation', usually presented as a self-explanatory matter of national pride and seldom investigated further. I start differently in this essay, one that also happens to be an account of the Indian cinema in a sense, with the assumption that this statement could well be less assertion and more a point of departure for some (possibly uncomfortable) questions. I do not expect to resolve most of these questions in the words that follow. What follows is the outline of an argument, an agenda, for researching both the Indian cinema itself and for addressing larger questions of film theory in general.

It is of course true that the terrain that cinema spans in India can be of astonishing dimensions: an approximate 23 million people, over 2 per cent of our total national population (and possibly half the population of many established film-making nations), go to the cinema every *day*. It is also the case that this audience has been, over the broad part of this century, remarkably resistant to the cultural invasion of Hollywood. Right now the Indian film-goer's seeming resistance to non-local forms of entertainment is spilling

I thank Tejaswini Niranjana for her help and support, without which I might never have brought this essay to completion. I am indebted to several colleagues in Hyderabad, notably S.V. Srinivas, Susie Tharu, R. Srivatsan and Satish Poduval for the intensive debates that followed an earlier version (entitled 'The Four Looks and the Indian Cinema'), and arguments with Paul Willemen, Madhava Prasad, Vivek Dhareshwar and Ravi Vasudevan which helped me further some of the arguments and abandon others.

over into several new areas such as cable television and music video, and indeed forming something of a precedent to the Indian consumer's attitude to the recent flood of multinational goods as one premium brand after another, from cars to cigarettes and cornflakes, discovers the difficulties of making inroads into the Indian market without substantially adapting itself to local conditions. In the cinema itself, we have recently seen a renewed but—to say the least—only moderately successful, and sometimes embarrassing, assault on local film markets with Hindi dubbed versions of top-of-the-line American productions (such as *Speed*, *Cliffhanger* and *Richie Rich*) vying with local produce in predominantly B-movie distribution sectors.

Instead of assuming, as much writing on the subject does, that an entirely sufficient explanation for this resistance can be found in nationalist indigenism, let us start with a different premise which assumes, *prima facie*, that there is nothing determinedly indigenist in the political values of Indian film spectators at large, that it's simply that they like local products more than imported ones, and ask instead the question: what constitutes the Indian spectator as a film-viewing *category*? If it is indeed a category of some kind, with what kind of political and cultural values is it constituted, and where—culturally —is it constituted? Is it, so to say, a kind of 'special knowledge', an ability, and an invitation, to read texts in certain ways? Or is it better seen from the other end as something of a *mode of address* that identifies 'spectators' in a certain fashion, which then might in turn be placed alongside and in some kind of dialogue with the cultural-political determination of Indian subjects? Whatever the case, given the largely complete, time-honoured and self-sustaining account of film spectatorship—that after a certain moment in the cinema's history when it became a fully industrialized entity, it put together something that Noel Burch (1990: 2) calls a 'reading competence' that has been taught for fifty years and more as the 'Language of Cinema' and is now, as he says, 'universal among the young in industrial societies'—it would be fair to argue that the Indian film-going experience is now a large enough, sufficiently complex area to severely complicate the question of what constitutes 'reading competence' in the case of cinema, and—if Burch is right in making the link—to also complicate the relationship between this competence and industrialism, and to suggest a need to rethink the issue on the terrain of film theory itself.

This essay seeks to extrapolate from a number of arguments on how Indian viewers see Indian films. In that extrapolation is a larger agenda that, contrary to my evidence and area, is not in any special way 'about' the Indian cinema. What I want to do here is to try and put together not so much an 'Indian' film theory (as against, typically, a 'western' one) but rather the outlines of a *theory of the cinema that can account for the Indian cinema.* In doing so, I start with the assumption extended recently by Tejaswini Niranjana (1997) that the category 'Indian' may no longer be limited to national boundaries, given that it is continuously produced, and implicated, in local cultural formations in places as removed from our shores as Trinidad and South Africa. In this sense the category 'Indian spectator' too may be seen as a category deployed in, and attractive to, a range of spectator formations in parts of both the 'West' and the 'Third World', wherever people—whether ancestrally of Indian origin or not—see Indian films. This is an area on which little work has been done, so it is impossible right now to answer the often vexed question of whether those who see Indian films appear, when it comes to seeing Indian cinema, to require a faculty that seems to be either not accessible, or simply not interesting, to most other film viewers, and what this might then mean.

In all this, it has still to be worked out what relation the Indian cinema edifice has to what has recently been extensively investigated, notably in the USA, as the 'narrative' or 'story' film, which replaced an earlier diverse and chaotic period usually exemplified by the fairground and the era of the nickelodeon, and at a date on which all film historians are agreed: 1914. The institution of an economy of film narration, with the arrival of several techniques of shooting and editing that are now commonplace but which at that time de-froze the otherwise static, frontal relation between the screen and the film-viewer, is often equated with the triumph of industrial capital as evident in the term 'Industrial Mode of Representation' (or IMR) that goes along with Burch's 'reading competence'. By this argument, and others that have been repeatedly made (and continue to be made) in India, the cinema here has simply not mastered the 'classic' story-telling idiom. The mainstream Indian cinema has often been remarked upon with wonder at the number of songs in it, the ingredients of the 'masala' that move from comic routines to fight sequences, with the plot itself—if there is one—providing the barest outline for all that goes on in the film. Given that Indian films do depend, in some fashion, upon the Hollywood mode of story-telling, the question whether the Indian 'spectator' is simply what we might call an insufficiently 'Hollywoodized' audience, or whether the Indian cinema's modes of making and showing the moving image should be used to severely problematize the notion of 'reading competence' itself, remains indecisive and controversial.

Let me start with the category of the *institution of the cinema*. At one level, in doing so, I speak of the film industry itself, but one that for all its scale has still not been recognized as an industrial institution by entities such as the Union Finance Ministry, banks and corporations, and does not therefore have access to banking or corporate finance.[1] It still stands perceived as a low-technology, low-capital, labour-intensive cottage industry comprising mainly of independent production houses.

At another, related, level, I speak of the 'institution of the cinema' in the sense in which Christian Metz (1982) uses the category as comprising an institution of systematizing a well-established chain of exchanges between film-going spectators, the screen itself, and the filmed and projected moving image, each component existing as an articulate sector better known in simpler language as production, distribution and exhibition. Metz interprets this institution as comprising, not so much a 'reading competence', but rather the management of an encounter between on one side, an agency that 'releases' and then in some ways guarantees the film through its camera-projector-viewer axis, and on the other side, another agency that 'receives' the film and 'who may therefore see what the text does not want me to see'.[2] Here the many determinations of cinematic realism thus come together with the spectator's freedom to configure him/herself, from the one extreme of a voyeuristic 'not me', to the commoner 'me' devoid of my ego as I become a pure mechanism of looking, to the far more complex self that the film assembles as the entity 'for whom it was made'. Metz's insight here is one I want to further frame into a specific question that is not part of his argument: one of cultural/spectatorial *rights*. Who is it that decides what 'I'—the agent, in his language, of the film's release mechanism—shall see? What control do I, in my more modest avatar of individual spectator, have over that decision? How does this exercise of discipline constitute me, and what say do I have in that category, of my 'constituted' self? All of these happen to be, I submit, pivotal questions underpinning the very existence of the cinema in India, and certainly the context of a number of major battles to which entire careers have been devoted and lives lost.[3]

Let me arrive at a third level with the suggestion that the resistance that the Indian film spectator puts up to what has been called the 'Hollywood Mode of Production' also extends to, or certainly informs, the Indian cinema's own resistance to turning into a properly capitalist industry. The 'self' that the spectator constitutes over the duration of a film's narrative, I submit, relates in some fashion to what Vivek Dhareshwar (1995: 318) has recently called the 'ways in which the political present is disposed to theorize itself'. I am seeking a rather more complex connection here, between what I would see as the possible larger paradigms of institutionalization that the 'cinematic institution' covers and that the film spectator negotiates, by taking a slight detour into what Dhareshwar presents as the very premise of *intelligibility* itself. For Dhareshwar, the entire process of making sense of what we see of reality emerges out of an impasse into which we find ourselves in India: the 'inability of the history that has constituted our present to "go forward", as it were', at a time when the instruments of such definition—of cultural and political self-understanding—do not seem to provide the conditions for rendering key concepts, such as citizenship, rights, democracy, secularism, the nation, as intelligible.

The crucial question . . . is how the 'who' (of 'culture') and 'what' (of 'politics') relate to each other. This question lies at the heart of the concept of the citizen subject. What is involved in the *translation* of political idioms? How to characterise the resulting imbrications? Are there any 'pre-requisites of citizenship?—economic, cultural, or gender? Are the problems and antagonisms generated in the process of putting citizenship (and other related concepts such as rights) into practice contingent by-products, or are they internal to it?

It is my contention here that the cinematic institution in India has a great deal to say about all of this. In a technically precise sense it is possible to argue that within the Metzian 'exchange' between the agencies of 'release' and 'reception', the cinema is always *about the present*, always situated, literally, in the present tense. This faculty has over the years demonstrated its astonishing ability to literally render history itself, as *itihasa* or 'thus it was', as seen for instance in the power of both actual and simulated documentary footage. Put more simply, as any film editor would testify, the basic shot before it is edited *prima facie* consists of both its immediate textual 'subject-matter' and a kind of excess spillover that can potentially take the meaning of its subject-matter into a number of directions. To yoke that meaning into, let's say, its commonest axis of realism—where the shot of a tree would have to look like a tree on screen—requires a number of further processes to come into place: you need to shoot the tree from a certain angle and distance, you need to let the shot last only for a certain duration, you might need to further transit from that shot into another where the volumes established in the shot are not completely violated by the next. In this situation, in a technically basic sense, the process of 'rendering intelligible' in the cinema requires in part at least a process of containment, where what is shown becomes acceptable to viewers as containing only what meaning the narrative imputes to the subject-matter of a shot, and can mean nothing else.

We are perhaps more familiar with the broader historical and aesthetic dilemmas posed by this aspect of the cinema—by its tendency to both create authoritative subject-matter and simultaneously to exceed that subject-matter—but are perhaps less aware of what this might mean to the terrain on which Dhareshwar locates the problematic of intelligibility. Cinematic narration is persistently reduced in popular discourse to its 'story' but remains elusive to precisely this horizon of the economic. From this basic fact the entire history of cinema could be written up. It could be viewed as a series of contests over, and efforts to 'contain', the spillover involved in the very category of the moving (as against still) image. This drive contrasts with efforts—mainly in mass culture and the cinematic avant-gardes—to point to this excess and even at times, to articulate the possibility of an intervention of some kind into the economic base itself. Not for nothing, I might say in passing, does the cinema feature so prominently in this entire century in revolutionary political movements from the Soviet to the Latin

American, and in nationalist efforts at decolonization throughout the 'Third World'.

That argument will have to be made elsewhere. At this moment, I shall restrict it to its relatively well-charted component in India: to the specific history in which it was sought to be an ally of the state's project of deploying, in Dhareshwar's words, 'both sovereignty and discipline to institute modernity, including the institutions and practices of political modernity'. If indeed such a connection could be made, not only on an administrative level featuring, say, NFDC and Doordarshan but in the deeper political sense that Dhareshwar is trying to get at, then the resistance of both the global popular and avant-garde cinemas to *this* project of containment—the resistance, in the instance of the former, of spectators to the process of the cinema being converted into a fully capitalist enterprise—can also be explored in the terms Dhareshwar uses: in the cinema's constitution of 'not-yet-citizens', and most of all perhaps, in its remarkable ability to address collectives, communities, and groups, on the terrain of an address apparently constituted only to fully formed citizens/individuals in the Noel Burch sense of a universalized reading competence.

In this essay I shall argue that just as the concepts of democracy and citizenship became, in the way they were understood and deployed, factors of mediation and negotiation in the setting up of an indigenous, modernist, sovereign state/subject, so it was that the cinema's deploying and thematizing of concepts drawn from capitalist systems of production led to the founding of an institution around a 'narrative contract' between spectators and producers, and between the spectators themselves. The second category is not only contiguous to the first, but it displays an astonishing reliance on the first to create the very terms of filmic narrative.

## THE CONTRACT OF CINEMA

This is a brief diversion summarizing an important argument by Sudipta Kaviraj (1995) which makes a forceful point about how Indian nationalism 'received' the discourses of western liberalism. Kaviraj starts by suggesting that in the colonial period, but perhaps even since, 'western concepts (e.g. of democratic theory) . . . are brought into Indian political discourse through a dual process'. This duality has consisted of, first, an assimilation of the official discourse itself, read precisely as such, as something *official* in the sense in which the state guarantees it as such. As we move this concept into greyer areas, I shall later attribute this 'official' category with a certain *interpretative* status: as qualified to provide precisely *authoritative* interpretations for both the contextual transfer of the category itself but also to interpret whatever problems might arise in its local implementation. Then there was a second level of assimilation: which Kaviraj calls the 'vernacular' variation, where once the concept 'enters the vocabulary of the colonial peoples and comes to figure in their imagination' their meanings, their implications and consequences 'begin to diverge significantly from the trajectories analysed within traditions of western theory'. His argument locates the two discourses as eventually residing in two worlds in India, one embodying the traditionally dominant language of secular liberal opinion and which literally speaks in English, the second, of nationalism and democracy and which speaks in a range of hybrid vernaculars. In my version of this, with which Kaviraj may not agree, the two discourses, 'official' and 'vernacular' are in time *both* converted into distinct and recognizable categories and, as such, *both* indigenized to various degrees. What persists is precisely the preciously maintained duality, which it seems to be in the interest of everyone concerned to hang on to, even as different values and faculties are imputed to each, which open up a space for something of a *transactional* relationship between the two. Like two sides of a coin, neither has existence except in relation to the other; each mediates, and even occasionally invents, the other in its self-image.

In this negotiation, and assimilation, lies the resolution of a key issue: the concept of the citizen. It is here that Kaviraj outlines a move that, I think, fundamentally skews the dualism between 'official' and 'vernacular'—or 'inside/outside', 'home/world', 'material/spiritual' or even plain and simply 'us/them'—and sends the dualism spinning off into a radically new direction. Nationalist writers often evoked arguments of democracy and self-determination, but all of this was

to make a fundamentally different case. The liberal argument that the rationality of man must be construed to mean that each human being is the best judge of his own interests and therefore deserved the right to individual autonomy was simply transferred, to the considerable embarrassment of utilitarian theorists, to the national community . . . (and meant) primarily the collective freedom of the Indian people from British rule, a translation of the question of liberty entirely, unproblematically, into the question of national sovereignty.

The consequences of this move for India after Independence have only now come to be clarified. In part at least, the attribution of individual liberty to something as abstract as a nation led, after Independence, to widespread acceptance of the concept that it was the *nation* (rather than the people who lived in it) that had won freedom. The state, which stepped into the 'domain of the public' and took over the right to be the sole legitimate user of the 'official' language of liberty and freedom, in turn created a set of *further* conduits for the disbursing of both that language and the rights that underpinned it.

If India has never had a 'developed individualist conception of society', then it certainly does have one now. In fact it is demonstrable that the transactions that take place between the state and the agents of civil society on the one side, and groups, collectives and communities on the other, is precisely over the terrain of individual rights as India internalized these and as these came to reside in the nation and its hypothesized citizen-subject. It is better therefore, for our purpose, to regard the category of the 'individual citizen' as something of an omnibus category that works primarily as a *transactional* site, and a mechanism, for all the actions that collectively comprise what in India we call 'democracy'—in short, as precisely the beginnings of a structure of narration. As Kaviraj goes on to suggest, it is 'better not to treat democracy as a governmental form. . . . A better strategy, in the case of the Third World, is to treat it, more problematically, as a *language*'. This language in turn, he argues elsewhere (Kaviraj 1992: 33), underpins something like a narrative: the narrative of institutionalization, best seen in this context as not universal (a category to which narrative structures do sometimes aspire) but as local and particular, as a *contract*:

The telling of a story brings into immediate play some strong conventions invoking a narrative community. Ordinarily these are coincident in terms of their frontiers with social communities of some form . . . To some extent, all such communities, from the stable to the emergent, use narrative as a technique of staying together, redrawing their boundaries or reinforcing them. Participating in a movement quite clearly involves accepting something like contractual obligations and, I suspect, some of this affiliation of individuals to movements counter-acting a monadic individualism is accomplished by narrative contracts.

Let me now start gradually mapping this political model borrowed from Indian democracy theory to the cinema. I shall do this through shifting three categories discussed above into direct parallel with the cinema. These are the categories of 'narrative contract', 'citizen' and 'civil society'.

The difficulty Indian (and generally non-western) film-makers have with the concept of 'story-telling' as in Hollywood cinema has already been mentioned. And yet anyone who knows how the mainstream Indian cinemas function would also know that in fact the *story*—or at least what is written down in advance by people like screenplay and dialogue writers—is *crucial*, both to producers and distributors. For what they have invested in the film's launch is, apart from stars and music director, precisely the story (the 'property' as Hollywood and even some Hindi cinema calls it). The story is crucial as well to audiences, whose cinephiliac dissection of what they have seen, concentrates overwhelmingly on this component, not as exclusive from but somehow containing the entire film-going experience.

Plainly, in this sense, the difficulty of 'telling a story' lies less in the mechanics of narration itself and far more in what we have already called the economy of narration: economy, or even econom-ism, in the sense in which the story, and the universe of its evidence, claims to provide not only a complete explanation for all that goes on inside a movie theatre but also discredits all evidence exterior to this universe as irrelevant to what story-telling *enacts*. It is also well known that behind all this baggage lies the considerable legacy of realism: realism, in the cinema, being a combination of the refer-ents of reality that endorse the image as 'realistic', the conventions of 'rendering plausible' whatever is shown, and the entirely self-sustaining diegetic nature of the 'industrial mode of representation'.

Indian cinema has a great deal to say about all these categories. One possible mode of enquiry into this might be to, first of all, treat the 'story' as a rather more comprehensive category in which are provided certain explicit guarantees, as in a contract, and also as a system for putting in place the actual mechanics of a *narrativized site for spectators, to enact a series of transformations in the way it actual-*

*izes them.* Let me explore this further with a second transposition from the political model mentioned above to the cinema: a shift this time from the category 'citizen' to the category 'viewer'. The historical relationship between citizen and viewer in the formation of a public sphere is well known. I want to explain this further with the help of Partha Chatterjee's new work on the subject: work that helps me explore the components of cinematic story-telling that are literally contracted to be instruments of negotiation.

It is well known that 'interpellation' was defined by its author as something of a 'double constitution': in the first move, it demarcates the 'category of subject' as 'constitutive of all ideology', but in the second, limits, or specifies, this action to its 'constituting concrete individuals as subjects' (Althusser 1994). For my purpose I shall understand this double constitution as follows: while at one level, the democratic constitution of the citizen literally consists of *naming* all the actual, existing, members of a nation as such, at another there is also the ideological process of putting in place what is basically an abstraction: the subject, constitutive of 'all ideology', which actual members of society are differentially invited to identify with, assimilate, approximate to. Following Chatterjee's work (Chatterjee 1997), the first 'naming' category can be defined as 'democratic': it is one where people are 'classified, described, enumerated'. And the second a category of 'modernity', where people are invited, sometimes coerced, to transform themselves and gradually, over time, approximate to the codes of the abstract 'national' subject.

This constitutes a key dichotomy which is often politically resolved through what we have seen as the concept of citizenship as a transactional site, and which is much more often *narratively* resolved through a process of enactment in a variety of forms. The 'narrative contract' in the cinema can now be understood as the following: in maintaining the concept of the category of the 'individual'—here the 'individual viewer' for whom the film has supposedly been made—as a necessary fiction, the narrative structure has to enact, and in various ways further aid, the transformation of that category, and the rights it underpins, into something like the bestowing of citizenship rights to what Chatterjee calls 'political society'.

One final transposition further elaborating the category of the story: a shift from the category 'civil society' to that of 'realism' as its privileged narrative mode. Earlier I had argued that the category of 'citizen as nationalist' was mobilized, as authentic and legitimate, mainly for the purpose of authenti*cating* and legitim*ating* certain discursive constellations as against others—in its negotiations between what we had earlier called 'official' and 'vernacular'—as ·speaking 'for' the Indian state or in its 'official' self-image. I shall now go further and suggest that, in its deployment as a category of legitimation in Indian cinema, realism performs not only a 'pedagogical mission in relation to the rest of society'—one that involves tutoring people into the protocols of 'how to see films' as fully formed members of civil society see them—but, and as an extension of this function, also works, on behalf of the state, as the dominant overseer for the narrative contract of cinema as a whole. We are familiar with its relatively more limited instances of 'actually functioning realism' in, say, a Shyam Benegal film where its place in the 'pedagogical mission' of modernity is self-evident as is the fact that it purports to address fully formed members of civil society, functioning under the authority of their gaze, and usually constitutes an invitation to such audiences to, as it were, participate in and sit in judgement over whatever moral or ethical contradictions it presents to them in its presentation of 'reality'. (One path for this mediation is that of 'psychological' realism and projective identification translating into concepts of bourgeois subjectivity and literally residing in the 'sphere of the patriarchal, conjugal, family' as its given audience.)

This aspect of what we might call 'NFDC' realism—so named after the Indian government institution that usually funds such cinema—is more familiar than the extension of this paradigm over the cinematic institution as a whole. Here too, in the film industry, we have, in general, a set of persistent assumptions that repeatedly evoke realist conventions to authenticate what's going on: that the cinema only addresses *individuals*, the protection of whose interest justifies the very existence of institutions such as the Censor Board; that these individuals in the movie theatre see films in a 'realist way', in other words 'identify with' certain situations within the fiction (so that what is commonly considered wrong with the mainstream cinema is that impressionable people identify with the wrong things, the cinema provides immoral 'role models' for our youth).

Realism's legitimatory capacities are then often extended to oversee disputes between the film industry and the Censor Board when, typically, such-and-such scene considered objectionable is argued as being 'necessary to the plot', or when female stars say that they might agree to reveal their bodies 'if the story requires it'.

What is entirely missed when we accept realism's own definitions of its function under such circumstances—circumstances that are by now self-evidently far removed from the more standard European contexts of realism theory—is why it remains a crucial category for *audiences*. I shall argue that the ability of audiences to recognize, and slot into the narrative contract, the 'ideal(ized)' viewer for whom, so to say, 'this film has been made', and the way that this category—guaranteed and endorsed by institutions of the state as containing, and capable of disbursing, the rights of citizenship— features as a site for *further* negotiations within the wider arena of cinephilia, is in fact the actual 'reading competence' of the Indian film-goer watching Indian cinema. What actual audiences do with this idealized category forms the subject of the rest of this enquiry.

## LOOKING IN CINEMA

Let me begin by partially repeating the proposition made above in more conventional 'reception theory' terminology. I first propose that all the 'textual readings' that are these days politically correctly described as 'context activated' are in fact fundamentally dependent on their own manufacture of the text's 'idealized' reader. In doing this, I am inserting a rather more live political dimension to what is otherwise a relatively straightforward phenomenon: that real-life readers and viewers of any text at some level usually try to comprehend and put in place some abstracted category of 'who this text is meant for', and engage with this category as part and parcel of any textual reading.

There is a common argument that in some ways, film theory's tendency to elide the actual people who go to see films in favour of a textually driven theory of spectatorship is ahistorical. Paul Willemen (1994), for instance, forcefully argues that

for the purposes of formalism, real readers are supposed to coincide with the constructed readers. Should they have the temerity to consider the text as a profoundly unstable economy of discourses . . . these readers will be accused of running the risk of distorting or simply failing to recognize the aesthetic structure as a self-regulating system that makes sense only from a particular vantage point.

While holding (I believe) on to what he calls the 'locus of struggle', I think it is nevertheless worth asserting the equal possibility that 'real' viewers who have paid to see a film themselves have a major stake in wanting to prop up the coincidence between their gaze and its fictional 'vantage-point' that inscribes their gaze into the text. Extending this latter submission, I wish to investigate the possibility that it is not only readers who read against the grain who risk something. Risk is involved *even* when actual viewers attempt to assimilate a fictional vantage-point of the 'ideal' reader: for even in this attempt lies a struggle and a possibility of failure that actual viewers are usually aware of, and what's more, that film *narratives* are aware of. This is, at least in part, the struggle that renders the text as a 'profoundly unstable economy of discourses' in the first place. Examining *why* this is so, and what is the nature of that instability, is one, perhaps the more useful, way of approaching the problem, rather than the commoner assumption that the problem lies not so much in the text but in the 'historico-ideological' space that the viewer inhabits.

A technical point about this space in cinema, that the viewer inhabits. An interesting aside that recent research into early cinema provides is how long it took, and how many experiments (mainly on fairgrounds) were involved before the now-universal system of audience seating was arrived at. Today films are shown worldwide under roughly identical conditions: spectators sit unidirectionally facing a screen, and the projector is behind them, over their heads. If this is now a universal law, it follows that all screenable films therefore must constitute, at base, a frontal address, the one addressed to all those who are looking unidirectionally at the screen. What I shall for now call this *baseline* address is in fact a crucial one, because unless that frontal address is shifted in some way, the film will simply be stuck with an actual audience, one not very different from say, the experience of projecting still-image slides. This is, I am sure, readily acceptable, but its corollary may not be. And that is that *all* films, and especially films working with a figurative structure and attempting to narrativise or simply temporalize this address, in fact *require* and *acknowledge* in various ways this baseline in their structuring; that it forms a crucial component of their effort to shift it into a different register—and further, that the requirement is in the nature of a tacit agreement that this baseline of address is always to an actual viewer, to somebody sitting there in front of the screen. The filmic frame is marked in the camera and that frame is replicated on screen, and that is what people see when they sit in a movie theatre. It is in the cinema's acknowledgement and possible reiteration that this is so that brings us to the launching moment of a second category of viewer: the 'inscribed' viewer, constructed or 'marked in' by the film/text.

For inscribed viewers who 'move' with or are 'moved by' the film, on the other hand, do not appear to face this limitation of being stuck with a unidirectional frontal address, but can very well acquire another, more negotiable, more flexible, site: a site that comes close to what we, paraphrasing Metz, might call 'outside the frame but within the fiction'—a category similar to, if not quite, the well-known out-of-frame character whose subjective look determines the angle of the camera in so much 'story-telling' film. Inscribed viewers, in other words, permit actual ones to disclaim, negate or renounce—in Freudian terms *disavow*—the fact that it is always and at all times within the duration of a film *they* who are watching it.

It seems to me that, seen in this light, the 'actual' and 'inscribed' viewer dichotomy then cannot be something that arrived in the cinema with the 'story-telling' system, contrary to standard assumptions. Reversing a standard question film-goers ask each other, it is rather more like, 'What does this film make of you?' For very much the reasons that Metz mentions, which are that since what you are seeing does not (unlike in theatre) physically exist, it follows that both the pressure upon actual viewers to 'own up' to the camera-projector-viewer baseline gaze which they see as simply theirs alone—their 'identification with the camera/projector'—or to disavow it and find ways of doing so, it must also follow that this is *basic to the moving image itself* even though it is true that this was later what the Hollywood-mode IMR institutionalized into its most familiar forms. Seen in this light, it is possible to excavate a considerably longer-term history of how cinema dealt with this problem in its earliest days and in ways that have proved influential ever since, and certainly it opens up the possibility of investigating how local cinemas the world over internalized this technology through bringing to it their own terms of reference. In this history, it would perhaps be possible to show other kinds of conventions that brought these categories together, not only to pluralize the history of film viewership itself but also to question the apparent claims of self-sustaining autonomy and fully internalized 'inscribed' viewer categories by Hollywood-derived narratives. In both (the French) Lumiere and (Indian) Phalke, there is no real instance of camera placement that uses editing to categorically shift the linear frontal baseline axis of camera-projector-*actual* viewer, to create, say, the point-of-view of an offscreen character. In both, however, once viewers got over the initial shock, incredulity, astonishment and so on, there was clearly inaugurated the process of *acknowledgement* that this is the case—that 'real' people sitting in front of the screen are watching this—and then, having said that, of *characterizing* this axis with a further set of values that have proved influential beyond their times in the traditions to which these film-makers belong. In Lumiere's case this was in effect the assertion that 'what the camera sees is true, and therefore what you are seeing actually happened', and in Phalke's, 'Do you recognize what the camera is showing you?' Phalke's question in a sense includes Lumiere's assertion, even though it shifts its subject-matter somewhat.

Even so basic a point as the one I have made above, nevertheless finds me stumble right in the middle of one of the most hallowed debates in film theory. Writers from both *Cahiers du Cinema* and *Screen* in the 1960s–70s have gnawed on different aspects of this problem, which for them, in turn, originated in previous debates around 'reality' in the film—in brief, around the problematic status of 'actual', 'physical' or 'pro-filmic' reality once the cinema has given it a working over. Jean-Louis Comolli (1980: 124) summarized a famous debate around deep-focus cinematography in Bazin and Mitry, to eventually suggest that the best place to look for the 'reality-effect' might be on its impact on viewers: on their 'desire' to believe while not being deluded in the least by the fiction machine, which makes them not just passive and alienated receivers but as 'players, accomplices, masters of the game'.

My intention here is to revisit a few of these formulations but with a slight, if crucial, change in the rules of the 'game' that spectators play, and I am of course, thinking mainly of Indian spectators here. Earlier I had pointed via Chatterjee's writing to how a double process was enacted in India's categorization of the citizen. Transferring these categories into film, we can equate the first category of the double constitution—where actual people are named as possessors of certain democratic rights—with the 'actual' viewer of film. We can now start seeing why the cinema came to mean so much to Indian people at large. Those basic 'enumerative' rights of democracy—the right to be counted, the right to receive welfare—are precious, since these are often the only kind of rights that people in general basically have in a place like India, and people, to different degrees, are aware of and 'recognize' this. And similar rights are unshakably, unambiguously, at all times, present in the *film-going experience itself*, independently of the actual film they go to. This is what, to recall Comolli's 'game', they *know*.

In other words, a crucial value of a political order is added on to what I have called the baseline of the cinema—the unambiguous, unshakable *fact* that, in one sense, the camera's point of view and hence that of the projector, can be nothing other than the view of the actual viewer, and the ensuing *need* to let the viewer recognize this, and then to reassert, acknowledge, this fact at various points in the narrative structuring process. At this level, therefore, when the viewer purchases a ticket, enters the auditorium and 'releases' the film saying 'I am here' ('I am present . . . I help it to be born'), what the cinema is also doing is to incarnate one of the most fundamental, even if ambiguous at times, rights of democracy.

If this is so, then the second category of 'inscribed' viewer can also be explained by the second political move: of putting that abstracted ideological category of citizen in place. Here in the cinema, unlike in political society's battles with the state, there can be no coercion (not obviously, anyway). The inscribed viewer category comes in precisely through the invitation to viewers to identify it, and then identify *with* it: hence both statements, 'It is true' and 'Do you recognize what you see?'; or even, in admittedly different kinds of political contexts, 'You see this/You own this'. What is to be 'recognized' is not necessarily what is on screen: what is also recognized is the abstract category of *viewer* whom the film is, so to say, 'supposed to' be addressing (in the terms used say, by the Censor Board). This is crucial: if you do not succeed, then the local IMR has simply failed, as it does when foreign film-goers proclaim themselves mystified by Prakash Mehra's or Manmohan Desai's films.

Let me consolidate this with another argument by Metz, on what the spectator of film 'identifies with'. The spectator, he says, identifies with the 'character of the fiction' and, at some points can also 'identify with the actor', but neither concept explains fully what's going on. For identification with the 'human form appearing on the screen . . . still tells us nothing', also because *actually* there is no object out there—in human form or otherwise—to identify with. A spectator of the cinema has therefore to be credited with a special knowledge, dual but unique. The spectator 'identifies with *himself*', with himself 'as a pure act of perception', as the 'condition of possibility of the perceived and hence as a kind of transcendental subject'.

To put it in my terms of the 'double constitution', an already formed spectator who exists before the film is made and shown, enters a movie theatre with considerable guarantee—to which he can and does apply if the film, let's say, proves 'scary' ('it's just the camera')—that his already formed ego will not be violated. He then identifies with himself, as a pure act of perception—as a possible transcendental subject which can, for the first time, propose a different way of being perceived by those in authority. The actual viewer enters the movie theatre, and identifies with—not the film's hero or heroine—but with *himself*, his 'inscribed' self, but this time round a self that has become narrativized, and therefore, one that can imagine itself as something like a fully formed subject of society. Such a transformation cannot, as we shall see, be admitted to occur within the tenets of realism, where the actual and inscribed self have necessarily to be assumed to be the same thing, or so the form tells its privileged viewer. Most 'mainstream' films usually borrow this idea for their own purpose, making it often difficult for viewers to claim otherwise. Nevertheless, it is when this is not so, when actual viewers make themselves into something else, that is the truly interesting part of this specifically cinematic phenomenon.

If this argument has any truth in it whatsoever, then it is apparent that we now have to reverse gears a bit in terms of film theory. It is generally the case that most enquiries into 'story-telling' cinema and its 'classic' variety have concentrated on analysing the efficient organization of the intra-diegetic system, or the choreographing of spaces, looks, gestures, and the paraphernalia of camera, editing and sound that assembles all of these things into a coherent and meaningful story: the history of how all of these were put together. On the way, it is often assumed that achieving diegetic coherence is the first principle of story-telling cinema. It is further assumed that there is something destinal about this evolution—that the American cinema 'aspired', from its origins almost, to diegetic realism; and finally, that in some ways the cinema evolved from its origins to gradually, and after many false starts, fit into and successfully reproduce a spectatorial gaze that either pre-existed it or, at any rate, existed independently of the cinema.

If this argument means anything at all, we need to now open the possibility that the cinema's development as a language *coincides with* the assembly of systems of how to look at it; that since these systems do not pre-exist cinema but rather develop alongside it, it inevitably follows that different systems of institutionalizing cinema must also have explored different sets of political-liberatory possibilities in assembling what I have called the 'narrative contract'. At the base of all this, it seems to me, we need to at least account for the possibility that diegetic action can also be seen as existing at the service of the spectator's look, its purpose—initially at least— one of efficiently managing the requirements of the *viewer's* gaze.

## The First Three Looks

In her famous essay 'Visual Pleasure and Narrative Cinema', Laura Mulvey (1975/1989) was concerned mainly with this problem as a question of gender, as is well known: the 'I' who am watching a movie was, she wanted to show, coded mainly into a male viewer and a male gaze. Her basic argument, with a few minor shifts into a different political context—shifts to which I believe the argument itself would be hospitable—allows me to further expand my actual/inscribed viewer argument. In that essay, famously, she identified not two but *three* looks 'associated with all cinema':

the camera as it records the pro-filmic event, that of the audience as it watches the final product, and that of the characters at each other within the screen illusion.

So *first* look: camera looks at reality, at the outside, selects from the outside a frame. *Second* look: spectators look at screen, and *third* look, characters within the film look at each other. It is this last, third, look that is assumed to orchestrate the entire range of intra-diegetic action in a film, which was first put together in the origins of 'classic story-telling' cinema, encoded into an IMR and institutionalized into the 'Hollywood mode of production'. It also happens to be the look that has historically posed the greatest difficulties to Indian, and generally non-western, cinemas. Mulvey, for valid reasons of her own, repeats the standard assumption that the third look asserts its supremacy over the first two. 'The conventions of narrative film', she writes,

deny the first two [looks] and subordinate them to the third, the conscious aim being always to eliminate intrusive camera presence and prevent a distancing awareness in the audience. Without these two absences (the material existence of the recording process, the critical reading of the spectator), fictional drama cannot achieve reality, obviousness and truth.

As a consequence, she says,

The camera becomes the mechanism for producing an illusion of Renaissance space, flowing movements compatible with the human eye, an ideology of representation that revolves around the perception of the subject; the camera's look is disavowed in order to create a convincing world in which the spectator's surrogate can perform with verisimilitude.

Mulvey's well-known project was to demonstrate the inherently unstable nature of this model which 'constantly endangers the unity of the diegesis and bursts through the world of illusion' by pointing to the 'female image as a castration threat . . . an intrusive, static, one-dimensional fetish'. Let me further explore the instability of the fiction in my terms by mapping *my* two looks onto Mulvey's first (camera looks at pro-filmic 'reality') and second (spectator looks at screen) looks before we come to her third look.

My argument is instantly faced with considerable difficulty. For if, as I say, the *actual* viewer's look at screen is, at its base, *identical* with that of the camera, then where does the difference lie between Mulvey's first and second looks? They are in fact the same thing. Let me posit for the moment the suggestion that the second look in Mulvey's sense is not merely the look of spectator to the screen in some mechanistic fashion, but already incorporates the look of the inscribed spectator ('outside the frame but within the fiction').

What this slight shift does is open up a substantial gulf between the actual and inscribed viewer categories: the gulf of the apparatus itself. Even in basic technical terms, the most untutored, dunderheaded, film viewer would know that what you are seeing on screen is *not* identical to what the camera saw: that image, captured on film, edited, and with a mixed soundtrack has to be accounted for if my 'narrative contract' is to work. Indeed, the constant addition of effects to the apparatus, from Dolby to DTS, 35 mm to Scope to 70 mm to, most recently, IMAX, it seems that the entire apparatus of cinema now exists mainly to separate out these two categories from ever meeting. Let me reiterate, without solving the problem right now, the presence in this of two distinct curvilinear trajectories into the pro-filmic action: the one that *endorses* audience 'recognition' or 'release' of what they see and, in reverse, of their place in the auditory-visual machine as 'receiver' of that experience, and the one that *permits their disavowal* from the fact that it is their gaze that the apparatus has basically assembled. Let me also suggest that we would understand all this better if we were to replace the metaphor 'camera' which still tends to stand in for 'apparatus' with its allied, but less popular variant: the film *frame*.

With these instruments let us approach one of the most ubiquitous arguments in film theory. Mulvey says, and it is generally assumed, that the third look—which characters exchange at each other—in story-telling cinema subordinates the first two into its fold. It incorporates, inducts, the first two, making them invisible. On the other hand, I now suggest that when, *if*, the third look announces its intentions to subordinate the first two looks into its domain, this action on its part—which is anyway much less common in cinema than people think—is preceded by a *quid pro quo* that, so to say, sets up the conditions under which the narrative will perform this act, this coup.

In this initial negotiation, the first look (which we now see as camera-to-reality, *endorsing* audience recognition) *conspires* with the second (viewer looking at cinematic artifice, denying link with reality) to produce a prior transaction to which the narrative is forced to *respond*. In this transaction, the frame's *disciplining* of uncontrolled, untamed, reality 'outside' into first a pro-filmic and then an *enframed* image, constitutes a prior domination that *viewers* are invited to assimilate for themselves. This initial act of triumph, extended to a transformation in the viewer's status in all of this, allows actual viewers to enable themselves to become what I might call a triumphant, *spectacularized* audience, capable of acting upon that authority. It is in some sense once this has been achieved, that the cinematic apparatus then demonstrates all its spectacular equipage, in the service of newly ensconced spectacularized authority.

The nature of this triumphal nexus has meant different things in different times in the cinema's history. Its most famous instance is of course when the cinema industry shifted from being 'an anarchic cottage industry to a monopolistic branch of American Business', when the triumph of a bourgeois-modernist audience over the often unequal and anti-democratic tendencies of nineteenth-century capitalism led to the rise of the 'downtown palace and admission charges so prohibitive that they effectively displaced the working class as the cinema's allegedly primary spectator/subject', and a prolonged contest over 'unequal development of productive relations, spectatorship and individual authorship (that) left traces of resistance in the films themselves'. One of these resistances indeed, was the already mentioned loss of deep-focus cinematography since the late silent period. I think it is arguable that the replacement of the 'always objective' zero-to-infinity field depth with a narrow focus field literally allows the viewer's gaze to bestow meaning to that part of the field in focus, i.e. that part of reality upon which they choose to bequeath their attention. The transaction actually taking place is of course the reverse of this: the camera's ability to focus is extended to the valorization of the second look.

Whatever its status, the second look is not any longer merely that of the viewer looking at the screen: it is that of *empowered* viewer deriving considerable authority through that look: an empowerment that springs directly from the presence of the frame as itself something imposing disciplinary coherence upon whatever the viewer is seeing. It is, to continue the early American cinema instance, likely that this notion of the second look was in evidence much more obviously in what Gunning/Gaudreault (Gunning 1990) call the 'cinema of attractions', and that it was mistrusted by the guardians of morality who characterized nickelodeons as dens of iniquity. If so, it is further arguable that story cinema and the consequent narrative inscription of viewer—the 'induction' of his/her look into the diegesis—in fact, constitutes something like putting in place a system of control over that power accumulation.

In fact more and more recent work on Hollywood has tended to demonstrate how long it took, and the extent to which the 'story-telling' mode was literally policed, through the 1930s and indeed until 1960. Overturning the common assumption that D.W. Griffith structured narrative and formalized the industry with the 'story-telling' mode towards the end of the first decade, so to say 'once for all', Mike Cormack's remarkable book (1994: 147–8) shows the extent to which the 'story-telling mode' was quite literally policed by state agencies during the complex and troubled relationship between Hollywood and the American state through the 1930s, starting with the Wall Street Crash in 1929, Roosevelt's New Deal presidency in 1932, the Payne Fund and the institution of the Production Code (better known as the Hays Office) in the period 1930–2, and the fact that it was only around 1939 when an 'ideological need for unity answered by strong subjectivity—the unified American viewer' that finally saw a greater autonomy devolve upon both the industry itself and its codes of signification. Likewise, the infamous House Committee on UnAmerican Activities (HUAC) crackdown on Hollywood in 1951, according to Peter Wollen (1992: 45) accounts for the death of the musical genre after *Singin' in the Rain* (1951).

I believe that it was McCarthyism, in the broad sense of the term . . . that first tragically limited the MGM musical and eventually brought it to a halt. [T]he tragedy remains that Hollywood allowed itself to be intimidated into . . . humiliating conformity and compromise which enervated and destroyed its creative energy right through to the 1960s.

This process of negotiating the first look into the second—of transforming the actual viewer into something that I might call the 'enabled viewer'—is itself not only problematic to an external cultural/political authority: it is also internally problematic because it is an inherently unstable one and this has its own political consequences. Indeed, this is the key instability in the entire cinematic contract. For this transition itself has to be managed, literally like something of a managing agency written into that contract. So crucial is this transformation, and so pivotal the role of the 'ensconced' second look in film viewing, that whatever the formulaic norms of story-telling, *every* film has to literally address this all over again and take no precedent for granted in the process of 'informing' the viewer of the specific faculties, the rights, that this look possesses, the conditions under which it may 'donate' that look to certain kinds of intra-diegetic action and the terms under which it will get it back. For I believe it is demonstrable that audiences never surrender, or donate, their gaze to an intra-diegetic agency in any unproblematic fashion. When they do so, it is implicitly under certain terms, and almost always premised on the assumption that they will receive it back in an enhanced version. There are also important instances where film-goers do not surrender their gaze, *period* .

## THE NARRATOR

We can now define with perhaps greater clarity the function of yet another key category in film theory: the *narrator*, or narrative agency, usually understood as the voice of the 'story-teller', the guide to viewers through the looking maze. It is well known that in many situations in the early cinema, this story-teller—or lecturer— was some person physically present in the auditorium. Gaudreault says (1992) that this person was present in American film more or less until 1910; in Japan the *benshi* and in Korea the *byunsa* extended this into an independent performance art. Gunning (1994: 92, 206) describes his function further: 'the film lecturer endowed the film image with narrative order and legibility, a reading at the service of linear storytelling. . . . The lecturer could supply such values only as a supplement, an additional aid, rather than as an inherent organic unity'. For Gunning, 'this system of providing added realism and narrative clarity through an exterior supplement contra- dicted the traditional diegetic realism to which American film aspired', and hence it was, he writes, that systems like parallel editing came about, 'creat[ing] the filmic equivalent of an omniscient and omnipotent narrator who selects and shapes the information conveyed to the spectator, playing with expectations through effects of irony and suspense'.

Gunning's definition, now considered standard, seems to overlook an important slippage here. Clearly when the narrator was physically present as a lecturer/story-teller, it was evident that this entity was different from the film's diegetic universe: it was an 'exterior supplement' and even, as Gunning says above, one that 'contradicted' the aspirations of American film towards realism. However, when the narrator was inducted into the story-telling mechanism itself, within the film, this distinction was assumed to have been fully integrated into the story-telling. In fact, I think, the contradiction that early cinema demonstrated so graphically between narrator and diegesis remains in later film and is crucial, even in the most sophisticated story-telling systems available.

The narrator is clearly a figure of authority, the one who will tell you 'how to look'. Originating in part in the novel form, and therefore, at least partly contextualized by what Edward Said has shown as the 'imperialist vision' through his book *Culture and Imperialism* (1993), the authority of the narrator in the cinema derives through the cinematic apparatus itself. In other words, it incarnates a narrativizing agency upon the disciplinary gaze that the camera exerts upon reality, extending only from there to the entire recording-mixing-projection apparatus. Crucial to the exercise of this authority, and preceding the 'how to look' one, this entire equation is put in place first and foremost to tell the viewer that 'it is you who is looking'. It is the agency in the film that endorses the viewer's gaze, and it therefore follows that the narrator is, at birth anyway, the apparatus responding to the *first* look: actual viewer looks at screen, and the narrator acknowledges this fact: the 'naming' component of interpellation is now complete.

Let us view this firmly established axis—frame-first look-narrator—from the other end, from the viewer's needs, and in particular from his/her deeply ambivalent response to this assertion that 'it is you who is looking'. If the narrator is indeed, as we have seen, the representative of the *apparatus* on the negotiation table between the two looks, then it must be the agents of *intra-diegetic action*—the characters, the plot—that appear at that same place as agents of the still-in-process, insecure, wanting-to-be-empowered not-quite second look. They begin, at least, the complicated proce-dure of negotiating the narrator's next and equally crucial assertion: 'no, it is not you who is looking'.

But there are a number of formal and legal problems involved: one, the two antagonists are not equal; it is not, to take a favourite phrase from India's pro-liberalization private sector, a 'level playing field'. Simply on the basic issue of viewership rights, the narrator cannot make, or rather, cannot be seen to make, both statements.

The dominant realist overseeing of the narrative contract quite definitely prohibits the narrator from acknowledging the needs of disavowal—as we see in the universal illegality of voyeurism. From the other end, for very good formal reasons, it is folly when any film assumes that it can assemble a fully formed second look at the expense of the first. Because the problem of viewership rights now collides with another problem: the second look emerges as something inherently unstable, capable almost at any moment of sliding into the first. So a horror movie, for instance, one of the genres that can, sometimes at least, appear to do away with realism, can also demonstrate that even, or especially, at moments when viewers are the most involved with what they see, the first look suddenly pops up, the 'pure act of perception' disintegrates before a more reassuring realization that one is 'only watching a film'. The second look is insecure, and threatens to slide at any time into the first: recognizing this is in a sense the first principle of narrative organization in film. This in part explains the several *further* responsibilities of the ever-enlarging cinematic apparatus and the narrator agency to *ensure* that precisely this unpredictable, eternally unstable, entity be properly managed. In most 'story-telling' cinema therefore, far from being merely a narrative grammar, various aspects like the 'shock of entry into narrative' are inevitably viewed as carefully orchestrated scenes.

At any rate, assuming that the full negotiation of actual spectator into his/her inscribed category—or first look into 'empowered' second—is something fragile, and can be in theory disrupted any time; that it is the business of the narrator to see that this does not happen, and in this the narrator is backed and aided by the apparatus itself, let me now suggest a replacement of Mulvey's three-looks model with the following alternative. Instead of locating the third look as inevitably and permanently having subordinated and triumphed over, the first two, let me suggest that the role of the 'narrator' is best understood through a *relay* of differential emphases on the enframed image on the one side, and intra-diegetic action on the other. Rather than viewing the one as having, inevitably and permanently, assimilated the other, it is more useful for me to map a sort of oscillating movement between the two, with at times the first dominating, at other times the second reigning supreme.

In conclusion, I therefore propose the following model which,

I believe, substantially reworks the standard mould provided by film theory. It seems to me a globally prevalent norm that whenever the cinema assumes its 'pedagogical mission in society'—whenever an effort is made, for whatever reason, to re-instruct viewers in 'how to see films'—the narrative *frame* almost inevitably surfaces as the dominant organizing force, and directly provides the authority to a narrator structure which also functions best under such conditions. I speak of 'frame' here in its full technical specificity: as literally the piece of masking that determines the screened image. Later we can disaggregate the frame into a set of numerous component parts within it, both technical (e.g. the horizon, the focus field) and narrational (e.g. conventions like 'direct-to-camera' looks etc.) Right now, I would point only to the wide prevalence of such uses of the frame globally in film industries, whether in Hollywood (e.g. in films like Hitchcock's *Psycho*, 1960, or Spielberg's *Jaws*, 1975), or in what came to be known as the 'new' or 'art' cinema movements in places as divergent as Latin America (e.g. the Cinema Novo in Brazil in the 1950s, the movements associated with film-makers like Godard and Fassbinder in Europe, Oshima in Japan or Park Kwang-Su in Korea) whenever the cinema undertakes the enterprise of reforming spectators. In most of these instances, we see an appeal made to the narrator's authority and behind the authority of the apparatus itself, the ambiguously *assertive* component of film narrative. Placing a broad interpretation upon this, I shall hazard the following conjecture: that the surfacing of the frame coincides with circumstances when it is required that the 'actual' viewer be asserted, reconstituted, re-ensconced, as a fully formed entity, a citizen subject who fully incarnates his symbolic authority. Such an assertion can occur in the cinema all on its own, but it can successfully also (and more effectively) occur at times when the *state* steps in and concretely underwrites this symbolic unity between 'actual' and 'inscribed' viewer.

Wherever it happens, and however it happens, it appears to be generally the case that once such critical moments pass and both the narrative structuring, as well as the spectator's authority to view and interpret is relatively more secure as to what this authority consists of, what we have is, precisely, a *de-privileging* of the frame as the sole, or even main, carrier of the spectator's authority, as more sophisticated 'second looks', interpellative and identificatory systems step in and perform the same tasks, incarnate the same 'contract', with greater effectivity than the frame can do. At this other end of the spectrum, what we get is not so much an identifiable extreme situation but differential degrees to which the frame is de-privileged, secondarized, through the instituting of other modes of address, interpellation and identification—and then crucially *disavowal*—as the 'actual' audience admits—in part or in full—the valid presence of narrative structures which can exist, so to speak, on their behalf. Given that the narrator agency works best, and is at its most authoritative, when it is directly backed by the authority of the film frame, standing in for the apparatus as a whole, it is also true that as the narrat*ive* takes over from the narrat*or* the viewer's anxieties and allows for more complex forms of disavowal. Indeed, as the cinema becomes a more local language in different contexts the world over, what is disavowed is *precisely* the frame. This is literally demonstrable: it is only when 'you are not looking' that the frame too is not dominating the screened action, when it gives way, and is replaced by, more complex, locally derived, interpellative and identificatory devices and gets more and more difficult to understand for people who are not tutored into those systems. This leads to an important and key contradiction: since the narrator is there mainly to combine and pull together into an apparently unified entity, the look of apparatus with that of viewer, and since more sophisticated interpellative systems appear to lead, precisely, to viewers' disavowal of the *apparatus* (of which the frame is only a stand-in, like the camera) it also follows that every time the cinema moves too far from disciplinary Realism, the narrator gets weaker, more diffuse and contested, sometimes unrecognizable in its 'classic' avatar. Here, in this process, what is in fact happening is that the interpellative machinery incorporates paradigms from *democratic* functioning—democratic in the sense in which Partha Chatterjee uses the word. This often provides at least one context in which disciplinary Realism steps in and reasserts control. In such situations, when Realism's commitments to civil society and modernity can, as Chatterjee shows, directly conflict with democratic systems, the baseline axis of cinema—an evaluative category rarely presented by other (cultural, political) sites for other versions of the same conflict—becomes a crucial device for both film-goers and film theorists to identify in order to understand what's going on.

## NOTES

1. This is especially an issue at the time of writing, when following the gangland assassination of producer Gulshan Kumar, the second film producer to be killed this year, the Indian government's 'shortsightedness' in this regard—which, it is claimed, has 'forced' the industry to take recourse to illegal funding—has been virulently critiqued by most of the mainstream press.

2. Metz describes the cinematic apparatus as replicated within the spectator's gaze as comprising two sites of looking, one of the spectator 'duplicating the projector', a second the spectator 'duplicating the screen'.

When I say that 'I see' the film, I mean thereby a unique mixture of two contrary currents: the film is what I receive, and it is also what I release, since it does not pre-exist my entering the auditorium and I only need to close my eyes to suppress it. Releasing it, I am the projector (which itself duplicates the camera), receiving it I am the screen . . . (p. 51).

Elsewhere in the same book in his famous essay on voyeurism, Metz further divides these two currents into two categories within the film itself: the institution of cinema, which knows that I am watching, and which acknowledges the importance of the actual viewer's presence, and the text, or the story, which disavows, 'doesn't want to know', that it is being watched (p. 95).

3. The instance of the Chunduru massacre on 6 August 1991 has become notorious in the annals of Indian film history. On July 4 of that year, a dalit graduate, Govatota Ravi, bought a ticket in the 'chair' class, forbidden by local convention to dalits, and apparently touched another viewer with his legs, leading to arguments and finally violence. See Samata Sanghatana's report (1991). On a very different plane, the ideal of 'dying in the cause of cinema' is incarnated in the death of film-maker John Abraham, whose itinerant existence in his last years extended into the way he made his last film *Amma Ariyan* (1986). See Rajadhyaksha/Willemen (1995) for entries on both the film-maker and the film.

## REFERENCES

Althusser, Louis, 1994. 'Ideology and Ideological State Apparatuses (Notes Towards an Investigation)', in Slavoj Zizek (ed.), *Mapping Ideology*, London: Verso.

Burch, Noel, 1990. *Life to those Shadows*, London: British Film Institute.

Chatterjee, Partha, 1997. 'Beyond the Nation? Or Within?', *Economic & Political Weekly* 32(1/2), 4–11 January: 30–4.

Comolli, Jean-Louis, 1980. 'Machines of the Visible', in Stephen Heath/Teresa du Laurentis (ed.), *The Cinematic Apparatus*, London: Macmillan.

Cormack, Mike, 1994. *Ideology and Cinematography in Hollywood 1930–39*, New York: St Martin's Press.

Dhareshwar, Vivek, 1995. ' "Our Time": History, Sovereignty and Politics', *Economic & Political Weekly* 30(6), 11 February.

Gaudreault, Andre, 1992. 'Showing and Telling: Image and Word in Early

Cinema', in Thomas Elsaesser (ed.), *Early Cinema: Space, Frame, Narrative*, London: BFI Publishing.

Gunning, Tom, 1992. 'The Cinema of Attractions: Early Film, its Spectator and the Avant-Garde', in Thomas Elsaesser (ed.), *Early Cinema: Space, Frame, Narrative*, London: BFI Publishing.

Gunning, Tom, 1994. *D.W. Griffith and the Origins of American Narrative Film: The Early Years at Biograph*, Urbana: University of Illinois Press.

Kaviraj, Sudipta, 1992. 'The Imaginary Institution of India', in Partha Chatterjee/Gyanendra Pandey (ed.), *Subaltern Studies VII: Writings on South Asian History and Society*, New Delhi: Oxford University Press.

—————, 1995. 'Democracy and Development in India', in Amiya Bagchi (ed.), *Development and Democracy*, New Delhi: Sage.

Laclau, Ernesto and Chantal Mouffe, 1985. *Hegemony and Socialist Strategy: Towards a Radical Democratic Politics*, London: Verso.

Metz, Christian, 1982. *Psychoanalysis and the Cinema: The Imaginary Signifier*, London: Macmillan.

Michelson, Annette (ed.), 1984. *Kino-Eye: The Writings of Dziga Vertov*, Berkeley: University of California Press.

Mulvey, Laura, 1989. 'Visual Pleasure and Narrative Cinema', *Screen* 16(3), 1975, repr. in Mulvey, *Visual and Other Pleasures*, London: Macmillan.

Niranjana, Tejaswini, 1997. 'Left to the Imagination', *Small Axe* 1(2), September.

Rajadhyaksha, Ashish and Paul Willemen, 1995. *Encyclopaedia of Indian Cinema*, London and New Delhi: BFI and Oxford University Press.

Said, Edward, 1993. *Culture and Imperialism*, New York, Alfred A. Knopf.

Samata Sanghatana, 1991. 'Upper Caste Violence: Study of Chunduru Carnage', *Economic and Political Weekly* 26(36): 2079–84.

Willemen, Paul, 1994. 'Notes on Subjectivity', in *Looks and Frictions*, London/ Bloomington: BFI/Indiana University Press.

Wollen, Peter, 1992. *Singin' in the Rain*, London: BFI Publishing.

# 11 | *Devotion and Defiance in Fan Activity*

S.V. SRINIVAS

THREE THOUSAND FANS' ASSOCIATIONS (FAs) with a membership varying between 10 and 500 members, spread across all the three regions that comprise Andhra Pradesh, are devoted to Chiranjeevi, the most popular Telugu movie star today.[1] Every major 'hero' and 'heroine' has a fan association, with numbers that roughly correspond to their popularity. In this essay I shall discuss fan club activity, explore its relationship with stardom, and examine some of the implications of such activity to the culture industry. For the purposes of my argument, I shall restrict my use of the term 'fan' to refer to one who is an actual member of an association. Most of my observations are based on my interactions with Chiranjeevi fans in Vijayawada and Hyderabad, although I shall use insights gained from discussion with fans of other stars and from other parts of the state.

I focus on Chiranjeevi (Konidela Sivashankar Varaprasad) fans because, the popularity of the star apart, his rise to prominence corresponds roughly with the exit of N.T. Rama Rao (NTR) from the industry (1982–83: although he continued to make films

Presented at the Cultural Studies Workshop on Modernity, organized by CSSS, Calcutta, at Mysore, November 1995. I thank all those whose views and arguments I have used in this essay. In addition, I am grateful to Hussain, Devender and 'Sudha' for giving me copies of letters from other fans as well as other material. Chiranjeevi and Allu Aravind not only spent hours with me but also gave me valuable material. I thank them for their encouragement and cooperation. I am grateful to Vivek Dhareshwar, Ashish Rajadhyaksha and Ravi Vasudevan for commenting on earlier drafts of this essay. This is a part of my Ph.D. project and I thank Tejaswini Niranjana, my supervisor, without whose support I may never have ventured out of English Literature.

sporadically over the next decade), and the eclipse of Krishna, who, after NTR, had by far the largest fan following in the state. This also coincides with the introduction of the 'slab system' of tax on film exhibition, in 1983, which in turn enhanced the economic importance of organized fan activity, as we shall see. The year also saw the release of *Khaidi* (A. Kodandarami Reddy, 1983), a turning-point in Chiranjeevi's career as the most popular star, which also saw a vast increase in his fan following.

It has been argued that FAs were created by the film industry, following their successful promotion of M.G. Ramachandran (MGR) in Tamil Nadu. Motivated by profit, the industry encouraged and funded FAs of both NTR and A. Nageswara Rao in the hope that fans would provide free publicity to the actors and their projects. The production companies and studios that actively manufactured the star system in the 1950s and 1960s, therefore, created fans' associations as a logical extension of that activity.[2]

However, when the slab system of taxation was introduced, theatres were graded and a flat tax was imposed regardless of tickets actually sold (Grade A paid 28 per cent of capacity, B 18 per cent, C 14 per cent). Distributors had to bear these expenses as well as the increasing rent of theatres. In consequence, they began losing money for all screenings of less than 50 per cent of capacity. For them, the safest bet was a film that ran to packed houses simultaneously in a number of halls, even if only for a few weeks. Distributors, who generally bought films under production, had to rely entirely on common categories like the star's 'image', the music, the promise of 'action', the 'comedy track', etc., in order to estimate the film's potential worth. These are elements that conventionally attract the 'repeat audience' or those who watch a film more than once. Fans became important in this scheme because their active participation on the opening day attracted crowds who then returned to see the film, as well as, more directly, because the fans themselves constitute a major part of the repeat audience.

Two recent books have addressed the fan phenomenon in Tamil Nadu: M.S.S. Pandian's *The Image Trap* (1992) and Sara Dickey's *Cinema and the Urban Poor in South India* (1993b). In Tamil Nadu it has been the active political participation of fan clubs, especially the use of film by the Dravidian movement, that remains the focus of scholarly attention (Hardgrave and Neidhart 1975;

Pandian 1991, 1992; Dickey 1993a, 1993b). Although in itself a major phenomenon that seems to radically distinguish the south Indian variety of fandom, it is possible that the unprecedented involvement of fans in party politics in Tamil Nadu has restricted debate on fans as being (potential) political cadres, and therefore, reduced political debate itself to its narrow implications. In Andhra Pradesh, despite the presence of FAs from the 1950s, and despite their demonstrable effectiveness in the political careers of NTR and others, like Krishna himself, Jamuna (a Lok Sabha MP), Mohan Babu (Rajya Sabha MP), Nutan Prasad and Rao Gopala Rao (both members of the state Legislative Council for a term), the phenomenon has received little critical attention. Although I am concerned with the political implications to the extent that I am interested in questions of power (to define, to control), my study does not restrict itself to the kind of fan activity that furthers potential politicians, or fans as potential political cadres. I shall instead argue that fans constantly negotiate between what is *expected* from them by the industry (and by the stars themselves) and what empowers them. Fans deploy the vocabulary of excess, hyperbole, adulation/devotion/admiration often in order to articulate their own social-political, cultural and economic aspirations. Even if it is true that FAs were created by the industry, fans have today come a long way from being unpaid servants of the industry. My endeavour would be to show the process and the result of fan activity overcoming its 'original' functions.

In the first part of this essay I discuss stardom and its expectations from fans as well as the occasionally uncomfortable relationship between a star and his fans. The second part deals with how the fans' aspirations are worked into their FA activities, and the results of those activities.

## 'STARDOM IS A BLESSING'—CHIRANJEEVI

Chiranjeevi, whose first film was *Pranam Khareedu* (K. Vasu, 1978), has acted in over 120 films, including three in Hindi. His films have been dubbed into Tamil and Hindi. He has been reputedly the highest paid star in Telugu, and even, briefly, the country, starring in productions that could cost between Rs 3.75 and 5 crore. He has repeatedly stated that he has no intentions of entering politics. Remarkably, he has been associated with few scandals and has received very little 'negative' publicity in the film press.

On screen, he introduced a new form of dance with quick, vigorous, choreographed steps, which stood in stark contrast to the more leisurely style of his predecessors. He did his own stunts, often in a far more spectacular fashion than the norm in early 1980s' Telugu films. Fans often mention his portrayal of the wronged and angry fugitive fighting feudal oppression in *Khaidi* as his 'most important' early hit.

Chiranjeevi has himself asserted that a 'star' is not necessarily a 'hero' but anyone who can draw audiences to theatres (Interview, Madras, 22 January 1995). This emphasis on the *business* prospects of stardom exists, primarily, in relation to fans. Chiranjeevi realized that he was a star when he 'saw devotion in the eyes of [his] admirers' (he used the word *abhimani*: literally admirer, 'fan' and *abhimani* being considered synonymous. Interview, Hyderabad, 19 July 1995). Stardom brings wealth, prestige and enormous satisfaction and, as Chiranjeevi said, 'Anybody can be a (good) actor if he tries hard enough. But there are very few stars. . . . Only one or two in a generation' (Interview, Madras).

Affirming that fans ensure a sustained interest in the star, he said that indeed they are a 'bulwark against changing audience taste' (Interview, Hyderabad, 19 July 1995). Their commitment to the star is unquestionable and they stand solidly by him when he needs them. For example, in May 1995, when women's and students' groups called for the banning of his film *Alluda Majaaka* (E.V.V. Satyanarayana, 1995), his fans took out a large procession in Hyderabad and threatened to immolate themselves. The film was not banned.

In my interviews with him, Chiranjeevi mentioned several instances of 'hero worship' and the forms this took. His fans often cut their thumbs to smear their blood on his forehead; they have died in accidents on their way to one of his public meetings; they are undeterred by police cane-charges; they remain prepared to get physical with anyone who passes a derogatory remark against him; they imitate his hairstyle, use his gestures and phrases from films, etc. Given this devotion, and in this environment, his responsibility is to provide them not only with two-and-a-half hours of entertainment (comparable to a 'six-course meal') that enables them to 'forget everything else', but also ensure that his films have the right 'message' (Interview, Madras).

Unfortunately Chiranjeevi's 'message' movies—*Swayamkrushi* (K. Vishwanath, 1987), *Rudraveena* (K. Balachander, 1988) and *Apadbandhavudu* (K. Vishwanath, 1992)—despite winning critical acclaim (and occasionally awards), have not been very successful commercially. Nor has his recent *S.P. Parashuram* (Raviraja Pinisetty, 1994) done well, although he plays the role of an honest police officer fighting corrupt politicians. His fans claim they enjoyed the first three films (it was *others* who didn't) and argue that he ought not to have made the last one, since its Hindi original had been seen by most town- and city-dwellers. They blamed the actress, Sridevi, and asserted that films with a policeman hero rarely do well in Andhra Pradesh. In short, for the first three 'class' movies they blamed the audience, and for the fourth, found plenty of reasons for its failure but stopped short of blaming the star.[3]

Despite their commitment, fans are a constant source of anxiety to the star. They write angry letters and make abusive long-distance calls when they are unhappy with him. They also reject some films. This unease, and effort to 'discipline' the star leads to occasional attempts, in turn, to discipline the fans, trim fan responsibilities and activity to meet certain criteria. A crucial attempt in this was the establishment of the fanzine *Megastar Chiranjeevi*.

The first issue was published in August 1989. Although announced as a monthly, the journal publishes only three or four issues annually, usually on occasions like the star's birthday or the release of a film. Edited by Vijaya Bapineedu, a prominent film director who calls himself a fan of the star, and published by Allu Aravind, a major producer and Chiranjeevi's brother-in-law, it has an average print run of 15,000 copies, extended to 40,000 for special issues. It is usually published as three booklets, including at least one glossy pin-up, colour photographs, information about forthcoming Chiranjeevi releases, biographical notes, chronicles of the star's achievements, fan mail, and lyrics from unreleased titles. The inaugural issue called for photographs of FAs along with details of the nature of social service rendered by each. These were published in subsequent issues. Priced at between Rs 15 and Rs 20, it is easily the most expensive film-related journal in Telugu. Despite this, it has reportedly sustained an aggregate loss of Rs 1.5 lakh. According to its publisher, it remains the first 'official' fanzine in Andhra Pradesh.

The inaugural incarnated Chiranjeevi as the 'Mega' star, explaining that mega meant ten raised to the power of six. 'If anyone in the industry imagines himself to be ten times greater than others, Chiranjeevi is many times greater than him' (inside cover, inaugural issue). The establishment of this periodical constituted the first major effort to consciously harness fan energies, to ensure that they performed controlled, 'productive' activities. The stress on social service is common (cf. Dickey 1993b: 148–72), and it is aimed at using the FAs to earn the star some goodwill as well as delegitimizing some—although not all—of fandom's 'excesses'. The magazine, like other popular productions including those by the fans themselves, tries to collate the 'real' Chiranjeevi in order to create a real-hero figure. The July 1991 issue, for instance, chronicled his concern for the victims of a cyclone. There are, however, both legitimate and well-established modes to compare, or construct, this figure as well as illegitimate ones, as the official mouthpiece makes clear.

The April 1992 issue published a letter from an angry fan and Chiranjeevi's signed response. Though it is possible that these letters were manufactured by the editorial staff of the magazine, the point is not the authenticity of the exchange but the *need* for it. This example needs to be read in the light of the tense relationship between the star and his fans and not as a historical event. The fan was scandalized and angry that the actress Nagma is seen to abuse Chiranjeevi during a song in *Gharana Mogudu* (K. Raghavendra Rao, 1992, unreleased at the time of publication). The fan sought the withdrawal of the song as this damaged the image of the 'Megastar's Natakishore' (a play on two of the actor's titles). The fans of other stars were ridiculing the song, the letter said, to the extent that the letter writer was insulted and wished to die.

Chiranjeevi's response asserted that it was only in the 'acting' that he was insulted, and not in real life. *In the film* the abuse is addressed to the character's husband Raja, not to himself. He pleaded, 'Watch *Gharana Mogudu*. Even after doing so if you feel the song denigrates me, write to me.' He added:

Don't pick fights with the fans of other stars. It is not good to do so. I have said so a number of times. Here (in the industry) all the heroes are very friendly and cordial with each other. You fans, being the admirers of heores, should not abuse each other.

So, hereafter, I hope you will be an admirer I admire. Don't even think of committing suicide. (*Megastar Chiranjeevi*, April 1992)

Chiranjeevi is not the only star who has had to convince his fans not to indulge in violence: Venkatesh and Nagarjuna, the other leading male stars in Telugu, have also asked their fans to stop fighting amongst themselves. Krishna indeed issued newspaper advertisements appealing to his fans not to boycott *Varasudu* (E.V.V. Satyanarayana, 1993) in which he played a 'negative' role.

Part of the problem stems from the fans' perception of themselves as guardians of the star's image. In Chiranjeevi's words, 'even the man who pays three or four rupees thinks he owns the star and has a right over him' (Interview, Madras). There is tremendous pressure on the star to maintain and reinforce this image. R. Nandakumar, in his essay on the star system, argues that

On the part of the spectator, it is not the individual roles in which the star is cast so much as the one cumulative image that emerges from the totality of his various performances that comes in handy to be accepted. This consciously maintained image of the star is enforced on the spectator as a concrete reality through the whole paraphernalia of its popular culture—*mammoth hoardings, the rosy fan adulations, slushy gossip, glossy advertisements* and so on *that crowd on him breaking all resistance*. (Nandakumar 1992: 44; emphasis mine.)

While correctly drawing attention to the importance of reinforcement, and therefore of the 'totality' of performances, Nandakumar assumes (i) that the 'spectator' is essentially a pitiable, but passive, victim; and (ii) that fans are agents of the industry's propaganda. The second assumption is evidently incorrect, as my essay seeks to show. As for the first, I wish to argue that it forecloses the entire possibility of any site for contest, or even struggle, against the manipulative designs of the industry (as a political and cultural entity). I shall argue, instead, that once a star's image begins to gain currency—in itself by no means a 'natural' consequence of its creation—it is very difficult for either the star or the industry as a whole to maintain control over it, or to manipulate it at will (cf. also Seiter et al. 1989; Lewis 1992; Cashmore 1994 for elaborate accounts of the larger problem of control).

Stardom exists within a complex network of fan/audience

expectations which, in part, result from what Nandakumar calls the 'cumulative image'. These expectations are not restricted to the star's image, but in fact extend to the cinema itself. They do not spring from a specific set of films ('starring' the star) but from a larger set of cinematic and cultural referents. Chiranjeevi says of his fans, 'They expect me to dance like Michael Jackson and fight like Jackie Chan' (Interview, Madras). Far from being willing slaves of their masters, fans can be 'like cane-wielding school masters', ready to punish and difficult to please.

Pandian's *The Image Trap* correctly draws attention to the careful and systematic orchestration of images that, in turn, construct the figure of the 'real' hero: a generous MGR who fights oppression and is a friend of the poor (Pandian 1992: 95, 99, 102). Such orchestration is evident in the case of Chiranjeevi as well, although the image projected is somewhat different. It is perhaps indicated by the fact that Chiranjeevi remains untouched by scandal, by the striking similarities between the 'official' life-story and popular print biographies produced by fans, providing evidence for the success of the enterprise.[4]

However, even as it alerts us to the manner in which popular culture is (always/already?) a site for the production of ruling-class ideologies, Pandian's book offers an insight that comes more as a surprise than as a logical extension of his study:

The fact that politics is always a contested terrain and that even among the devoted followers of MGR there exist indelible marks of dissent, however emasculated they may be, are quite important. Therein lies the possibilities (*sic*) of constituting the 'other' of MGR-style politics and creating a new progressive common-sense. (p. 145)

Dickey's work (1993a, 'Fans and Politics', 1993b) takes up the question of how fan club activity is related to the daily lives of fans and the social and political spaces it provides. Her failure in designating what these are, and the possibilities they offer, is summed up in her own conclusion:

Like the movie themes that oscillate between promising the poor wealth in the future and telling them they have true (i.e. moral) wealth now these activities express a tension between the desire of poor people to be other than they are and to be proud of who they are. (Dickey 1993b 172)

Is this tension a dead-end? Or does it manifest itself in something we could call subversion, or defiance?

## USING THEIR ILLUSION

'A fan is the only selfless supporter'—Vijaya Bapineedu

Fans are a distinct section of the audience. In addition to their 'loyalty' over a period of time, fans are characterized by their excess, hyperbole and even obsession. A fan is never 'objective' in his/her assessment of the star's performance. Commitment and 'excessive' admiration are integral to fandom (norms in this regard are set by the middle-class audience). This excess, surplus investment becomes evident in the fan's response which is almost always a public statement—be it the imitation of the hairstyle or a charcoal sketch of the star.

Fans and other sections of the audience iconize the star (who is in any case an already iconized figure) around whom the 'meaning' of a film revolves. The star has a set of attributes at any given point of time which may change over a period of time. A villain can thus become a hero (like Mohan Babu) and hero a 'character-actor', etc. These attributes are not limited to the star's screen performances but also to his 'real' life. Fans suppress and contest the circulation of anything ranging from a film to a biographical detail, that is perceived as being 'damaging' to the star.

The icon assumes crucial importance to fans possibly because they deploy it to negotiate their social, political and cultural location in the public sphere. In the process they often invest the star-icon with a valency that has little to do with the 'real' or official version of the star. Not surprisingly, Chiranjeevi became the rallying point of Kapu youth in coastal Andhra during the 1980s, although he himself never associated himself with Kapu mobilization.[5]

Most FAs have ten to twelve members each. These are almost always young males, between sixteen to thirty years, belonging to a wide cross-section of castes. The caste composition of an average FA depends on a variety of factors, including the star's caste, his/her political affiliations and, in turn, the caste equations and antagonism at play in the FA's area of operation. A few members hold regular white-collar jobs. Some organizers are businessmen and most have had some formal education—graduates are not uncommon, illiterates are. Every association has a president and a secretary, and many other office-bearers. Most associations function autonomously, though they do interact and coordinate their activities with other FAs sharing the same affiliations as theirs.

None of the FAs I visited in Hyderabad and Vijayawada had conventional office space. They usually meet in public places: bylanes, tea-shops, cycle-repair shops and usually ensure that their meeting-places are in the vicinity of cinema halls. Shopkeepers and their assistants in these areas know the important figures by name as well as their working hours. However small the FA, it usually describes itself as a town-wide, state-wide or nation-wide organization, depending on where it is located. A number of FAs have their own letterheads, and their office-bearers have printed visiting cards.

Why do young people join FAs? Dickey quotes a fan, 'to promote and support the star' (Dickey 1993b: 163). She does not ask why anyone would want to do that, but the answer would usually be, 'because I/we admire/like the star'. That these answers reinforce what a fan is expected to say and are not explanations is clear when we contrast them with the response of Parachuri Vijayalakshmi, the only female member of an FA that I have ever come across. Vijayalakshmi, a graduate, is president of the All-India Vijayashanti Cultural Organization, Vijayawada. Vijayashanti is perhaps the most popular female star in the state today. Asked why she had organized the FA, Vijayalakshmi said, 'Of course I like Vijayashanti, but I started this association because someone [in the industry who is a friend of the family] requested me to' (Interview, Vijayawada, 20 July 1994). She added that her fan activity would help her gain public exposure, which in turn, would help her enter politics.[6] (She wanted to contest as a municipal corporator.)

A dissimilar response from another fan would help further illustrate the point I am trying to make. Ramu Yadav, president, *Akhilandhra Chiranjeevi Yuvata*, is among the most prominent Chiranjeevi fans in Hyderabad, and also, as restauranteur, the wealthiest FA organizer I have met. He and his friends formed their association not only because they 'like watching Chiranjeevi', which they did on the opening day of any release, but because the FA gave its members access to tickets.

These non-standard responses come from atypical fans: Vijaya-lakshmi's gender and Ramu Yadav's economic status set them apart (in Yadav's case, apart from even the members of his own association). These distinctions made it necessary for both to provide explanations in terms of practical benefits, something most fans prefer not to discuss. Their responses do however alert us to the unstated agendas of FAs, which become clearer as we examine their actual activities.

Recent studies on fans in the West have focused on their productivity, rather than their passivity (Vermorel 1985; Grossberg 1992). They discuss how fandom helps fans cope with the pressures of life, how it makes socialization possible (Hobson 1989), how it is potentially empowering (Brower 1992; Grossberg 1992). These studies, however, address either unorganized, or informally organized, fan associations which usually operate in contexts far removed from mine.

The most striking thing here about fan activity is its sheer 'excess' (cf. Jenson 1992; Fiske 1992, on the supposed excesses of fans). The number of times they watch their stars' films, the ease with which they pick quarrels or fights to defend their nominee; their obsession with the most trivial details of stars' lives and their films; the superlatives they use in describing/praising their stars. Practically all that they are seen or heard doing is usually sneered at by 'decent, reasonable, respectable' people as being unnecessarily extravagant, hyperbolic, excessive.

Implicit in the condemnation is the norm, or what constitutes the permissible response to actors/stars on screen. Those who would see no point in defending these responses, or more usually, of using them to condemn fans on this account, could note that (i) fan activity usually takes place 'without regard' to social (i.e. middle-class) acceptability, and (ii) in the fans' own domain there is intense competition between groups and individuals to surpass whatever has been considered the 'limit' in terms of a public expression of their adulation. Since a fan is defined and recognized by his/her active participation in the whole business of film-seeing, the spectacular act of 'devotion' is in itself evidence of commitment. The intensity of FA activity is in direct proportion to its local influence. Participation in this activity itself sets privileged fans apart from others with possibly similar socio-economic backgrounds but without access to its organized response. As is evident in the letterheads printed by fans, admiration and hero-worship is inextricably linked to the fan's own quest for social recognition and power. Fan activity is supposed to exist in order to project a star's image, to advertise their latest films. Less wealthy FAs plaster walls with handwritten posters announcing new releases or praising their merits. Others with more access to funds print posters, hang banners, place plywood cut-outs in the vicinity of cinema halls. Some compose collages from stills in cheap fan magazines which are then used to decorate movie theatre lobbies. Thousands of flyers are distributed elaborating a film's merits or cele-brating its success. Prominent in each is the name of the association, its office-bearers and, occasionally, the entire list of its members.

FAs actively contribute to the mood of celebration with which new releases are greeted. A quiet first day spells financial disaster for the product. When fans do not participate in these activities, their 'boycott' not only sends a clear message to the general audience but also changes the atmosphere within which new films are watched. Fans thus *create* a space for themselves not only in the transaction between the movie and its viewer, but also in the broader social cultural context of film-watching. They take over public spaces and literally leave their signatures across the entire urban space within which they operate. Etched in public toilets for instance, you could see a cryptic 'NBK ZBD', i.e. 'Nandamuri Balakrishna Zindabad' (Balakrishna is NTR's son and current star). Charcoal and brick drawings of major stars are a common sight, though these could be by individual, i.e. 'unorganized' fans. Their regular meeting-places are no more owned by them than the movie theatres that they take over, quite literally, when the occasion demands.

This tendency to take over, in various ways, public spaces that do not acknowledge their presence in official transactions with the public is an important aspect of fan assertion. In Vijayawada it has led to the carving up of parts of the city into fan territories. These territories usually reflect, with some accuracy, the control over the city's centres by political parties to which the FAs are affiliated. (Disputes over these spaces have sometimes occurred even between FAs with otherwise identical affiliation.) In Vijayawada city, Chiranjeevi associations succeeded in driving away their rival

Balakrishna fans and their allies from the Gandhinagar area, which has thirteen theatres. As a result, Balakrishna fans cannot perform fan activity in and around the theatres of this area. In the past, when tensions within FAs resulted in a split, it was the more powerful splinter that retained the 'office'/meeting place. Translated into day-to-day functioning, territorial limits impose severe restrictions on FAs: they may not be in a position to, for example, defend themselves in the competition for wall or hoarding space, or exert influence over theatre managements outside their 'areas'.

The influence FAs exert over theatre managements is an important indication of their 'clout', another important example of fan assertion. The prestige attached to this assertion relates to the power theatre managements have, over the years, arrogated to themselves. It is not unusual in parts of coastal Andhra for guards to indulge in cane-charges to control crowds, or for ushers and other staff to abuse and manhandle members of the audience.

In addition, influential FAs and their office-bearers have access to first day/week show tickets, otherwise impossible to acquire in the open market. Viewing a film on the day of its release is considered an achievement even by middle-class, upper-caste youth. When a star's film is released, hundreds of people approach FAs for tickets. Depending on the importance of the FA, a predetermined number of tickets are reserved for it. There have been occasions when violence has erupted over this issue when managers have refused to supply tickets to fans. Today, 'quotas' are treated as a matter of right.

In recent times, Chiranjeevi FAs in Vijayawada have become so influential that they organize special benefit shows on the opening day, booking an entire hall and selling tickets at high premiums. On special occasions (such as the 100th day mark) FAs buy all the tickets for the night shows and sell or distribute them, not always at a premium.

During such 'special' shows, and during the first day of the screening of the film, fans take over the cinema halls. Theatres are elaborately decorated by them, and there is much slogan-shouting during the show. Police frequently cane-charge crowds of unsuccessful ticket-hunters who attempt to storm the halls. Throughout the show, whistling and shouting drown the soundtrack. Fans once vandalized a theatre in Hyderabad when the management refused to replay a song-sequence (for the third time), and dispersed only after a cane-charge. Such incidents are common when fans 'liberate' cinema halls, as is the sight of rifle-wielding policemen patrolling aisles during the screening.

Theatre owners and distributors accuse FAs—only in private, off-the-record conversations—of extorting money. Fan-leaders, it is argued, use their associations as a pretext for making money. If true, it is further evidence of the links of fan activity with fan aspirations. If false, it means that the industry which supposedly created and funded FAs is discrediting them, an indication that fans are not just a repeat audience but also a threat.

Fan assertion often leads to friction with distributors. The immediate origin is disagreement over how long a star's film should run. As mentioned earlier, the distributor begins to suffer a loss whenever the occupancy rate falls below 50 per cent. When this happens, the distributor usually withdraws the film. Fans, on the other hand, ever-conscious of records and jubilees, insist that the film be allowed to run till it touches the 50- or 100-day mark. In early 1994, Balakrishna fans allegedly burnt a distributor's office over one such dispute. When a star's film fails, fans blame the distributor or producer for the failure, accuse them of withdrawing prints when collections did not warrant such an action, of poor publicity, poor timing of release, and so on.

Central to the conflict with the industry, whether manifested at the level of theatre managements, distributors or producers, is the question of who controls the medium itself. Fans create and use the opportunities they get to send the message that they matter. Acts of assertion are articulated in terms of commitment, admiration for the star, and their self-assigned responsibility to protect the star's image.

Fan assertion is a response to the film industry's indifference to and contempt for the audience. The industry does not have a mechanism for receiving audience opinion. The only feedback it receives, and is interested in, is collection figures. This does not prevent the industry from making claims on behalf of the audience about what 'they' want. Apart from petitioning the government to ban a film, members of the audience have few legitimate means of venting their grievances or seeking redressal. By virtue of being organized, FAs happen to be the only section of the audience that has not only forced the industry to listen to their views but to take them into consideration. So far, it must be added, FAs have not demanded 'clean' or 'socially committed' cinema. On the contrary, they have rallied against such demands when their star's film is involved. Their 'political incorrectness' is a consequence of their mode of articulation, and it is worth arguing that it will probably continue until they transform themselves so radically that they will no longer be fan associations. Battles with the industry over the degree of control exerted are not always open ones. Quieter, less spectacular, activities of FAs too become sites of this struggle. The communication network of an FA is one such site.

Fans functioning from different parts of the state keep in constant touch with each other by writing short letters at regular intervals. The letters inform fans in other areas about the performance of films (of all major stars) in their town/city, about the activities undertaken by their FA, the possibility of coordinating activities, or of visits to the star. More important FAs receive requests for stills from forthcoming titles, which are usually distributed by producers through FAs free of cost. Information regarding the performance of films can be inaccurate, but these letters do provide fans with a sense of belonging to a larger collective, one spread across parts of or even the whole state, and potentially a source of considerable strength. Other occasions, like public functions organized by producers to celebrate a film's success, also allow fans to gauge the extent of their community. Letters provide space for a more sustained interaction which is invisible to and independent of the industry.

Apart from letters, FAs provide members and non-members with a direct interaction on a daily basis. Most fans spend the better part of an evening at their regular meeting-places, meetings attended by unorganized fans and non-fans as well. Discussions are not restricted to cinema alone, but often revolve around it and films are analysed and judged.

When a film is discussed, participants assess the good and bad points of the film, as well as *how* it should be viewed and analysed. Films are broken up into compartments: star, story, dance, fight, music, photography, comedy track, etc.—each component compared with its counterparts in other films in Telugu and other languages, such as English and Hindi. Given the sheer number of films that the debators watch, the filmic intertext could be reasonably said to include the entire range of popular cinema available to a generation. In the light of this intertext, categories are invented, altered or reinforced ('class' films, 'mass' films, or 'class' elements of a 'mass' film). Cinema is watched in the light of the networks of this expectation.[7]

I do not claim that FA discussions are the only source of such expectations, or that fans are the only sections of the audience that invent them. FAs merely provide an institutional space for the creation and circulation of opinion and expectation. I would, however, venture to claim that opinions thus generated do have a much larger circulation, and also that there are significant differences between these and the products of non-fans who otherwise share similar socio-economic backgrounds. The crucial significance of the space provided by FAs lies in its autonomy, no matter how partial or limited, from the industry and its designs. The existence of such spaces goes a long way in preventing the industry from achieving total success in deciding the shape of the cinema to come.

Fan discussions, like their other activities, open up social and cultural spaces that may not even exist, and enable them to assert their importance *vis-à-vis* the industry itself and to gain some control over the medium. Acts of fan assertion are not always with reference to cinema, but address other fans and the rest of society as well— for example, the prestige of a fan among sections of the lower-class audience. The links between FAs and political parties in places like Vijayawada are evidence of yet another attempt by fans to seek larger and more meaningful roles for themselves. 'Social service', which I have only mentioned in passing, but which is today one of their official functions, may also be viewed in this light.

In Vijayawada, a number of Chiranjeevi fans are supporters of the Congress (I).[8] Some important fan organizers are former student activists of the party who established FAs even while they were active in student politics. An overwhelming majority of Balakrishna fans are Telugu Desam Party (TDP) supporters and continue to do party work (Balakrishna is NTR's son). Krishna and Nagarjuna fans are Congress (I) supporters. Suman fans are TDP supporters who work in tandem with Balakrishna fans, as do some Venkatesh fans. Interestingly, Chiranjeevi, Nagarjuna and Venkatesh have not openly declared their political sympathies so far.

The choice of both star and political party is partly influenced by caste factors. This is evident from the composition of both Chiranjeevi and Balakrishna FAs. During the mid-1980s, in Vijayawada, members of the Kapu caste, and some individuals from other castes which had an antagonistic relationship with the Kamma caste, joined or formed Chiranjeevi FAs and stayed away from or left Balakrishna FAs (formed largely by NTR fans). Chiranjeevi FAs also attracted anti-TDP and/or pro-Congress (I) youth regardless of caste. Parallel developments took place among Balakrishna FAs. All this resulted in a large concentration of Kapus and Congress (I) supporters in Chiranjeevi FAs and Kammas and TDP supporters in Balakrishna FAs.[9] Similar developments are evident in other coastal Andhra towns. While caste and party affiliations do not fully explain the reasons for the 'choice' of a star, the very fact that they played, and continue to play, any role at all, should caution us against treating fans as passive victims of mass-produced images.

The reasons given by fans themselves for joining or supporting political parties vary from the chance such affiliations offer to 'serve the people better', to the protection that party affiliation offers, both from other fans as well as from theatre managements and the police. Most fans, when asked why they did not become (or continue as) full-time activists, were unanimous in their answer: it was too dangerous. Vijayawada's party politics, an extension of gang rivalry, can be extremely violent even by Andhra standards. There have been dozens of murders of party activists and leaders in the past fifteen years.

There are interesting similarities between fans and party activists, especially at the lower levels. Both are largely poor or lower-middle-class youth who belong to Sudra 'forward' castes (Kapu, Kamma) or to backward castes, and a significant number are dalits. Few hold regular white-collar jobs—and their activities, including distribution of pamphlets, flyers, wall writing, posters, hanging banners, slogan shouting, and even processions, are often common to both.

It would, however, be wrong to assume that fans are future political cadres, or that FA activities prepare fans to enter conventional politics. Regardless of the success of their star in the political arena, and in spite of the similarities between FA activities and those of political parties, not all fans involve themselves directly in party politics. Most NTR fans became Balakrishna fans, not TDP activists; and the few who did, went beyond the lowest levels of the party. On the other hand, minor Congress (I) activists became major Chiranjeevi fans.

While it is not surprising that some fans sought places for themselves in conventional politics and FAs did, at times, become fronts for political activities, it must be stressed that the transformation is neither natural nor a one-way process. FAs and political parties attract people from similar socio-economic backgrounds, who share a common quest for social recognition and power. The leaking of one activity into the other is perhaps due to these factors, and not because fans and their associations evolve in any inevitable way into party cadres and political parties. It is difficult to disentangle fandom in its present form from criminality. This is not to suggest that FA members are criminals. They are constructed and perceived as criminals by respectable (middle-class, upper-caste) citizens. 'Rowdy' is a term frequently used with reference to fans. One police officer actually described a major fan organizer in Vijayawada as a 'noted rowdy-sheeter'. Indeed, the fan in question is an accused in a murder case, a carry-over from his past involvement in party politics. Interestingly, the 'rowdy' is a central figure in party politics of Vijayawada (as well as other parts of the country).

Dhareshwar and Srivatsan's analysis of the rowdy-sheeter offers useful insights to this shadowy figure. They argue,

In the middle-class imagination the 'rowdy' inhabits the dark zone of the city [the 'basti'], trafficking in illegal, immoral activities, a zone that is always in need of law and order, and always threatening to spread to the safer, cleaner habitat of the city (Dhareshwar and Srivatsan 1996: 202).

The rowdy or 'lumpen' is the subhuman 'other' of the globalizing, upper-caste, middle-class 'citizen' and is invoked to explain 'all that the [middle-class] find[s] disturbing in the social and political life of the nation'(p. 2).

It is not surprising that the rowdy makes an appearance in FAs. The fan is a rowdy not only because he breaks the law in the course of his assertion or his association with 'criminalized' politics—the fan becomes a rowdy by overstepping the line which demarcates the legitimate, 'constructive', permissible excess, and the illegitimate. As I have argued, a fan may cross this line and become a criminal. It is irrelevant whether a particular fan actually has a criminal record (rowdy-sheet). As far as the 'citizen' is concerned, the fan is a blind hero-worshipper (devoid of reason) and a villain. The rowdy/fan is an agent of politics which is de-legitimized.

In this essay I have tried to show that there is no such thing as 'pure' hero-worship. Fan activity neither constitutes the surrender of young people to the will of the industry, nor prevents them from articulating aspirations, which fans share with other members of their caste and class groups.

I would like to conclude this essay with a summary of one of my interviews. Ambati Venkateswara Rao, a dalit Congress activist and a former fan, argues that unlike the past, present-day fans lack discipline, are motivated by selfishness and caste loyalties instead of admiration. They are interested in money, and in projecting themselves as leaders. He condemns the degeneration of fans and laments that fans are getting involved in politics (Interview, Vijayawada, 9 July 1994). I hope my essay conveys the fact that I do not share his nostalgia and disgust.

## NOTES

1. Approximate figures based on estimates by Vijaya Bapineedu, editor of *Megastar Chiranjeevi* (Interview, Madras, 23 January 1995).

2 . This explanation was provided by K. Narasaiah, journalist and former film distributor. Two other distributors agreed with this view (Interviews, Vijayawada, 19 January 1994, 20 July 1994).

3. See Pandian (1992: 124) for a parallel response of MGR supporters blaming others for the failures of his government.

4. Compare Chiranjeevi's 'Autobiographical Note', for a forthcoming biographical sketch by director Mahesh Bhatt, with K. Kasivisweswara Rao's *Mighty Megastar Dynamic Hero Chiranjeevi Sachitra Jeevita Charita* (1994).

5. See Amin (1984) for a discussion on how peasants in UP made the iconized figure of Gandhi central to their social and political agenda. Amin points out that the peasants' 'ideas about Gandhi's "orders" and "powers" were often at variance with those of the local Congress-Khalifat leadership and clashed with the basic tenets of Gandhianism itself' (p.55). The point I am trying to make with the comparison is that the popular classes' interpretation of cultural or political signifiers has a great deal to do with their subalternity.

6. Vijayalakshmi distanced herself from fan activity later in 1995. She cites inadequate response to and recognition for her work by the star. She did not get a TDP nomination in the municipal corporation elections.

7. See Srinivas (1994) for a discussion of *Roja* (Mani Ratnam, 1992) in the context of audience expectations.

8. Congress (I) and the Telugu Desam Party (TDP) will be used rather loosely for the purposes of this essay to include any of their respective student or youth wings. In Vijayawada, most young people's links with these parties are through student organizations, United Independents (UI) and United Students' Organization (USO), which later became a part of the Congress (I) and TDP when their founders joined these parties. These organizations have little or no presence in other parts of the state.

9. After the split in TDP in 1995, most Balakrishna fans in Vijayawada aligned themselves with the official TDP (led by N. Chandrababu Naidu) which is supported by Balakrishna. Some stayed loyal to the NTR TDP (led, at the time of writing, by his widow, Laxmi Parvathi) because of their loyalty to their local patron and MLA, Devineni Rajasekhar. They shifted to the Congress (I) when Devineni Rajasekhar joined Congress (I) in 1996.

# REFERENCES

Ang, Ian, 1990. 'The Nature of the Audience', in Downing et al., pp. 155–65.

Amin, Shahid, 1984, 'Gandhi as Mahatma: Gorakhpur District, Eastern UP, 1921–22', in Ranajit Guha (ed.), *Subaltern Studies III*, New Delhi: Oxford University Press, 1989.

Brower, Sue, 1992. 'Fans as Tastemakers: Viewers for Quality Television', in Lewis, pp. 163–84.

Cashmore, Ellis, 1994. *And There Was Television*, London: Routledge.

Chiranjeevi, 1994. 'Autobiographical Note', unpublished.

Dhareshwar, Vivek and R. Srivatsan, 1996. 'Rowdysheeters: An Essay on Subalternity and Politics', in Shahid Amin and Dipesh Chakraborty, *Subaltern Studies IX*, New Delhi: Oxford University Press, pp. 201–31.

Dickey, Sara, 1993a. 'The Politics of Adulation: Cinema and the Production of Politicians in South India', *The Journal of Asian Studies* 52(2), May: 340–72.

————, 1993b. *Cinema and the Urban Poor in South India*, Cambridge: Cambridge University Press.

Downing, John, Ali Mohammed and Annabelle Sreberni-Mohammed, 1990. *Questioning the Media: A Critical Introduction*, New Delhi: Sage Publications.

Fiske, John, 1992. 'The Cultural Economy of Fandom', in Lewis, pp. 30–49.

Grossberg, Lawrence, 1992. 'Is there a Fan in the House?: Effective Sensibility of Fandom', in Lewis, pp. 50–65.

Hardgrave, Robert L. Jr. and Anthony C. Niedhart, 1995. 'Films and Political Consciousness in Tamilnadu', *Economic and Political Weekly* 10(1/2), January: 27–35.

Hobson, Dorothy, 1989. 'Soap Operas at Work', in Seiter et al., pp. 150–67.

Jenson, Joli, 1992. 'Fandom as Pathology: The Consequences of Characterization', in Lewis, pp. 9–29.

Lewis, Lisa A. (ed.), 1992. *Adoring Audience: Fan Culture and Popular Media*, London: Routledge.

*Megastar Chiranjeevi* (Telugu), August 1989, April 1992 issues.

Nandakumar, R., 1992. 'The Star System: A Note Towards its Sociology', *Deep Focus* 4(2): 44–5.

Pandian, M.S.S., 1991. '*Parasakthi*: Life and Times of a DMK Film', in this volume.

—————, 1992. *The Image Trap: M.G. Ramachandran in Film and Politics*, New Delhi: Sage Publications.

Rao, Kaasivisweswara K., 1994. *Mighty Megastar Dynamic Hero Chiranjeevi Sachitra Jeevita Charita* (Telugu), Rajahmundry: Sri Devi Publishers.

Seiter, Ellen et al., 1989. *Remote Control: Television, Audience and Cultural Power*, London: Routledge.

Srinivas, S.V., 1994. '*Roja* in "Law and Order" State', *Economic and Political Weekly*, 29(20), May: 1225–6.

Vermorel, Fred and Judy, 1985. *Starlust: The Secret Fantasies of Fans*, London: W.H. Allen.

## Interviews (in Telugu)

Allu Aravind: Madras, 23 January 1995.

Ambati Venkateswara Rao: Vijayawada, 9 July 1995.

Chiranjeevi: Madras, 22 January 1995, Hyderabad, 19/20 July 1995.

Gogineni Naidu: Vijayawada, 25 July 1994.

K. Jagadish: Vijayawada, 17 July 1995.

K. Narsaiah: Vijayawada, 19 July 1994.

K. Satyanarayana: Vijayawada, 20 July 1994.

M. Ramesh: Vijayawada, 20 July 1994.

M. Suresh Babu: Vijayawada, 18 July 1994.

P. Vijaylaxmi: Vijayawada, 20 July 1994.

Ramu Yadav: Hyderabad, 14 July 1994.

R. Swami Naidu: Hyderabad, 19 July 1995.

Vijaya Bapineedu: Madras, 23 January 1995.